YOUR PERSONAL HOROSCOPE 2013

JOSEPH
POLANSKY

YOUR PERSONAL HOROSCOPE 2013

Month-by-month forecast for every sign

The only one-volume horoscope you'll ever need

The author is grateful to the people of STAR ★ DATA, who truly fathered this book and without whom it could not have been written.

© 2012 by Star ★ Data, Inc.

This 2012 edition is published for Barnes & Noble, Inc. by HarperCollins*Publishers*

ISBN: 978-1-4351-4517-7

Manufactured in Great Britain by Clays Ltd, St Ives plc.

2 4 6 8 10 9 7 5 3 1

Cover illustration © Sally Taylor

Contents

Introduction

Welcome to the fascinating and intricate world of astrology!

For thousands of years the movements of the planets and other heavenly bodies have intrigued the best minds of every generation. Life holds no greater challenge or joy than this: knowledge of ourselves and the universe we live in. Astrology is one of the keys to this knowledge.

Your Personal Horoscope 2013 gives you the fruits of astrological wisdom. In addition to general guidance on your character and the basic trends of your life, it shows you how to take advantage of planetary influences so you can make the most of the year ahead.

The section on each sign includes a Personality Profile, a look at general trends for 2013, and in-depth month-by-month forecasts. The Glossary (page 5) explains some of the astrological terms you may be unfamiliar with.

One of the many helpful features of this book is the 'Best' and 'Most Stressful' days listed at the beginning of each monthly forecast. Read these sections to learn which days in each month will be good overall, good for money, and good for love. Mark them on your calendar – these will be your best days. Similarly, make a note of the days that will be most stressful for you. It is best to avoid booking important meetings or taking major decisions on these days, as well as on those days when important planets in your horoscope are retrograde (moving backwards through the zodiac).

The Major Trends section for your sign lists those days when your vitality is strong or weak, or when relationships with your co-workers or loved ones may need a bit more effort on your part. If you are going through a difficult time, take a look at the colour, metal, gem and scent listed in the 'At a Glance' section of your Personality Profile. Wearing a piece of jewellery that contains your metal and/or gem will strengthen your vitality, just as wearing clothes or decorating your room or office in the colour ruled by your sign, drinking teas made from the herbs ruled by your sign or wearing the scents associated with your sign will sustain you.

Another important virtue of this book is that it will help you to know not only yourself but those around you: your friends, co-workers, partners and/or children. Reading the Personality Profile and forecasts for their signs will provide you with an insight into their behaviour that you won't get anywhere else. You will know when to be more tolerant of them and when they are liable to be difficult or irritable.

In this edition we have included foot reflexology charts as part of the health section. So many health problems could perhaps be avoided or alleviated if we understood which organs were most vulnerable and what we could do to protect them. Though there are many natural and drug-free ways to strengthen vulnerable organs, these charts show a valid way to proceed. The vulnerable organs for the year ahead are clearly marked in the chart. It's very good to massage the whole foot on a regular basis, as the feet contain reflexes to the entire body. Try to pay special attention to the specific areas marked in the chart. If this is done diligently, health problems can be avoided. And even if they can't be completely avoided, their impact can be softened considerably.

I consider you – the reader – my personal client. By studying your Solar Horoscope I gain an awareness of what is going on in your life – what you are feeling and striving for and the challenges you face. I then do my best to address these concerns. Consider this book the next best thing to having your own personal astrologer!

It is my sincere hope that *Your Personal Horoscope 2013* will enhance the quality of your life, make things easier, illuminate the way forward, banish obscurities and make you more aware of your personal connection to the universe. Understood properly and used wisely, astrology is a great guide to knowing yourself, the people around you and the events in your life – but remember that what you do with these insights – the final result – is up to you.

A Note on the 'New Zodiac'

Recently an article was published that postulated two things – the discovery of a new constellation, Ophiuchus, making a thirteenth constellation in the heavens and thus a thirteenth sign, and the statement that because the Earth has shifted relative to the constellations in the past few thousand years, all the signs have shifted backwards by one sign. This has caused much consternation, and I have been receiving a constant stream of letters, emails and phone calls from people saying things like: 'I don't want to be a Taurus, I'm happy being a Gemini', 'What's my real sign?' or 'Now that I finally understand myself, I'm not who I think I am!'

All of this is 'much ado about nothing'. The article has some partial truth to it. Yes, in two thousand years the planets have shifted relative to the constellations in the heavens. This is old news. We know this and Hindu astrologers take this into account when casting charts. This shift doesn't affect Western astrologers in North America and Europe. We use what is called a 'tropical' zodiac. This zodiac has nothing to do with the constellations in the heavens. They have the same names, but that's about it. The tropical zodiac is based on the Earth's revolution around the Sun. Imagine the circle that this orbit makes, then divide this circle by twelve and you have our zodiac. The Spring Equinox is always 0 degrees (Aries), and the Autumn Equinox is always 0 degrees (Libra). At one time a few thousand years ago, these tropical signs coincided with the actual constellations – they were pretty much interchangeable, and it didn't matter what zodiac you used. But in the course of thousands of years the planets have shifted relative to these constellations. Here in the West it doesn't affect our practice one iota. You are still the sign you always were.

In North America and Europe there is a clear distinction between an astrological sign and a constellation in the heavens. This issue is more of a problem for Hindu astrologers. Their zodiac is based on the actual constellations – this is called the 'sidereal' zodiac. And Hindu astrologers have been accounting for this shift all the time. They keep close tabs on it. In two thousand years there is a shift of 23 degrees, and they subtract this from the Western calculations. So in their system many a Gemini would be a Taurus and this is true for all the signs. This is nothing new – it is all known and accounted for, so there is no bombshell here.

The so-called thirteenth constellation, Ophiuchus, is also not a problem for the Western astrologer. As we mentioned, our zodiac has nothing to do with the constellations. It would be more of a problem for the Hindus. But my feeling is that it's not a problem for them either. What these astronomers are calling a new constellation was probably considered a part of one of the existing constellations. I don't know this as a fact, but I presume it is so intuitively. I'm sure we will be getting articles by Hindu astrologers explaining this.

Glossary of Astrological Terms

Ascendant

We experience day and night because the Earth rotates on its axis once every 24 hours. It is because of this rotation that the Sun, Moon and planets seem to rise and set. The zodiac is a fixed belt (imaginary, but very real in spiritual terms) around the Earth. As the Earth rotates, the different signs of the zodiac seem to the observer to rise on the horizon. During a 24-hour period every sign of the zodiac will pass this horizon point at some time or another. The sign that is at the horizon point at any given time is called the Ascendant, or rising sign. The Ascendant is the sign denoting a person's self-image, body and self-concept – the personal ego, as opposed to the spiritual ego indicated by a person's Sun sign.

Aspects

Aspects are the angular relationships between planets, the way in which one planet stimulates or influences another. If a planet makes a harmonious aspect (connection) to another, it tends to stimulate that planet in a positive and helpful way. If it makes a stressful aspect to another planet, this disrupts the planet's normal influence.

Astrological Qualities

There are three astrological qualities: *cardinal*, *fixed* and *mutable*. Each of the 12 signs of the zodiac falls into one of these three categories.

Cardinal Signs	Aries, Cancer, Libra and Capricorn The cardinal quality is the active, initiating principle. Those born under these four signs are good at starting new projects.
Fixed Signs	Taurus, Leo, Scorpio and Aquarius Fixed qualities include stability, persistence, endurance and perfectionism. People born under these four signs are good at seeing things through.
Mutable Signs	Gemini, Virgo, Sagittarius and Pisces Mutable qualities are adaptability, changeability and balance. Those born under these four signs are creative, if not always practical.

Direct Motion

When the planets move forward through the zodiac – as they normally do – they are said to be going 'direct'.

Grand Square

A Grand Square differs from a normal Square (usually two planets separated by 90 degrees) in that four or more planets are involved. When you look at the pattern in a chart you will see a whole and complete square. This, though stressful, usually denotes a new manifestation in the life. There is much work and balancing involved in the manifestation.

Grand Trine

A Grand Trine differs from a normal Trine (where two planets are 120 degrees apart) in that three or more planets are involved. When you look at this pattern in a chart, it takes the form of a complete triangle – a Grand Trine. Usually (but not always) it occurs in one of the four elements: Fire, Earth, Air or Water. Thus the particular element in which it occurs will be highlighted. A Grand Trine in Water is not the same as a Grand Trine in Air or Fire, etc. This is a very fortunate and happy aspect, and quite rare.

Houses

There are 12 signs of the zodiac and 12 houses of experience. The 12 signs are personality types and ways in which a given planet expresses itself; the 12 houses show 'where' in your life this expression takes place. Each house has a different area of interest. A house can become potent and important – a House of Power – in different ways: if it contains the Sun, the Moon or the 'ruler' of your chart; if it contains more than one planet; or if the ruler of that house is receiving unusual stimulation from other planets.

1st House	Personal Image and Sensual Delights
2nd House	Money/Finance
3rd House	Communication and Intellectual Interests
4th House	Home and Family
5th House	Children, Fun, Games, Creativity, Speculations and Love Affairs
6th House	Health and Work
7th House	Love, Marriage and Social Activities
8th House	Transformation and Regeneration
9th House	Religion, Foreign Travel, Higher Education and Philosophy
10th House	Career
11th House	Friends, Group Activities and Fondest Wishes
12th House	Spirituality

Karma

Karma is the law of cause and effect which governs all phenomena. We are all where we find ourselves because of karma – because of actions we have performed in the past. The universe is such a balanced instrument that any act immediately sets corrective forces into motion – karma.

Long-term Planets

The planets that take a long time to move through a sign show the long-term trends in a given area of life. They are important for forecasting the prolonged view of things. Because these planets stay in one sign for so long, there are periods in the year when the faster-moving (short-term) planets will join them, further activating and enhancing the importance of a given house.

Jupiter	stays in a sign for about 1 year
Saturn	2½ years
Uranus	7 years
Neptune	14 years
Pluto	15 to 30 years

Lunar

Relating to the Moon. See also 'Phases of the Moon', below.

Natal

Literally means 'birth'. In astrology this term is used to distinguish between planetary positions that occurred at the time of a person's birth (natal) and those that are current (transiting). For example, Natal Sun refers to where the Sun was when you were born; transiting Sun refers to where the Sun's position is currently at any given moment – which usually doesn't coincide with your birth, or Natal, Sun.

Out of Bounds

The planets move through the zodiac at various angles relative to the celestial equator (if you were to draw an imaginary extension of the Earth's equator out into the universe, you would have an illustration of this celestial equator). The Sun – being the most dominant and powerful influence in the Solar system – is the measure astrologers use as a standard. The Sun never goes more than approximately 23 degrees north or south of the celestial equator. At the winter solstice the Sun reaches its maximum southern angle of orbit (declination); at the summer solstice it reaches its maximum northern angle. Any time a planet exceeds this Solar boundary – and occasionally planets do – it is said to be 'out of bounds'. This means that the planet exceeds or trespasses into strange territory – beyond the limits allowed by the Sun, the Ruler of the Solar system. The planet in this condition becomes more emphasized and exceeds its authority, becoming an important influence in the forecast.

Phases of the Moon

After the full Moon, the Moon seems to shrink in size (as perceived from the Earth), gradually growing smaller until it is virtually invisible to the naked eye – at the time of the next new Moon. This is called the waning Moon phase, or the waning Moon.

After the new Moon, the Moon gradually gets bigger in size (as perceived from the Earth) until it reaches its maximum size at the time of the full Moon. This period is called the waxing Moon phase, or waxing Moon.

Retrogrades

The planets move around the Sun at different speeds. Mercury and Venus move much faster than the Earth, while Mars, Jupiter, Saturn, Uranus, Neptune and Pluto move more slowly. Thus there are times when, relative to the Earth, the planets appear to be going backwards. In reality they are always going forward, but relative to our vantage point on Earth they seem to go backwards through the zodiac for a period of time. This is called 'retrograde' motion and tends to weaken the normal influence of a given planet.

Short-term Planets

The fast-moving planets move so quickly through a sign that their effects are generally of a short-term nature. They reflect the immediate, day-to-day trends in a horoscope.

Moon	stays in a sign for only 2½ days
Mercury	20 to 30 days
Sun	30 days
Venus	approximately 1 month
Mars	approximately 2 months

T-square

A T-square differs from a Grand Square in that it is not a complete square. If you look at the pattern in a chart it appears as 'half a complete square', resembling the T-square tools used by architects and designers. If you cut a complete square in half, diagonally, you have a T-square. Many astrologers consider this more stressful than a Grand Square, as it creates tension that is difficult to resolve. T-squares bring learning experiences.

Transits

This refers to the movements or motions of the planets at any given time. Astrologers use the word 'transit' to make the distinction between a birth or Natal planet (see 'Natal', above) and the planet's current movement in the heavens. For example, if at your birth Saturn was in the sign of Cancer in your 8th house, but is now moving through your 3rd house, it is said to be 'transiting' your 3rd house. Transits are one of the main tools with which astrologers forecast trends.

YOUR PERSONAL HOROSCOPE 2013

Aries

♈

THE RAM

*Birthdays from
21st March to
20th April*

Personality Profile

ARIES AT A GLANCE

Element – Fire

Ruling Planet – Mars
   Career Planet – Saturn
   Love Planet – Venus
   Money Planet – Venus
   *Planet of Fun, Entertainment, Creativity
     and Speculations* – Sun
   Planet of Health and Work – Mercury
   Planet of Home and Family Life – Moon
   Planet of Spirituality – Neptune
   *Planet of Travel, Education, Religion
     and Philosophy* – Jupiter

Colours – carmine, red, scarlet

*Colours that promote love, romance and social
   harmony* – green, jade green

Colour that promotes earning power – green

Gem – amethyst

Metals – iron, steel

Scent – honeysuckle

Quality – cardinal (= activity)

Quality most needed for balance – caution

Strongest virtues – abundant physical energy, courage, honesty, independence, self-reliance

Deepest need – action

Characteristics to avoid – haste, impetuousness, over-aggression, rashness

Signs of greatest overall compatibility – Leo, Sagittarius

Signs of greatest overall incompatibility – Cancer, Libra, Capricorn

Sign most helpful to career – Capricorn

Sign most helpful for emotional support – Cancer

Sign most helpful financially – Taurus

Sign best for marriage and/or partnerships – Libra

Sign most helpful for creative projects – Leo

Best Sign to have fun with – Leo

Signs most helpful in spiritual matters – Sagittarius, Pisces

Best day of the week – Tuesday

Understanding an Aries

Aries is the activist *par excellence* of the zodiac. The Aries need for action is almost an addiction, and those who do not really understand the Aries personality would probably use this hard word to describe it. In reality 'action' is the essence of the Aries psychology – the more direct, blunt and to-the-point the action, the better. When you think about it, this is the ideal psychological makeup for the warrior, the pioneer, the athlete or the manager.

Aries likes to get things done, and in their passion and zeal often lose sight of the consequences for themselves and others. Yes, they often try to be diplomatic and tactful, but it is hard for them. When they do so they feel that they are being dishonest and phony. It is hard for them even to understand the mindset of the diplomat, the consensus builder, the front office executive. These people are involved in endless meetings, discussions, talks and negotiations – all of which seem a great waste of time when there is so much work to be done, so many real achievements to be gained. An Aries can understand, once it is explained, that talks and negotiations – the social graces – lead ultimately to better, more effective actions. The interesting thing is that an Aries is rarely malicious or spiteful – even when waging war. Aries people fight without hate for their opponents. To them it is all good-natured fun, a grand adventure, a game.

When confronted with a problem many people will say, 'Well, let's think about it, let's analyse the situation.' But not an Aries. An Aries will think, 'Something must be done. Let's get on with it.' Of course neither response is the total answer. Sometimes action is called for, sometimes cool thought. But an Aries tends to err on the side of action.

Action and thought are radically different principles. Physical activity is the use of brute force. Thinking and deliberating require one not to use force – to be still. It is not good for the athlete to be deliberating the next move; this will only slow down his or her reaction time. The athlete must act instinctively and instantly. This is how Aries people tend to behave in life. They are quick, instinctive decision-makers and their decisions tend to be translated into action almost immediately. When their intuition is sharp and well tuned, their actions are powerful and successful. When their intuition is off, their actions can be disastrous.

Do not think this will scare an Aries. Just as a good warrior knows that in the course of combat he or she might acquire a few wounds, so too does an Aries realize – somewhere deep down – that in the course of being true to yourself you might get embroiled in a disaster or two. It is all part of the game. An Aries feels strong enough to weather any storm.

There are many Aries people who are intellectual. They make powerful and creative thinkers. But even in this realm they tend to be pioneers – outspoken and blunt. These types of Aries tend to elevate (or sublimate) their desire for physical combat in favour of intellectual, mental combat. And they are indeed powerful.

In general, Aries people have a faith in themselves that others could learn from. This basic, rock-solid faith carries them through the most tumultuous situations of life. Their courage and self-confidence make them natural leaders. Their leadership is more by way of example than by actually controlling others.

Finance

Aries people often excel as builders or estate agents. Money in and of itself is not as important as are other things – action, adventure, sport, etc. They are motivated by the need to support and be well-thought-of by their partners. Money as a way of attaining pleasure is another important motivation. Aries function best in their own businesses or as managers of their own departments within a large business or corporation. The fewer orders they have to take from higher up, the better. They also function better out in the field rather than behind a desk.

Aries people are hard workers with a lot of endurance; they can earn large sums of money due to the strength of their sheer physical energy.

Venus is their money planet, which means that Aries need to develop more of the social graces in order to realize their full earning potential. Just getting the job done – which is what an Aries excels at – is not enough to create financial success. The co-operation of others needs to be attained. Customers, clients and co-workers need to be made to feel comfortable; many people need to be treated properly in order for success to happen. When Aries people develop these abilities – or hire someone to do this for them – their financial potential is unlimited.

Career and Public Image

One would think that a pioneering type would want to break with the social and political conventions of society. But this is not so with the Aries-born. They are pioneers within conventional limits, in the sense that they like to start their own businesses within an established industry.

Capricorn is on the 10th house (career) cusp of Aries' Solar horoscope. Saturn is the planet that rules their life's work and professional aspirations. This tells us some interesting things about the Aries character. First off, it shows that, in order for Aries people to reach their full career potential, they need to develop some qualities that are a bit alien to their basic nature: they need to become better administrators and organizers; they need to be able to handle details better and to take a long-range view of their projects and their careers in general. No one can beat an Aries when it comes to achieving short-range objectives, but a career is long term, built over time. You cannot take a 'quickie' approach to it.

Some Aries people find it difficult to stick with a project until the end. Since they get bored quickly and are in constant pursuit of new adventures, they prefer to pass an old project or task on to somebody else in order to start something new. Those Aries who learn how to put off the search for something new until the old is completed will achieve great success in their careers and professional lives.

In general, Aries people like society to judge them on their own merits, on their real and actual achievements. A reputation acquired by 'hype' feels false to them.

Love and Relationships

In marriage and partnerships Aries like those who are more passive, gentle, tactful and diplomatic – people who have the social grace and skills they sometimes lack. Our partners always represent a hidden part of ourselves – a self that we cannot express personally.

An Aries tends to go after what he or she likes aggressively. The tendency is to jump into relationships and marriages. This is especially true if Venus is in Aries as well as the Sun. If an Aries likes you, he or she will have a hard time taking no for an answer; many attempts will be made to sweep you off your feet.

Though Aries can be exasperating in relationships – especially if they are not understood by their partners – they are never consciously or wilfully cruel or malicious. It is just that they are so independent and sure of themselves that they find it almost impossible to see somebody else's viewpoint or position. This is why an Aries needs as a partner someone with lots of social graces.

On the plus side, an Aries is honest, someone you can lean on, someone with whom you will always know where you stand. What he or she lacks in diplomacy is made up for in integrity.

Home and Domestic Life

An Aries is of course the ruler at home – the Boss. The male will tend to delegate domestic matters to the female. The female Aries will want to rule the roost. Both tend to be handy round the house. Both like large families and both believe in the sanctity and importance of the family. An Aries is a good family person, although he or she does not especially like being at home a lot, preferring instead to be roaming about.

Considering that they are by nature so combative and wilful, Aries people can be surprisingly soft, gentle and even vulnerable with their children and partners. The sign of Cancer, ruled by the Moon, is on the cusp of their solar 4th house (home and family). When the Moon is well aspected – under favourable influences – in the birth chart, an Aries will be tender towards the family and want a family life that is nurturing and supportive. Aries likes to come home after a hard day on the battlefield of life to the understanding arms of their partner and the unconditional love and support of their family. An Aries feels that there is enough 'war' out in the world – and he or she enjoys participating in that. But when Aries comes home, comfort and nurturing are what's needed.

Horoscope for 2013

Major Trends

Ever since Uranus, one of the most dynamic of planets, moved into your sign in March of 2011, change – sudden and dramatic – has been the theme of your life. By the time Uranus is finished with you in about five years' time, you will be in radically different conditions and circumstances than you are now. All of you are feeling the changes, but those of you born early in the sign of Aries (March 20 to April 5) are feeling it the strongest. Part of this is not so pleasant. Sometimes we cling unconsciously to negative situations, relationships or mental patterns – we cling to a status quo that is actually destructive to us – and so Uranus has to take dramatic measures to release us from this bondage. Sometimes it is an earthquake, a tsunami, or some other natural disaster that does the trick. Sometimes other dramatic events happen. None of this is punishment, only liberation. With Uranus involved there is little we can do consciously to prevent the change; these things are not something you can plan for. The events are generally sudden and unexpected – things you wouldn't dream of in a million years. With Uranus you can only expect the unexpected. But when the change happens, suddenly you are in a new life; suddenly you are free to follow the true desire of your heart. This is the blessing here.

The last two years were very challenging, filled with crises. Happily you got through; the worst is over with. Most of the long-term planets have moved from their stressful aspect to you, and there should be a tremendous increase in your health and energy in 2013. More on this later.

Saturn moved into your 8th house in October of 2012 – a very nice transit for you as it moved away from its stressful position. This year you need to scrutinize your sexual activity more closely. There is a need to focus more on quality than quantity. Saturn knows how to do this.

Last year, on February 4, Neptune made a major move out of your 11th house and into your spiritual 12th house. The spiritual life is much more emphasized than usual and this will be a long term trend.

Your main areas of interest in the year ahead are the body, the image and personal pleasure; communication and intellectual interests (until June 27); home and family (from June 27 onwards); sex, death and rebirth, reincarnation, past life regression, occult studies and personal reinvention; career; spirituality.

Your paths of greatest fulfilment in the year ahead are communication and intellectual interests (until June 27); home and family (from June 27 onwards); sex, death and rebirth, reincarnation, past life regression, occult studies and personal reinvention.

Health

(Please note that this is an astrological perspective on health and not a medical one. In days of yore there was no difference, these perspectives were identical. But now there could be quite a difference. For a medical perspective, please consult your doctor or health practitioner.)

Health and energy is much, much improved over the past few years. If you got through 2011 and 2012, you will coast ahead this year; you will be stronger than ever. Your 6th house of health is basically empty this year, with no long-term planets there. The short-term planets will move through briefly, but these transits are temporary and not trends for the year. I count this empty 6th house as a positive for health. You don't have much of a need to focus here as nothing is wrong. You can sort of take good health for granted.

Good though your health is, you can make it even better. Give more attention to the following organs: the head, face and scalp (regular scalp and face massage is always a powerful therapy for you, craniosacral therapy likewise – the bones in the skull sometimes get out of alignment and need to be re-aligned); the lungs, small intestine, arms, shoulders and respiratory system. Arms and shoulders should be regularly massaged, and air purity tends to be more important for Aries than for most. Since these are the most vulnerable areas keeping them healthy and fit is sound preventive medicine.

Uranus is in your own sign now for the long term. This tends to make you experimental with the body. You are into 'testing' its limits. Basically this is a good thing. This is how we learn about ourselves; this is how we expand our physical limits, expand athletic performance, expand physical strength and endurance. But this testing needs to be done in a mindful way; disciplines such as yoga, tai chi and other martial arts would be good. You can test the body and expand its limits but in a safe and controlled way. This trend is in effect for many more years.

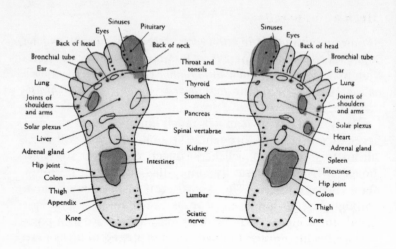

Reflexology

Try to massage the whole foot on a regular basis, but pay extra attention to the points highlighted on the chart. When you massage, be aware of 'sore spots', as these need special attention. It's also a good idea to massage the ankles and top side of the feet.

Mercury is your health planet (a great health planet to have by the way) and this is his natural domain. He is strong and powerful on your behalf. In the physical body he rules the lungs, small intestine, arms, shoulders and respiratory system – hence their importance in overall health. Our regular readers know that Mercury is a fast-moving planet. In the course of the year ahead he will move through all the signs and houses of your Horoscope. Thus, there are many short-term trends in health, depending on where Mercury is and the aspects he receives, that are best dealt with in the monthly reports.

Home and Family

Your 4th house of home and family becomes strong – and in a happy way – from June 27, as Jupiter moves into that house and stays there well into 2014. Jupiter moving through the 4th house brings good fortune in the purchase or sale of a home, and often it shows a move – a happy move to larger and better quarters. But one doesn't need physically to move to achieve happiness and more space in the home. Often a renovation will do. Sometimes the addition of a new frill or accessory 'expands' the home and makes it different. Sometimes people buy additional homes or properties. However, whether you move or not, the opportunity to move will come to you – and when this happens you can decide what to do.

Jupiter in the 4th house shows happiness and pleasure from the family. There is good family support this year. You are generous with the family and vice versa. It brings prosperity to the family as a whole, but especially to one of the parents or parent figures in your life.

This aspect also shows the 'expansion of the family unit'. Generally this happens through birth or marriage. Sometimes through meeting people who are 'like' family to you; people who support you unconditionally. Perhaps the best thing that happens is that the emotional life will be up and optimistic. Good moods draw good events.

Not everything is rosy with the family. In-laws are having a rough time with surgeries, perhaps near-death kinds of experiences and dramatic personal changes. But somehow the family bands together and stays optimistic. There is a 'can do' spirit in the family.

Aries of childbearing age are much more fertile than usual this period. This is so in 2014 as well.

You have the kind of chart of someone who hosts religious services, scripture studies, or prayer meetings at the home – especially after June 27. In fact the family as a whole seems more religion oriented.

If you're planning renovations (and especially construction) any time after June 27 would be good, but July 13 to

August 28 is best. If you're beautifying the home, redecorating or repainting, June 3 to June 28 is good.

Siblings and sibling figures in your life are prospering this year. Overall they are having a good year, but don't seem likely to move. If they have been single, they seem involved in a serious romance. Parent figures could be having cosmetic-type surgery (although this could have already happened). Children are not likely to move this year. They want to, but they are better off making better use of the space they have.

Finance and Career

Your 2nd house of finance is not a house of power this year. You are coming off a banner financial year in 2012 and seem more or less satisfied. This is a status quo kind of year. You have no special need to make dramatic changes. However, there is a Solar Eclipse on May 10 that occurs in your money house and this will create some change. This will be short term though.

Fast-moving Venus is your financial planet, thus there are all kinds of short-term trends depending on where she is and the aspects she receives. These are best dealt with in the monthly reports. In general though, money tends to come to you in a variety of ways, through a variety of people. You are very flexible when it comes to earnings.

With Venus as your love planet as well as your financial planet, your social connections are of utmost importance in finance. Basically Aries is an independent sort who likes to chart his or her own destiny, but when it comes to finance, they need others.

With Venus as the financial planet you can never measure the native's wealth just by their financial statements. Their real wealth is in who they know, in the relationships that they have built up. In the corporate world they often place a monetary amount on this 'goodwill', above and beyond the actual physical assets that the company has.

Though the money house is empty this year there will be periods when the short-term planets move through there and activate it temporarily. These will be peak financial periods for the year. This year it happens from April 20 to May 31.

Your spouse, partner or current love is feeling financially stressed this year. They need to reorganize their finances. If they juggle things around a little, they will find that they have all the resources they need. Over the next two years they will become financially healthier; they'll get rid of a lot of waste and learn to manage their money better. It's not always pleasant but is really a cosmic workshop in financial management.

Career – professional status and prestige – is much more important than mere money this year. Money and career tend to be related, but not always. Many people will sacrifice earnings for a more prestigious position. Not everyone is like that but many are, and you are one of them.

Pluto the planet of transformation, death and rebirth, has been in your 10th house of career for some years now, while Saturn, your career planet, moved into your 8th house of transformation, death and rebirth in October 2012. So we have a double message here. Your company, your industry, your profession is undergoing deep transformation, being completely reformed. This process has been going on for some years but is accelerating now. In coming years these might not even be recognizable – it will be as if you were in a new company, industry or profession.

There are many scenarios as to how these things happen, too many to list here. But sometimes there are major leadership changes in your company or industry. Sometimes the top people have surgeries or near-death kinds of experiences. Sometimes there is a bankruptcy or near bankruptcy of the company. Sometimes the government creates new rules and regulations that reform an industry. We have mentioned only a few. But the stresses in the career are the birth pangs of something new and wonderful. Birth was never an easy or painless process.

Love and Social Life

Your 7th house of marriage and partnerships is not a house of power this year. This tends to the status quo, with nothing special happening in the love life. Singles will most likely stay single; married couples will most likely stay married. Sure, there will be periods in the year when the love life will be more active as the short-term planets activate this house, but these are short-term trends, not trends for the year. This year these periods will be from August 16 to October 23 and from December 7 to the end of the year.

Though your 7th house is empty, the social life in general seems much improved over the past two years. In 2009–2011 Saturn was moving through this house. Love was tested and there were many a divorce or separation. Serious relationships and friendships were also severely tested. The good ones survived – they always do – but the less than perfect, the ones that were flawed from the beginning didn't survive. This is the purpose of these testings. If your marriage or relationship survived the past few years, it will probably survive anything. You've got something very special. The testing is over with and you can enjoy each other again. Those of you recovering from a divorce are probably not in the mood to marry so soon.

We have been speaking mainly of those in or working on the first or second marriages. Those working on the third marriage had romance last year and possibly even a marriage. The aspects look great in the year ahead too. There are tests and trials but they seem survivable. What I like here is that love is seeking you out. The beloved seems very devoted to you. There is a strong commitment here and this tends to survival.

Aries is in a season for exploring personal freedom. This is generally not so good for committed kinds of relationships. A committed relationship could work if freedom and change is allowed within the relationship. Those of you involved with an Aries in a romantic way need to understand this. Grant them as much freedom as possible so long as it isn't destructive.

Whatever marriage you are working on this seems more of a 'friendship' year than a romantic one. Friends seek you out. Friends are devoted to you. Friends put your interests ahead of their own.

These are the general trends for the year. There will be many short-term love trends depending on where Venus is and the aspects she receives, but these are best dealt with in the monthly reports.

Self-improvement

With Uranus in your sign for some years to come, there is a need to learn to cope with change. We may have mentioned this last year, but this lesson is still very much in effect. Change is the law of the universe. If you can learn to flow with the changes and not resist them, you will go through this very easily and harmoniously. If change is a law of the universe, then change actually – truly – is your friend, for the universe is for us, not against us. Change tends to bring insecurity and this is another area that needs to be dealt with. If the universe takes away one cherished toy, rest assured that it will replace it with a better toy. It is always working for our good.

With Uranus in the sign of Aries there is a mood of rebellion in the world. No one is feeling this more than Aries. Sometimes rebellion – especially against real oppression – is called for. But usually it is not. There are positive, constructive ways to change things. The positive way is to produce a better system, methodology, arrangement than what is current. It is not about loud yelling, bombast or violence. If you don't like the way your company is run, create a better way on your own. Show it. Demonstrate it. If you are lucky enough to live in a democracy, exercise your rebellion with your vote and with political activism for what you do support.

The danger is that one can get into 'blind rebellion' – rebellion for the sake of rebellion. It doesn't matter what the real issues are; authority is evil, merely because it is authority. This can have negative consequences both for the rebel and for the one he or she is rebelling against.

This mood will be especially prevalent with Aries children. They will be more difficult to handle. If you have Aries children the first step is to give them as much freedom as possible so long as it isn't destructive. Encourage them to get into creative hobbies where they can express their originality and rebellious urges in safe, constructive ways. If you want them to do something avoid the 'authoritarian' approach. Let them know the logic, the rationale behind your request – and not just 'because I said so'.

Month-by-month Forecasts

January

Best Days Overall: 8, 9, 17, 18, 26, 27, 28
Most Stressful Days Overall: 4, 5, 10, 11, 24, 25, 31
Best Days for Love: 4, 5, 8, 9, 18, 19, 29, 30, 31
Best Days for Money: 4, 8, 9, 12, 18, 19, 20, 22, 29, 30, 31
Best Days for Career: 6, 7, 10, 11, 14, 15, 24, 25

You begin your year with 70 per cent and sometimes 80 per cent of the planets above the horizon in the upper part of the Horoscope. Your 10th career house is very powerful all month, but especially until the 19th. You are in the midst of a yearly career peak. You are in the noon time of your year. Focus on the career and your outer, worldly objectives. You can safely let go of home and family issues for a while. You can best serve your family by succeeding in the outer world. This is a month of great career progress: pay rises and promotions are likely.

Last month the planets began to shift from the Western, social, sector of your chart to the Eastern sector. This month, on the 19th, the shift is even stronger. The Eastern, independent, sector is now dominant. As our regular readers know, this is a time to take charge of your destiny, to shape conditions and circumstances the way you want them to be to create your personal nirvana. You have the power to do it now. Others will most likely go along with you, but if not, you can go it alone. After six or so months with the planets in the West, where you were forced to adapt to situations, you can readily see what needs changing and can now set about fixing things.

During this month 90 per cent of the planets are in forward motion, and by the end of the month ALL the planets will be forward. So this is a fast-paced kind of month and you should see rapid progress towards your goals.

This is a very good month for both love and money. Venus, both your financial planet and your love planet, is in Sagittarius until the 19th. This indicates increased earnings, luck in speculations and a generally upbeat attitude to finance. Sure, there are some problems, but you have the faith and the confidence to deal with them. After the 19th Venus crosses the Mid-heaven and moves into your 10th house of career. This shows pay raises. Financial opportunity comes from your good professional reputation and from the financial favour of bosses, elders and authority figures – perhaps even from the government. If you have issues with the government it might be advisable to handle them after the 19th. The financial planet in Capricorn after the 19th indicates a sound financial judgement, a good long-term perspective on finance. Before the 19th you are a free spender, perhaps an impulse spender. Afterwards you seem more responsible.

Your spouse or current love is making dramatic financial changes these days. He or she seems stressed. You seem the bigger earner right now. For singles there are love opportunities in foreign lands and in educational or religious-type settings. Until the 19th you are impulsive in love, but caution and perhaps testing will come after the 19th. The question is, can you restrain your ardour while your love planet is in Capricorn?

Health is good overall, but this is not one of your best months. Rest and relax more until the 19th. Happily you seem focused more on health this month and this is good news.

February

Best Days Overall: 5, 13, 14, 23, 24
Most Stressful Days Overall: 1, 7, 8, 20, 21, 22, 27, 28
Best Days for Love: 1, 9, 10, 18, 19, 27, 28
Best Days for Money: 9, 10, 15, 16, 17, 18, 19, 27
Best Days for Career: 2, 3, 7, 8, 11, 12, 20, 21

Career is still successful and a major focus, but the interest is fading somewhat. Generally this is because many short-term goals have been achieved and it's now time to focus on other things. Since the 19th of last month, your 11th house of friends has been powerful and this continues until the 18th of this month. You are in a strong social period, but it's not necessarily a romantic period. It's more about friendship and group activities. Your understanding of technology increases this month, and when Venus enters your 11th house on the 2nd, you seem to be spending on hi-tech gadgets.

The planetary momentum is overwhelmingly forward. Until the 18th all the planets are moving forward. Thus this is an excellent period for starting new projects or launching new products – the 10th to the 18th is the best time (the Moon will be in her waxing cycle).

On the 18th your career planet, Saturn, starts to retrograde. If you need to negotiate with bosses or the government or make other important career decisions, it's best to do this before this date.

The finances of your spouse, partner or current love seem improved this month, but he or she is not out of the woods. There needs to be a re-organization and restructuring there.

This month is a spiritual kind of month. Mars, your ruling planet, moves into your 12th house of spirituality on the 2nd. From the 3rd to the 5th it will travel (conjunct) with your spiritual planet Neptune. On the 5th, Mercury will move into the 12th house; on the 18th the Sun will move into this house, and on the 26th Venus will join the party. This is a month for spiritual-type breakthroughs. The invisible world is very close to you and unusually active in your affairs. This is a period for supernatural kinds of experiences – synchronicities, enhanced ESP and prophetic-type dreams. Those of you on a spiritual path will make great progress this month, and many of you will actually experience the things that you are reading about in books or hearing at the lectures or seminars.

When Mars is conjunct with Neptune (from the 3rd to the 5th), it's best to avoid alcohol or drugs. You are naturally high that period and these things could put you over the edge. The intuition will be sharp all month, but especially that period.

The element of Water will be very strong all month, but especially after the 18th; 60 per cent and sometimes 70 per cent of the planets will be in water signs. Thus people around you will be much more sensitive than usual. They will react to seemingly insignificant things – voice tones, body language and facial expressions. Take more care with other people's feelings now, especially those of children.

March

Best Days Overall: 4, 5, 12, 13, 14, 22, 23, 31
Most Stressful Days Overall: 1, 6, 7, 20, 21, 27, 28
Best Days for Love: 1, 2, 3, 10, 11, 21, 22, 27, 28, 31
Best Days for Money: 1, 2, 3, 8, 9, 10, 11, 15, 16, 17, 18, 21, 22, 27, 28, 31
Best Days for Career: 2, 3, 6, 7, 10, 11, 20, 21, 29, 30

Many of the trends that we wrote of last month are still very much in effect. The Water element continues to be strong. Until the 20th, up to 70 per cent of the planets are in water signs. Keep in mind our previous discussion. When water is strong people tend to get depressed more easily. They view the world – the future – according to the mood of the moment. Logic is completely over-ridden. Understanding this – and this is what astrology is really all about – will help you to handle this better.

The planets are now at their maximum Eastern position in your chart, so your personal independence, your personal power, is at its maximum right now. Now it's time to have life on your terms. Let the world adjust to you for a change. (Of course others are always to be treated with respect, but you can go your own way as long as you are not being destructive to others.)

Health and energy are excellent this month, and especially after the 20th as the Sun enters your sign. You have all the energy you need to achieve anything you set your mind to. You can enhance health even further by giving more attention to the feet; regular foot massages will be unusually powerful this month. Your health planet went retrograde on February 23 and will be retrograde until the 19th, so avoid making major dietary changes, or changes to the health regime, until after the 19th. Be more careful in communication as well. A thoughtless word can have all kinds of repercussions that you never imagined.

Your spiritual 12th house is still powerful until the 20th, so bear in mind last month's discussion. Now would be an excellent time to review the past year, evaluate your progress (or lack of progress), correct mistakes, forgive those who need to be forgiven and set your goals for the year ahead. Your birthday is your personal new year and is a very important time astrologically speaking. You want to start your new year with a clean slate.

Mars will be conjunct to Uranus towards the end of the month, from the 27th to the 30th (although you will be feeling the effects before this). Avoid daredevil kinds of stunts and watch the temper. Aries children (who have been rebellious for a few years now) are more rebellious than usual. Avoid rush and impatience now, although it will be difficult – you are energetic and raring to go. Be more mindful on the physical plane.

April

Best Days Overall: 1, 9, 10, 19, 20, 27, 28
Most Stressful Days Overall: 2, 3, 16, 17, 23, 24, 29, 30
Best Days for Love: 1, 9, 10, 21, 22, 23, 24, 29, 30
Best Days for Money: 1, 4, 5, 9, 10, 11, 12, 14, 15, 21, 22, 23, 24, 29, 30
Best Days for Career: 2, 3, 6, 7, 16, 17, 25, 26, 29, 30

Since the Sun went into your sign on March 20, life has been good. You are having your way. You are strong. (Whatever your age or stage in life, you have more energy than usual.) The physical appearance shines. The libido roars. You do the work of ten people and in half the time. Love and financial opportunities are seeking you out. This has been the case since March 22 and will continue until the 15th of this month. No need to search far and wide for love – you can't avoid it! There's no need to indulge in all the stratagems that most people employ, you just need to show up. Just go about your daily routine. Love seems happy this month, and especially from the 5th to the 9th as Venus travels with Mars, your personal planet. For singles this shows an important love meeting. For the already attached it indicates a more romantic period with the beloved.

Health and energy are still very good. I would say they are at the maximum for the year ahead. So you have all the fire power to achieve whatever you want to achieve. Until the 14th enhance the health through foot massage. Spiritual techniques are very powerful during this period too. After the 14th you respond very well to scalp and face massage. Vigorous physical exercise (which you seem to be into anyway) also enhances the health. The main danger health-wise (as it was last month) is from accident or injury due to haste or impatience. When we rush we lose our awareness and thus become more vulnerable to these things.

The Sun is in Aries and the planetary momentum is over-whelmingly forward: 90 per cent of the planets are moving forward this month. Thus you are in the best 'starting energy' of your year. This is another good period to launch those new products or projects into the world. I especially like the 10th to the 19th – the Sun and Mars are in Aries and the Moon is waxing.

On the 19th the Sun enters your money house and you begin a yearly financial peak. Mars will enter this house a day later on the 20th. So you are in a period of peak earnings. You are focused here and we tend to get what we focus on. Now is the time to build up the bank balance and investment portfolio. There is luck in speculations, but also other lucky breaks in your financial life as well. Your spouse, partner or current love (and your social circle in general) is supportive of your financial goals. You manage to combine business and pleasure this period. You socialize with the people you do business with and do business with friends. After the 20th, your spouse, partner or current love's finances also improve. There are still many changes going on but this period is a 'respite', a financial vacation.

There is a Lunar Eclipse on the 25th. Take things nice and easy during that period. Avoid speculations and be more patient with children and children figures in your life. Family members should also avoid risky kinds of activities.

May

  Best Days Overall: 6, 7, 16, 17, 25, 26
  Most Stressful Days Overall: 13, 14, 15, 21, 22, 27, 28
  Best Days for Love: 10, 11, 21, 22, 29, 30
  Best Days for Money: 2, 3, 8, 9, 10, 11, 12, 21, 22, 29, 30
  Best Days for Career: 4, 13, 14, 23, 27, 28, 31

On March 20 the planets began to shift from the upper to the lower half of your Horoscope. Last month the shift got even stronger. This month 60 per cent and sometimes 70 per cent of the planets are below the horizon of your chart. Your career goals have more or less been attained and now it is time to focus more on the home and family and to get this area of life in order. Career is still very important but you can shift some attention to the home and to your emotional life. There is a need now to find (and function from) your personal point of emotional harmony. When this is found, the career will go well in very natural ways. If you've been ignoring the family recently now is the time to start mending fences and restoring harmony.

You are still very much into a yearly financial peak until May 20. Prosperity is happening but there are some bumps along the way. A Solar Eclipse on the 10th occurs in your money house, and this indicates dramatic financial changes. These changes probably needed to be made long ago but now the eclipse forces the issue. The changes seem good in the long term, but in the short term they are not comfortable.

Health and energy are still very good, but it won't hurt to reduce your schedule during the eclipse period. This Solar Eclipse also affects children or children figures in your life. Often it brings life-changing kinds of events in their lives. They are forced now to redefine their image, their personality and the way they think of themselves. Generally this leads to wardrobe changes – changes in hair style, hair colour and overall presentation.

There is a Lunar Eclipse on the 25th in your 9th house. Though the eclipse is basically benign to you, it won't hurt to take things easier. Like every Lunar Eclipse the home and family are affected (so it is good that you are focusing more here). Family members can be more temperamental, so more patience is needed. Often there is a need for repairs in the home as hidden flaws come out. Students seem affected strongly by this. There can be changes of school or changes in courses or educational plans. There will be dramatic, life-changing kinds of events with the people at your place of worship or with a religious organization you belong to.

On the whole though, the month ahead looks good. Venus will be travelling with Jupiter towards the end of the month (from the 27th to the 29th); this indicates a nice payday, a nice financial windfall or opportunity. For singles this shows a happy love meeting. For those who are married it indicates more romance with the present partner.

June

Best Days Overall: 2, 3, 12, 13, 21, 22, 30, 31
Most Stressful Days Overall: 10, 11, 17, 18, 23, 24
Best Days for Love: 10, 17, 18, 19, 20, 27, 28
Best Days for Money: 5, 6, 8, 9, 10, 17, 18, 19, 20, 26, 27, 28
Best Days for Career: 1, 10, 19, 23, 24, 27

The planets are now at their maximum lowest position in the chart. You are in the 'midnight hour' of your year, which is considered a very 'magical' hour of the day. The old day is over with and a new day has begun – only it is not yet apparent to the senses. Midnight is not for outer kinds of activities but for the activities of the night: sleep, and the collecting of forces for the new day. This is the time to work on your outer goals by 'interior' methods – though dreaming, visualizing and entering into the 'inner condition' of what you want or where you want to be. This is the necessary prelude for attaining any goal. You are like a seed germinating in the ground. Mighty things are happening, only they cannot be seen. But when the daytime of your year comes around (in a few months' time) they will be seen. The seedling will burst from the earth and flower in visible, tangible reality.

Early in the month the focus is on communication and intellectual interests. A good time to catch up on those letters, emails and phone calls you owe, and great for taking courses in subjects that interest you – for expanding your knowledge base and exercising the mind. But after the 21st, the Sun enters Cancer, your 4th house of home and family. Jupiter will enter here on the 27th too. Now is the time for focusing on the family.

This is a month for making psychological kinds of breakthroughs. You will tend to be more nostalgic this period, to reminisce more. Often people from your past come back into the life and jog the memory. You will have a greater interest in history as well; not just your personal history but history in general.

Though career is not that important right now, much career progress is happening. Your career planet, Saturn, is receiving beautiful aspects. There is much success – and perhaps promotion and pay rises – happening, only it will manifest later on. Your career planet is retrograde.

Neptune, your spiritual planet, is also receiving very beautiful aspects. So, for those on the spiritual path there are important breakthroughs happening, revelations from on high. Your intuition is super.

Health needs more watching after the 21st. As always, rest and relax more: avoid burning the candle at both ends. Enhance the health through a right diet and give more attention to the stomach. Women should give more attention to the breasts. Emotional health is very important this month. Avoid depression like the plague. Keep the moods peaceful and constructive.

Love and money are close to home. Family connections play an important role in both. Family seems very supportive these days. A parent figure enters a two-year cycle of prosperity.

July

Best Days Overall: 1, 9, 10, 11, 19, 20, 27, 28
Most Stressful Days Overall: 7, 8, 14, 15, 21, 22
Best Days for Love: 1, 10, 11, 14, 15, 19, 20, 29, 30
Best Days for Money: 1, 2, 3, 7, 8, 10, 11, 16, 17, 19, 20, 25, 29, 30
Best Days for Career: 7, 16, 17, 21, 22, 25

Many of the trends we wrote of last month are still very much in effect. So review our discussion of last month.

Last month, on the 21st, the planetary power shifted from the East to the West. This month, on the 18th, Mars, your ruling planet, also shifts to the West. The social, Western sector is now dominant for the next five or six months. Hopefully, you have already made the personal changes that you needed to make. Hopefully, you have already created the conditions that you wanted to create. Now, it is time to live with your creation. If you have created wisely, it is a time to enjoy it. If you have made mistakes, well, now you experience the consequences of the mistakes. It's not so easy as it was to have your way. Now you have to adapt to situations as best you can and cultivate your social skills. The good graces of others are the most vital thing right now, in finance, love and career.

Health still needs watching until the 23rd. We don't see major problems here, but this is not your best health period. Energy is not up to its usual standard and thus you are more vulnerable to problems. Enhance the health in the ways mentioned last month. Your health planet Mercury is retrograde until the 21st, so avoid making major changes to the health regime without more research. Diet is important now, but study the matter thoroughly before making changes. Health and vitality will return after the 23rd.

Like last month career is not that important, but in spite of this many wonderful, behind-the-scenes things are happening. On the 8th your career planet starts to move forward, and thus there is more clarity about the career.

The spiritual life is also satisfying and successful. The spiritual faculties – ESP, intuition, etc. – are very much enhanced.

Mars travels with Jupiter from the 18th to the 24th, which is a very happy transit. A foreign trip is happening. Students have success in their studies or in getting into a good school or college. A nice financial windfall or opportunity comes, and people in authority look upon you with favour.

Love is happy this period. Singles are meeting people they can have fun with, rather than making serious commitments. Until the 23rd you seem to 'leap before you look' – you are a 'love at first sight' kind of person. But after that date you become more cautious (and rightfully so). Venus in Virgo from the 23rd onwards is not one of her favourite positions. She becomes too analytical – and romance is to do with the heart, not the head. You will have to exert more effort in showing love and warmth to others after the 23rd.

August

Best Days Overall: 6, 7, 15, 16, 23, 24
Most Stressful Days Overall: 3, 4, 10, 11, 12, 17, 18, 30, 31
Best Days for Love: 8, 9, 10, 11, 12, 19, 25, 26
Best Days for Money: 3, 8, 9, 13, 14, 19, 21, 22, 25, 26, 30, 31
Best Days for Career: 3, 13, 17, 18, 21, 30

Last month on the 22nd you entered a yearly personal pleasure peak, which is still in effect for the rest of the month ahead. Enjoy. This is a time for exploring the joys of life, for leisure-type activities and recreation. Aries of childbearing age have been fertile since last month, and now even more so. Enjoy your life, but don't get too carried away by 'irrational exuberance' – especially on the 1st and 2nd. Drive more carefully, try to avoid risky kinds of activities and watch the temper. If you read the newspapers on those days you'll understand what we're referring to.

The element of Water is still very strong this month, so be more mindful of other people's feelings. Everyone is more sensitive these days.

This is a time of year when people like to travel abroad, but this doesn't seem advisable this period. Try especially to avoid foreign travel from the 18th to the 25th. The journeys that are favourable now are 'interior' ones into your past or past lives; emotional and mental journeys rather than actual physical ones. Legal issues can take a surprising turn from the 18th to the 25th. Students make changes to educational plans this period.

Venus is still in Virgo until the 16th. This is not the best aspect for love. Like last month you will have to work harder to project warmth and love to others. You (or the people you attract) can be overly perfectionist in love, overly critical and analytical. This attitude will kill romantic moments and opportunities. It is good to want perfection in love – you deserve it – but you need to go about it in the right way, in a constructive way.

Love will be much happier when Venus moves into her own sign of Libra on the 16th. Here she is strong on your behalf. The social magnetism will be stronger than usual. You are in a more romantic mood. You attract more romantic kinds of people. A serious relationship is not indicated here – you are in a fun-loving mood – but the opportunities for it are there.

Until the 16th, money is earned the old-fashioned way, through work and practical service to others. After the 16th, the social dimension (always important for you) becomes even more important in finances. Social connections and your ability to get on with others improve the bottom line. Job seekers have good fortune this month. Your 6th house of work becomes powerful after the 22nd. Those who employ others will find suitable employees if they need them.

Health is good all month.

September

Best Days Overall: 2, 3, 11, 12, 20, 21, 29, 30
Most Stressful Days Overall: 1, 7, 8, 13, 14, 27, 28
Best Days for Love: 7, 8, 17, 18, 27, 28
Best Days for Money: 1, 8, 9, 10, 17, 18, 19, 22, 23, 27, 28
Best Days for Career: 1, 9, 10, 13, 14, 18, 27

The planetary power makes an important shift this month. By the 22nd, the upper half of the Horoscope (the sector of career and outer activities) becomes stronger than the lower half (home, family and emotional issues). Dawn is breaking in your year. It is time to wake up and be about, time to work on your career and outer goals by the methods of day – through overt physical action. Family life will still be very important, but you can shift more attention to the career now. This is the best way to serve your family.

You are still very much in a creative, fun kind of period. But less so than last month. Work has been important since August 22. This is a time to be more productive at work, to handle all those boring, detail-oriented jobs like getting your accounts in order, proof-reading your letters or reports, getting your files in order – things of this nature. It is still a favourable time for job seekers and for those who employ others.

On the 22nd you enter your yearly social peak. Romance is on your mind. You are in the mood for it and opportunities are abundant. While a marriage is not likely, there are still happy romantic experiences and opportunities happening. In general, you are going out more, attending more parties and gatherings.

The month ahead seems hectic. You are trying to balance many, many conflicting interests: an active social life, the need for fun and entertainment, your spiritual life, home and career. You've got a full plate this month. Also it seems that you are involved in some major, complicated project – launching a new business or institution. These big projects always tend to be complicated. Thus, you need to rest and relax more and pay more attention to health. Until the 9th, health is enhanced by paying more attention to the small intestine. Right diet is still an issue for you. After the 9th, give more attention to the kidneys and hips. Regular hip massage will be wonderful. Discord in love or with friends can be a cause of health problems, so work to maintain harmony here. From the 29th onwards, give more attention to the colon, bladder and sexual organs. Safe sex and sexual moderation is important then.

In spite of all the stress the month ahead seems prosperous. Your spouse, partner or current love is having a good

month, both personally and financially. There is still a financial re-organization going on but this month things seem
easier. He or she seems more financially supportive as well.
Friends in general are more financially supportive. There is a
nice payday happening on the 27th–28th as Venus makes
fabulous aspects to Jupiter. This also brings a very happy
romantic meeting or social opportunity.

October

Best Days Overall: 1, 8, 9, 17, 18, 27, 28
Most Stressful Days Overall: 4, 5, 11, 12, 24, 25, 31
Best Days for Love: 4, 5, 7, 8, 17, 18, 27, 28, 31
Best Days for Money: 6, 7, 8, 15, 16, 17, 18, 19, 20, 24,
   25, 27, 28
Best Days for Career: 6, 7, 11, 12, 15, 16, 24, 25

Like last month the pace of life is frenetic, and you are
working hard to balance many competing interests. Continue to rest and relax more; it is difficult right now but if
you shift the rhythm of life a bit you can do it. Instead of go-
go-go, make it go-go-rest. Often we can maximize energy by
letting go of trivial things and focusing on the essentials.
Like last month you can enhance the health by giving more
attention to the colon, bladder and sexual organs. Safe sex
and sexual moderation continue to be important. The month
ahead seems more sexually active than usual, but if you
listen to your body (and not your mind) you will know
when enough is enough. Mercury, your health planet, goes
retrograde on the 21st, so avoid making major changes to
the diet or health regime after that period. Health and vitality should improve after the 23rd.

Your spouse, partner or current love is in a yearly financial peak from the 23rd onwards. But still there are many
dramatic financial changes going on – it seems to me they
are for the better though.

The work load is frenetic this month, but after the 15th,
as Mars enters your 6th house, you have a strong work ethic

and you seem able to handle it. Job opportunities need more research after the 21st. Read all the fine print in contracts. Ask questions. Resolve any doubts. Happy career opportunities are happening after the 23rd. Children or children figures also have career success during this period.

You are still in a yearly social peak until the 23rd. After then, your 8th house of transformation becomes powerful. The interests shift to personal transformation and reinvention, past lives and life after death. On the financial level, you are focused on debt and taxes.

A Lunar Eclipse on the 18th is strong in its effect on you, so reduce your schedule. Like every Lunar Eclipse the home and family are affected. If there are hidden problems in the home (or with family members) they come out now so that they can be dealt with. This eclipse occurs in your own sign. Those born later in the sign of Aries – April 13–20 – seem most affected. There is a redefinition of your image and personality happening. You are going to present a 'new you' to the public. Students make important changes in educational plans. Legal issues start to move forward, either positively or negatively (but the aspects seem mostly positive now).

November

Best Days Overall: 5, 6, 13, 14, 23, 24
Most Stressful Days Overall: 1, 7, 8, 20, 21, 22, 28, 29
Best Days for Love: 1, 7, 16, 17, 26, 27, 28, 29
Best Days for Money: 3, 4, 7, 11, 12, 16, 17, 21, 22, 26, 27, 30
Best Days for Career: 3, 4, 7, 8, 11, 12, 20, 21, 30

The Solar Eclipse on the 3rd is basically benign to you, but it won't hurt to reduce your schedule anyway. It occurs in your 8th house of transformation, which often shows a need to deal with issues of death. Not necessarily personal physical death; sometimes it brings encounters with death or near-death kinds of experiences, and most of the time these encounters are on the psychological level. There is a need to overcome fears about it, to get a deeper understanding of it.

The eclipse also indicates more financial changes for the spouse, partner or current love. This has been going on all year, but now it is intensified. In general, though, this is a good financial month for this person. The Sun rules children generically. In your chart, as Lord of the 5th house, it is the actual ruler of children. So there are dramas, life-changing kinds of events, in the lives of the children (or children figures) in your life. These events need not necessarily be bad, but they are important and change your relationship with them. Those of you ready to give birth around this time (and many of you are) need to take care.

Health and energy are very good this month, and will get even better when the Sun moves into Sagittarius on the 22nd. You have all the energy you need to achieve your goals.

Love is happy but complicated this month. On the one hand, you are mixing with the high and mighty – people above you in status. You have a knack for meeting people socially who can help your career. Love is high on the agenda after the 5th and this focus leads to success. There are romantic opportunities with bosses and your superiors this month. The problem is that you seem too practical about love. It is more difficult to show your natural warmth to others. You seem slow and cautious about love and find it difficult to give your heart to another. Those involved with Aries romantically need to be more patient with them. From the 14th to the 16th Venus makes aspects to Pluto and Uranus, and this can shake things up a bit – a lover's spat, a quarrel, or abrupt mood changes in love. This is short term and might even lead to good later on. The air gets cleared.

Finances are good this period. Bosses, elders, parents or parent figures are supportive financially. There could be pay rises (official or unofficial) happening. Sometimes the boss doesn't give you an actual raise but instead arranges things so that you make more. You and your spouse, partner or current love seem in financial harmony and are cooperating with each other.

December

> Best Days Overall: 2, 3, 10, 11, 12, 20, 21, 22, 30, 31
> Most Stressful Days Overall: 4, 5, 12, 18, 19, 25, 26
> Best Days for Love: 4, 5, 13, 14, 23, 24, 25, 26
> Best Days for Money: 1, 4, 5, 8, 9, 13, 14, 18, 19, 23, 24, 28, 29
> Best Days for Career: 1, 4, 5, 8, 9, 18, 19, 28, 29

A happy and successful month ahead. Until the 21st, your 9th house is powerful. Thus foreign lands call to you. Keep in mind though that Jupiter is retrograde, so foreign travel might not be so advisable. If you must travel, protect yourself. Insure your tickets and don't schedule connecting flights too tightly. Allow more time to get to and from your destination. Religion, philosophy and higher education are important this month as well. Students at the college or postgraduate level should do well this month. Learning need not be a chore. It is actually one of the great pleasures of life, as you will learn this month.

Health is very good until the 21st. After the 5th give attention to the liver and thighs. Regular thigh massage is powerful. After the 24th, as Mercury moves into Capricorn, give more attention to the spine, knees and skin. Regular back massage will be powerful. If you feel under the weather a visit to the chiropractor or osteopath might be a good idea. Health becomes more delicate after the 21st. Try to rest and relax more. You seem very busy, more than usual, so this will be a challenge. However, if you drop the trivia from your life and focus on what is really important you will have all the energy you need to achieve your goals. In previous months you could afford to be profligate with your energy, but not now.

This month, on the 21st, the planets start to make an important shift from the Western sector to the Eastern sector of the chart. From this point onwards – well into next year – you will be becoming more independent day by day. You once again enter a cycle where you can have things your way. No need to compromise or 'people please'; your destiny, your happiness is in your own hands.

On the 21st you enter a yearly career peak. Family is still important, but the main focus should be on the career. You owe it to your family to be successful. There is much success, much progress happening here.

Be patient with finances this month. Your financial planet Venus is in Capricorn, and so the financial trends that we wrote of last month are still in effect. Pay rises are still likely. But now you should take a long-term view of wealth. Avoid the 'quick buck'. Build wealth methodically over time. This is a very good month to set up a financial plan, or long-term savings or investment plan. Your financial planet will go retrograde on the 21st, so avoid major purchases or important financial decisions after the 21st. Do your holiday shopping early this year!

Love is a mixed picture. On the one hand, you are active here – aggressive in love. You seem popular as well. Yet, you seem out of synch with the beloved. You will have to work harder to make things work. He or she seems on top right now, calling the shots, and this could be hard to handle.

Taurus

♉

Birthdays from
21st April to
20th May

Personality Profile

TAURUS AT A GLANCE

Element – Earth

Ruling Planet – Venus
  Career Planet – Uranus
  Love Planet – Pluto
  Money Planet – Mercury
  Planet of Health and Work – Venus
  Planet of Home and Family Life – Sun
  Planet of Spirituality – Mars
  Planet of Travel, Education, Religion
    and Philosophy – Saturn

Colours – earth tones, green, orange, yellow

Colours that promote love, romance and social
  harmony – red–violet, violet

Colours that promote earning power – yellow,
  yellow–orange

Gems – coral, emerald

Metal – copper

Scents – bitter almond, rose, vanilla, violet

Quality – fixed (= stability)

Quality most needed for balance – flexibility

Strongest virtues – endurance, loyalty, patience, stability, a harmonious disposition

Deepest needs – comfort, material ease, wealth

Characteristics to avoid – rigidity, stubbornness, tendency to be overly possessive and materialistic

Signs of greatest overall compatibility – Virgo, Capricorn

Signs of greatest overall incompatibility – Leo, Scorpio, Aquarius

Sign most helpful to career – Aquarius

Sign most helpful for emotional support – Leo

Sign most helpful financially – Gemini

Sign best for marriage and/or partnerships – Scorpio

Sign most helpful for creative projects – Virgo

Best Sign to have fun with – Virgo

Signs most helpful in spiritual matters – Aries, Capricorn

Best day of the week – Friday

Understanding a Taurus

Taurus is the most earthy of all the Earth signs. If you understand that Earth is more than just a physical element, that it is a psychological attitude as well, you will get a better understanding of the Taurus personality.

A Taurus has all the power of action that an Aries has. But Taurus is not satisfied with action for its own sake. Their actions must be productive, practical and wealth-producing. If Taurus cannot see a practical value in an action they will not bother taking it.

Taurus' forte lies in their power to make real their own or other people's ideas. They are generally not very inventive but they can take another's invention and perfect it, making it more practical and useful. The same is true for all projects. Taurus is not especially keen on starting new projects, but once they get involved they bring things to completion. Taurus carries everything through. They are finishers and will go the distance, so long as no unavoidable calamity intervenes.

Many people find Taurus too stubborn, conservative, fixed and immovable. This is understandable, because Taurus dislikes change – in the environment or in their routine. They even dislike changing their minds! On the other hand, this is their virtue. It is not good for a wheel's axle to waver. The axle must be fixed, stable and unmovable. Taurus is the axle of society and the heavens. Without their stability and so-called stubbornness, the wheels of the world (and especially the wheels of commerce) would not turn.

Taurus loves routine. A routine, if it is good, has many virtues. It is a fixed – and, ideally, perfect – way of taking care of things. Mistakes can happen when spontaneity comes into the equation, and mistakes cause discomfort and uneasiness – something almost unacceptable to a Taurus. Meddling with Taurus' comfort and security is a sure way to irritate and anger them.

While an Aries loves speed, a Taurus likes things slow. They are slow thinkers – but do not make the mistake of assuming they lack intelligence. On the contrary, Taurus people are very intelligent. It is just that they like to chew on ideas, to deliberate and weigh them up. Only after due deliberation is an idea accepted or a decision taken. Taurus is slow to anger – but once aroused, take care!

Finance

Taurus is very money-conscious. Wealth is more important to them than to many other signs. Wealth to a Taurus means comfort and security. Wealth means stability. Where some zodiac signs feel that they are spiritually rich if they have ideas, talents or skills, Taurus only feels wealth when they can see and touch it. Taurus' way of thinking is, 'What good is a talent if it has not been translated into a home, furniture, car and holidays?'

These are all reasons why Taurus excels in estate agency and agricultural industries. Usually a Taurus will end up owning land. They love to feel their connection to the Earth. Material wealth began with agriculture, the tilling of the soil. Owning a piece of land was humanity's earliest form of wealth: Taurus still feels that primeval connection.

It is in the pursuit of wealth that Taurus develops intellectual and communication ability. Also, in this pursuit Taurus is forced to develop some flexibility. It is in the quest for wealth that they learn the practical value of the intellect and come to admire it. If it were not for the search for wealth and material things, Taurus people might not try to reach a higher intellect.

Some Taurus people are 'born lucky' – the type who win any gamble or speculation. This luck is due to other factors in their horoscope; it is not part of their essential nature. By nature they are not gamblers. They are hard workers and like to earn what they get. Taurus' innate conservatism makes them abhor unnecessary risks in finance and in other areas of their lives.

Career and Public Image

Being essentially down-to-earth people, simple and uncomplicated, Taurus tends to look up to those who are original, unconventional and inventive. Taurus people like their bosses to be creative and original – since they themselves are content to perfect their superiors' brainwaves. They admire people who have a wider social or political consciousness and they feel that someday (when they have all the comfort and security they need) they too would like to be involved in these big issues.

In business affairs Taurus can be very shrewd – and that makes them valuable to their employers. They are never lazy; they enjoy working and getting good results. Taurus does not like taking unnecessary risks and they do well in positions of authority, which makes them good managers and supervisors. Their managerial skills are reinforced by their natural talents for organization and handling details, their patience and thoroughness. As mentioned, through their connection with the earth, Taurus people also do well in farming and agriculture.

In general a Taurus will choose money and earning power over public esteem and prestige. A position that pays more – though it has less prestige – is preferred to a position with a lot of prestige but lower earnings. Many other signs do not feel this way, but a Taurus does, especially if there is nothing in his or her personal birth chart that modifies this. Taurus will pursue glory and prestige only if it can be shown that these things have a direct and immediate impact on their wallet.

Love and Relationships

In love, the Taurus-born likes to have and to hold. They are the marrying kind. They like commitment and they like the terms of a relationship to be clearly defined. More importantly, Taurus likes to be faithful to one lover, and they expect that lover to reciprocate this fidelity. When this doesn't happen, their whole world comes crashing down. When they are in love Taurus people are loyal, but they are also very possessive. They are capable of great fits of jealousy if they are hurt in love.

Taurus is satisfied with the simple things in a relationship. If you are involved romantically with a Taurus there is no need for lavish entertainments and constant courtship. Give them enough love, food and comfortable shelter and they will be quite content to stay home and enjoy your company. They will be loyal to you for life. Make a Taurus feel comfortable and – above all – secure in the relationship, and you will rarely have a problem.

In love, Taurus can sometimes make the mistake of trying to control their partners, which can cause great pain on both sides. The reasoning behind their actions is basically simple: Taurus people feel a sense of ownership over their partners and will want to make changes that will increase their own general comfort and security. This attitude is OK when it comes to inanimate, material things – but is dangerous when applied to people. Taurus needs to be careful and attentive to this possible trait within themselves.

Home and Domestic Life

Home and family are vitally important to Taurus. They like children. They also like a comfortable and perhaps glamorous home – something they can show off. They tend to buy heavy, ponderous furniture – usually of the best quality. This is because Taurus likes a feeling of substance in their environment. Their house is not only their home but their place of creativity and entertainment. The Taurus' home tends to be truly their castle. If they could choose, Taurus people would prefer living in the countryside to being city-dwellers. If they cannot do so during their working lives, many Taurus individuals like to holiday in or even retire to the country, away from the city and closer to the land.

At home a Taurus is like a country squire – lord (or lady) of the manor. They love to entertain lavishly, to make others feel secure in their home and to encourage others to derive the same sense of satisfaction as they do from it. If you are invited for dinner at the home of a Taurus you can expect the best food and best entertainment. Be prepared for a tour of the house and expect to see your Taurus friend exhibit a lot of pride and satisfaction in his or her possessions.

Taurus people like children but they are usually strict with them. The reason for this is they tend to treat their children – as they do most things in life – as their possessions. The positive side to this is that their children will be well cared for and well supervised. They will get every material thing they need to grow up properly. On the down side, Taurus can get too repressive with their children. If a child dares to upset the daily routine – which Taurus loves to follow – he or she will have a problem with a Taurus parent.

Horoscope for 2013

Major Trends

Last year, 2012, was basically a good year. The long-term planets were not stressing you out and were mostly friendly towards you. Health should have been good and overall energy was basically high. However, late in the year, in October, Saturn moved into Scorpio and into stressful alignment with you. Those of you born early in the sign of Taurus – from April 20 to May 5 – are feeling this most strongly. Those of you born later in the sign are feeling it now but will feel it more intensely in 2014. So, there is more resistance now. This stress is not enough to cause failure, but it does slow you down a bit. Your energy needs to be watched and there is more resistance to your goals. More on this later.

Saturn's move into Scorpio was also a move into your 7th house of love and social activities. Current marriages or serious kinds of relationships are getting a good testing; business partnerships too. In general there is less social activity in the year ahead – more on this later.

Neptune, the most spiritual of all the planets, made a major move into your 11th house of friends last year. He will be there for another 13 or so years, and so this is a long-term trend. Your social sphere, your friendships are getting spiritualized and more refined. You will be attracting more spiritual types into your life as a result. More details on this later.

In March of 2011 Uranus made a major move into your 12th house of spirituality and will be there for another five years or so – another long-term trend. Uranus is your career planet, thus this transit has important implications in your career which we will discuss later on. Mostly though, it indicates dramatic, radical change in your inner, spiritual life. Taureans are basically traditional, conservative people, but not in spiritual matters now. You are experimental and scientific now. You are changing teachers, regimes and practices, probably multiple times. Those of you who have never been involved in spirituality will probably get involved this year or in coming years. Those of you already on the path will be changing that path. There is much ferment and upheaval in this area of life. There is also much upheaval in charitable or altruistic organizations that you are involved with.

Your most important areas of interest this year are finance (until June 27); communication and intellectual interests (from June 27 onwards); love and social activities; religion, philosophy, foreign travel and higher education; friends, groups, group activities, organizations; and spirituality.

Your paths of greatest fulfilment will be finance (until June 27); communication and intellectual interests (after June 27); love, romance and social activities.

Health

(Please note that this is an astrological perspective on health and not a medical one. In days of yore there was no difference; these perspectives were identical. But these days there could be quite a difference. For a medical perspective, please consult your doctor or health practitioner.)

As we mentioned, the long-term planets are mostly kind to you this year. Only Saturn is giving long-term stress. So health should continue to be good, although perhaps not quite as good as last year. Saturn by himself is not enough to cause serious problems – it's when the planetary power starts to 'gang up' on you that we get concerned.

The fact that your 6th house of health is empty is also a good sign. You are not overly focused on health issues because you have no need to be: nothing major is wrong.

Good though your health is, you can make it even better. Give more attention to the kidneys and hips (hips should be regularly massaged); the neck and throat (neck massage is always beneficial for you, tension tends to collect there and needs to be released regularly; craniaosacral therapy is especially good for you too, as is it works on the vertebrae of the neck as well as the bones in the skull. These vertebrae need to be kept in right alignment, singing and chanting mantras or the five vowel sounds, which will release much tension and harmonize the throat and entire body); and the heart.

In fact the heart is a vulnerable area for you this year. If you are of appropriate age regular check-ups might be in order. More important than that is the avoidance of worry and anxiety, the spiritual root causes of heart problems. Give this some serious thought. If there is something positive and constructive to be done about a problem, then by all means it should be done. But if there is nothing constructive that can be done how does the worry help your situation? It not only doesn't help, but makes matters even worse – especially if you understand the metaphysical laws of the universe. From a health perspective, worry only puts more strain on

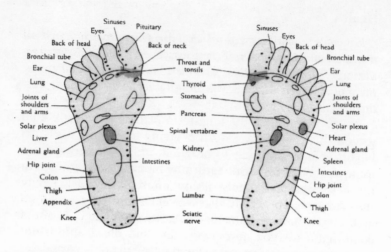

Reflexology

Try to massage the whole foot on a regular basis, but pay extra attention to the points highlighted on the chart. When you massage, be aware of 'sore spots', as these need special attention. It's also a good idea to massage the ankles and top side of the feet.

the heart. From the worldly perspective worry is natural and normal. After all, everybody does it. But from the spiritual perspective worry is a mental pathology and the root cause of many a physical pathology.

Venus, as our regular readers know, is your health planet. In the physical body she rules the kidneys, hips, neck and throat – hence their importance in overall health. Venus is also the generic planet of love. (In your chart, Pluto is your actual love planet, but in general Venus is the ruler.) Thus problems in love tend to be the spiritual root causes of health problems. Since love is challenging this year (it is getting a real testing) you will have to work harder than usual to maintain harmony. Perhaps a relationship will need to dissolve. If so let it be in the most harmonious way possible, with minimum pain or rancour. This is easy to say, but not so easy to do. But if health problems arise (God forbid) it will need to be done.

Venus is a fast-moving planet. She will move through all the signs and houses of your Horoscope in the coming year. Thus there are many short-term health trends (depending on where she is and the aspects she receives) that are best dealt with in the monthly reports.

Home and Family

Next year will be a different story, but this year the 4th house of home and family is not a house of power. Basically this indicates contentment with the status quo, with no great need to make dramatic changes. Of course, you always have free will – you never lose that – but the cosmos is not impelling you one way or another.

Parents or parent figures are better off not moving in the year ahead, although it is most likely that they want to. If they do there will be many delays and glitches involved. They are better off making better use of the space they have, re-organizing the home, moving the furniture around, things of this nature. They seem to be buying health equipment for the home or installing health equipment there.

A parent or parent figure is undergoing many personal changes and dramas. Perhaps there is surgery or a near-death kind of experience. This parent or parent figure seems in conflict with the spouse, partner or current love as well. Neither approves much of the other. This is not helping the love life and is one of the challenges in love this year.

However, this same parent or parent figure (the gender of the parent depends on whether you are male or female) has dream job opportunities coming up. If he or she hires others, there is an expansion of the workforce indicated.

Children or children figures in your life are successful this year. They are having a banner career year. There is elevation, honour and recognition happening. But a move is not likely this year. If it does happen it will most likely be in the latter half of the year, after June 27.

Grandchildren are experiencing great instability in the home and with family this year. They are likely to have multiple moves. Sometimes it is not an actual move, but they live in different places for long periods of time and it is as if they had moved multiple times. They need to cultivate emotional equilibrium this year (and for many years to come). They seem unusually sensitive and temperamental. Yoga, meditation, or a spiritual discipline would do wonders for them right now.

If you are planning construction in the home – serious kinds of repairs – July 22 to August 23 and August 28 to October 15 are good times. If you are planning cosmetic kinds of changes, from June 28 to August 23 would be good. This latter period is also good if you are buying art or objects for the home.

There are many short-term family trends which we will cover in the monthly reports – the Sun, your family planet, is a fast-moving planet.

Finance and Career

Finance is always important to a Taurean, regardless of whether the money house is strong or weak. But this year your money house is strong, so you are more focused here than usual.

Ever since Jupiter moved into your sign in June 2011, you have been in a prosperity cycle. And this trend continues in the year ahead, until June 27. Finance will be good afterwards too, but you can sort of coast in this period. It doesn't require much of your attention.

Regular readers undoubtedly know that Jupiter moving through the money house is a classic indicator of prosperity. It expands earnings. It expands the financial horizons. It makes assets that you own more valuable. It brings happy financial opportunity as well. Most importantly, it brings a financial optimism – a 'can do' spirit. When Jupiter enters the money house 'lucky' things begin to happen – an unexpected client or job comes your way, or a tax refund is larger than expected. Often people win at the lottery or other kinds of gaming, and a cherished item that you wanted but couldn't afford suddenly becomes affordable. You invoice someone for x amount and they send you double and say keep the change. You feel the steady presence of Lady Luck (who is under Jupiter's command, by the way).

Jupiter in the money house (and the feeling of optimism that it brings) makes you a bigger spender this year. You are more generous with others as well. You spend, you give, because you feel that you can afford to (and this is so whether the cash is on hand or not!). Overspending is perhaps the greatest financial danger right now. Of course, spend for what you need, but sometimes the spending can be gratuitous and this should be avoided.

In your Horoscope Jupiter rules the 8th house of transformation. Thus in many cases there are inheritances occurring, and they seem substantial. (This could have happened last year too.) Often you are named in someone's will, or collect on trust funds, or are named the executor of a will. If you have issues with an insurance company, the outcome seems fortunate. Debt seems easy to make this year – a mixed blessing. The corporate world is fuelled by debt and if debt dries up, business is in crisis. But for you there doesn't seem to be a problem. You have good access. The real problem is to avoid the abuse of debt. Don't take money merely for the sake of taking it – it should be for some legitimate business purpose. If you have good ideas this is a good year to attract investors to your projects.

Death is not a pleasant subject and people are understandably squeamish about it. But for you there is profit here. Like last year you can profit from troubled properties or troubled companies – perhaps even bankrupt companies or repossessed properties. You have a knack – an instinct – for value here.

If you are an investor I like the bond market this year, especially bonds for communication, media and transportation companies.

On June 27 Jupiter will enter your 3rd house of communication. Thus a new car and communication equipment is coming to you. Sales and marketing become important financially. You need to make good use of the media.

Love and Social Life

This is a challenging love and social year, as we mentioned. Saturn moving through the 7th house of love is severely testing existing relationships. This would be difficult enough, but there are also two eclipses in this house this year: a Lunar Eclipse on April 25 and a Solar Eclipse on November 3. Add to this mix Uranus's Square to Pluto, your love planet (which will be very exact for a few months in the year ahead), and you have the recipe for extreme volatility in love. True love will always prevail, but it won't be easy. Anything less than perfection will probably dissolve.

We never really know if love is real when everything is harmonious and honeymoonish. When things are going well it is only natural to feel content. It is in the tough times that we learn the depth of our love. If conditions are hellish and you still want each other, most likely your love is real. If you are willing to confront all the challenges and not run for the hills, love is real. This is the cosmic purpose behind all of this. In the stresses of the testing, the tough times, reality emerges. The cosmos wants only the best for you – anything less will not do.

There are other positive things that emerge from a testing. When a company is producing a car they road test it so that – they subject it to above normal stresses – much more than the average driver will ever face. In these tests any hidden problems are revealed and can be corrected. Thus the final product will be superior. So it will be in your relationship. The testing will reveal the hidden fault lines and you will be able to correct them and have a better relationship than before. Admittedly, this is not a pleasant experience – it's good, but not pleasant.

Singles, especially those of you working on the first marriage, are better off not marrying now. In fact the social life should be re-organized now. Focus on quality rather than quantity. Better fewer dates but quality ones, than hordes of lacklustre dates. Learn to enjoy your own company. If you enjoy your company, others will too.

For singles there is an attraction for older, more established people. There is a feeling of stability and comfort that you get with them. They need to be highly educated and refined and established in their business or profession. You have the aspects of someone who falls in love with the professor, the minister, the mentor, or the guru. There are love opportunities in foreign lands, with foreigners, in educational and religious-type settings.

Those in or working on the second marriage have an easier time, but friendships and business partnerships are still getting tested. There is strong opportunity for a second marriage after June 27. The same is true for those working on their third marriage. Jupiter will start to make beautiful aspects to Neptune around that time.

Self-improvement

With Jupiter in your money house during the first half of the year, your finances will improve on their own. There's nothing special that you need to do – just receive the largesse and act on the opportunities that will surely come. The love situation is another story however. Here, your actions and attitudes can either exacerbate problems or soften them. There will definitely be problems; the issue is how you handle them.

In the next two years it is good to understand and apply the Principle of Least Pain, Least Damage. Troubled relationships are painful whether they dissolve or survive. This seems unavoidable. But the challenge for you is to follow the path of least pain, least damage. Often, unfortunately, the tendency is to inflict maximum pain on those who have wronged us. This will only create a cycle of more and more pain. Everyone will suffer more than is needed. Further, it will delay future relationships. And, if a person understands the karmic law, the present condition will tend to repeat and repeat, until the lesson is learned. The Cosmic schoolroom, though full of love and compassion, is still unremitting law, and will keep you in first grade forever if need be, until the lessons of first grade are mastered.

If a relationship is to dissolve, and often this is necessary, do it in the least painful way. If a relationship is to survive, work out the differences in the least painful way as well. Exactly what this way is, you must discern for yourself; there are no rules, every situation is unique and special.

Practising the art of forgiveness is also very important for the next two years. Holding grudges blocks the spiritual energy from flowing in and often has health consequences. Forgiveness will come easier if we understand that we forgive the person, not the actions. The wrong actions are wrong. Full stop. But the people did these actions under all kinds of inner compulsions. And, who knows, if we were in their shoes, we might have acted the same too. Forgiveness will happen with time. But why prolong the process and increase the suffering?

Uranus, as we mentioned, is now in your 12th house of spirituality for the long term. This is a very important transit. Many are under the misconception that 'spirituality' is some compartmentalized area that has nothing to do with 'practical' life. Nothing could be further from the truth. This outer 3D world is a world of 'pure effect', not a cause for anything. All the outer events that we observe with our senses are merely the side effects of 'internal' forces. Thus when a person starts to change the internal conditions – the thoughts and feelings – the outer conditions inevitably change. Right now, huge inner changes are happening, and in due course you will see them manifest in your outer life. You are in a process of creating 'inner freedom' – freedom of thought and feeling – and this will inevitably lead to outer freedom, the breaking of many outer ties. Be patient, the process takes time.

Month-by-month Forecasts

January

Best Days Overall: 2, 3, 10, 11, 19, 20, 29, 30
Most Stressful Days Overall: 6, 7, 12, 13, 26, 27, 28
Best Days for Love: 2, 3, 6, 7, 8, 9, 10, 11, 18, 19, 20, 29, 30
Best Days for Money: 2, 3, 4, 10, 11, 12, 21, 22, 23, 31
Best Days for Career: 8, 12, 13, 17, 26, 27

You begin your year with 80 per cent and sometimes 90 per cent of the planets above the horizon of your chart. On the 19th you enter a yearly career peak. So this is a time to be focused on the career and on outer achievement. Family is important to you, but even the family is supportive of the career goals. They are urging you on. There is little of the usual conflict between family life and the career these days and this is good. This is a month of success and forward progress.

The planetary momentum is forward this month. Until the 30th, 90 per cent of the planets are moving forward, and after the 30th ALL of them will be going forward. This is an excellent time – and especially from the 11th to the 27th – to launch new projects or products into the world. Forward progress should be more rapid than usual.

This month, beginning on the 19th, the planetary power will shift from the West to the East, from the social sector of your chart to the sector of the self. This produces psychological changes. You enter a period of greater personal independence. You have more power and ability to create conditions as you desire them to be, to have life your way on your terms. In the past six months you've been forced to adapt to situations, to compromise and to 'people please'. By now you know what situations are unpleasant and what needs to be changed, and now you can start making the changes. Happiness is up to you and you alone.

Health and vitality are basically good until the 19th, but afterwards you need to rest and relax more and maintain high energy levels. If you drop the trivia from your life and focus on what's really important you will discover that you have all the energy you need to achieve your goals. Enhance the health in the ways mentioned in the yearly report. But until the 10th also give more attention to the liver and thighs. Regular thigh massage will be good. After the 10th your health planet moves into Capricorn, so more attention needs to be given to the spine, knees, teeth, bones, skin and overall skeletal alignment. Regular back and knee massage will be powerful. If you feel under the weather, a visit to the chiropractor or osteopath might also be good. Detox regimes are powerful until the 10th, while after that date metaphysical therapies – prayer, positive visualization – will be powerful.

The main career challenge now comes from your spouse, partner or current love. There seems to be some opposition here. Perhaps he or she feels that you are too focused on your outer life and not enough on your relationship. This will be a challenge all year. Somehow you have to balance career duties with your relationship. Love is challenging this year, but especially this month until the 19th. A current relationship is being severely tested.

You are in a cycle of prosperity now. The money is rolling in. But the prosperity will be even stronger after the 19th.

February

Best Days Overall: 7, 8, 15, 16, 17, 25, 26
Most Stressful Days Overall: 2, 3, 9, 10, 23, 24
Best Days for Love: 2, 3, 7, 8, 9, 10, 15, 16, 18, 19, 25, 26
Best Days for Money: 1, 9, 11, 12, 18, 19, 21, 22, 27
Best Days for Career: 4, 5, 9, 10, 13, 23

The planets are still mostly above the horizon of the chart this month; until the 15th 90 per cent of them are above the horizon, after which the percentage drops to 80 per cent.

You are still very much in a yearly career peak, so go for it. Keep the focus. Pay rises and promotions were likely last month and could still happen in the month ahead. Family is still supporting your career activities, and seem actively involved here. The nice thing is you don't have the usual conflicts of family vs. career that most people have. The two areas merge nicely. Like last month your challenge is to balance the love life – the marriage, the social life – with the career. It's going to take work but somehow you have to win the support of the beloved and friends. You will figure out a way.

The planetary momentum is forward this month. Until the 18th all the planets are moving forward (highly unusually). Retrograde activity will increase later in the month, but the number will never be more than 20 per cent retrograde. So this is still a good month to launch new products or projects, especially from the 10th to the 18th.

You are still in a prosperity cycle, but finances are more challenging this month. On the 5th, Mercury, your financial planet, moves into Pisces in stressful aspect with Jupiter. This could cause over-spending or over-confidence. A healthy confidence is always a good thing, but sometimes it is unrealistic and causes people to take unnecessary risks. Mercury will go retrograde on the 23rd, so try to make important purchases or financial decisions before then. After the 23rd a healthy review of the financial life is in order. It is a time for attaining mental clarity about your finances.

Mercury travels with Neptune on the 6th and the 7th, so be alert for financial intuition on those days. Financial information and guidance will come through dreams, psychics, ministers, or spiritual channels. This is a spiritual period anyway – Mars, your spiritual planet, is travelling with Neptune from the 3rd to the 6th – so there is help available from the invisible world.

Health still needs watching until the 18th. Until the 2nd give more attention to the spine, knees, teeth, bones, skin and overall skeletal alignment, like last month. After the 2nd give more attention to the ankles and calves. These should be regularly massaged. After the 26th the feet become important and regular foot massage will be beneficial.

March

Best Days Overall: 6, 7, 15, 16, 24, 25, 26
Most Stressful Days Overall: 2, 3, 8, 9, 22, 23, 29, 30
Best Days for Love: 2, 3, 6, 7, 10, 11, 15, 16, 21, 22, 24, 25, 29, 30, 31
Best Days for Money: 1, 2, 3, 8, 9, 10, 11, 17, 18, 19, 20, 21, 27, 28, 29, 30
Best Days for Career: 4, 8, 9, 12, 13, 22, 31

Though your yearly career peak is mostly over with, there are still nice things happening here. Success continues. Your career planet, Uranus, receives intense and positive stimulation towards the end of the month, and as most of the planets are still above the horizon, the outer world is still the focus. Mars conjuncts with your career planet from the 18th to the 21st. This indicates that you are working hard and being aggressive in career matters, together with confidence and quick achievement. (It can also bring some conflicts too.) The Sun also conjuncts with Uranus from the 27th to the 30th, which shows good family support for the career, and that family or family connections are creating opportunities. Probably you will be working more from home during that period. Venus is also conjunct to Uranus from the 26th to the 29th. This shows personal success, elevation, and someone who is 'on top' of their world. These aspects are also bringing happy career opportunities.

The Water element is very strong until the 12th – up to 70 per cent of the planets are in water signs. People are unusually sensitive these days, so be more mindful about this. They will not only react to words, but to gestures, body language, voice tones and facial expressions. Seemingly little things can provoke unexpected responses. Some extra precautions can prevent much heartache and hurt feelings later on.

This is a very spiritual kind of month. Until the 20th there are many planets in the sign of Pisces, and after that date the Sun, Mars and Venus move into Aries – your 12th house of spirituality. Many of you will make important spiritual breakthroughs. Spiritual practice should go better as well. You are close to the invisible world and the invisible world is close to you. You can expect a hyperactive dream life and many kinds of supernatural experiences. It is a good month to be involved in charities and altruistic causes.

Finances are still a bit delicate however. Your financial planet is retrograde until the 17th, so continue to review your financial life. This is still a period for gaining mental clarity on your finances, not for actually doing things. When Mercury starts to move forward on the 17th clarity should be there and it will be safer to make important financial decisions and moves then. The financial planet in Pisces indicates good financial intuition. But while Mercury is still retrograde you need to double check your intuition. After the 17th it becomes more trustworthy.

Financial opportunities come through friends, groups and group activities. Online activities also boost the finances. It is very important to stay up to date with the latest technology: your technological skills are important for the bottom line.

Love is reasonable until the 20th. After that it gets rather stormy. A current relationship hangs by a thread.

April

Best Days Overall: 2, 3, 11, 12, 21, 22, 29, 30
Most Stressful Days Overall: 4, 5, 19, 20, 25, 26
Best Days for Love: 1, 2, 3, 9, 10, 11, 12, 21, 22, 25, 26, 29, 30
Best Days for Money: 4, 5, 7, 8, 14, 15, 19, 23, 24, 27, 28
Best Days for Career: 1, 4, 5, 9, 10, 19, 20, 27, 28

The planets are now in their maximum Eastern position for the year. This trend will continue next month as well. This is the time to create the conditions that you want in your life. You have the power to do this. You know your own mind better than anyone else, and you should act on it. You can and will have life on your terms this month.

This month after the 19th, the planets will start to shift from the upper half to the lower half of the Horoscope. The shift will not be complete until next month, but you are already starting to feel it. Career goals have more or less been achieved and it is time to start focusing on the home, the family and your emotional well being. It is dusk in your year. The Sun is just getting ready to set. It is not yet dark, but getting there. Tie up loose ends in the career and get ready to get the home in order.

The planetary momentum is still strongly forward this month. It is a very good time, especially from the 10th to the 25th, to launch new products or ventures. The New Moon of the 10th seems the optimum time for these things.

Until the 19th you are still in a very spiritual kind of period, so review our discussion of this last month.

Love is still problematic. Only a very strong relationship can survive this testing. Your beloved is not only in conflict with your career, but with both parent figures and perhaps with the family as a whole. Things will get a bit easier after the 15th, but the situation still seems stressful.

Mercury, your financial planet, is still in mystical Pisces until the 14th. So the financial intuition is very good now and can be trusted. Taureans are very practical, down-to-earth people, but this is a month where you go deeper into the supernatural sources of supply rather than the natural sources. Money will come to you in unexpected ways, and not because of your personal effort or smart business tactics. It will just come. It will force you to ponder what wealth is really all about and where it really comes from.

After the 14th, as Mercury moves into Aries, you need to be careful about rash financial decision-making. If you have attained some mental clarity during the planet's retrograde period it won't be such a problem, but if not, it can be.

On the 19th the Sun crosses the Ascendant and enters your own sign; Mars enters the next day. You are now in a yearly personal pleasure peak – a time to enjoy all the delights of the senses and the body, and a time to get the body and image into shape. Though love has been stressful, you still attract the opposite sex. You look great and have greater than usual personal charisma. Health and energy are super.

A Lunar Eclipse on the 25th affects especially those of you born early in the sign (April 21–May 1), so reduce your busy schedule at this time. This eclipse will test the current relationship, and cars and communication equipment.

May

    Best Days Overall: 8, 9, 10, 18, 19, 27, 28
    Most Stressful Days Overall: 2, 3, 16, 17, 23, 24, 29, 30
    Best Days for Love: 8, 9, 10, 11, 18, 19, 21, 22, 23, 24, 27, 28, 29, 30
    Best Days for Money: 2, 3, 8, 9, 10, 11, 12, 21, 22, 29, 30
    Best Days for Career: 2, 3, 6, 7, 16, 17, 25, 26, 29, 30

When Mercury enters your sign on the 1st of the month, the planetary shift below the horizon of your chart is established; up to 70 per cent of the planets will be in the lower half of the Horoscope, the maximum for the year. Career is still important, but now it is time to work on the career by interior methods – by the methods of the night rather than the methods of the day. Visualize what you want and where you want to be. Fall asleep with this image. Work inwardly to attain the 'feeling' of the desired result. This is a form of day dreaming that is under your conscious control. Let go of the world of appearance – you are after an 'inner state' – and in truth, no outer appearance has the power to obstruct your entry. As you live in the feeling of what you want, eventually (and especially when the planets shift again) the inner state will 'objectify' and become manifest.

When Mercury enters your sign you start to receive nice financial windfalls. This is a prosperous month. Financial opportunities will seek you out without the need to run after them. Your personal appearance and overall demeanour seems very important in finances this month and thus you spend more on your image.

Health and energy are still very good. In fact this abundance of energy could actually create some problems. You tend to be more in a hurry now. You want everything to happen quickly, and so impatience could make you careless. Temper could be a problem too. It can invite undesirable or needless conflict. Make haste but be mindful about it.

We have two eclipses this month. The first, the Solar Eclipse of the 10th, is the stronger one. It occurs in your own sign. Make sure you reduce your schedule then. All Taureans will feel this, but those born between April 5 and April 15 will feel it strongest. Often these eclipses bring detoxes of the body, especially if you haven't been careful in dietary matters. It causes a need to redefine the personality and image. Outer events will happen that will force this. You will start to think differently about yourself and present a new image to the world. Often this brings changes of hairstyle and wardrobe. The family seems affected by this eclipse as well. There are shake-ups there, with life-changing kinds of events in the lives of family members (or those who are like family to you). If there are hidden flaws in the home, you find out about them now and will be forced to make repairs and corrections.

The Lunar Eclipse of May 25 brings dramas in the lives of siblings or sibling figures in your life. Cars and communication equipment will get tested and will often need replacement. Your spouse, partner or current love will be forced to make dramatic financial changes.

June

Best Days Overall: 5, 6, 15, 16, 23, 24
Most Stressful Days Overall: 12, 13, 19, 20, 25, 26
Best Days for Love: 5, 6, 10, 15, 16, 19, 20, 23, 24, 27, 28
Best Days for Money: 1, 7, 8, 9, 10, 11, 17, 18, 19, 20, 26, 27, 28
Best Days for Career: 2, 3, 12, 13, 21, 22, 25, 26, 30

Last month on the 20th, you entered a yearly financial peak – Taurus heaven! This continues until the 21st of this month. The money is rolling in and financial objectives are being attained. By the 27th, as Jupiter leaves the money house, your interests will shift to the mind, to learning, communicating, teaching and intellectual interests. It's time to take a financial breather and take stock. Your financial planet goes retrograde on the 26th and this is the time to take that break. Avoid making major financial commitments or decisions after the 26th. Focus more on fact-gathering and doing your financial homework.

Jupiter moving into your 3rd house of communication will bring a new car and new communication equipment to you – if not this month, in the year ahead.

Finance is the major focus this month until the 21st. After that, it is good to build up your knowledge base and expand the mind – take courses in subjects that interest you, build up your vocabulary, catch up on the phone calls, letters or emails that you owe. This will not only be pleasurable in its own right, but with your financial planet in your 3rd house all month this will have a good bottom-line effect as well.

Love continues to be problematic this month, especially after the 21st. There have been problems here all year, but in the past two months things should have been quieter. Now they flare up again. The current relationship is in crisis. Sometimes it is not the fault of the actual relationship; there can be dramatic, life-changing events – a personal crisis – in the life of your spouse, partner or current love and the problems stem from that.

Affairs of the heart are complicated. It is difficult to give rules as every situation is unique, but as a general principle we could say to follow the path of least pain. A stormy relationship is going to be painful no matter what, but you can maximize that pain or minimize it. Do your best to minimize it.

Love is stressful, but the overall social situation looks happy. New and important friends are coming into the picture this month.

A boss, parent or parent figure – an authority figure in your life – could have surgery or near-death kind of experience this month. And a parent or parent figure has a financial windfall between the 19th and the 21st. There are also opportunities to move, buy additional homes, or renovate the present home during this period.

Legal matters are delayed but the end result looks successful. There are happy travel opportunities this month, but allow more time getting to and from your destination.

July

Best Days Overall: 2, 3, 12, 13, 21, 22, 29, 30
Most Stressful Days Overall: 9, 10, 11, 17, 23, 24
Best Days for Love: 1, 2, 3, 10, 11, 12, 13, 17, 19, 20, 21, 22, 29, 30
Best Days for Money: 4, 5, 6, 7, 8, 16, 17, 25, 26
Best Days for Career: 1, 12, 13, 21, 22, 23, 24, 27, 28

In order to manifest the desires of your heart, the cosmos has sometimes to shake things up, sometimes in dramatic ways. This is what is happening this month. Love continues to be severely tested all month. There are important career changes happening. And the family situation also seems unstable. All these changes will ultimately be good, but while they are happening they are not so pleasant.

Part of the family stress can be attributed to a move, renovation or other home improvement. It is good that you are focusing on the home and family now. Career issues will take time to resolve and there is no quick solution there. Your career planet goes retrograde on the 17th and will be retrograde until December 17 – almost the balance of the year ahead. Appearances are deceptive now. Avoid judging the career by what 'seems' to be; work now to attain mental clarity here – this is the most important thing.

Your 3rd house of communication is still very powerful until the 22nd. This is a very nice transit for students below college level. Learning is fun. There is success in their studies. A sibling or sibling figure enters a two-year period of prosperity and overall success.

This is a hectic, active month. Happily health is good until the 22nd and you have all the energy you need to deal with all this activity. After the 22nd though, you need to rest and relax more and do whatever you can to maintain your high energy levels. Spend more time at the health spa. Get massages. Until the 23rd you can enhance your health by paying more attention to the heart. Avoid worry and anxiety as much as possible. Right diet also seems important. After the 23rd pay more attention to the small intestine – see the reflexology chart on page 58.

For singles this is a good month for practising unconditional love. Those working on the second marriage have very nice love opportunities now (and last month as well). A foreign trip could materialize from the 12th to the 19th, but with your travel planet Saturn still retrograde, allow more time for getting to and from your destination.

There are important financial changes happening this month. Your financial planet Mercury camps out in square aspect to Uranus from the 17th to the 21st. However, it's best to make the changes after the 21st when Mercury is going forward once more.

The planetary power is starting to shift from the East to the West – the social sector of the chart. So your period of personal independence is starting to end. The shift is not yet complete but it is in process. You are starting to shift psychological gears; the focus is now on other people rather than your own personal interests.

August

Best Days Overall: 8, 9, 17, 18, 25, 26, 27
Most Stressful Days Overall: 6, 7, 13, 14, 19, 20
Best Days for Love: 8, 9, 13, 14, 17, 19, 25, 26
Best Days for Money: 1, 2, 3, 4, 13, 14, 15, 16, 21, 22, 24, 25, 28, 29, 30, 31
Best Days for Career: 6, 7, 15, 16, 19, 20, 23, 24

By the end of the month the planetary shift to the Western sector will be complete, and between 60 and 70 per cent of the planets will be in the West. It's time to down play the self and focus on the needs of others. Hopefully, you've already created good conditions for yourself – now is the time to road test them. If you built well, you will be enjoying your creation. If not, you will see the flaws and be able to correct them during your next cycle of personal independence, next year.

Your 10th house of career is basically empty this month, while your 4th house of home and family is strong all month. So the focus is on the home, as it should be. Your emotional harmony, your family focus, will actually help your career this month. Bosses will be looking at this.

Finances look good this month. Mercury now moves very speedily through three signs and houses of your Horoscope. This shows financial confidence and fast progress. The changes you made last month seem to be working out. Mercury is in Cancer until the 8th and then moves into your 4th house of home and family until the 24th. Thus you are spending more on the home and family this period, but can also earn here too. Family members are financially supportive, family connections and parent figures likewise. Most likely you are earning from home as well, doing more work from home. Mercury in Leo indicates that money is earned in happy ways and that you are enjoying the wealth that you have. On the other hand it can make you more speculative and risk-taking. If you overdo this, it can hurt. This speculative tendency continues even after the 24th as your financial planet enters your 5th house. The children in your life inspire you to earn more, and often they have good financial ideas: 'out of the mouths of babes ...'

Health is much improved after the 22nd. But until then continue to rest and relax more. Review our discussion of last month. Health can be enhanced by giving more attention to the small intestine (like last month) until the 16th. After that, give more attention to the kidneys and hips. Hip massage will be especially beneficial. Keeping harmony in the love life is always important for you from the health perspective, but especially so after the 16th. If you feel under the weather, bring harmony back into the love life as much as you can. With love so stressed this won't be easy, but as we mentioned, you can choose to minimize the negativity rather than maximize it.

September

Best Days Overall: 4, 5, 6, 13, 14, 22, 23
Most Stressful Days Overall: 2, 3, 9, 10, 15, 16, 29, 30
Best Days for Love: 4, 5, 8, 9, 10, 13, 14, 17, 18, 22, 23, 27, 28
Best Days for Money: 1, 5, 6, 9, 10, 15, 16, 18, 19, 24, 25, 26, 27, 28
Best Days for Career: 2, 3, 11, 12, 15, 16, 20, 21, 29, 30

On August 22 you entered one of your yearly personal pleasure peaks, one of your cosmic vacation periods and a time for recreation and the enjoyment of life. You are still very much in this peak until the 22nd of this month. No matter the problems we face or the complications, life can still be enjoyed – and the joy itself alleviates many of the problems. This is the lesson of the month ahead.

For the past two months Taureans of child-bearing age have been at their most fertile for the year. This trend continues this month. (In 2014 they will be even more fertile than now.)

On the 22nd as the Sun enters your 6th house of health and work, you enter a more serious, work-oriented period. You have a need to be productive. It's a very good period for job seekers. There is good fortune now. If you are a job seeker, family connections should be explored.

This month we have a very dynamic Grand Square in the heavens. It began on August 16 and will be in effect all this month. This indicates a challenging kind of period. You are involved in some huge, complicated undertaking and this tends to be stressful. You want to manifest something big in the world. Many competing interests have to be balanced and harmonized – love, career, personal interests, work, home and family. Each pulls you in a different direction. Each demands their due. When things are this complicated it is best to handle each day as it comes. Handle the needs of the day – the needs of the hour – and try not to project too far into the future. If today is handled right, tomorrow will also be handled right.

Love is once again being severely tested. As we mentioned, this has been going on all year, but the severity tends to wax and wane. Now it is more severe than in the past. You won't be able to completely eliminate the negativity, but you can minimize it as much as possible. The good news is that your 7th house of love is very strong right now. Most of the planets are still in the Western, social sector of the Horoscope. Thus love and social activities are very important to you. You are focused here, and willing to overcome all the challenges – and this tends to success.

There are more dramatic financial changes happening from the 9th to the 29th. But you will get through. Your good work ethic and your social connections will be a big help.

Health is basically good. This too is a help. With high energy levels you can cope with all the hectic activity happening. You can enhance the health even further by giving more attention to the kidneys and hips (like last month) until the 11th, and to the colon, bladder and sexual organs after the 11th. Detox regimes are powerful after the 11th.

October

Best Days Overall: 2, 3, 11, 12, 19, 20, 29, 30
Most Stressful Days Overall: 1, 6, 7, 13, 14, 27, 28
Best Days for Love: 2, 3, 6, 7, 8, 11, 12, 17, 18, 19, 20, 27, 28, 29, 30
Best Days for Money: 6, 7, 15, 16, 22, 23, 24, 25
Best Days for Career: 1, 8, 9, 13, 14, 17, 18, 27, 28

This month the planetary power shifts once again. This time the shift is from the lower portion of the Horoscope to the upper – to the sector of career and outer achievement. It is morning in your year, and time to wake up and focus on the outer world – especially the career. The shift begins on the 23rd. From here on in, for the rest of the year ahead, you can let go of family and emotional issues and focus on your outer goals.

On the 23rd you enter a yearly social peak. The love life, which has been stressed all year, gets easier and more active. You still need to be choosy about your friends and the invitations you accept, but the ones that happen now are of a higher quality. Singles are dating more but are not likely to marry. Those working on the second or third marriage had very nice opportunities last month, and there are more on the way. A vindictive spouse or lover seems to be harming your good professional reputation, or wants to. The truth will eventually prevail.

The pace of life is less hectic than last month, especially after the 23rd. The major project going on seems to have made progress and requires less effort. Your health still needs watching, and happily you are on the case. The important thing is to get more rest after the 23rd. Enhance the health through detox regimes all month. Until the 7th colon detoxing is powerful; after that, liver detoxing. Safe sex and sexual moderation are important until the 7th. After the 7th regular thigh massage will be powerful.

A Lunar Eclipse on the 18th occurs in your 12th house of spirituality. It also impacts on Jupiter, the planet of religion and metaphysics. This suggests that important spiritual and philosophical changes are happening now. You change your spiritual regime and discipline, perhaps your teachers as well. There can be dramatic, life-changing kinds of events with people at your place of worship and in spiritual organizations that you are involved with. With Jupiter (the ruler of your 8th house of transformation) involved here you could be having encounters (generally psychological) with death. There is a need to come to terms with it, to understand it better. Your spouse, partner or current love is forced to make dramatic financial changes. Cars and communication equipment get tested.

Your financial planet will be in your 7th house of love all month. Thus there can be business partnerships or joint ventures happening. The opportunities come to you. Social connections play an important role in earnings. You seem to have good access to outside money this month, to credit or outside investors.

Mercury goes retrograde on the 21st. Try to make important purchases and financial decisions before then. Afterwards more homework is needed. It might seem to you that your financial life is going backwards instead of forwards but this is illusory. You just need to slow down a little and review the financial life.

November

Best Days Overall: 7, 8, 16, 17, 25, 26, 27
Most Stressful Days Overall: 3, 4, 9, 10, 23, 24, 30
Best Days for Love: 3, 4, 7, 8, 16, 17, 25, 26, 27, 30
Best Days for Money: 3, 4, 11, 12, 18, 19, 20, 21, 22, 30
Best Days for Career: 5, 6, 9, 10, 13, 14, 23, 24

This is not one of your best health periods, so continue to rest and relax more and give more attention here. Review our discussion of last month. A Solar Eclipse on the 3rd does not help matters either. Until the 5th give more attention to the liver and thighs, as we mentioned last month. After the 5th pay attention to the spine, knees, teeth, bones, skin and overall skeletal alignment. Regular back massage, regular visits to a chiropractor or osteopath will be powerful. Health will improve dramatically after the 22nd.

The Solar Eclipse of the 3rd affects you strongly, so reduce your schedule for a few days before and after. Spend more quiet time at home and avoid risk-taking and stressful kinds of activities. The love life has been stressed all year and this eclipse puts more pressure on it. A current relationship is in serious trouble. Even a basically good relationship is getting tested. (The bad ones have collapsed long ago.) If your relationship survives this period, it will probably survive anything.

Every Solar Eclipse affects your family and this one is no different. The Sun is the ruler of your 4th house of home and family, so there are family upheavals – dramatic, often life-changing events in the lives of family members. Perhaps even near-death kinds of experiences. Sometimes family members are undergoing dangerous kinds of surgery (or it is recommended to them). If there are flaws in the physical home or in the family relationship you find out about them now; everything gets uncovered so you can deal with it – while it was hidden there wasn't much you could do about it.

The financial trends that we wrote of last month are still in effect this month. However, your financial planet will start to move forward on the 10th and financial clarity will return. Decision-making will be much easier (and safer) after the 10th. This should be a prosperous month. Mercury receives beautiful aspects from Jupiter and Neptune. Your financial intuition is good (especially after the 10th) and access to outside money is even better than last month. Debt is easier to obtain this month, but also easier to repay.

For singles there are happy romantic opportunities from the 14th to the 16th but they are unlikely to be very enduring.

December

Best Days Overall: 4, 5, 13, 14, 23, 24
Most Stressful Days Overall: 1, 6, 7, 20, 21, 22, 28, 29
Best Days for Love: 1, 4, 5, 13, 14, 23, 24, 28, 29
Best Days for Money: 1, 8, 9, 10, 11, 15, 16, 17, 18, 19, 21, 22, 28, 29
Best Days for Career: 2, 3, 6, 7, 10, 11, 20, 21, 30, 31

Your 8th house of transformation became powerful on the 22nd of last month, and is still powerful until the 21st of this month. Thus this is a period for detoxing on all the various levels – mental, emotional and physical. Over time the body accumulates all kinds of material. It was not necessarily evil or toxic at the time, but if it stays in the body it can become that way, so it is good to have a clean out. The same is true with material possessions. We tend to hang on to all kinds of things we no longer need. It's time for a good house cleaning. Get rid of the clutter. Sell it or give it to charity. Many of us also carry emotional patterns from the dim past, from childhood. Perhaps these patterns were once useful, but now they have outlived their usefulness and are probably holding you back. Let them go. This is what transformation and resurrection is all about. When the unneeded and the outgrown are got rid of, resurrection naturally happens.

Love is more active this month, but again it's highly unstable. Expect the unexpected. Mood changes in love are difficult to handle. All your life you have been working for stability in love and now you are getting just the opposite. It is difficult to know where you stand from moment to moment.

Although the love life has been stressed and marriage is most likely not happening these days, the sex life seems active now. Your needs are being met.

Health is good this month and gets even better after the 21st. Enhance the health in the ways mentioned last month.

After the 8th we have another Grand Square pattern forming. This indicates a hectic period. Again this big project seems important. No big things ever happen without stress and struggle and this is the situation now. Happily you have the energy to handle it.

Your 9th house is powerful after the 21st and foreign travel is much easier now that Saturn is moving forward again. Students do better in school now.

There are very dynamic aspects from the 23rd to the 31st. Drive more carefully, avoid arguments, be more mindful on the physical level and avoid daredevil-type stunts. This is not a time for these sorts of things.

Gemini

♊

Personality Profile

GEMINI AT A GLANCE

Element – Air

Ruling Planet – Mercury
  Career Planet – Neptune
  Love Planet – Jupiter
  Money Planet – Moon
  Planet of Health and Work – Pluto
  Planet of Home and Family Life – Mercury

Colours – blue, yellow, yellow–orange

Colour that promotes love, romance and social harmony – sky blue

Colours that promote earning power – grey, silver

Gems – agate, aquamarine

Metal – quicksilver

Scents – lavender, lilac, lily of the valley, storax

Quality – mutable (= flexibility)

Quality most needed for balance – thought that is deep rather than superficial

Strongest virtues – great communication skills, quickness and agility of thought, ability to learn quickly

Deepest need – communication

Characteristics to avoid – gossiping, hurting others with harsh speech, superficiality, using words to mislead or misinform

Signs of greatest overall compatibility – Libra, Aquarius

Signs of greatest overall incompatibility – Virgo, Sagittarius, Pisces

Sign most helpful to career – Pisces

Sign most helpful for emotional support – Virgo

Sign most helpful financially – Cancer

Sign best for marriage and/or partnerships – Sagittarius

Sign most helpful for creative projects – Libra

Best Sign to have fun with – Libra

Signs most helpful in spiritual matters – Taurus, Aquarius

Best day of the week – Wednesday

Understanding a Gemini

Gemini is to society what the nervous system is to the body. It does not introduce any new information but is a vital transmitter of impulses from the senses to the brain and vice versa. The nervous system does not judge or weigh these impulses – it only conveys information. And it does so perfectly.

This analogy should give you an indication of a Gemini's role in society. Geminis are the communicators and conveyors of information. To Geminis the truth or falsehood of information is irrelevant, they only transmit what they see, hear or read about. Thus they are capable of spreading the most outrageous rumours as well as conveying truth and light. Geminis sometimes tend to be unscrupulous in their communications and can do both great good or great evil with their power. This is why the sign of Gemini is symbolized by twins: Geminis have a dual nature.

Their ability to convey a message – to communicate with such ease – makes Geminis ideal teachers, writers and media and marketing people. This is helped by the fact that Mercury, the ruling planet of Gemini, also rules these activities.

Geminis have the gift of the gab. And what a gift this is! They can make conversation about anything, anywhere, at any time. There is almost nothing that is more fun to Geminis than a good conversation – especially if they can learn something new as well. They love to learn and they love to teach. To deprive a Gemini of conversation, or of books and magazines, is cruel and unusual punishment.

Geminis are almost always excellent students and take well to education. Their minds are generally stocked with all kinds of information, trivia, anecdotes, stories, news items, rarities, facts and statistics. Thus they can support any intellectual position that they care to take. They are awesome debaters and, if involved in politics, make good orators. Geminis are so verbally smooth that even if they do not know what they are talking about, they can make you think that they do. They will always dazzle you with their brilliance.

Finance

Geminis tend to be more concerned with the wealth of learning and ideas than with actual material wealth. As mentioned, they excel in professions that involve writing, teaching, sales and journalism – and not all of these professions pay very well. But to sacrifice intellectual needs merely for money is unthinkable to a Gemini. Geminis strive to combine the two. Cancer is on Gemini's solar 2nd house (of money) cusp, which indicates that Geminis can earn extra income (in a harmonious and natural way) from investments in residential property, restaurants and hotels. Given their verbal skills, Geminis love to bargain and negotiate in any situation, and especially when it has to do with money.

The Moon rules Gemini's 2nd solar house. The Moon is not only the fastest-moving planet in the zodiac but actually moves through every sign and house every 28 days. No other heavenly body matches the Moon for swiftness or the ability to change quickly. An analysis of the Moon – and lunar phenomena in general – describes Gemini's financial attitudes very well. Geminis are financially versatile and flexible; they can earn money in many different ways. Their financial attitudes and needs seem to change daily. Their feelings about money change also: sometimes they are very enthusiastic about it, at other times they could not care less.

For a Gemini, financial goals and money are often seen only as means of supporting a family; these things have little meaning otherwise.

The Moon, as Gemini's money planet, has another important message for Gemini financially: in order for Geminis to realize their financial potential they need to develop more of an understanding of the emotional side of life. They need to combine their awesome powers of logic with an understanding of human psychology. Feelings have their own logic; Geminis need to learn this and apply it to financial matters.

Career and Public Image

Geminis know that they have been given the gift of communication for a reason, that it is a power that can achieve great good or cause unthinkable distress. They long to put this power at the service of the highest and most transcendental truths. This is their primary goal, to communicate the eternal verities and prove them logically. They look up to people who can transcend the intellect – to poets, artists, musicians and mystics. They may be awed by stories of religious saints and martyrs. A Gemini's highest achievement is to teach the truth, whether it is scientific, inspirational or historical. Those who can transcend the intellect are Gemini's natural superiors – and a Gemini realizes this.

The sign of Pisces is in Gemini's solar 10th house of career. Neptune, the planet of spirituality and altruism, is Gemini's career planet. If Geminis are to realize their highest career potential they need to develop their transcendental – their spiritual and altruistic – side. They need to understand the larger cosmic picture, the vast flow of human evolution – where it came from and where it is heading. Only then can a Gemini's intellectual powers take their true position and he or she can become the 'messenger of the gods'. Geminis need to cultivate a facility for 'inspiration', which is something that does not originate in the intellect but which comes through the intellect. This will further enrich and empower a Gemini's mind.

Love and Relationships

Geminis bring their natural garrulousness and brilliance into their love life and social life as well. A good talk or a verbal joust is an interesting prelude to romance. Their only problem in love is that their intellect is too cool and passionless to incite ardour in others. Emotions sometimes disturb them, and their partners tend to complain about this. If you are in love with a Gemini you must understand why this is so. Geminis avoid deep passions because these would interfere with their ability to think and communicate. If they are cool towards you, understand that this is their nature.

Nevertheless, Geminis must understand that it is one thing to talk about love and another actually to love – to feel it and radiate it. Talking about love glibly will get them nowhere. They need to feel it and act on it. Love is not of the intellect but of the heart. If you want to know how a Gemini feels about love you should not listen to what he or she says, but rather, observe what he or she does. Geminis can be quite generous to those they love.

Geminis like their partners to be refined, well educated and well travelled. If their partners are more wealthy than they, that is all the better. If you are in love with a Gemini you had better be a good listener as well.

The ideal relationship for the Gemini is a relationship of the mind. They enjoy the physical and emotional aspects, of course, but if the intellectual communion is not there they will suffer.

Home and Domestic Life

At home the Gemini can be uncharacteristically neat and meticulous. They tend to want their children and partner to live up to their idealistic standards. When these standards are not met they moan and criticize. However, Geminis are good family people and like to serve their families in practical and useful ways.

The Gemini home is comfortable and pleasant. They like to invite people over and they make great hosts. Geminis are also good at repairs and improvements around the house – all fuelled by their need to stay active and occupied with something they like to do. Geminis have many hobbies and interests that keep them busy when they are home alone.

Geminis understand and get along well with their children, mainly because they are very youthful people themselves. As great communicators, Geminis know how to explain things to children; in this way they gain their children's love and respect. Geminis also encourage children to be creative and talkative, just like they are.

Horoscope for 2013

Major Trends

You've had many years of sudden, dramatic changes. One minute things are a certain way and then, all of a sudden, life is completely different. Many have experienced these kinds of things, but for you it has been non-stop. Things have settled down a bit the past two years – Uranus has moved away from its stressful aspect to you – but you've learned by now how to live with insecurity, and this was the whole point. Nothing on this earthly plane is ever permanent and we need to learn how to handle impermanence.

Last year two important transits happened. Neptune made a major move from your 9th house into your 10th house of career, and Jupiter moved into your own sign. Both of these affect finance and career. Jupiter's move into Gemini in June 2012 initiated a two-year cycle of prosperity. So the year ahead is prosperous. Neptune's move into your career house indicates more idealism in career matters. You tend to be idealistic about your career anyway, but now even more so. You will be known more for your charitable activities, your spiritual attainments, than for your outer career achievements. There are more details about this later.

Saturn moved into your 6th house of health and work last year and will be there for another two years. It indicates a need to work harder and in a more disciplined kind of way. The job situation seems difficult to handle, and many of you have changed jobs. This also had an impact on your health and health regime. More on this later.

Geminis of child-bearing age are more fertile this year. Weight in general needs more attention. However, love is blooming this year. It was good last year too, but this year it is perhaps even better. See later for details.

Your most important interests in the year ahead are the body, image and personal pleasure (until June 27); finance (from June 27 onwards); health and work; sex, occult interests, personal reinvention, past lives, life after death; career; friends, groups, and group activities. You have many interests this year; be careful not to disperse your energies. Try to select the most important things and focus on them.

Your paths of greatest fulfilment this year are the body, image and personal pleasure (until June 27); finance (after June 27); health and work.

Health

(Please note that this is an astrological perspective on health and not a medical one. In days of yore there was no difference, these perspectives were identical. But now there could be quite a difference. For a medical perspective, please consult your doctor or health practitioner.)

Health is vastly improved compared with the previous few years. This year, there is only one long-term planet stressing you out – Neptune – and this is not enough to cause major problems. Health should be good. Sure, there will be periods in the year when your health is less easy than usual, but these things are caused by short-term planetary transits, and these are temporary and not trends for the year; when they pass your normal good health and energy return.

Saturn in your house of health all year shows many things. One, you are more focused on health this year. You are willing to take on disciplined, tough health regimes. Since health looks good, I read this as working to maintain good health. It also indicates a need to give more attention to the spine, knees, teeth, bones, skin and overall skeletal alignment. Pluto, your health planet, is in the sign of

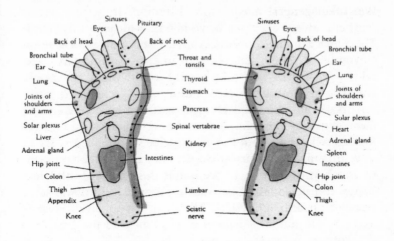

Reflexology

Try to massage the whole foot on a regular basis, but pay extra attention to the points highlighted on the chart. When you massage, be aware of 'sore spots', as these need special attention. It's also a good idea to massage the ankles and top side of the feet.

Capricorn all year (and for many years to come) and Capricorn rules these same areas. Regular visits to a chiropractor or osteopath would be a good idea. The vertebrae need to be kept in right alignment. Yoga, Alexander Technique, Pilates and Feldenkrais are excellent for the spine; regular back massage would be wonderful too. Give the knees more support when exercising or playing sports. If you are out in the sun for a long time, use a strong sunscreen – your skin is more sensitive than usual.

Saturn rules your 8th house of transformation, and Pluto, your health planet, rules surgery on a generic level. So surgery seems indicated in the year ahead, although it doesn't seem for life-threatening kinds of things. It may be recommended to you and should you choose this route, it seems successful. However, you also benefit from detox regimes. Often these achieve the same ends as surgery, only they take longer.

There are two eclipses in your house of health this year. There is a Lunar Eclipse on April 25 and a Solar Eclipse on November 3. These will tend to produce health scares, but with your overall health so good, they are likely to be only scares and nothing more. Often these eclipses indicate important, fundamental changes in the health regime and diet, generally for the better. These changes have long needed to be made, but the eclipse gives the needed push.

With Jupiter in your 1st House since June 2012 you need to watch your weight, as we mentioned. Basically this is a happy transit. It brings sensual pleasures, the fulfilment of carnal fantasies and desires. The main danger healthwise is excess – too much of a good thing. Enjoy all the pleasures that Jupiter brings by all means, but try not to overdo it. There is a price to be paid for this. Listen to your body – it will tell you when enough is enough.

Your most vulnerable health periods this year will be from February 18 to March 20; August 23 to September 22; and November 22 to December 21. These are times to rest and relax more and in general pay more attention to your health.

Home and Family

Your 4th house of home and family is pretty much empty this year; it is not a house of power. Generally, as our regular readers know, this indicates a basic contentment with the status quo. You have more free will in this area than usual, but will you use it? Generally people do not.

A parent or parent figure is entering a very spiritual kind of period. The body is being refined and spiritualized. If they are not on a spiritual path they should embark on one. Sometimes this shows a tendency to abuse alcohol or drugs, but this should be avoided as the body can overreact to this. Exercises such as yoga and tai chi – spiritual kinds of exercises – are very good for this person. It will assist the process of elevating the body more than other kinds of exercises. This person is making very dramatic financial changes, perhaps involving new ventures or 'start ups'. They are likely to move, renovate the existing home or acquire additional homes. (This could have happened last year too.) If the parents or parent figures are married, the relationship seems stable this year. There will be periods where it will be more stressful (when Mercury comes into stressful alignment with Neptune) and periods that are less stressful (when Mercury is in harmonious alignment with Neptune), but these are all short-term trends and they pass quickly.

Siblings and sibling figures are experiencing emotional volatility. They don't seem happy with the home. They feel cramped and restricted. However a move this year is not advisable.

Children in your life are making excellent psychological progress. They are dealing with deep psychological issues and seem successful here. There are renovations going on in their room (if they live with you) or in their home (if they are of an appropriate age). Grandchildren of an appropriate age most likely moved last year. This year they seem content with the status quo.

If you are planning major repairs or renovations, October 15 to December 7 is a good time for this. If you are merely redecorating, making cosmetic kinds of changes or buying art objects for the home, July 22 to August 16 and August 23 to September 22 are good times.

Finance and Career

We mentioned earlier that ever since Jupiter moved into your sign in June of last year, you were in a cycle of prosperity. This year you are still in the early stages of the cycle, so wealth is increasing at a good pace. You are enjoying the good life, you are travelling more than usual, and basically you are optimistic about yourself and your future. And you have the wherewithal to enjoy all the carnal pleasures. Lady Luck has camped out in your aura and you are catching the lucky breaks. Often we see this in the little things as well as the big – you get an unexpectedly large tax refund; you get a bargain at the shops; gamblers discover that they are luckier at the casino; people win substantial sums on lotteries. These are the little signals that Jupiter is working his magic on you, that the heavenly doors of affluence are open.

Jupiter moving through your own sign until June 27 will also bring happy educational opportunities, and it seems wise to take them. Students should be successful in their studies. College applicants do very well – colleges are looking for you rather than vice versa.

On June 27 Jupiter enters your money house, bringing more prosperity. Stocks you own go up in value. Your home is probably worth more than you think. Your financial horizons get expanded. Your financial goals are bigger and you have more power to attain them. They are no longer beyond your reach. Happy financial opportunities come as well.

Jupiter is your love planet. Translated into financial terms this indicates a lucrative and happy business partnership or joint venture. Companies often merge or get sold under this aspect. Your spouse, partner or current love is financially supportive, much more than usual. Social connections are important financially. Friends seem rich and supportive as well. They bring happy financial opportunities. When the love planet is involved in finances we can never judge a person's wealth by financial statements, or by merely looking at tangible assets. Geminis' wealth these days is much more than this. Who they know is as important as how much they have. Wealth of friendships, as regular readers know, is a valid form of wealth.

When Jupiter moves into Cancer on June 27 it will start to make fabulous aspects to your career planet Neptune. This aspect is most exact in July, but is in effect afterwards too. This brings career elevation. Generally there are pay rises and promotions, but it also brings honours, recognition and an elevation of your status in your company, profession or industry. Your partner and friends are supportive of your career and bring opportunities. Your ability to get on with others seems to be a big factor in your success. When Jupiter moves into Cancer there will be a Grand Trine in the Water signs – and your career planet is involved with this. So the year ahead is successful careerwise.

With Neptune, your career planet, now in the spiritual sign of Pisces, you need a meaningful kind of career. It's not just about making money and outer success. Your career has to have some spiritual value to it – it has to be something that truly benefits the world. This is your main challenge now and in the coming years. There's more on this later.

Love and Social Life

Last year, and especially the second half of it, was a banner love year, and the trend continues perhaps even more strongly in 2013. Singles will not be single for too long. Perhaps they won't actually marry, but it will be 'as if' they had married. They will be involved in a serious romantic relationship with strong marriage potential.

Jupiter, the love planet, is moving through your sign. Love is coming to you. You are not likely to escape it. It seems unavoidable. This person finds you, woos you, courts you. You are having love on your terms this year. The beloved caters to you, is devoted to you, is totally on your side. He or she puts your interests ahead of his or her own. You are the most important thing in their life. This kind of devotion is difficult to withstand.

You are lucky in finances this year, but perhaps even luckier in love.

This love will get tested later on in the year in August. Jupiter will move into Square aspect with Uranus, but this relationship seems to have a lot of cosmic help. I feel it can survive this.

What we said about love also applies to friendships. Friends – and happy social opportunities – seek you out, and you are in demand socially. We have often compared the effect of a planetary transit to the action of a drug. It is as if you have taken a cosmic aphrodisiac. You exude love and grace. You look good. You are always smart and intellectual, but now the love force emanates from you and people respond to this. This is a year of great popularity.

After June 27, as Jupiter moves into your money house, you are working to combine an active social life with an active financial life. You do business with your friends, the people that you socialize with, and you socialize with the people you do business with. You find love and social opportunity as you pursue your normal financial goals and with people who are involved in your finances.

Before June 27 it is the physical aspects of love that attract – the charms of the body, the right image, the right look. The beloved has to fit your image of love and vice versa. Love is expressed physically, not just through sex but through hugging, touching, massage and things of this nature. After the 27th wealth becomes an important attraction. You are attracted to the rich, the good providers, the people who can help you financially. Love is expressed in material ways, through material gifts or financial support. This is how you feel loved and this is how you express it.

Self-improvement

Saturn, as we have mentioned, is now in your 6th house of health for the next two years. We discussed some of the physical aspects of this in the health section, but there is more to it.

Saturn in your 6th house shows that you gravitate to traditional, orthodox medicine. You want the therapies that have stood the test of time. Even those of you who like alternative therapies will probably gravitate to the very ancient systems – acupuncture, acupressure and so on. The new and the untried, no matter how trendy, are not for you.

The good point about this is that you are not into 'quick fixes' healthwise. You want long-term cures, long-term solutions. Generally this involves lifestyle changes, adopting a healthier type of life. You seem willing to do this now.

You are very prosperous in the year ahead. It could be that you are merely working harder, putting in more hours. You have good luck with you, but you are also putting in the work. Those of you who hire others are probably laying off people this year, making the workforce leaner but more productive. Those of you who work for others are probably seeing the same phenomenon in your own company. There are job changes in the year ahead, changes in working conditions and the workplace.

Neptune on the Mid-heaven makes you very idealistic about your career, as we mentioned. It also indicates a spiritual type of career for many of you. Those involved in a mundane worldly career (and there's nothing wrong with this) might want to spend more time with charities and altruistic kinds of causes. It will not only give you much personal satisfaction, but will actually enhance your career and public image. Of course, you shouldn't do this for personal benefit, but this will be the natural side effect.

In many case, spirituality itself will become the career. Spiritual development will be the mission (a valid one, by the way). Practices that seem solitary such as meditation, or breathing exercises, are really not solitary at all. They affect in a positive way everyone around you. Spiritual practice changes families, communities, and even the world.

Month-by-month Forecasts

January

Best Days Overall: 4, 5, 12, 13, 21, 22, 23, 31
Most Stressful Days Overall: 2, 3, 8, 9, 14, 15, 29, 30
Best Days for Love: 4, 8, 9, 12, 18, 19, 22, 29, 30, 31
Best Days for Money: 2, 3, 4, 10, 11, 12, 21, 22, 24, 25, 31
Best Days for Career: 6, 14, 15, 24

You begin your year with most of the planets in the Western, social sector of your Horoscope. Relationships are important now. Your good (with the exception of romance) comes to you by the good graces of others and not so much because of your personal abilities or personal actions. Thus there is a need to cultivate the social skills and adapt more to situations. If conditions are not pleasant, make a note, and get ready to change them when you enter your period of personal independence. It is not yet time for forcing issues. Let others have their way, so long as it isn't destructive.

The upper half of the Horoscope contains 70 and sometimes 80 per cent of the planets. So you are in a cycle where your career, your outer world objectives are dominant. You are focused here and thus success is more likely. We get what we focus on. Next month you will enter a yearly career peak and success will be even greater.

The planetary momentum is overwhelmingly forward at the moment – 90 per cent of the planets are moving forward and on the 30th all of them will be forward. This is an excellent time to launch new projects or products into the world. The 11th to the 27th is especially favourable for these launches.

Your 8th and 9th houses are the most powerful this month. Until the 19th, the 8th house of transformation is strong. Thus it is good for detox regimes on all levels, physical, emotional, mental and financial. Your efforts at personal transformation – creating the person that you want to be –

will also go better. After the 19th, as the Sun moves into your 9th house, it is good for religious and metaphysical-type breakthroughs, and for scheduling foreign trips. Students should do better in school too. If you are involved in legal issues, try to schedule them after the 19th.

Love is excellent all month, but especially after the 19th. This is a good period to schedule a wedding or other kind of party, and especially after the 30th.

Finances are reasonable this month; nothing special one way or the other. In general you should earn more from the 11th to the 27th. You have more financial energy and enthusiasm that period than either before or after.

Health is much improved over last month. The main danger is overindulgence. This can create weight problems. Enhance the health in the ways described in the yearly report.

February

Best Days Overall: 1, 9, 10, 18, 19, 27, 28
Most Stressful Days Overall: 5, 11, 12, 25, 26
Best Days for Love: 5, 9, 10, 18, 19, 27
Best Days for Money: 1, 9, 10, 18, 20, 21, 22, 27
Best Days for Career: 2, 11, 12, 20

Last month on the 19th you entered a mini love peak for the year. You have others coming later on, but this was one of them, and it continues until the 18th of this month. Most of you seem involved in some serious relationship, but if not, this is a period for meeting a special someone. Your love planet Jupiter was retrograde most of last month until the 30th. Now it is moving forward and so social confidence and judgement are good. Mental clarity on love issues is back, so it's safe now to make important love decisions.

In most areas of life you need to compromise and adapt to others, but in love you are having things your way and on your terms. After the 5th be more patient with the beloved. You seem in some minor disagreement.

Until the 18th all the planets are moving forward. Thus you are in another good period for launching new projects or products into the world. The 10th to the 18th seem best. On the 18th (and you will begin to feel this earlier) you enter a yearly career peak. Career is active and successful and promotions now wouldn't be a surprise. The 6th–7th, 11th–12th and the 19th–21st are especially successful. If you have issues with your boss or with the government, these are good times to deal with them.

Health and energy are wonderful until the 18th. After that, try to rest and relax more. With the career so active it will probably be difficult, but if you drop the trivia from your life you will find it easier. Enhance health in the ways mentioned in the yearly report and do whatever is possible to maintain high energy levels. Your health is basically good this year, but this is not one of your best periods.

The planetary power begins to shift from the West to the East, from the social sector to the personal sector, on the 18th. Thus you will start becoming more independent day by day. You will have the power to create what you desire in your life, to go your own way and to find your own happiness. Others will start to adapt to you.

Mars conjuncts your career planet Neptune from the 3rd to the 5th. A friend is very successful and supportive of you. Friends in general are opening career doors. Your high-tech expertise seems very important during this period.

Finances are strongest from the 11th to the 25th as the Moon is in her waxing phase, although finance doesn't seem like a big deal this month. Status and prestige – being number one – seem more important.

March

Best Days Overall: 1, 8, 9, 17, 18, 19, 27, 28
Most Stressful Days Overall: 4, 5, 10, 11, 24, 25, 26, 31
Best Days for Love: 1, 2, 3, 4, 5, 8, 9, 10, 11, 17, 18, 21, 22, 27, 28, 31
Best Days for Money: 1, 2, 3, 8, 9, 10, 11, 17, 18, 20, 21, 22, 27, 28, 31
Best Days for Career: 1, 2, 10, 11, 20, 29

Mercury, the Lord of your Horoscope, and a very important planet in your life, went retrograde on February 23 and will be retrograde until the 17th of this month. You are successful but seem to lack direction. This is a period for gaining mental clarity about your personal goals and family issues. Perhaps you are not sure of the kind of image you want to project, so take the time to do homework on these things. Clarity will come after the 17th.

You are definitely in charge in the romance department. You seem above the beloved, calling the shots. Often this creates problems. It is wonderful to have authority, but if it is abused there will be love problems. Friends might not take too kindly to this either. The beloved (and friends in general) are in conflict with their families and this is adding to the stress. The love and social life improves dramatically after the 20th and next month will be even better.

The Sun will be in Aries from the 20th onwards. This is considered the best starting energy of the year. Spring is when the plants start to grow and nature resurrects. In addition the planetary momentum is overwhelmingly forward, especially after the 17th, so this is another great time to begin new ventures. The 20th to the 27th is the best time to begin things.

Your health still needs watching until the 20th. Review our discussion of this last month. Health and energy roar back after the 20th.

On the 20th your 11th house of friends becomes powerful. Thus it is a strong social period. You are involved with

friends, groups, group activities and professional organizations. It is a very good time to upgrade your technology or to
increase your general knowledge here. Foreign trips are also
likely after the 20th as Uranus (your travel planet) gets
intense stimulation. Group tours seem more favourable than
solo travel.

Pluto, your work planet, receives stressful aspects after
the 20th and so there are probably job changes afoot. This
could be with your present company or with another one.
Also the conditions of work are changing. Those of you who
employ others experience employee turnover and instability
these days. You will also be making dramatic changes to the
health regime and diet.

April

Best Days Overall: 4, 5, 14, 15, 23, 24
Most Stressful Days Overall: 1, 6, 7, 8, 21, 22, 27, 28
Best Days for Love: 1, 4, 5, 9, 10, 14, 15, 21, 22, 23, 24,
    27, 28, 29, 30
Best Days for Money: 1, 4, 5, 9, 10, 14, 15, 16, 17, 21, 23,
    24, 29, 30
Best Days for Career: 6, 7, 8, 16, 25

The Sun is in Aries and the planetary momentum is still
overwhelmingly forward. If you have new products or
projects to launch and you haven't yet done so, this is still a
great period to do it. The New Moon of the 10th is particularly good, but the 10th to the 25th – the waxing Moon
period – is reasonable.

Pluto, your health planet, is receiving some stressful
aspects until the 20th. Often this brings a health scare.
However, overall health looks excellent this period (and for
the year ahead) so this is likely to be nothing more than a
scare. Like last month we see job changes and changes in the
conditions of work. Employers are experiencing employee
turnover. Job seekers need to be more patient this month.
With Pluto going retrograde on the 12th, job opportunities

need more research – not everything the recruiter says is actually so. Read the contract. Study the fine print. This applies to health insurance or health care plans as well.

A Lunar Eclipse on the 25th reinforces much of what we say above. It brings job changes, instability with employees and perhaps a health scare. It also shows dramatic financial changes.

Most of the planets are still above the horizon and your 10th career house is still powerful until the 14th, so keep your focus on the career. There is still much success and positive developments happening here. It is safe to downplay home and family issues now. In fact, the family seems very supportive of your career. The family as a whole seems elevated in status over the past few months, and a parent or parent figure seems very active on the social level.

The planetary power is approaching the maximum Eastern position this month (the absolute maximum occurs next month), so there is no need to compromise these days. Create your life – the conditions and circumstances – as you would like them to be. This is the time for having things your way. You need to decide your path of greatest happiness, not others. You are in a period where personal initiative and personal ability matter. Make the most of it. Later on in the year it will be more difficult to change conditions.

Your 11th house of friends is still powerful all month, so review our discussion of this from last month. Foreign travel, especially group travel, seems to be happening.

On the 19th, your 12th house of spirituality becomes powerful. This is a period for spiritual-type breakthroughs and for interior revelation. The growth that is happening now is interior, covert, behind the scenes, but the results will be clear next month. Every spiritual breakthrough leads inevitably to a physical or material breakthrough. Things always happen first in the spiritual world.

Finances are not that big of a deal, as has been the case since the beginning of the year. But earnings (and your mood for finance) will be stronger from the 10th to the 25th.

Love is still very happy, and a child in your life has a happy romantic experience from the 5th to the 9th.

May

Best Days Overall: 2, 3, 11, 12, 21, 22, 29, 30
Most Stressful Days Overall: 4, 5, 18, 19, 25, 26, 31
Best Days for Love: 2, 3, 10, 11, 12, 21, 22, 26, 29, 30
Best Days for Money: 2, 3, 8, 9, 10, 11, 12, 13, 14, 15, 19, 20, 21, 22, 29, 30
Best Days for Career: 4, 5, 13, 23, 31

We have two eclipses this month, which ensures that the month ahead will be turbulent and full of change. If you read the newspapers this month you will see what I mean here. However, in spite of this, your life is going well. You will not be affected too much and you will be in a good position to help others through this period. Things might not be going so well for them.

The Lunar Eclipse of the 25th occurs in your 12th house of spirituality. This indicates changes in your spiritual practice and attitudes. Generally this comes as a result of interior revelation. People often change teachers, teachings and paths under this kind of eclipse. There will be shake-ups in a spiritual or charitable organization that you are involved with. The Moon is your financial planet, so every Lunar Eclipse brings dramatic financial changes. This one is no different. People seldom make necessary changes voluntarily; events have to force them, and this is the function of the eclipse. Generally we face some major 'financial fear' and need to overcome it. Cars and communication equipment will get tested – often they need replacement or repair. There are dramas in the lives of siblings or sibling figures. Friends, too, seem affected.

The Solar Eclipse of the 10th occurs in your 7th house of love. Generally this indicates a testing of love, and the beloved is more temperamental this period. Often it indicates a change in the marital status. In your case, with the love life so good, it could signal marriage – taking your relationship a step further. This eclipse will also test cars and communication equipment and bring dramas and life-changing kinds of events to siblings, sibling figures and neighbours. Neptune, your career planet, is very affected by this eclipse, thus there are career changes happening, and changes in your industry and corporate hierarchy. Parents, parent figures or bosses experience life-changing events.

Overall, however, this is a happy month. On the 20th you enter a yearly personal pleasure peak. You have been having much personal – carnal – pleasure all year, but this month even more so. You have much energy and charisma now. Your personal appearance shines, and your self-confidence and self-esteem are very healthy now – in fact problems could come from too much of a good thing!

Your financial energy is strongest from the 10th to the 25th as the Moon waxes. Finance is basically OK. The eclipse brings changes, and you will see the result of this next month.

June

Best Days Overall: 7, 8, 17, 18, 25, 26
Most Stressful Days Overall: 1, 15, 16, 21, 22, 27, 28
Best Days for Love: 8, 9, 10, 17, 18, 19, 20, 21, 22, 26, 27, 28
Best Days for Money: 7, 8, 9, 10, 11, 17, 18, 26, 27
Best Days for Career: 1, 10, 19, 27, 28

The eclipses last month brought financial and career changes and this month you will see the positive results of these. On the 21st you enter a yearly financial peak. On the 27th Jupiter enters your money house and will be there for a whole year. This might be more of a lifetime peak than a yearly peak. The money is rolling in – a good time to build up your bank balances and investment portfolio now. Managing your wealth can be as important as earning. Your spouse, partner or current love will also be prospering greatly later in the month. He or she seems generous as well; likewise parents or parent figures. Wonderful career opportunities are happening at the end of the month.

Until the 21st you are still in one of your yearly personal pleasure peaks. All the pleasures of the senses are open to you and you have the wherewithal to indulge yourself. The only problem here is excess. Overindulgence carries a price tag.

On the 27th, as Jupiter enters your money house, a (very lucrative) business partnership seems in the works. It might not happen this month, but it will happen in future months – the opportunity will come. Your spouse, partner or current love is financially supportive, and friends in general are cooperating financially. The most important thing is that you are focused here, which is something that we haven't seen all year. This focus is what tends to bring success. Your personal appearance – your overall demeanour – is important financially. You are probably investing in your wardrobe or accessories.

Health is excellent all month. You have all the energy you need to achieve anything you set your mind to. You can enhance your health further in the ways mentioned in the yearly report on page 92.

On May 20 the planetary power shifted from the upper half of your Horoscope to the lower half. There are still very nice career opportunities coming to you, and there is still much success happening, but now you can shift some attention to the home, family and your emotional well being. You will start to be more fussy about career opportunities. No matter how good they seem, if they violate your emotional harmony or place family or domestic stress on you, you are likely to pass on them.

July

Best Days Overall: 4, 5, 6, 14, 15, 23, 24
Most Stressful Days Overall: 12, 13, 19, 20, 25, 26
Best Days for Love: 1, 7, 8, 10, 11, 16, 17, 19, 20, 25, 29, 30
Best Days for Money: 7, 8, 16, 17, 18, 25, 27
Best Days for Career: 7, 16, 17, 25, 26

The Water element became very strong last month, especially after the 21st. Now 60 per cent (and sometimes 70 per cent) of the planets are in Water signs. This heightens the emotional sensitivities in people. Little things, voice tones, body language, a seemingly innocent remark can upset people, so be more mindful this month. There are also strong positives with all this water. People are more tender and compassionate with each other – the love life especially is more tender. Personal creativity is also stronger. On a metaphysical level, it is easier to attain the 'feeling' of what you desire, and thus easier to manifest and create it.

Planetary retrograde activity is greatly increased now; 40 per cent of the planets are retrograde until the 8th and from the 17th to the 20th, and 30 per cent are retrograde after the 20th. We are at the maximum level of retrograde activity for the year right now. So be patient with all the minor glitches and complications that this brings. Slow down and be more methodical in everything that you do.

You are still very much in a yearly financial peak. Finances are very good right now. You are catching the lucky breaks and have the financial support of your beloved. The social circle is supportive as well. The New Moon of the 8th marks a particularly strong financial day, and this New Moon will clarify the finances as the month progresses. All the information you need will come to you.

Your 3rd house of communication and intellectual interests becomes powerful on the 22nd. Thus you are in Gemini heaven. The cosmos impels you to do what you most love – learn, teach, read, communicate, sell, trade and market.

Thus this is a successful and enjoyable period for you. The mind is sharper than usual, likewise your communication skills.

For singles (if there are still any of you out there) love opportunities come as you pursue your financial goals, and perhaps with people involved in your finances. Social opportunities come this way as well. Love is shown in material, practical ways through financial support or material gifts. This is how you show love and this is how you feel loved. They say that love can't be bought, but right now for Geminis this isn't so. The wealthy in general attract you.

Health and energy are excellent. You can enhance the health further in the ways mentioned in the yearly report. Job changes are afoot this month too.

August

Best Days Overall: 1, 2, 10, 11, 12, 19, 20, 28, 29
Most Stressful Days Overall: 8, 9, 15, 16, 21, 22
Best Days for Love: 3, 8, 9, 13, 14, 15, 16, 19, 21, 22, 25, 26, 30, 31
Best Days for Money: 3, 4, 6, 7, 13, 14, 15, 16, 21, 22, 25, 30, 31
Best Days for Career: 3, 13, 21, 22

The element of Water is still very strong this month, although not as strong as in the past two months. Review our discussion of this from last month.

Very beautiful career developments are happening. This has been the trend for the past few months and it continues. There is much success happening, much opportunity for advancement. However, with most of the planets still below the horizon, and with your 4th house of home and family becoming powerful after the 22nd, your main focus is your emotional life and your family situation. You need to set up the interior conditions for career success to happen. The opportunities are there but you need to be emotionally ready for them. As the saying goes, you need to be ready for prime time. Your career planet Neptune has been retrograde since June 7, so study career offers carefully – there is no rush.

Your 3rd house of communication and intellectual interests is still powerful until the 22nd. Your naturally sharp mind is even sharper now. You inhale information. All your natural communication skills are magnified now. This is a great period for writers, teachers, journalists and media people. Students should do well too. After the 22nd the focus moves to the home and family. This is a time to get your physical house in order, to spend more time with the family and to make psychological progress.

Health and energy are still excellent, but after the 22nd start to rest and relax more. The Sun in Virgo does not show one of your best health periods. Enhance your health by maximizing energy and in the ways mentioned in the yearly report (page 93).

Love is still very happy. Your spouse, partner or current love continues to prosper and continues to be generous with you. His or her prosperity will be stronger after the 22nd than before but it is basically good all month. Singles still find love as they pursue their normal financial goals. Finances are good this month and for the rest of the year. Earning power will tend to be strongest from the 6th to the 23rd as the Moon is waxing.

Mars squares Uranus on the 1st and 2nd. Drive more carefully and be more mindful on the physical plane. This applies to friends as well. Jupiter squares Uranus from the 18th to the 23rd. The beloved can be more temperamental in this period. Be patient. He or she should drive more carefully and avoid arguments. Jupiter squares Pluto from the 4th to the 13th and the same advice applies.

September

Best Days Overall: 7, 8, 15, 16, 24, 25, 26
Most Stressful Days Overall: 4, 5, 6, 11, 12, 18, 19
Best Days for Love: 1, 8, 9, 10, 11, 12, 17, 18, 19, 27, 28
Best Days for Money: 1, 4, 5, 9, 10, 13, 14, 18, 19, 24, 27, 28
Best Days for Career: 1, 9, 17, 18, 19, 27

On August 22 the planetary power shifted from the East to the West of the Horoscope, from the sector of the self to the social sector, the sector of other people. Thus there is a psychological shift happening. You are forced to cultivate your social skills now: personal ability is not that important, instead the 'likeability' factor is vital. Success depends on others now. Hopefully you have created conditions as you desire them to be over the past months – now it is time to road test your creation. It is more difficult to create now, you have to adapt to existing conditions as best you can. From now until the end of the year make a note of conditions that are disturbing and need to be changed. When your next period of personal independence comes next year, you will be able to make these changes with more ease and less stress.

Your career planet is still retrograde; most of the planets are still below the horizon of the chart and your 4th house of home and family is still powerful. All this is giving a very clear message. Like last month, keep the focus on the home and family and the emotional life. Keep working to build the interior conditions for success, to be emotionally ready for it. There are many positive career opportunities coming your way but don't jump into anything without doing more homework. Your instinct will tell you whether something is right or not. The career opportunity has to be 'emotionally comfortable' and family friendly.

Health still needs watching until the 22nd, but afterwards improves tremendously. On the 22nd you enter another yearly personal pleasure peak. You will be working harder than usual, but in spite of this you will manage to have some fun. Geminis of child-bearing age are in their most fertile period of the year.

Last month, on the 16th, a rare Grand Square formed in the heavens. This Grand Square is in effect all of this month as well. You and perhaps your spouse, partner or current love could be involved in a major undertaking and are more stressed out than usual. If you are involved in legal matters they seem stressful and complicated now. Foreign travel is not advisable during this period, unless it is in the line of duty. Elective foreign travel is better off being re-scheduled.

Prosperity is still happening this month – and next month will be even better. Your strongest earning period will be from the 5th to the 19th, as the Moon is waxing. This is when you have the greatest enthusiasm for financial matters.

Love is more delicate after the 22nd. The beloved seems more stressed than usual and seems in disagreement with you. This is a short-term problem and will pass by the 29th.

October

Best Days Overall: 4, 5, 13, 14, 22, 23, 31
Most Stressful Days Overall: 2, 3, 8, 9, 15, 16, 29, 30
Best Days for Love: 6, 7, 8, 9, 15, 16, 17, 18, 24, 25, 27, 28
Best Days for Money: 4, 5, 6, 7, 13, 14, 15, 16, 23, 24, 25
Best Days for Career: 6, 15, 16, 24

There is much power in the Water element this month. There will always be at least half of the planets in Water signs, and at times up to 70 per cent of them. Keep in mind our previous discussions of this. Be more mindful of the sensitivities of others (this month they are likely to be hypersensitive). When the Water element is this strong people become nostalgic and sentimental. Moods override logic. At times like this clear thinkers such as you are more needed than ever. A dose of rational thinking (communicated in a sensitive way) is what the world needs right now.

The Grand Square in the heavens that we mentioned last month is still in effect until the 23rd. This presages a hectic, active period – personally, for the beloved, for friends and for the world at large. Big things are manifesting now. But, like last month, you still manage to have fun in spite of the hectic pace. You are still in one of your yearly personal pleasure peaks until the 23rd.

There is a Lunar Eclipse on the 18th that occurs in your 11th house of friendship. Basically the eclipse is benign to you, but it might not be so benign to the people around you, so it's best to take things a bit easier. As always, do what needs to be done, but re-schedule what you can, especially if the activities promise to be stressful. This eclipse brings financial changes, which will turn out well in the long run. It brings dramas in the lives of friends and friendships can be tested. This eclipse impacts on Jupiter, your love planet, so your current relationship has a brief rough spot. The beloved will likely be more temperamental so be patient. Don't take things too personally. Basically there is harmony between you and the beloved and you will get through this period.

The situation at work still seems highly unstable. This has been the case all year, but now it seems particularly intense. Uranus' square to Pluto, your work planet, is very exact now. The good news is that you are very focused on work all month and so you seem willing to overcome all the various challenges and changes. Job seekers have excellent aspects all month, but especially after the 23rd. In spite of all the instability at work, the overall career seems very good. The career trends that we have been discussing for the past few months are still in effect.

Health is good this month. Also you seem more focused here, giving it a lot of attention. Your state of health dramatically impacts on your personal appearance these days and this is not always the case, so staying healthy does more for your looks than all the perfumes and cosmetics in the world. This seems the reason for the focus – not ill health.

November

Best Days Overall: 1, 9, 10, 18, 19, 28, 29
Most Stressful Days Overall: 5, 6, 11, 12, 25, 26, 27
Best Days for Love: 3, 4, 5, 6, 7, 11, 12, 16, 17, 21, 22, 26, 27, 30
Best Days for Money: 3, 4, 11, 12, 20, 21, 22, 23, 30
Best Days for Career: 3, 11, 12, 20, 30

This month, after the 22nd, the planetary power starts to shift to the upper half of the Horoscope. The shift won't be complete until next month, but you start to feel the change after the 22nd. Hopefully, you have got your family and emotional life in order, as it is now time to focus on your outer life – your career and outer world goals.

The situation at work continues to be unstable. Probably there are many layoffs at your company and perhaps other changes in the workplace. Uranus' square to your work planet is still very exact. A Solar Eclipse in your 6th house of work is also signalling job changes and upheavals at the workplace. Have no fear though: your overall career is not affected, it is still blossoming this month.

The Solar Eclipse of the 3rd will test cars and communication equipment. Every Solar Eclipse tends to have this effect as the Sun is your communication planet. It brings dramatic events in the lives of siblings, sibling figures and neighbours. Often there are disruptions in your neighbourhood. Letters don't get mailed or get sent to the wrong address. Glitches at the post office or with your email are normal under a Solar Eclipse. This eclipse impacts on Saturn, the ruler of your 8th house of transformation. Thus it brings dramatic financial changes in your spouse or partner's finances. It can also bring encounters with death (generally on the psychological level). Sometimes people have dreams about death. Sometimes someone they know dies and there are funerals to attend. Sometimes it is an actual near-death kind of experience. The purpose here is to gain a deeper understanding of death so that life can be lived better.

Inheritance has been in your chart since June 27 and it is in the chart again this month. Hopefully no one needs to actually die. It can indicate that you are named in someone's will, or receive a trust fund or insurance payment.

On the 22nd you enter a yearly love and social peak. The unattached are likely to meet someone special. Those already attached should have more romance within the relationship. In general there will be more going out, more parties and more social interaction.

Health becomes more delicate after the 22nd. There's nothing serious afoot, it's just not one of your best periods. Enhance health in the ways mentioned in the yearly report.

Earning power will be strong all month, but especially from the 3rd to the 17th.

December

    Best Days Overall: 6, 7, 15, 16, 17, 25, 26
    Most Stressful Days Overall: 2, 3, 8, 9, 23, 24, 30, 31
    Best Days for Love: 1, 2, 3, 4, 5, 8, 9, 13, 14, 18, 19, 23, 24, 28, 29, 30, 31
    Best Days for Money: 1, 2, 3, 8, 9, 11, 12, 18, 19, 22, 23, 28, 29
    Best Days for Career: 1, 8, 9, 18, 28

Mercury, the Lord of your Horoscope, seems in exile this month, especially from the 5th to the 24th. He is far, far away from his natural home. This more or less describes you. You are far from home, in strange circumstances and not as confident as you normally are. Perhaps this is a good thing. With so many planets in the West, and with so much riding on the good graces of others, a little humility is in order now. It plays well socially. You seem very popular this month. Your 7th house of love is strong until the 21st and Mercury is in your house of love from the 5th to the 24th. This shows that you are going out of your way for others. You are putting the interests of others ahead of your own. You are a good friend to have these days. Others notice this and appreciate it.

Jupiter, your love planet, went retrograde on the 7th of last month. So social confidence is not what it should be – another reason that you are putting yourself out for others. The retrograde of Jupiter is not going to stop the social life – it only slows things down a bit. Singles will still date and have fun, but important love decisions are best delayed. On the 21st Venus will also start to retrograde (this is relatively rare, happening once every two years or so). Thus the two love planets in your chart will be retrograde at the same time. More caution in love (or with business partnerships) is called for. It might seem to you that your love life or current relationship is going backwards instead of forwards, but it is merely a 're-evaluation' that is happening. A breather now might be a healthy thing. Regardless of the complications in your love life this seems a sexually active kind of month. Regardless of your age or stage in life, the libido is stronger than usual.

With the 8th house of transformation powerful after the 21st, your spouse, partner or current love is in a yearly financial peak and is likely to be more generous with you. This is a good period to pay down debt or to borrow if you need to. There is better access to outside capital this month.

Health still needs watching until the 21st. After that your natural health and vitality return.

There are some very dynamic aspects towards the end of the month, so avoid risk-taking activities then. Mars will be square to Uranus and Pluto (a very dynamic energy) from the 23rd to the 31st. And Mercury (your ruler) will be square to these planets from the 29th to the 31st and to the Sun on the 30th and 31st. Drive more carefully, and avoid arguments whenever possible. Watch the temper and be more mindful on the physical plane.

Cancer

♋

THE CRAB
Birthdays from
21st June to
20th July

Personality Profile

CANCER AT A GLANCE

Element – Water

Ruling Planet – Moon
   Career Planet – Mars
   Love Planet – Saturn
   Money Planet – Sun
   Planet of Fun and Games – Pluto
   Planet of Good Fortune – Neptune
   Planet of Health and Work – Jupiter
   Planet of Home and Family Life – Venus
   Planet of Spirituality – Mercury

Colours – blue, puce, silver

Colours that promote love, romance and social harmony – black, indigo

Colours that promote earning power – gold, orange

Gems – moonstone, pearl

Metal – silver

Scents – jasmine, sandalwood

Quality – cardinal (= activity)

Quality most needed for balance – mood control

Strongest virtues – emotional sensitivity,
tenacity, the urge to nurture

Deepest need – a harmonious home
and family life

Characteristics to avoid – over-sensitivity,
negative moods

Signs of greatest overall compatibility – Scorpio,
Pisces

Signs of greatest overall incompatibility – Aries,
Libra, Capricorn

Sign most helpful to career – Aries

Sign most helpful for emotional support – Libra

Sign most helpful financially – Leo

Sign best for marriage and/or partnerships –
Capricorn

Sign most helpful for creative projects – Scorpio

Best Sign to have fun with – Scorpio

Signs most helpful in spiritual matters – Gemini,
Pisces

Best day of the week – Monday

Understanding a Cancer

In the sign of Cancer the heavens are developing the feeling side of things. This is what a true Cancerian is all about – feelings. Where Aries will tend to err on the side of action, Taurus on the side of inaction and Gemini on the side of thought, Cancer will tend to err on the side of feeling.

Cancerians tend to mistrust logic. Perhaps rightfully so. For them it is not enough for an argument or a project to be logical – it must feel right as well. If it does not feel right a Cancerian will reject it or chafe against it. The phrase 'follow your heart' could have been coined by a Cancerian, because it describes exactly the Cancerian attitude to life.

The power to feel is a more direct – more immediate – method of knowing than thinking is. Thinking is indirect. Thinking about a thing never touches the thing itself. Feeling is a faculty that touches directly the thing or issue in question. We actually experience it. Emotional feeling is almost like another sense which humans possess – a psychic sense. Since the realities that we come in contact with during our lifetime are often painful and even destructive, it is not surprising that the Cancerian chooses to erect barriers – a shell – to protect his or her vulnerable, sensitive nature. To a Cancerian this is only common sense.

If Cancerians are in the presence of people they do not know, or find themselves in a hostile environment, up goes the shell and they feel protected. Other people often complain about this, but one must question these other people's motives. Why does this shell disturb them? Is it perhaps because they would like to sting, and feel frustrated that they cannot? If your intentions are honourable and you are patient, have no fear. The shell will open up and you will be accepted as part of the Cancerian's circle of family and friends.

Thought-processes are generally analytic and dissociating. In order to think clearly we must make distinctions, comparisons and the like. But feeling is unifying and integrative.

To think clearly about something you have to distance yourself from it. To feel something you must get close to it. Once a Cancerian has accepted you as a friend he or she will hang on to you. You have to be really bad to lose the friendship of a Cancerian. If you are related to Cancerians they will never let you go no matter what you do. They will always try to maintain some kind of connection even in the most extreme circumstances.

Finance

The Cancer-born has a deep sense of what other people feel about things and why they feel as they do. This faculty is a great asset in the workplace and in the business world. Of course it is also indispensable in raising a family and building a home, but it also has its uses in business. Cancerians often attain great wealth in a family business. Even if the business is not a family operation, they will treat it as one. If the Cancerian works for somebody else, then the boss is the parental figure and the co-workers are brothers and sisters. If a Cancerian is the boss, then all the workers are his or her children. Cancerians like the feeling of being providers for others. They enjoy knowing that others derive their sustenance because of what they do. It is another form of nurturing.

With Leo on their solar 2nd house (of money) cusp, Cancerians are often lucky speculators, especially with residential property or hotels and restaurants. Resort hotels and nightclubs are also profitable for the Cancerian. Waterside properties allure them. Though they are basically conventional people, they sometimes like to earn their livelihood in glamorous ways.

The Sun, Cancer's money planet, represents an important financial message: in financial matters Cancerians need to be less moody, more stable and fixed. They cannot allow their moods – which are here today and gone tomorrow – to get in the way of their business lives. They need to develop their self-esteem and feelings of self-worth if they are to realize their greatest financial potential.

Career and Public Image

Aries rules the 10th solar house (of career) cusp of Cancer, which indicates that Cancerians long to start their own business, to be more active publicly and politically and to be more independent. Family responsibilities and a fear of hurting other people's feelings – or getting hurt themselves – often inhibit them from attaining these goals. However, this is what they want and long to do.

Cancerians like their bosses and leaders to act freely and to be a bit self-willed. They can deal with that in a superior. They expect their leaders to be fierce on their behalf. When the Cancerian is in the position of boss or superior he or she behaves very much like a 'warlord'. Of course the wars they wage are not egocentric but in defence of those under their care. If they lack some of this fighting instinct – independence and pioneering spirit – Cancerians will have extreme difficulty in attaining their highest career goals. They will be hampered in their attempts to lead others.

Since they are so parental, Cancerians like to work with children and make great educators and teachers.

Love and Relationships

Like Taurus, Cancer likes committed relationships. Cancerians function best when the relationship is clearly defined and everyone knows his or her role. When they marry it is usually for life. They are extremely loyal to their beloved. But there is a deep little secret that most Cancerians will never admit to: commitment or partnership is really a chore and a duty to them. They enter into it because they know of no other way to create the family that they desire. Union is just a way – a means to an end – rather than an end in itself. The family is the ultimate end for them.

If you are in love with a Cancerian you must tread lightly on his or her feelings. It will take you a good deal of time to realize how deep and sensitive Cancerians can be. The smallest negativity upsets them. Your tone of voice, your irritation, a look in your eye or an expression on your face can cause great distress for the Cancerian. Your slightest gesture is registered by them and reacted to. This can be hard to get used to, but stick by your love – Cancerians make great partners once you learn how to deal with them. Your Cancerian lover will react not so much to what you say but to the way you are actually feeling at the moment.

Home and Domestic Life

This is where Cancerians really excel. The home environment and the family are their personal works of art. They strive to make things of beauty that will outlast them. Very often they succeed.

Cancerians feel very close to their family, their relatives and especially their mothers. These bonds last throughout their lives and mature as they grow older. They are very fond of those members of their family who become successful, and they are also quite attached to family heirlooms and mementos. Cancerians also love children and like to provide them with all the things they need and want. With their nurturing, feeling nature, Cancerians make very good parents – especially the Cancerian woman, who is the mother *par excellence* of the zodiac.

As a parent the Cancerian's attitude is 'my children right or wrong'. Unconditional devotion is the order of the day. No matter what a family member does, the Cancerian will eventually forgive him or her, because 'you are, after all, family'. The preservation of the institution – the tradition – of the family is one of the Cancerian's main reasons for living. They have many lessons to teach others about this.

Being so family-orientated, the Cancerian's home is always clean, orderly and comfortable. They like old-fashioned furnishings but they also like to have all the modern comforts. Cancerians love to have family and friends over, to organize parties and to entertain at home – they make great hosts.

Horoscope for 2013

Major Trends

You have come through two very rough years. You were 'paying your dues', getting tougher and stronger; everything you got was earned by the sweat of your brow. 2011 was more challenging than 2012, but 2012 was also difficult. This year, you start to see the rewards of your efforts and hard work. It will seem to you that you have become lucky, but the truth is that you are merely harvesting the seeds planted in the past two years.

Many of you have high aspirations, and this is good. But in order to achieve these aspirations, the spiritual and mental muscles needed to be developed. The reflexes had to be trained – hence the reason for the difficult period. No one would expect to run in the Olympics without training, and this was what you were going through.

During the first half of the year your growth is spiritual and internal. Jupiter will be in your 12th house of spirituality. Many powerful things are happening – secret things, sacred things – but they are not overt. When Jupiter moves into your own sign on June 27, you will start to see this inner growth manifest itself tangibly. Others will see it too.

Because the obstructions that have been hindering you are taken away, and your muscles are stronger, you should see rapid progress to your goals. It will be a successful year ahead, prosperous too. More on this later.

Health was challenging in 2011 and 2012 as well. This year the whole situation is different. Health will be good. If there have been problems you will hear good news about them. More details later.

There are dramatic job and career changes this year – I feel for the better. But since these things happen suddenly, there could be some stress involved. Ever since Uranus moved into your 10th house of career in 2011, your career has been unstable. There have been changes already and will be many more to come. See below for details.

Your most important interests this year are spirituality (until June 27); the body, the image and personal pleasures (from June 27 onwards); children, creativity and leisure; love and romance; religion, metaphysics, higher education and foreign travel; career.

Your paths of fulfilment in the coming year are spirituality (until June 27); the body, image and personal pleasures (from June 27); children, creativity and leisure.

Health

(Please note that this is an astrological perspective on health and not a medical one. In days of yore there was no difference, these perspectives were identical. But now there could be quite a difference. For a medical perspective, please consult your doctor or health practitioner.)

If you came through 2011 and 2012 with health intact you did very well. In contrast, 2013 will be a breeze. You still need to be careful healthwise, though; two powerful long-term planets are still in stressful alignment with you, but this is nothing compared to what you've experienced previously.

Towards the end of last year, in October, Saturn moved away from his stressful aspect and is now making harmonious aspects to you, and Neptune also moved away from a neutral aspect to a harmonious one in 2012. This year, Jupiter will move through your own sign, which is a harmonious and happy aspect. So health, if not good, is much improved. You are getting stronger and stronger day by day. Perhaps some new doctor, therapy or medicine will get the credit for this – things often happen that way. But the truth is the planetary alignments have shifted and thus more cosmic healing power, or life force, or *chi* (whatever name you want to call it) has come into you. This produced the improvement.

Health still needs watching this year but it seems that you are doing it. Jupiter, your health planet, will move into your

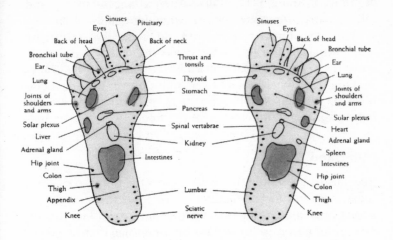

Reflexology

Try to massage the whole foot on a regular basis, but pay extra attention to the points highlighted on the chart. When you massage, be aware of 'sore spots', as these need special attention. It's also a good idea to massage the ankles and top side of the feet.

sign on June 27. Your 6th house of health is more or less empty this year, but your health planet will be powerfully placed. Thus there is a focus here.

There are many things that can be done to improve the health. The first and most important is to maintain high energy levels. Rest and relax more. Don't allow yourself to get overtired: delegate those tasks that can be delegated. A little thought and planning can show you how to achieve more with less effort.

Next, give more attention to the heart (avoid worry and anxiety, the main spiritual root causes of heart problems); the stomach and breasts, especially after June 27 (the right diet is always more important for you than for most people; pay attention to what you eat, and also to how you eat – meals should be taken in a calm relaxed way with a feeling of gratitude and appreciation); the liver and thighs; and the lungs, small intestine, arms, shoulders and respiratory system, until June 27 (arms and shoulders should be regularly massaged, and air purity is more important than usual). Since these are the most vulnerable areas in the year ahead, keeping them healthy and fit is sound preventive medicine. Most of the time problems can be prevented, or at least reduced and modified to a great degree.

Home and Family

Regular readers know that with Cancer the home and family is an important focus regardless of whether the 4th house is strong or weak. Family is the whole purpose of life. But the amount of power in the 4th house shows whether in a given year there will be more or less focus here. It is a matter of degree. This year the house is more or less empty this year and the focus is less than usual – unlike in the past few years where the focus was greater and this area of life was much more challenging.

Now that Saturn has left your 4th house of home and family, you can breath a little easier. The main problems seem to have been resolved. In the past two years you had to take on extra family burdens and responsibilities. There was a need to re-organize the home, the family relationships and the daily domestic routine. Many of you felt cramped or stifled in the home, both on a physical and psychological level. Many of you redecorated, bought art objects and otherwise beautified the home. The whole social life seemed centred around the home and with the family.

This year the focus is more on the children and those who play that role in your life. It is a serious period in their life now, especially for the oldest. Self-esteem and self-confidence are not what they should be. He or she seems depressed and pessimistic; things look dark and black for this child. He or she seems fearful of 'letting the light shine', though in truth a low profile is in order these days. However, one can let one's light shine in a quiet, low key way. This is the challenge for this child or child figure. School seems a challenge and he or she feels burdened by it. Perhaps there are problems with a sibling. Overall energy is not what it should be and there could be health problems. The social life is perhaps not up to par. However, there are good points here too. The child is more disciplined and serious about life (although perhaps too serious). Try to make sure that he or she has some fun, that it's not all work, work, work. If this child needs to lose weight this is a good year for it. It is a good year for getting involved in disciplined health regimes and getting the body in shape.

Aside from the above, there are two eclipses that affect this child. So there are many disruptive changes in the life.

In general, your challenge is to learn to apply a wise discipline upon the children and children figures. Let them know their limits – be very clear about this – but within the limits grant freedom. Though you love them you can't just let them have their way these days; there has to be limits.

If you're planning major repairs or renovations, after December 7 is a good time. If you plan to make cosmetic changes or to redecorate, August 16 to September 11 and September 22 to October 23 are good times.

Finance and Career

Finances have been more or less stable over the past few years – now this is about to change. On June 27 Jupiter will enter your own sign, initiating a multi-year cycle of prosperity. In the meantime you are getting ready for it. Be patient. When a seed is buried in the ground there is no discernable activity. But the truth is that tremendous, dynamic activity is taking place underground. The seed is being transformed and one fine day, buds and shoots will appear above the ground. Ever since Jupiter moved into your 12th house of spirituality in June of last year, beautiful and mighty interior growth has been taking place within you. Psychics and seers can see it, but to the ordinary person nothing is happening.

But as Jupiter crosses the Ascendant the buds begin to bloom naturally, normally, effortlessly. Suddenly, the whole picture changes; the invisible becomes visible.

Our regular readers know that when Jupiter moves into your own sign he brings the good life with him. All kinds of limitations fall by the wayside. Suddenly success is within your grasp. Lucky things start to happen. People often win lotteries or sweepstakes under this aspect. They travel to foreign countries. They eat in good restaurants. They go to fine clubs. They buy (or receive) expensive clothing or accessories. They fulfil many of their carnal fantasies. Most importantly, they seem to have the wherewithal to do this. More important than the actual physical things that happen is the feeling of optimism that comes – the 'can do' spirit. You feel rich. You feel lucky. And thus, lucky events start to happen. You start to attract wealth and wealth opportunities.

Jupiter is your work planet. Thus his move across your Ascendant is very fortunate for job seekers. It indicates that dream jobs, happy jobs, come to you. There's no need to pound on doors. The job is coming to you. Most likely you won't even escape it even if you tried. (You always have free will – you can decline it if you choose – but you won't escape the opportunity.)

In the meantime, while Jupiter is still in your 12th house, job seekers should look in spiritual or altruistic kinds of settings. Work in a non-profit type organization or a spiritual organization seems likely. Some of you might want to volunteer your time in one of these organizations and this will lead to actual job opportunities.

The career has been exciting ever since Uranus moved into your 10th house in March 2011. Much change is happening there, and in truth you seem to like it that way. There is great instability, perhaps some insecurity, but a lot of freedom and excitement too. Freelance work seems more favourable now. You have a need for constant change as you get bored much too quickly. Even if you are in a corporate kind of environment, you need different and varied kinds of assignments. Learning to be comfortable with insecurity in career matters is the major lesson these days.

There is much change and upheaval in your company and in your industry. The rules of the game keep changing. The ups and downs of the career are extreme these days. When success happens it is unusually great, but there can be deep dry spells as well. You are being set free (and this will be a multi-year process) to follow the career of your dreams. As time goes on the barriers that prevented this will fall. Suddenly the path is open. Obstructions and barriers sometimes need dramatic actions to break them and the cosmos will supply this.

You will end the year richer than when you began – and 2014 will be even better.

With the Sun, a fast-moving planet, as your financial planet there will be many short-term trends in finances, depending on where the Sun is and the aspects he receives. These are best discussed in the monthly reports below.

Love and Social Life

Now that Pluto is in your 7th house of love for many years to come, this is an important area of life and an area of great focus. Love has been challenging for the past two years. It is still challenging this year, but less so. If your relationship weathered the past two years it will survive the year ahead too.

In 2011 and 2012 (and much of 2010) your love planet Saturn was in stressful aspect with both Pluto and Uranus. Love was severely tested. Anything less than perfection, which is what the cosmos wants for you, probably dissolved. This applied to business type partnerships as well as romantic ones. But the worst of the stress seems over with.

Your love planet is now in the 5th house of children and fun for the next two years, in the sign of Scorpio. Love attitudes have shifted now. Sexual magnetism seems the most important thing – you've had enough stress, now you want relationships that are enjoyable. You want that 'honeymoon' feeling. You will start to attract this kind of thing in the year ahead, only keep in mind that honeymoons don't last for ever, as much as we try to make them. To expect a relationship to be a constant honeymoon is just not realistic.

Sexual chemistry is a vital component of any romantic relationship. However, this can be overdone. And this might be the case this year. Your love planet is in sexy Scorpio and Pluto, the generic ruler of sex, is in your 7th house of love. Good sex covers many sins, but of itself it is not enough to hold a relationship together. My experience has been that even the best of sexual chemistries have a life span of 9 to 12 months. So there is a need to look deeper into things and to take more things into account. On the other hand, singles don't seem that serious about love this year, and with long-term commitment not a big issue right now their approach might be right – have fun, and when it's over it's over.

If your marriage or relationship weathered the past two years it's time to have some fun together and perhaps go on a second honeymoon. If you are single and working on your first marriage, you find love at the usual places – clubs, resorts, places of entertainment. If you are working on the second marriage, love is in spiritual-type settings – meditation seminars, yoga kirtans, prayer meetings or charity events. Mere good sex will not be enough for you; you are looking for spiritual compatibility, a spiritual soul mate, and this kind of relationship is, most definitely, coming to you – most likely in the latter part of the year. Those working on the third marriage have a status quo kind of year.

In general, and this is a long-term trend, your love life, your social sphere, is getting a cosmic detox. Detoxing is seldom pleasant but the end result is good. Impurities in love, as with physical impurities in the body, need to be removed from the system so that healthy love can happen. You are in process of giving birth to the love life, the marriage, of your dreams. The problems and challenges are merely birth pangs.

Self-improvement

Jupiter, as we mentioned, has been in your spiritual 12th house since June of 2012. This shows a year of intense spiritual development. Much of this development will be about health and healing – it is a period where you go deeper into the spiritual dimensions of healing. Many of you have already gained a good understanding of this, especially in the past two years, but there's always more to learn and you're going deeper into it.

Spiritual healing is a bit different than the 'mind–body' connection: it's higher and deeper. I remember a time when even the mind–body connection was not accepted, but thanks to the yoga people and many other pioneers it is now pretty much mainstream. Make no mistake: this was great progress for the world.

Mind–body medicine has to do with positive thinking, positive affirmations, thinking and visualizing thoughts of health and desired physical performance. But in spiritual healing, we aim higher. The object in spiritual healing is to access a power – a force – that is essentially above and beyond the mind. The mind is used, but the power that produces the healing is beyond the mind, and has nothing to do with thinking as we understand it. It is a force that knows only perfection, and when it is allowed to operate in the mind and body, it will immediately start to create perfection.

This power is accessed through prayer, meditation and invocation. And there are no limits as to what this power can do in the body and it is not wise to place limits on it. The limitations that we experience are personal ones, the limitations of our beliefs. But the power itself has no limits. There is nothing that it cannot cure. In 2011 especially, and in 2012, many of you were forced to call on this power. Events were just too overwhelming.

When this power is invoked it not only starts to deal with the physical problems, but also the spiritual root causes behind the problems. It cures at the core, the root, and often this takes time. The issues can be very deep. Many of you understand clearly what we're talking about here. Now it is time to go deeper into it.

Month-by-month Forecasts

January

Best Days Overall: 6, 7, 14, 15, 24, 25
Most Stressful Days Overall: 4, 5, 10, 11, 17, 18, 31
Best Days for Love: 6, 7, 8, 9, 10, 11, 14, 15, 18, 19, 24, 25, 29, 30
Best Days for Money: 2, 3, 4, 10, 11, 12, 21, 22, 26, 27, 28, 31
Best Days for Career: 4, 5, 12, 13, 17, 18, 22, 23, 31

You begin your year with 70 and sometimes 80 per cent of the planets in the social Western sector of the chart. Your 7th house of love is very powerful all month, but especially until the 19th. You are in the midst of a yearly social peak. Self-interest and personal desires are best downplayed; relationships are the most important thing now. Though I doubt whether singles will marry this month, they are likely to meet people they would consider marrying. The aspects for actual marriage are much better later on in the year, in July and August. However, it looks like a sexually active kind of month. Libido is roaring.

Last month the planetary power made a shift from the lower to the upper half of your Horoscope. By the 10th the shift is complete – at least 80 per cent of the planets are above the horizon of your chart. So, though home and family are always important to you, you are in a period for focusing on the career and your outer worldly objectives. This is now the best way to serve your family. Your outer success will actually enhance your family life rather than detract from it.

Your social grace, your ability to get on with others, is important on the financial level. Your social connections are playing a huge, positive role in earnings until the 19th. You socialize with the people you do business with (and a lot of your social activity is business related), and like doing business with people you are friendly with. On the 19th the Sun moves into your 8th house of transformation and this shows that your spouse, partner or current love is entering a yearly financial peak. Thus he or she is likely to be more generous.

Your financial planet in the 8th house from the 19th onwards shows an ability to pay down or take on debt. Both happen relatively easy. It just depends on what your need is. A good financial detox is in order after the 19th. Get rid of excessive or wasteful expenses, extra bank accounts, extra credit cards and so forth. It is a time for prospering by 'pruning'. Of course, necessities shouldn't be pruned – just extraneous things. It's a good idea to go through the home and get rid of belongings – clothing or furniture – that you don't use. Sell them or give them to charity. This will clear the channels for new supply to enter.

Health is delicate until the 19th. Be sure to rest and relax more. Enhance the health in the ways mentioned in the yearly report.

February

Best Days Overall: 2, 3, 11, 12, 20, 21, 22
Most Stressful Days Overall: 1, 7, 8, 13, 14, 27, 28
Best Days for Love: 2, 3, 7, 8, 9, 10, 11, 12, 18, 19, 20, 21
Best Days for Money: 1, 9, 10, 18, 20, 23, 24, 27
Best Days for Career: 1, 11, 12, 13, 14, 20, 21, 22

The planetary momentum is overwhelmingly forward this month. Until the 18th ALL the planets are moving forward, which is highly unusual. The pace of life is faster. Results happen more quickly. Thus it is a good period for launching new ventures or products into the world. From the 10th to the 18th – as the Moon waxes – would be the best time, but all month is basically good.

Your house of transformation is still powerful until the 18th, so review our discussion of this last month. Many of you are involved in personal transformation, personal reinvention, and this is a good period to make progress here.

With Jupiter still in your spiritual 12th house, the spiritual life has been very important. Spiritual phenomena will increase this month as there are many planets in Pisces. Your already good psychic abilities increase even further. The dream life will be unusually active: take note of your dreams on the 6th and 7th as these seem especially significant.

The Water element – your native element – is very powerful this month from the 18th onwards. This is basically good for you. The world at large is more feeling oriented, more 'touchy-feely'. Logic, rationality, matter little. It is the mood of the moment – the feeling – that is important. You are very comfortable with this.

On the 18th (and you will feel it before this) your 9th house becomes ultra powerful. Opportunities for foreign travel will come and they seem happy. There is also travel related to the career from the 3rd to the 5th. Happy educational opportunities will come and these should be taken. Your mind is more philosophically oriented; it easily grasps higher learning. This is a good period for students, especially those at college or at postgraduate level. It is also a period for religious and philosophical-type breakthroughs.

Love gets more complicated this month as your love planet goes retrograde on the 18th. You have experienced this many times in your life. Saturn retrogrades for a few months every year. This doesn't stop your love life; it only slows it down a bit. Important love decisions should not be made for the next few months; it is a time for review and re-evaluation. But aside from this minor complication love seems happy, especially after the 18th. Saturn is receiving beautiful aspects from many planets. Singles have many romantic opportunities and are dating more. Those of you who are married attend more parties and gatherings. It's great to enjoy these things in a non-committal kind of way.

Finances are good this month and get even better after the 18th. The financial intuition is super after that date, and especially from the 19th to the 21st.

Health is wonderful this month.

March

Best Days Overall: 2, 3, 10, 11, 20, 21, 29, 30
Most Stressful Days Overall: 1, 6, 7, 12, 13, 14, 27, 28
Best Days for Love: 2, 3, 6, 7, 10, 11, 20, 21, 22, 29, 30, 31
Best Days for Money: 1, 2, 3, 8, 9, 10, 11, 17, 18, 22, 23, 27, 28, 31
Best Days for Career: 2, 3, 11, 12, 13, 14, 22, 31

The planets are still mostly in the upper half of your chart, and on the 20th you enter a yearly career peak. Go for gold now. Focus on the career. Family issues don't need much attention now. In fact the family is supporting your outer ambitions. There is much success happening. Pay rises (either overt or achieved more subtly) are happening. Your good professional reputation helps the bottom line. This will be a prosperous month. Elders, bosses, parents or parent figures are not only supporting your career, but your financial goals as well.

This career focus could stress your health if you allow it. Health becomes more delicate after the 20th as at least half, and sometimes more, of the planets will be in stressful alignment with you after that date. Give the career all the attention it needs, but do it in a way that maximizes your energy. Take breaks when you feel tired. Let go of the trivia in your life. Integrate a health regime into your work schedule and get massages as often as you can. Enhance the health in the ways mentioned in the yearly report on page 127.

This month the planets will make an important shift from the Western sector, where they have been so far this year, to the East. The shift will begin on the 20th but will become more established next month. Thus you are entering a cycle of personal independence. Other people are always important, but they become less so these days. Your own personal initiative and personal abilities are what matter now. Hopefully over the past few months you've noted the conditions that irk you. Now over the coming months it is time to make changes, to create your conditions as you desire them to be. You have more personal control than usual.

Mercury has been retrograde since February 23, and this continues until the 17th of this month. This affects your spiritual intuition. It needs more verification this period. Intuition is always right, but sometimes the human mind does not interpret it correctly. This is the main problem now. Also, take more care in communicating. Make sure that you say what you mean and that others get the real message. The reverse is also true. In your chart, the retrograde of Mercury affects you more than the average person. Mercury is not only the generic ruler of communication, but in your chart is the actual Lord. So be patient when phone calls are missed, or computers act up, or letters don't get delivered. These are typical phenomena. You just have to be philosophical about these things.

Your spouse, partner or current love seems more generous on the 1st and 2nd. He or she has a nice payday. Important financial changes are happening from the 27th to the 30th – some shock or surprise. It's a very short-term issue and you will handle it. Parents or parent figures need to drive more carefully from the 18th to the 21st and also need to avoid risky kinds of activities. There may be shake-ups in your corporate hierarchy (or industry) over that period as well.

April

Best Days Overall: 6, 7, 8, 16, 17, 25, 26
Most Stressful Days Overall: 2, 3, 9, 10, 23, 24, 29, 30
Best Days for Love: 1, 2, 3, 6, 7, 9, 10, 16, 17, 21, 22, 25, 26, 29, 30
Best Days for Money: 1, 4, 5, 9, 10, 14, 15, 19, 20, 21, 23, 24, 29, 30
Best Days for Career: 1, 9, 10, 21, 29, 30

On the 14th, as Mercury moves eastward, the planetary shift to the East is confirmed. For the next six months or so you are in a period of personal independence. You can and should have things your own way, so long as you are not harming others. If others don't go along with your plans you have the power and the wherewithal to go it alone if necessary. Now there are no excuses – personal happiness is in your hands.

The main headline this month is the power in your 10th house of career. It was strong last month and even stronger now, with 60 per cent of the planets moving through this house this month. This shows a lot of focus and lot of activity. Pay rises could have happened last month and can still happen now – the 14th to the 20th seems a likely time for this. Bosses, elders and parent figures are supporting your financial goals. As we mentioned, it is not always a literal pay rise that happens: earnings can be increased in more covert kinds of ways.

This is a very successful month. Generally a focus on the career detracts from family life, but not so for you. The family seems very supportive – actually pushing and promoting your career goals.

Finances are good this month too. Avoid speculations at the beginning of the month. Be more careful with debt and read all the small print attached to any loans you take out. A child or child figure in your life could create some sudden expense at this time. However, these are small, short-term bumps on the road. Prosperity is strong. The New Moon on the 10th brings career opportunity and financial increase. It will also clarify career issues as the month progresses.

Health still needs attention until the 19th so keep in mind our discussion of this last month. Health and energy will improve dramatically after that date. Enhance the health in the ways mentioned in the yearly report.

The planetary momentum is mostly forward and the Sun is in Aries, the best starting energy of the zodiac. If you have new projects or products to release, this is the month to do it. The New Moon of the 10th is the best time, but anytime until the 25th is good.

A child or child figure in your life is enduring a stressful period. He or she seems rebellious and difficult to handle. Have patience here. He or she could use more attention as well. A Lunar Eclipse on the 25th reinforces this. Do your best to keep children or children figures out of harm's way. Reduced your schedule if possible – both yours and that of the children.

Love seems more challenging after the 19th. Perhaps there are financial disagreements with the beloved, or perhaps your career focus is detracting from the romance. None of these is the real reason: the beloved is just more stressed out and perhaps more irritable after the 19th.

May

Best Days Overall: 4, 5, 13, 14, 15, 23, 24, 31
Most Stressful Days Overall: 6, 7, 21, 22, 27, 28
Best Days for Love: 4, 10, 11, 13, 14, 21, 22, 23, 27, 28, 29, 30, 31
Best Days for Money: 2, 3, 8, 9, 10, 11, 12, 16, 17, 19, 20, 21, 22, 29, 30
Best Days for Career: 6, 7, 8, 9, 10, 18, 19, 27, 28

Two eclipses this month ensure that the month ahead will be eventful, both personally and for the world at large. Humans are powerful creatures with the gift of free will, which enables them to veer off from the Divine Plan for their lives.

It takes the events brought on by an eclipse – an earthquake, a natural disaster, a near-death kind of experience – to bring them back in line. You are affected by these eclipses more than most. With the Moon as your ruling planet, the Lunar Eclipse tends to be strongest. However, the Solar Eclipse is powerful in that it affects your financial life. However, the eclipses of this month are mild in comparison to some that you have already gone through. Not many other planets are affected here. They also make either harmonious or non-destructive aspects to you. Still, it won't hurt to reduce your schedule during these periods.

The Lunar Eclipse of the 25th will bring a redefinition of the personality and the self-concept. You are changing the way you think about yourself and the way you want others to perceive you. This is basically healthy. You are upgrading and polishing your image. If you haven't been careful in dietary matters these Lunar Eclipses can bring a detox of the body (this is not disease, though the symptoms seem the same). This eclipse occurs in your 11th house of friends. Thus friendships can be tested. Sometimes it is the basic relationship that is the problem; sometimes it is due to dramatic events that happen in the lives of friends. Your hi-tech equipment and gadgetry gets tested too (it would be a good idea to upgrade your anti-virus software now). Mars, your career planet, is affected by this eclipse, so there can be shake-ups in the career or in the lives of people involved with your career. Parents or parent figures need to take it easy during this period.

The Solar Eclipse of the 10th brings financial changes. These are basically good and probably needed to be made long ago. (It takes the dramas brought on by the eclipse to force these changes.) This eclipse occurs in your 6th house of health and work, and thus could bring a health scare or a job change. Since your health is basically good, this will most likely be nothing more than a scare. Neptune, the ruler of your 9th house, is affected by this eclipse and so it is probably not a good idea to travel abroad this period if it can be avoided. Students have dramas at school or with teachers.

There are dramatic, life-changing events with the people at your place of worship. Often this kind of eclipse brings crises of faith and your fundamental beliefs about life and the meaning of life get tested.

June

Best Days Overall: 1, 10, 11, 19, 20, 27, 28
Most Stressful Days Overall: 2, 3, 17, 18, 23, 24, 30
Best Days for Love: 1, 10, 19, 20, 23, 24, 27, 28
Best Days for Money: 7, 8, 9, 12, 13, 17, 18, 26, 27
Best Days for Career: 2, 3, 7, 8, 17, 18, 25, 26, 30

Last month was a very spiritual-type month, especially from the 20th onwards. In light of the two eclipses that happened this was a good thing. In times of distress we need to call upon our spiritual resources, and most likely this is what happened for you. These resources are more than adequate to handle any kind of crisis on the material plane. Your spiritual period continues until the 21st of this month. It is a time for spiritual breakthroughs. Your access to the invisible world of spirit and energy is much better now than at other times. It's good now to review the past year, atone for mistakes, forgive yourself and others, and set your goals for the year ahead which begins on your birthday – your personal new year.

You are on the cusp of great and glorious things. Things might seem dark at the beginning of the month, but as they say, it is always darkest before dawn. Momentous things are happening now. Jupiter will move into your sign on the 27th, initiating a two-year period of prosperity, happiness and good fortune. You start to catch the lucky breaks in life. You are lucky in speculations. You are up and optimistic. Things that were once daydreams or fantasies will actually start to happen.

The planetary power is now at its maximum Eastern position in your chart. Thus, you are in a period of maximum personal independence. You can and will have things your way. You can and will create the conditions for happiness and fulfilment. It's up to you now. Though health is still delicate – you still have two powerful long-term planets stressing you – after the 21st it improves immeasurably. With more energy all kinds of new possibilities open up.

The love life, which was merely so-so up to now, really takes off after the 21st. Singles are meeting significant others. Marriage would not be a surprise, though next month is better for that. Romance is in the air.

With the Sun and Venus moving through your sign, you look great. You are magnetic and charismatic. You dress with style and elegance. You look wealthy as well – you have the image of a prosperous person. But it's more than just image; when the Sun crosses your Ascendant on the 21st he will bring sizeable financial windfalls. In the year ahead you will be living a higher kind of lifestyle. With Jupiter it matters little whether you actually have the cash to support this lifestyle – you will live 'as if' you were rich.

Travel is happening later in the month too. However, keep in mind that Neptune, your travel planet, goes retrograde on the 7th, so allow more time for getting to and from your destination.

July

Best Days Overall: 7, 8, 17, 25, 26
Most Stressful Days Overall: 1, 14, 15, 21, 22, 27, 28
Best Days for Love: 1, 7, 10, 11, 16, 17, 19, 20, 21, 22, 25, 29, 30
Best Days for Money: 7, 8, 9, 10, 11, 16, 17, 18, 25, 27
Best Days for Career: 1, 5, 6, 16, 17, 25, 26, 27, 28

You've had a few very rough years, but now comes the positive payback. You are in one of the best periods of your whole life. All of you are feeling this now, but those born early in the sign of Cancer (from June 21 to July 1) feel it the most. Do you still face a few challenges? Certainly. But the good, the harmony, is much, much stronger.

Last month you entered a yearly personal pleasure peak on the 21st. This personal pleasure peak is much stronger than usual as benevolent Jupiter has joined the party. All of you are getting financially richer now – some more than others. All the planets in your own sign – the Sun, Venus, Mercury, Mars and Jupiter – indicate that you live 'as if' you were rich and affluent. You are living the high life now and your sensual fantasies are being fulfilled. Students are successful in school. Those applying to colleges hear very good news now. In general, Lady Luck sits beside you in most of the affairs of your life.

After going through such difficult years it would be natural to over-indulge in the good life. A little over-indulgence is understandable, but try to keep it in check. This is the main health danger right now. Weight needs watching now. Otherwise health and energy are super. You have all the energy you need to attain your goals.

Cancerians of child-bearing age have entered a period of great fertility. It is strongest now, but will be strong for the rest of the year. Many positive developments happen on the love front as well. Your love planet, Saturn, starts moving forward on the 8th after many months of retrograde motion. So there is now forward momentum in the social life. More importantly, Saturn receives beautiful aspects from Jupiter (and many other planets) this month. He is part of a rare Grand Trine in the Water element. So love is in the air now. There is romance for those who want it and marriage opportunities as well.

The whole month is financially prosperous. On the 22nd you enter a yearly financial peak.

Last month, on the 21st, the planetary power began to shift from the upper to the lower half of the Horoscope. This month the shift becomes even stronger. So it is time to focus on your first love – your home, family and emotional life. In spite of this shift there are still happy career opportunities happening between the 19th and 24th. But now you can afford to be choosier about what offers you will accept; they need to be emotionally comfortable and not cause family upheaval.

August

Best Days Overall: 3, 4, 13, 14, 21, 22, 30, 31
Most Stressful Days Overall: 10, 11, 12, 17, 18, 23, 24
Best Days for Love: 3, 8, 9, 13, 17, 18, 19, 21, 25, 26, 30
Best Days for Money: 3, 6, 7, 13, 14, 15, 16, 21, 22, 25, 30, 31
Best Days for Career: 3, 4, 13, 14, 22, 23, 24

The yearly financial peak that began last month gets even stronger this month, as more of the short-term planets join the Sun in your 2nd money house. The money is rolling in from many different sources. The heavenly gates of abundance have opened and it is pouring down on you – a most marvellous experience.

We still have a rare Grand Trine in Water, your native element. This tends to emotional harmony as people become more sensitive. It is also very comfortable for you.

Career opportunities are seeking you out, rather than vice versa. You are a 'hot commodity' now. You are not too focused on your career, yet it is still going well. (This proves the adage that too much personal interference can actually ruin a good thing. Sometimes it is best to allow the good to happen rather than trying to force it.) In terms of creating your personal conditions of happiness it would be right to take the initiative – but in career matters just now, it is not.

Foreign travel is still likely this month, but keep in mind that your travel planet Neptune is retrograde, so allow more time for getting to and from your destination. Students are still successful and getting into good schools. They probably have an abundance of schools to choose from and this will require more homework. Take time to make the choice.

Even non-students are having happy educational opportunities these days – and they should take them. There are religious and philosophical breakthroughs happening as well.

Health and energy continue to be good. Like last month the danger is over-indulgence in the good life. The good news here is that Mars spends most of the month (until the 28th) in your own sign. This indicates that you are more involved in physical exercise and sports.

Mars will square Uranus on the 1st and 2nd, which is a dynamic aspect. Avoid losing your temper (you are more susceptible to this now) and undue risk-taking, and drive more defensively. This applies to parents or parent figures as well. There can be shake-ups at the top levels in your company or industry during this period.

Love is good, as we mentioned, but your spouse, partner or current love seems more stressed out than usual. He or she needs to rest and relax more. This stress can complicate what is basically a good relationship.

September

Best Days Overall: 1, 9, 10, 18, 19, 27, 28
Most Stressful Days Overall: 7, 8, 13, 14, 20, 21
Best Days for Love: 1, 8, 9, 10, 13, 14, 17, 18, 27, 28
Best Days for Money: 1, 2, 3, 4, 5, 9, 10, 13, 14, 18, 19, 24, 27, 28, 29, 30
Best Days for Career: 2, 3, 11, 12, 20, 21, 29, 30

The planetary power is now at its maximum lowest point in the Horoscope this month – Cancerian paradise! Career goals have more or less been achieved and now you can focus on your true love, the home and family. This situation will not exist for ever; the planets will shift again in a few months, so enjoy the period while it lasts. A career break now will be the pause that refreshes, allowing you to gather your forces for the next career push in a few months' time. This is the midnight hour of your year. The body is still – outer activities are more or less in abeyance – but inwardly mighty processes are happening. And it is precisely these processes that enable the body to function when it is time to wake up.

The planetary power makes another important shift on the 22nd. The Western, social sector of the chart once again predominates. Your period of personal independence is about over with and now it is more difficult to have things your own way. Indeed, your way is probably not the best way these days. Getting things done by consensus and social skills is the pathway now. It is more difficult now (possible, but difficult) to create conditions as you want them to be, so it's best to adapt to existing conditions. Hopefully you've used the past five months to create things as you desire. Now you get to road test your creation.

The home and family are now the centre of life. There is more socializing at home and with family members and more entertaining from home. Even the love life is more or less centred round the home. Venus, your family planet, starts to travel with your love planet after the 11th. Love opportunities occur close to home and through family members and family connections.

Finances are good this month. Until the 3rd buying, selling, trading or retailing seem important. Sales and marketing – getting the word out about your product or service – seems important. After the 22nd, as your financial planet moves into the 4th house of home and family, it is family connections that bring financial opportunity. Most likely you are working more from home as well. Job seekers have had wonderful aspects since June 27. Job opportunities are seeking you out rather than the reverse, and there is nothing much you need to do to find work – it will find you.

Health is more delicate after the 22nd so be sure to rest and relax more. Enhance the health in the ways mentioned in the yearly report on page 127.

October

Best Days Overall: 6, 7, 15, 16, 24, 25
Most Stressful Days Overall: 4, 5, 11, 12, 17, 18, 31
Best Days for Love: 6, 7, 8, 11, 12, 15, 16, 17, 18, 24, 25, 27, 28
Best Days for Money: 1, 4, 5, 6, 7, 13, 14, 15, 16, 23, 24, 25, 27, 28
Best Days for Career: 1, 8, 9, 17, 18, 19, 30

Every Lunar Eclipse affects you strongly. The Moon rules your chart and is a very important planet for you. But the Lunar Eclipse of the 18th is stronger than most, and certainly stronger than the ones in April and May. It makes stressful aspects to you so be sure to reduce your commitments that period. Spend more quiet time at home. Parents, parent figures and children also need to take things easy. This eclipse occurs in your 10th house of career (which also rules bosses, authority figures, parents or parent figures), thus there are career changes afoot and shake-ups in your company or industry. This eclipse also impacts on Jupiter, your work planet, so job changes are also afoot. There are important financial changes that need to be made as well and the eclipse forces the issue.

Since health is more delicate, there could be a health scare – especially if you're not on top of things. Every Lunar Eclipse forces you to redefine your image, personality and self-concept. This one is no different. You are in the process (and eclipse phenomena are in effect for six months) of projecting a new image into the world, a new you. Health and energy will improve from the 23rd onwards. But until then rest and relax more.

Though the planetary power is below the horizon, there are many happy career opportunities happening this month, especially after the 23rd. Some of these could have happened last month as well. But as we mentioned, you can be more choosy now. Choose the opportunity that is most 'family friendly' and most emotionally comfortable.

On the 23rd, the Sun enters your 5th house and you enter another yearly personal pleasure peak. This is a time for recreation and fun, and for enjoying your children (or the children figures) in your life. There is a sort of 'happy go lucky' attitude to life. Finances are super and you have the wherewithal to have fun – and probably expensive-type fun too. There is luck in speculations. More importantly, you are earning money in happy ways and enjoying your wealth. Not everyone can say this. There is an opportunity for a business partnership or joint venture after the 23rd too. (This can also happen next month.) Financial opportunity and increase can happen as you are having fun at some resort, or at the theatre or a party.

The love life continues to be happy. Astrologically speaking, you couldn't ask for better love aspects than what you have after the 23rd. Foreign travel is also likely, only keep in mind that your travel planet is still retrograde so there are likely to be delays and glitches here. On the 21st Mercury also goes retrograde. Thus, the two planets that rule travel in your Horoscope are retrograde at the same time. Best schedule your trips before the 21st.

November

Best Days Overall: 3, 4, 11, 12, 20, 21, 22, 30
Most Stressful Days Overall: 1, 7, 8, 13, 14, 28, 29
Best Days for Love: 3, 4, 7, 8, 11, 12, 16, 17, 20, 21, 26, 27, 30
Best Days for Money: 3, 4, 11, 12, 21, 22, 23, 24, 30
Best Days for Career: 7, 8, 13, 14, 16, 17, 26, 27

As far as eclipses go, the Solar Eclipse of the 3rd is relatively benign to you. It occurs in your 5th house of children, so there are dramatic, life-changing kinds of events in the lives of children and children figures in your life. Their lives have been turbulent all year, but now even more so. Do your best to keep them out of harm's way this period. Speculations are best avoided during this eclipse period as well. You are basically fortunate in speculations these days, but not at this time. Like every Solar Eclipse, there are dramatic financial changes going on. Whatever didn't get changed by the last Lunar Eclipse will get changed and adjusted now.

This eclipse impacts on Saturn, the love planet. So love is being tested. The love life is still very good, but impurities in it – things that have been swept under the rug or ignored – now surface for cleansing. The beloved can be more temperamental so be more patient. These eclipses show us the 'dark side' of the beloved, which we don't want to see. It's another way that love gets tested. The eclipse will probably take your present relationship to the next level. Marriages often happen when the love planet is eclipsed – it indicates a change in the marital status. Those who are married can divorce, singles can marry.

Until the 22nd you are still in one of your yearly personal pleasure peaks. True you are working, but you also manage to play. After the 22nd you enter a work period, a more serious period. Fun, games and recreation are wonderful, but they are not the be all and end all of life. Recreation enables us to be better workers, more productive in our chosen line of work. In general this would be a good period for job seekers, but your work planet Jupiter goes retrograde on the 7th. Job opportunities might not be all that they are made out to be: study things more carefully. Health regimes (especially new ones) also need more study and homework. This is a good period for doing all those boring but necessary tasks in life – your accounting, bookkeeping, filing and organizing.

Health is good this month. You can enhance the health further in the ways mentioned in the yearly report.

Finances are also good all month. The opportunity for a business partnership or joint venture comes between the 4th and the 7th. Social connections, your spouse or current love, are very supportive during that period. A nice payday and perhaps a job assignment comes from the 12th to the 14th. Speculations are favourable that period as well. From the 22nd to the 25th analyse all financial opportunities more carefully. The Sun is in adverse aspect with Neptune, which means that there are behind-the-scenes dealings that need to be understood.

December

   Best Days Overall: 1, 8, 9, 18, 19, 28, 29
   Most Stressful Days Overall: 4, 5, 10, 11, 12, 25, 26
   Best Days for Love: 1, 4, 5, 8, 9, 13, 14, 18, 19, 23, 24, 28, 29
   Best Days for Money: 1, 2, 3, 8, 9, 11, 12, 18, 19, 20, 21, 22, 23, 28, 29
   Best Days for Career: 4, 5, 10, 11, 12, 15, 16, 25, 26

A very active and very hectic kind of month; a lot of change. There is a Grand Square in the heavens after the 8th and this will get even stronger after the 21st. Health is more delicate this month, and especially after the 21st. Rest and relax more. Pace yourself. Focus on the really important things in life and let go of the trivia. Often this makes for tough decisions. You can't be everywhere; you can't do everything, even though the demands on you are greater than usual. Focus on the really important. Enhance the health in the ways mentioned in the yearly report on page 127.

Health and work are the dominant interests until the 21st. This is a time to achieve all your work goals. You are in the mood for work now and this gives extra energy. After the 21st you enter a yearly social peak. Romance has basically been good since July and now it gets even better. Singles are dating more than usual, and those in couples are having more romance within their present relationships.

Your career planet, Mars, moves into your 4th house of home and family on the 8th. This indicates that your mission these days is your family. Your purpose is them – they are your career. But it also indicates more work from home; following the career path from the home. This is just a temporary condition that will last for about a month. On the 21st, the planetary power shifts from the lower half to the upper half of your Horoscope, which means it is time to start paying more attention to the career and outer goals. By now, you will have found your point of emotional harmony (and if not you will find it in the coming month). Now it is time to translate this harmony into outer success.

The home needs to be made safer during this period, especially from the 23rd onwards. Keep sharp objects, matches or other dangerous objects out of the reach of children. This is always a good practice, but especially now. Parents or parent figures need to be more careful driving and should avoid risky kinds of activities. And you and children or children figures in your life should drive more carefully from the 29th to the 31st.

Until the 21st, money comes the old-fashioned way through work. You seem like a big spender until the 21st. After that date your financial judgement becomes more sound, more practical. The social circle – friends, spouse or current love – also play a huge role in the finances now. Perhaps you are spending more on the spouse as well.

Leo

♌

THE LION
Birthdays from
21st July to
21st August

Personality Profile

LEO AT A GLANCE

Element – Fire

Ruling Planet – Sun
   Career Planet – Venus
   Love Planet – Uranus
   Money Planet – Mercury
   Planet of Health and Work – Saturn
   Planet of Home and Family Life – Pluto

Colours – gold, orange, red

*Colours that promote love, romance and social
   harmony* – black, indigo, ultramarine blue

Colours that promote earning power – yellow,
   yellow–orange

Gems – amber, chrysolite, yellow diamond

Metal – gold

Scents – bergamot, frankincense, musk, neroli

Quality – fixed (= stability)

Quality most needed for balance – humility

Strongest virtues – leadership ability, self-esteem and confidence, generosity, creativity, love of joy

Deepest needs – fun, elation, the need to shine

Characteristics to avoid – arrogance, vanity, bossiness

Signs of greatest overall compatibility – Aries, Sagittarius

Signs of greatest overall incompatibility – Taurus, Scorpio, Aquarius

Sign most helpful to career – Taurus

Sign most helpful for emotional support – Scorpio

Sign most helpful financially – Virgo

Sign best for marriage and/or partnerships – Aquarius

Sign most helpful for creative projects – Sagittarius

Best Sign to have fun with – Sagittarius

Signs most helpful in spiritual matters – Aries, Cancer

Best day of the week – Sunday

Understanding a Leo

When you think of Leo, think of royalty – then you'll get the idea of what the Leo character is all about and why Leos are the way they are. It is true that, for various reasons, some Leo-born do not always express this quality – but even if not they should like to do so.

A monarch rules not by example (as does Aries) nor by consensus (as do Capricorn and Aquarius) but by personal will. Will is law. Personal taste becomes the style that is imitated by all subjects. A monarch is somehow larger than life. This is how a Leo desires to be.

When you dispute the personal will of a Leo it is serious business. He or she takes it as a personal affront, an insult. Leos will let you know that their will carries authority and that to disobey is demeaning and disrespectful.

A Leo is king (or queen) of his or her personal domain. Subordinates, friends and family are the loyal and trusted subjects. Leos rule with benevolent grace and in the best interests of others. They have a powerful presence; indeed, they are powerful people. They seem to attract attention in any social gathering. They stand out because they are stars in their domain. Leos feel that, like the Sun, they are made to shine and rule. Leos feel that they were born to special privilege and royal prerogatives – and most of them attain this status, at least to some degree.

The Sun is the ruler of this sign, and when you think of sunshine it is very difficult to feel unhealthy or depressed. Somehow the light of the Sun is the very antithesis of illness and apathy. Leos love life. They also love to have fun; they love drama, music, the theatre and amusements of all sorts. These are the things that give joy to life. If – even in their best interests – you try to deprive Leos of their pleasures, good food, drink and entertainment, you run the serious risk of depriving them of the will to live. To them life without joy is no life at all.

Leos epitomize humanity's will to power. But power in and of itself – regardless of what some people say – is neither good nor evil. Only when power is abused does it become evil. Without power even good things cannot come to pass. Leos realize this and are uniquely qualified to wield power. Of all the signs, they do it most naturally. Capricorn, the other power sign of the zodiac, is a better manager and administrator than Leo – much better. But Leo outshines Capricorn in personal grace and presence. Leo loves power, whereas Capricorn assumes power out of a sense of duty.

Finance

Leos are great leaders but not necessarily good managers. They are better at handling the overall picture than the nitty-gritty details of business. If they have good managers working for them they can become exceptional executives. They have vision and a lot of creativity.

Leos love wealth for the pleasures it can bring. They love an opulent lifestyle, pomp and glamour. Even when they are not wealthy they live as if they are. This is why many fall into debt, from which it is sometimes difficult to emerge.

Leos, like Pisceans, are generous to a fault. Very often they want to acquire wealth solely so that they can help others economically. Wealth to Leo buys services and managerial ability. It creates jobs for others and improves the general well-being of those around them. Therefore – to a Leo – wealth is good. Wealth is to be enjoyed to the fullest. Money is not to be left to gather dust in a mouldy bank vault but to be enjoyed, spread around, used. So Leos can be quite reckless in their spending.

With the sign of Virgo on Leo's 2nd house (of money) cusp, Leo needs to develop some of Virgo's traits of analysis, discrimination and purity when it comes to money matters. They must learn to be more careful with the details of finance (or to hire people to do this for them). They have to be more cost-conscious in their spending habits. Generally, they need to manage their money better. Leos tend to chafe under financial constraints, yet these constraints can help Leos to reach their highest financial potential.

Leos like it when their friends and family know that they can depend on them for financial support. They do not mind – and even enjoy – lending money, but they are careful that they are not taken advantage of. From their 'regal throne' Leos like to bestow gifts upon their family and friends and then enjoy the good feelings these gifts bring to everybody. Leos love financial speculations and – when the celestial influences are right – are often lucky.

Career and Public Image

Leos like to be perceived as wealthy, for in today's world wealth often equals power. When they attain wealth they love having a large house with lots of land and animals.

At their jobs Leos excel in positions of authority and power. They are good at making decisions – on a grand level – but they prefer to leave the details to others. Leos are well respected by their colleagues and subordinates, mainly because they have a knack for understanding and relating to those around them. Leos usually strive for the top positions even if they have to start at the bottom and work hard to get there. As might be expected of such a charismatic sign, Leos are always trying to improve their work situation. They do so in order to have a better chance of advancing to the top.

On the other hand, Leos do not like to be bossed around or told what to do. Perhaps this is why they aspire so for the top – where they can be the decision-makers and need not take orders from others.

Leos never doubt their success and focus all their attention and efforts on achieving it. Another great Leo characteristic is that – just like good monarchs – they do not attempt to abuse the power or success they achieve. If they do so this is not wilful or intentional. Usually they like to share their wealth and try to make everyone around them join in their success.

Leos are – and like to be perceived as – hard-working, well-established individuals. It is definitely true that they are capable of hard work and often manage great things. But do not forget that, deep down inside, Leos really are fun-lovers.

Love and Relationships

Generally, Leos are not the marrying kind. To them relationships are good while they are pleasurable. When the relationship ceases to be pleasurable a true Leo will want out. They always want to have the freedom to leave. That is why Leos excel at love affairs rather than commitment. Once married, however, Leo is faithful – even if some Leos have a tendency to marry more than once in their lifetime. If you are in love with a Leo, just show him or her a good time – travel, go to casinos and clubs, the theatre and discos. Wine and dine your Leo love – it is expensive but worth it and you will have fun.

Leos generally have an active love life and are demonstrative in their affections. They love to be with other optimistic and fun-loving types like themselves, but wind up settling with someone more serious, intellectual and unconventional. The partner of a Leo tends to be more political and socially conscious than he or she is, and more libertarian. When you marry a Leo, mastering the freedom-loving tendencies of your partner will definitely become a life-long challenge – and be careful that Leo does not master you.

Aquarius sits on Leo's 7th house (of love) cusp. Thus if Leos want to realize their highest love and social potential they need to develop a more egalitarian, Aquarian perspective on others. This is not easy for Leo, for 'the king' finds his equals only among other 'kings'. But perhaps this is the solution to Leo's social challenge – to be 'a king among kings'. It is all right to be regal, but recognize the nobility in others.

Home and Domestic Life

Although Leos are great entertainers and love having people over, sometimes this is all show. Only very few close friends will get to see the real side of a Leo's day-to-day life. To a Leo the home is a place of comfort, recreation and transformation; a secret, private retreat – a castle. Leos like to spend money, show off a bit, entertain and have fun. They enjoy the latest furnishings, clothes and gadgets – all things fit for kings.

Leos are fiercely loyal to their family and, of course, expect the same from them. They love their children almost to a fault; they have to be careful not to spoil them too much. They also must try to avoid attempting to make individual family members over in their own image. Leos should keep in mind that others also have the need to be their own people. That is why Leos have to be extra careful about being over-bossy or over-domineering in the home.

Horoscope for 2013

Major Trends

Most of 2012 was plain sailing. The long-term planets were either kind to you or leaving you alone. You had abundant energy, especially when compared to past years, and so overall success and the attainment of your goals was more likely. Towards the end of the year, in October, Saturn moved into a stressful alignment with you. This created more resistance to your will and goals, but not enough to thwart them. Saturn slowed you down a bit, but success should have still happened. This trend continues in the year ahead. Health is basically good, but needs a bit more watching this year – more on this later on.

Uranus, your love planet, has been in Aries for two years now. He makes harmonious aspects with your Sun and for the first half of 2012 was making nice aspects with Jupiter. So the love life was good. This trend also continues for the first half of 2013. More on this later.

Jupiter moved through your 10th house of career in 2011 and 2012. This brought much career success to you in the form of honour, elevation, pay rises, promotions and recognition. In June 2012 Jupiter moved into your 11th house of friends and is there for the first half of 2013. So the year ahead is a strong social year. You have met – and will meet – new and important friends. Your social circle is very much expanded now. You are enjoying your friends and they you. This expansion of the social circle continues until June 27 when Jupiter moves into your spiritual 12th house. Thus the latter half of the year ahead is a very strong spiritual year. Those of you already on a spiritual path will deepen your practice. There will be many spiritual breakthroughs during that period. This is a period of internal growth that will usher in a two-year prosperity cycle in 2014.

The sex life and sexual practices are becoming more refined and spiritualized. This trend began last year and will continue for many more years.

Your most important areas of interest this year are home and family; health and work; sex, personal reinvention, occult interests, death and rebirth, past lives; religion, philosophy, higher education and foreign travel; friends, groups and group activities (until June 27); spirituality (from June 27 onwards).

Your paths of greatest fulfilment are home and family; friends, groups and group activities (until June 27); spirituality (after June 27).

Health

(Please note that this is an astrological perspective on health and not a medical one. In days of yore there was no difference, these perspectives were identical. But now there could be quite a difference. For a medical perspective, please consult your doctor or health practitioner.)

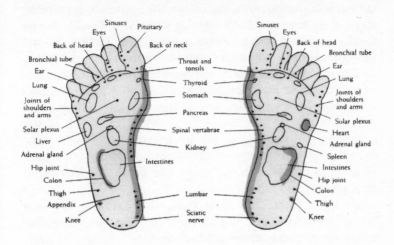

Reflexology

Try to massage the whole foot on a regular basis, but pay extra attention to the points highlighted on the chart. When you massage, be aware of 'sore spots', as these need special attention. It's also a good idea to massage the ankles and top side of the feet.

Health, as we mentioned, is basically good this year, although it is a tad more delicate than last year. Of all the long-term planets, only Saturn is in stressful alignment with you. This is not enough, by itself, to cause major problems. Still, it is good that your 6th house of health is strong and that you are paying attention to it this year. The danger would be in ignoring health issues and taking your health for granted.

As our regular readers know, there is much that can be done to enhance the health and prevent problems from developing. Pay attention to the heart (avoid worry and anxiety, the principal root cause of heart problems); the spine, knees, teeth, bones, skin and overall skeletal alignment (regular back massage is always good, especially if you massage alongside the spine, rather than directly on it, to strengthen the muscles that hold the spine in alignment; regular visits to a chiropractor or osteopath would also be good, as would yoga, Pilates, Alexander Technique and Feldenkrais; give the knees more support when exercising, and if you're at the beach use a good sun screen); and the colon, bladder and sexual organs. Safe sex and sexual moderation are important these days, especially since Pluto moved into your 6th house in 2009. Your health planet Saturn in the sign of Scorpio for the next two years reinforces what we're saying here. Colonics would be a good idea. Toxins tend to build up in the colon and can cause sluggishness and other problems.

Since these are the most vulnerable areas in the year ahead, keeping them healthy and fit is sound preventive medicine from the astrological perspective.

Saturn as we mentioned is the Health Planet, hence the importance of the spine, knees, teeth, bones, skin and overall skeletal alignment. Saturn rules health from the sign of Scorpio which governs the colon, bladder and sexual organs, so these are also important.

Saturn rules the health from the 4th house of home and family and this gives us many messages. First, the home and family situation needs to be in order and harmonious. Problems here will tend to impact on the physical health. If problems arise (God forbid), bring this area into harmony as quickly as you can. The 4th house rules the emotional life, everyday moods and feelings. Thus these should be kept positive and constructive. Depression, irritation and pessimism should be avoided like the plague. (By the way, Saturn in this house tends to depression, so be warned.)

The house of home and family (like the Moon, its natural ruler) is associated with the memory body. As readers know, this body contains the records of all past experiences, and not just from this life. If these get 're-activated' it can manifest as disease. Though I'm not a fan of past-life regression in general, if the health is affected, this might be a good idea this year.

The emotional life will tend to be volatile in the year ahead, so keeping your emotions positive and constructive will be a major challenge.

Home and Family

Your 4th house of home and family became a house of power last October. It will be important for two more years. This tends to be a difficult transit for home and family issues. The cosmos is re-organizing and re-structuring this whole area – the family, family relationships, your emotional life and the actual physical home. The end result will be a more organized and healthier home, but while it's happening it is much like having the kitchen redone – everything is disrupted and all over the place. However, after the upheaval and inconvenience is over with, the kitchen is perfect – better than before.

Every now and then a different part of life has to be re-organized. And this year – and next – it is the home. We see this in other ways too. There are two eclipses in the 4th house this year. There is a Lunar Eclipse on April 25 and a Solar Eclipse on November 3. These too lead to upheavals, shake-ups, sudden or unexpected repairs in the home, and dramas with family members and in the lives of family members. Sometimes the home is re-organized because of happy things – the birth of a child perhaps. A happy event (and it can easily happen for those of you of child-bearing age), but stressful nevertheless.

Saturn in the 4th house shows that you are taking on more responsibility in the home and with the family. These responsibilities seem unavoidable, and so the home life is more burdensome from the worldly perspective.

The health of a parent or parent figure seems of major concern. He or she is having a rough time these days. He or she will feel better after June 27, but before that life seems stressful.

You seem to be installing all kinds of health gadgets in the home. This has been a long-term trend, but this year even more so. The home is becoming as much like a gym or health spa as a home. In general you are working to make the home healthier. Sometimes people remove harmful toxins from paints, or asbestos (or other such substances) from the walls. Sometimes toxic build-ups are discovered beneath the home and these need to be cleared out.

If you are redecorating or beautifying the home in a cosmetic kind of way, September 11 to November 22 is a good time for this. Moves are not advisable this year, though you will be sorely tempted. But these seem fraught with delays and glitches.

Finance and Career

Your 2nd house of finance is not a house of power this year, so it's not a major focus or interest. You have free will in financial matters. The cosmos neither pushes you one way nor another. Generally the status quo prevails. In your case, the status quo seems good. You are just coming out of a very strong career year and you seem satisfied about your career and financial life.

Job seekers seem fortunate this year. Saturn (your work planet) and Pluto (your family planet) are in 'mutual reception' – each is a guest in the house of the other. This denotes great cooperation between the family and the job. Thus, family connections lead to work. Perhaps there is work in the family business or with family members. It is very likely that you can find jobs where you work from home too. Check these things out before you start pounding the pavements.

As we mentioned, Jupiter, is moving into your 12th house of spirituality on June 27 and will stay there well into 2014. This indicates you are in a preparation period for a new cycle of prosperity which will begin in 2014, most likely in the latter half of the year. Now is the time to clarify your financial goals, to pray and meditate for inner guidance here. Financial plans made by the intellect alone, which is always judging from the past, are generally unrealistic.

Intuition, which sees into the future, plus intellect are what is needed now.

Mercury, your financial planet, is a fast-moving planet and will move through all the signs and houses of your Horoscope in any given year. Thus there are many short-term trends in finance depending on where Mercury is and the aspects he is receiving. These are best dealt with in the monthly reports.

Mercury goes retrograde three times a year. These are periods where more caution is needed in financial matters. It's best not to sign contracts, make major purchases or investments, or take other important financial decisions during those periods. These are times for review and gaining clarity. This year these periods are from February 23 to March 16, June 26 to July 19 and October 21 to November 9. With Mercury as your financial planet, earnings come from communication, transportation, media activities, sales, marketing, PR, advertising, teaching and writing. Trading and retailing are also naturally good for you.

Career, as we mentioned, was very successful last year. This year it is basically a status quo kind of year. A Solar Eclipse on May 10 will shake things up a bit, but the effect is temporary.

One of the parents or parent figures in your life seems stressed, both personally and financially. However, the other parent or parent figure is prospering and picking up the slack. Children of an appropriate age are prospering, but they need to be careful not to abuse debt. Their financial intuition is super – perhaps it goes against logic – but it is good and should be followed. Your spouse, partner or current love, likewise. They are going deeper into the spiritual dimensions of wealth over the next few years.

Love and Social Life

We live in a moving universe. It doesn't stop for a second. So we are changing and evolving beings. This is so in all our affairs, and especially so in love. These changing needs and desires are the root causes for many relationship problems. We fell in love when we were a certain way and the object of our affections was a certain way. But as time went on, they changed and we changed – and so we are maybe not so keen about things as we once were. Adapting to the shifting changes in ourselves and those around us is not so easy, but astrology is a big help.

For about eight years, up to March 12, 2011, your love planet Uranus was in Pisces and in your 8th house of trans-formation. Sex appeal, sexual magnetism, the glamour, the fantasy were the allurements in love. Sex is always impor-tant to Leo, perhaps more than for any of the other signs (with the exception of Scorpio). But even so, it is not enough to hold a relationship together over time. Even the best sexual chemistry fades in a year or so. A good relation-ship needs more than that. Now that your love planet is in Aries and in your 9th house you are seeing this more clearly. You need a philosophical compatibility with the beloved. You need to share a similar world view and a similar perspective on the meaning of life. Philosophical differences as this stage of your life will subvert even the best sexual chemistry over time.

Of course you want to enjoy your relationship and to have fun – this is basic Leo philosophy. But you also want someone you can learn from, someone who can expand and enlarge your mental horizons. You have the aspects now of someone who falls in love with the college professor, mentor, guru or minister.

The Horoscope not only shows us the needs in love, but also how troubled relationships can be helped. If there are problems in your relationship, a trip to an exotic location – perhaps even a second honeymoon – might be in order. It is also good to worship and pray together and perhaps to take courses together as a couple. The bonds of the mind need to be strengthened.

For singles love opportunities happen in foreign lands or with foreigners in your own country. You are attracted to exotic types, and the more exotic the better. Love and social opportunities happen in educational and religious settings, at your place of worship or with members of your place of worship, in university or at university functions.

Love seems happy this year, especially in the first half. If you are in a relationship it will most likely continue. If you are single, you seem content with that. These trends apply to those in or working on the first or second marriages. Those working on the third marriage had wonderful romantic opportunities last year and in the year ahead as well. Marriage or something equivalent to marriage is likely.

Self-improvement

Saturn is now in your 4th house for the next two years. The home life, the family situation is not that happy. Things are going to work out here, but it needs time. Saturn in this aspect tends to depression. One feels that it is not safe to express one's true feelings and thus the tendency is to bury them and sweep them under the rug. When they do get expressed it is totally out of proportion to the event that triggered it. Thus a bad situation is made even worse.

Repressing negative feelings is also the root cause of many an illness. Negative feelings lodge in the body and eventually have to be discharged through a fever, or flu or some other malady. The body is throwing off the negativity and it isn't pleasant while it's happening.

So, there is a need to release these feelings in a non-destructive, safe way. If you have access to a therapist, this is a valid approach. If not, try writing about your feelings and 'outing' them from your system. Do this on a regular basis for the next two years, remembering to throw away or burn what you've written afterwards. When you feel upset or 'clogged' emotionally set aside a time – say half an hour – and just write down everything you are feeling. Don't hold back. When you've finished, take the papers (don't reread what you have written) and throw them in the bin. Some people like to burn the paper. You should feel that these energies are now in the 'cosmic dust bin', never to trouble you anymore. Or talk into a tape or digital recorder. Say whatever is on your mind and hold nothing back. When you finish – and you will feel an actual release as you are doing this – erase the recording. Don't listen to what you have said. Just erase it. It is out of you, and the emotional and physical health will start to improve. (In my book *A Technique for Meditation* we explain this in more detail and give other techniques as well.)

With Jupiter in your 12th house now, many of you are more deeply into spirituality. You are interested in the great supernatural realms within, the realms of the Divine. You will find that when you clear your clogged and negative emotions, your meditations will go much better, and prayer will be answered more quickly.

The sages say that the main reason that the answer to prayer is delayed is because of discord in the feeling body. The higher power needs harmony in order to flow properly, and by restoring harmony through the above methods the higher power will flow better.

Get used to an active dream life this year. Get used to supernatural kinds of experiences, to synchronicity and to unexplainable 'hunches' that prove to be right. Some people are frightened by these things, but you shouldn't be. Record your dreams and experiences in a journal. Don't judge. Just record them as if you were an impersonal reporter. Very important information will come to you in this way.

Month-by-month Forecasts

January

Best Days Overall: 8, 9, 17, 18, 26, 27, 28
Most Stressful Days Overall: 6, 7, 12, 13, 19, 20
Best Days for Love: 8, 9, 12, 13, 17, 18, 19, 26, 27, 29, 30
Best Days for Money: 2, 3, 4, 10, 11, 12, 21, 22, 29, 30, 31
Best Days for Career: 8, 9, 18, 19, 20, 29, 30

You begin your year with 80 and sometimes 90 per cent of the planets in the Western, social sector of your chart. In fact they are at their maximum Westerly point right now. You are in a strong social period. Your destiny seems in the hands of other people, which is a difficult position for a regal Leo to be in. Your personal gifts seem to matter little. It is likeability that matters now, in almost every area of life. Leos like to have their way and are used to having their way – but your way might not be the best way this period. Personal independence is not strong right now. This is a time to cultivate the social skills, to attain your ends by consensus and to adapt to situations as best you can. The King is far from his throne, in exile in a strange territory. He can't convey the full force of his will and personality. This is a temporary situation and will change in a few months. Right now adapt to things as best you can. Make a note of conditions that need to be changed, and when your period of personal independence comes you will be able to make those changes.

On the 19th you enter a yearly love and social peak. The love life is both active and happy. The main problem in love – and you will have this all year – is getting the family to accept the beloved and vice versa. There seems to be a lot of tension there.

Other things happen on the 19th as well. The planetary power shifts from the lower half of the Horoscope to the upper half. Thus dawn is breaking in your year. It is time to start focusing on your outer worldly objectives and to pursue them in physical and tangible ways. Your career planet will spend the month in your 7th house, thus others are very important in the career. Advancement depends on them. This also indicates that you further the career by social means, by attending or hosting the right kinds of parties and by developing the right social connections.

Health is more delicate after the 19th. As always the main preventive measure is to rest and relax more, to maintain high energy levels. Enhance the health in the ways mentioned in the yearly report on page 161.

Though you tend to be a speculator, money is earned the old-fashioned way through hard work until the 19th. This is not the chart of the lottery winner. However, Lady Luck returns to you from the 22nd to the 24th. There is a nice payday or some happy financial opportunity. The 25th to the 27th also seems fortunate in that department.

The planetary momentum is strongly forward this month: 90 per cent of the planets are moving forward until the 30th and after that ALL the planets are moving forward. Thus it is an excellent time to launch new products or ventures into the world. The 11th to the 27th is especially good.

February

Best Days Overall: 5, 13, 14, 23, 24
Most Stressful Days Overall: 2, 3, 9, 10, 15, 16, 17
Best Days for Love: 4, 5, 9, 10, 13, 18, 19, 23
Best Days for Money: 1, 9, 11, 12, 18, 21, 22, 25, 26, 27
Best Days for Career: 9, 10, 15, 16, 17, 18, 19

The planetary momentum is still overwhelmingly forward this month, and progress to your goals (and in the world at large) is swift. This is another good month to launch new products or projects. This month I like the 10th to the 18th the best, but the 18th to the 25th is pretty reasonable too – a solid second choice.

You are still very much in a yearly social peak until the 18th. Romance is in the air. While marriage is not likely, there are marriage opportunities happening. You meet people who are 'marriage material'. Singles have many types to choose from – athletic and military types, intellectuals, the rich and the powerful. Each has their particular allure. Your personal popularity is very strong these days. You seem very devoted to others; you are putting other people first (which is exactly what you should be doing now) and people respond to this.

The Western, social sector of your chart is still strong all month. Being in power is good, but being out of power also has its good points. This is a time to flow with life, to allow a higher power to take charge. Many of the problems in life come precisely because a human, very limited mind has been in charge, interfering with the perfect plan that wants to manifest itself. Now that the limited human self is less in charge, the higher plan can be revealed.

Health still needs watching until the 18th. Keep in mind our discussion of this last month. After the 18th health and energy improve dramatically. If there have been health problems, you hear good news on that score. Detox regimes are good all year, but especially after the 19th – your 8th house of transformation becomes powerful then. But detox should be carried further than the physical body. It should apply to the mind, the emotions and the financial life. The mind gets clogged with effete matieral (error and false information) and needs a good cleaning, and so do the emotions. In many cases there are habitual, knee jerk responses that perhaps were once good and useful, but are not any more. We tend to collect possessions that we don't need or use, and these things clog up the works and prevent proper functioning. This is a good month for a comprehensive clear out.

Love is still happy all month. The social life is less active after the 18th but love is still good. The month ahead is a sexually active kind of month, and for Leo this is wonderful.

Venus makes fabulous aspects to the Sun on the 6th and 7th and this brings career success and career opportunity.

Avoid speculations from the 8th to the 10th and from the 24th to the 26th. The dream life is also highly active on the 6th and 7th. Important spiritual information comes to you. There could also be a meeting with some sort of guru.

March

Best Days Overall: 4, 5, 12, 13, 14, 22, 23, 31
Most Stressful Days Overall: 2, 3, 8, 9, 15, 16, 29, 30
Best Days for Love: 2, 3, 4, 8, 9, 10, 11, 12, 13, 21, 22, 31
Best Days for Money: 1, 2, 3, 8, 9, 10, 11, 17, 18, 20, 21, 24, 25, 26, 27, 28, 29, 30
Best Days for Career: 2, 3, 10, 11, 15, 16, 21, 22, 31

The element of Water became very strong on February 18 and this situation continues until the 20th of this month. People are more sensitive now. So be more aware and avoid even the appearance of insensitivity. People will react (perhaps overly so) to little things, to voice tones, body language and facial expressions. There's no need to judge them – it's just the astrological weather.

Mercury, your financial planet, has been in your 8th house since February 5 and will be there the entire month of March. This shows a need to focus on the financial interests of other people. Their interests need to be taken into account in all business dealings – in fact they should come ahead of your own interests. As you succeed in prospering others, your own prosperity comes to you very naturally. Mercury went retrograde on the 23rd of last month and will be that way until March 17. This is a time for reviewing finances, not for making important moves. The object now is to attain mental clarity on your finances, and when this happens you will be in a better position to make moves after the 17th. Your financial intuition is basically good now, but until the 17th it needs more verification. The problem is not with this intuition but with the spin that you might be putting on it. Your spouse, partner or current love entered a yearly financial peak on February 19 and it continues until the 20th of this month. He or she should be more generous with you these days. This is a good month for detoxing on all levels – refer to our discussion of this last month.

Health is good all month. You have plenty of energy, plenty of vitality, plenty of zest to achieve all your goals. On the 20th the energy levels increase even further. This is a very successful period.

The planetary momentum is still very much forward. The Sun will move into Aries on the 20th and this is excellent 'starting' energy. So, if you have new products or projects this is a good month to launch them. The 20th to the 27th is the best time for this in the month ahead.

Your 9th house becomes very strong after the 20th. Thus the focus is on religion, philosophy and higher education. Foreign lands call to you and a foreign trip is very likely now. Students have success in their studies. When the 9th house is powerful, people will often prefer a theological discussion or the lecture of a visiting guru to a night out on the town. Mental and spiritual pleasures are more important than physical ones.

You had a yearly social peak from January 20 to February 18. But on the 20th, as many planets start to travel with Uranus, you have another yearly social peak. The love life becomes very active and happy. Singles have an important romantic meeting between the 26th and the 30th.

April

Best Days Overall: 1, 9, 10, 19, 20, 27, 28
Most Stressful Days Overall: 4, 5, 11, 12, 25, 26
Best Days for Love: 1, 4, 5, 9, 10, 19, 20, 21, 22, 27, 28, 29, 30
Best Days for Money: 4, 5, 7, 8, 14, 15, 19, 21, 22, 23, 24, 27, 28
Best Days for Career: 1, 9, 10, 11, 12, 21, 22, 29, 30

You have another window for starting new projects at the New Moon on the 10th, although the 11th is also good. You have all the aspects that you would want to have for this – many planets in Aries, a waxing Moon and a strong forward momentum of the planets (90 per cent are moving forward until the 12th).

Most of the planets are still above the horizon of your chart in the upper half of the Horoscope, and your 10th career house becomes very powerful after the 19th. You are entering a yearly career peak and there is much success and forward progress happening. Keep the focus on the career and let family and home issues go for a while. You can't completely ignore the home and the family, but you can shift your focus to your career. When the Sun, your ruling planet, crosses your Mid-heaven on the 19th you are on top; you are in charge. This situation doesn't last for too long – only about a month – so enjoy it while it's happening. You are like a celebrity in your world this month. You are looked up to, honoured and appreciated. Your career focus – and the fact that you are calling the shots – creates some tension with the family. Be patient with them and avoid being overbearing.

Your 9th house is still very powerful until the 19th, so review our discussion of this last month.

Your financial planet is now moving forward and will be in your 8th house until the 14th. Review last month's discussion of this. It's a good time to pay down or make new debt, according to your needs. In the past few months a lot of financial waste has been eliminated, thus when Mercury enters

Aries on the 14th your prosperity will be more solid. You are always a speculator and a risk-taker, but after the 14th even more so. You seem lucky in this department then. Mercury in Aries favours new ventures. It indicates financial confidence. Financial goals are attained quickly. Financial decisions are made quickly (perhaps too quickly). Financial opportunities come in foreign lands or with foreign companies or foreigners in general. People in your place of worship are also involved – in a positive way – with your finances.

Love is still happy. The unattached have wonderful opportunities now. Those already in relationships are closer to the beloved now. A second honeymoon or a romantic getaway to an exotic place seems in order. Romantic opportunities are pretty much as we have described in the yearly report.

A Lunar Eclipse on the 25th affects you strongly (especially those of you born early in the sign, the July Leos), so take it easy over the period. Be more patient with family members as they seem more temperamental. Do your best to maintain emotional equilibrium. This eclipse announces important changes in your spiritual life, in your practice and attitudes.

May

Best Days Overall: 6, 7, 16, 17, 25, 26
Most Stressful Days Overall: 2, 3, 8, 9, 10, 23, 24, 29, 30
Best Days for Love: 2, 3, 6, 7, 10, 11, 16, 17, 21, 22, 25, 26, 29, 30
Best Days for Money: 2, 3, 8, 9, 10, 11, 12, 18, 19, 21, 22, 29, 30
Best Days for Career: 8, 9, 10, 11, 21, 22, 29, 30

Two eclipses and a shifting of the planets show a tumultuous and hectic kind of month, both personally and for the world at large.

Health has been more delicate since April 19. No question that you need to rest and relax more, to pace yourself better.

Enhance the health in the ways described in the yearly report (page 161). You are very busy these days and so finding rest time will be a challenge. Scheduling mini breaks during your day might be good idea. The heart needs special attention until the 20th.

The Solar Eclipse of the 10th occurs in your 10th house of career and announces career changes. There are shake-ups at the top levels of your company or industry, and perhaps scandals as well. Unknown (and probably unflattering) knowledge comes to light. There are dramatic, life-changing events in the lives of parents, parent figures or authority figures in your life. There is a need to change tactics and strategy in the pursuit of career goals. Generally things happen that change the rules of the game.

You need to rest and relax more until the 20th and especially during the eclipse period. If you haven't been careful in dietary matters, a detox of the body could happen. Twice a year – every time there is a Solar Eclipse – you get a chance to redefine yourself, to create a 'new you' And this will be happening now. Keep in mind that eclipse phenomena are in effect for six months. These events might not happen immediately but over the course of the next six months.

The Lunar Eclipse of the 25th brings changes in the spiritual life: changes of teachers, teachings, practice and attitudes. Often it indicates shake-ups in a spiritual or charitable organization you are involved with. There are life-changing events in the lives of gurus or guru figures in your life. This eclipse occurs in your 5th house of children and thus shows dramatic changes in the lives of children or children figures. Often these changes are good – the child goes off to college or marries or gets a job – but they change the relationship. Children or children figures should avoid risky activities during this period. Speculations are not advisable then either. Many Leos are in the creative arts and entertainment fields, and this eclipse shows important changes and developments in their personal creativity.

On April 19 the planetary power began to shift from the West to the East. On May 1, as Mercury moved from the

West to the East, the shift was completed. Though the
Western, social sector of your Horoscope will be strong all
year, now you enter your period of personal independence.

June

   Best Days Overall: 2, 3, 12, 13, 21, 22, 30
   Most Stressful Days Overall: 5, 6, 19, 20, 25, 26
   Best Days for Love: 2, 3, 10, 12, 13, 19, 20, 21, 22, 25, 26,
      27, 28, 30
   Best Days for Money: 1, 8, 9, 10, 11, 15, 16, 17, 18, 19,
      20, 26, 27, 28
   Best Days for Career: 5, 6, 10, 19, 20, 27, 28

Retrograde activity is increasing this month. At the beginning of the month only 20 per cent of the planets are retrograde. By the end of the month the percentage doubles. Try
to do important things early in the month, before the 7th if
possible.

Your 11th house of friends became very powerful on the
20th of last month and is still powerful until the 21st. This
shows a social kind of month. You are involved with friends,
groups, group activities and organizations. These are not
only interesting in their own right, but also have strong
financial benefits. You hang around with wealthy people
and they seem supportive financially. They provide advice
and opportunity. Friends have been helpful financially all
year but especially now. Your financial planet in the 11th
house shows that technology is important on the financial
level, regardless of what business you do. Your technological
expertise is important. You are spending more on technology – staying up to date with the latest innovations – but
you earn from this as well.

Finances are good until the 21st but afterwards get more
complicated. Family expenses seem a problem. You don't
seem in financial synch with your spouse, partner or current
love, nor with a parent or parent figure either. But these are
short-term challenges and will pass by next month. There is

inheritance in the chart this month and this can take many forms. You can inherit money or things, sometimes from strangers. No one close to you need actually die. A friend whose spouse or family member has died can bring clothing or jewellery to you – things of this nature. If you need to borrow or meet with investors, the 19th to the 22nd is an excellent time. There is a nice payday happening then. Borrowing is also easier from the 21st onwards. Enterprising Leos can earn through creative financing. Your financial planet goes retrograde on the 26th, so avoid major financial decisions then.

On the 21st your 12th house of spirituality becomes very powerful. The year ahead is a very spiritual kind of year: Jupiter moves into your 12th house on the 27th and will spend the year ahead in there. Leos are party people, but from now on it's good to spend more time in self-examination away from others. This is a time for connecting with the Higher Power within and discerning its will and plan for your life. It is a time for a thorough review of the past year to assess what has and has not been accomplished – a time to identify past mistakes, make the proper corrections and set goals for the coming year, which begins on your birthday.

There is much growth and development happening now, but it is interior, behind the scenes. You might feel it but it is invisible to others. However next month (and next year) the growth will be visible and tangible.

The spouse, partner or current love has a nice payday between the 26th and the 28th. Children of the appropriate age had very good love aspects last month and this month. The whole year was good in the love department.

July

   Best Days Overall: 1, 9, 10, 11, 19, 20, 27, 28
   Most Stressful Days Overall: 2, 3, 17, 23, 24, 29, 30
   Best Days for Love: 1, 10, 11, 12, 13, 19, 20, 21, 22, 23,
      24, 27, 28, 29, 30
   Best Days for Money: 7, 8, 12, 13, 16, 17, 25, 26
   Best Days for Career: 1, 2, 3, 10, 11, 19, 20, 29, 30

The Water element became strong on June 21 and will be strong during all this month. You experienced this in February and March – people are more sensitive and more easily hurt. You need to be mindful about this. Avoid the smart wisecracks. There will be a price to be paid for these things later on.

You are still in a very spiritual, idealistic, altruistic kind of a period. This will be the case all year, but especially until the 22nd. It's easy to achieve your spiritual goals now, and good to be involved in spiritual practice – this will be much more powerful than usual – and in charitable or altruistic causes. On the 18th, Mars will enter your 12th house and this augers well for spiritual pilgrimages, travel of a religious or spiritual nature. This is a month (and a year) for spiritual breakthroughs and supernatural experiences.

Your altruism and spiritual orientation doesn't sit well with your spouse, partner or current love, but this is a short-term problem. By the 22nd there is harmony in love. The beloved is having very nice paydays these days. Prosperity will be good all year, but especially now. He or she is getting a new car and communication equipment this month.

Your financial planet went retrograde on June 26 and will stay that way until the 21st. In addition it camps out square to Uranus, so major, dramatic financial changes are happening from the 17th to the 24th. Try to make these changes after the 21st if possible. Job seekers have good success early in the month, but the entire year is good for job seekers too. The financial intuition is very sharp but needs more verification until the 21st.

The planets are now in their maximum Eastern position. Thus you are in your period of maximum personal independence. This is the time to take the bull by the horns and make those changes that you've wanted to make. You can act unilaterally if necessary (though keep in mind the sensitivities of others). There is much less of a need to adapt to situations. You can and should have life and conditions on your terms.

When the Sun crosses your Ascendant and enters your own sign on the 22nd you enter one of your yearly personal pleasure peaks. No one needs to instruct Leo on these things. Enjoy.

Love is more harmonious after the 22nd, as we mentioned, but it is still a bit complicated. Uranus, your love planet, starts to retrograde then. Your spouse, partner or current love lacks direction. Perhaps a current relationship lacks direction, in spite of the harmony. It is not advisable to make important love decisions one way or another after the 17th.

August

Best Days Overall: 6, 7, 15, 16, 23, 24
Most Stressful Days Overall: 13, 14, 19, 20, 25, 26, 27
Best Days for Love: 6, 7, 8, 9, 15, 16, 19, 20, 23, 24, 25, 26
Best Days for Money: 3, 4, 8, 9, 13, 14, 15, 16, 21, 22, 24, 25, 30, 31
Best Days for Career: 8, 9, 19, 25, 26, 27

You are still in the midst of a yearly personal pleasure peak, so this is a fun month – Leo heaven. Health is super and you have the energy of ten people. Even older Leos have more energy than usual. You look good, and self-confidence and self-esteem are at their peak for the year. Continue to create your life and the conditions of life as you desire them to be. The world will adapt to you these days.

The job situation seems stressful and perhaps unstable this month, but job opportunities abound for you. Your

financial planet Mercury crosses your Ascendant on the 8th
and enters your sign. This shows prosperity. Financial windfalls come and you spend more on yourself. Your personal
appearance seems important financially and thus you spend
on this.

On the 22nd you enter a yearly financial peak. Prosperity
is happening and from the 8th to the 24th there is luck in
speculations. Your spouse, partner or current love is also
prospering, although you need to work harder to create
financial harmony between you after the 24th. This is a good
month to fund your investment accounts and make financial
plans for the future.

Last month on the 22nd, the planetary power started to
shift from the upper half of your chart to the lower half. This
month the shift is complete and by the end of the month 60
per cent of the planets will be in the lower half of the chart.
Thus it is time to start focusing on the family, the home and
the emotional life and less on the career. This is a time for
working on the career by interior methods such as visualiza-
tions, to create the inner conditions for future career
success.

The beloved needs to drive more defensively on the 1st
and 2nd. He or she could be more temperamental that
period, so show more patience. Children or children figures
in your life need to avoid risky activities from the 4th to the
13th and from 18th to the 25th. Do your best to keep them
out of harm's way. Daredevil-type stunts need to be avoided.
This is not a time for speculations either.

A happy educational or travel opportunity comes after the
28th.

September

Best Days Overall: 2, 3, 11, 12, 20, 21, 29, 30
Most Stressful Days Overall: 9, 10, 15, 16, 22, 23
Best Days for Love: 2, 3, 8, 11, 12, 15, 16, 17, 18, 20, 21, 27, 28, 29, 30
Best Days for Money: 1, 4, 5, 6, 9, 10, 15, 16, 18, 19, 25, 26, 27, 28
Best Days for Career: 8, 17, 18, 22, 23, 27, 28

Mars will be in your own sign all month. This makes you more energetic, independent and forceful. It indicates that you are more athletic than usual and involved in exercise regimes. You achieve things very quickly. However, there is a downside here that needs to be watched. This transit can make you impatient and rash, which can lead to accidents or injury. Be more mindful on the physical plane. It can also increase your temper. You can be irritated too easily over delays or problems with others. This can lead to conflict, argument and sometimes actual physical violence. So be more careful now.

Like last month there are happy educational and travel opportunities happening. Students at college level seem to be doing well in their studies. Those seeking entrance to college are being pursued by schools.

You are still in the midst of a yearly financial peak. Financial goals are being achieved. This period is good for more than just 'earning' money, but also for making financial plans for the future, for funding your investment portfolio, setting up savings plans and so on – for all issues involving money. Sales, marketing, PR, advertising and using the media to good effect are always important for you on the financial level, but especially so after the 9th. Speculations are not advisable from the 15th to the 17th as important financial changes are happening then: perhaps your thinking or planning needs some revision.

Love seems stormy after the 22nd. You and the beloved are seeing things from opposite perspectives. There is validity to both perspectives; neither is right or wrong. The challenge will be to bridge the differences and to rise above them. One can have a difference of opinion yet still love the other person. In fact, the differences can lead to higher and better solutions if used properly. There is a solution that embraces both positions and it is through the conflict that you will find it. Part of the problem is that the beloved is going through a challenging time and this is affecting the relationship.

The planetary power is starting to shift to the West at the end of the month. The shift will be more pronounced next month. So your period of personal independence is finishing now. If there are still conditions to be corrected, try to do it early in the month. In coming months it will be more difficult.

October

Best Days Overall: 1, 8, 9, 17, 18, 27, 28
Most Stressful Days Overall: 6, 7, 13, 14, 19, 20
Best Days for Love: 1, 7, 8, 9, 13, 14, 17, 18, 27, 28
Best Days for Money: 2, 3, 6, 7, 15, 16, 24, 25, 29, 30
Best Days for Career: 7, 8, 17, 18, 19, 20, 27, 28

The shift of the planetary power to the Western sector of your chart is complete on the 23rd, when up to 80 per cent of the planets will be in the Western half of the chart – the maximum for the rest of the year. Hopefully you have created conditions according to your taste. Now it's time to road test your work. If you have created well, things will be comfortable. If not, you will experience pain and problems which should lead to better changes when your next period of independence comes. Pain is not a good thing, but good comes out of it. It is a message that something is amiss and needs correction.

The planets are now at the lowest point of your chart and you are in the midnight of your year. This is when the outer self, the body, is still but the interior processes are most active. This is the time to set up the 'inner conditions' for future success, to get emotionally prepared for the attainment of your goals. If you attained goals without the emotional preparation, they would be temporary. You would soon fall back.

Career is less important now. In fact, with the career planet in the 4th house since September 29 the home and family IS your career now. It's time to get this area of life in order. A stable home base is essential for career success. This is a month for psychological-type breakthroughs and understandings. It is a month to get the 'feeling body' – the emotional life – in order.

Saturn, your work planet, gets much stimulation this month. Thus this is an excellent period for job seekers. Jobs are close to home these days. Many of you will actually be working from home. Job opportunities seem to come through the family or family connections and the jobs that come now seem 'emotionally comfortable'.

Your financial planet will be in your 4th house all month, so family and family connections are important on the financial level as well. However, Mercury will go retrograde on the 21st, so try to make important purchases or investments before then.

There is a Lunar Eclipse on the 18th. This eclipse is basically benign to you; it occurs in your 9th house and shows changes in educational plans for students. Sometimes they change courses or schools. Like every Lunar Eclipse, this one indicates changes in the spiritual life – in practice and attitudes. Often it will bring shake-ups in a charitable or spiritual organization that you are involved with. The guru figures in your life experience dramas.

Love is still challenging, but will improve after the 23rd.

November

Best Days Overall: 5, 6, 13, 14, 23, 24
Most Stressful Days Overall: 3, 4, 9, 10, 16, 17, 30
Best Days for Love: 5, 6, 7, 9, 10, 13, 14, 16, 17, 23, 24, 26, 27
Best Days for Money: 3, 4, 11, 12, 21, 22, 23, 25, 26, 27, 30
Best Days for Career: 7, 16, 17, 26, 27

The main headline this month is the Solar Eclipse on the 3rd. Every Solar Eclipse affects you more than most as the Sun is the Lord of your Horoscope. You are very sensitive to these things. It occurs in the sign of Scorpio, in stressful alignment with you. So do reduce your schedule this period. In fact, a reduced schedule is advisable until the 22nd. This eclipse occurs in your 4th house of home and family, thus there are shake-ups in the home – perhaps some unexpected repairs or other problems. There are dramas in the lives of parents or parent figures. Family members are more temperamental this period; try not to make things worse. Like every Solar Eclipse, this one affects the body and image. It causes a redefinition of your self-concept, your presentation of yourself. You have a chance twice a year to upgrade your image and personality. Since this eclipse occurs very near Saturn, job changes are afoot too. There will also be changes in your health regime and practice.

Mercury your financial planet is still retrograde until the 10th, so avoid making important purchases or major financial moves until after that date. Your job now is to attain mental clarity on finances. Take your time with this. Once this happens financial decision-making will be easy. Mercury spends the month in your 4th house, like last month. Thus the family and family connections are a source of support and opportunity. You probably spend more on the home and family this period, but you earn from here as well. As we have been seeing all year, many of you are working and earning money from home. Investors will do well with real estate and industries that cater to the home. Bonds and the bond market also seem interesting.

Health has been more delicate since October 23. If you drop the unnecessary things from your life – and this requires tough choices – you will find that you have all the energy you need to achieve what is important to you. Continue to enhance the health in the ways mentioned in the yearly report. Health and energy improve dramatically after the 22nd.

Leos of child-bearing age are much more fertile these days than usual. In fact, you are in your most fertile period of the year right now. (It began on October 23.)

On the 22nd, as the Sun enters your 5th house, you enter another one of your yearly personal pleasure peaks. Sure, you will be working, but you will manage to have a lot of fun as well. Love is much happier now. Singles are having good romantic opportunities and those who are married are having more harmony in their relationships. Still, with your love planet retrograde, this is not a time for major decisions in love. Let love develop as it will. Don't try to force things.

December

> Best Days Overall: 2, 3, 10, 11, 12, 20, 21, 22, 30, 31
> Most Stressful Days Overall: 1, 6, 7, 13, 14, 28, 29
> Best Days for Love: 2, 3, 4, 5, 6, 7, 10, 11, 13, 14, 20, 21, 23, 24, 30, 31
> Best Days for Money: 1, 8, 9, 10, 11, 18, 19, 21, 22, 23, 24, 28, 29
> Best Days for Career: 4, 5, 13, 14, 23, 24

This is a time of year for parties and you are still in a personal party period – so everything is aligned for a fun kind of month. You are always the life and soul of the party, but this period even more so. Personal fertility is still very strong until the 21st (for those of child-bearing age), so a word to the wise is sufficient.

After the 21st you enter a more serious, work-oriented period. You're partied out. There are work goals that need to be attended to now. This is another excellent period for job seekers or for those who employ others. Taking on extra jobs this period would not be a surprise.

Though your health is basically good, you seem more focused here after the 21st. Most likely you are involved with the health of family members, and not necessarily your own.

Finances are excellent this month. Mercury is in lucky Sagittarius until the 24th. The only problem is overspending, which is likely. The financial optimism is so high that you feel you can afford everything. Financial expectations can be unreasonable or exaggerated this period. It is good to be generous, and few are as generous as you Leo, but try to keep it within bounds. After the 24th, as Mercury enters conservative Capricorn, the financial judgement is sound and down to earth. (Perhaps the bills are coming in and this sobers you up.) In truth, speculations are favourable until the 24th, but after that date they are not advisable.

The lower half of the Horoscope is still dominant, although this will change next month. For the moment it is still important to focus on the home and family and your emotional well being and stability, to create the inner conditions for success. Your career planet will make a rare (once in two years) retrograde move on the 21st, so your career will be under review now. It is a time for gaining mental clarity here. Take whatever time is necessary. There is no rush. Once you have mental clarity it will be easy to make the right career moves.

There are some very powerful planetary alignments at the end of the month from the 23rd to the 31st. You, the beloved and family members need to drive more carefully, and to avoid risky stunts and conflict. If you read the newspapers this period, you will understand what we're talking about here.

Virgo

ṃp

Personality Profile

VIRGO AT A GLANCE

Element – Earth

Ruling Planet – Mercury
  Career Planet – Mercury
  Love Planet – Neptune
  Money Planet – Venus
  Planet of Home and Family Life – Jupiter
  Planet of Health and Work – Uranus
  Planet of Pleasure – Saturn
  Planet of Sexuality – Mars

Colours – earth tones, ochre, orange, yellow

Colour that promotes love, romance and social harmony – aqua blue

Colour that promotes earning power – jade green

Gems – agate, hyacinth

Metal – quicksilver

Scents – lavender, lilac, lily of the valley, storax

Quality – mutable (= flexibility)

Quality most needed for balance – a broader perspective

Strongest virtues – mental agility, analytical skills, ability to pay attention to detail, healing powers

Deepest needs – to be useful and productive

Characteristic to avoid – destructive criticism

Signs of greatest overall compatibility – Taurus, Capricorn

Signs of greatest overall incompatibility – Gemini, Sagittarius, Pisces

Sign most helpful to career – Gemini

Sign most helpful for emotional support – Sagittarius

Sign most helpful financially – Libra

Sign best for marriage and/or partnerships – Pisces

Sign most helpful for creative projects – Capricorn

Best Sign to have fun with – Capricorn

Signs most helpful in spiritual matters – Taurus, Leo

Best day of the week – Wednesday

Understanding a Virgo

The virgin is a particularly fitting symbol for those born under the sign of Virgo. If you meditate on the image of the virgin you will get a good understanding of the essence of the Virgo type. The virgin is, of course, a symbol of purity and innocence – not naïve, but pure. A virginal object has not been touched. A virgin field is land that is true to itself, the way it has always been. The same is true of virgin forest: it is pristine, unaltered.

Apply the idea of purity to the thought processes, emotional life, physical body, and activities and projects of the everyday world, and you can see how Virgos approach life. Virgos desire the pure expression of the ideal in their mind, body and affairs. If they find impurities they will attempt to clear them away.

Impurities are the beginning of disorder, unhappiness and uneasiness. The job of the Virgo is to eject all impurities and keep only that which the body and mind can use and assimilate.

The secrets of good health are here revealed: 90 per cent of the art of staying well is maintaining a pure mind, a pure body and pure emotions. When you introduce more impurities than your mind and body can deal with, you will have what is known as 'dis-ease'. It is no wonder that Virgos make great doctors, nurses, healers and dieticians. They have an innate understanding of good health and they realize that good health is more than just physical. In all aspects of life, if you want a project to be successful it must be kept as pure as possible. It must be protected against the adverse elements that will try to undermine it. This is the secret behind Virgo's awesome technical proficiency.

One could talk about Virgo's analytical powers – which are formidable. One could talk about their perfectionism and their almost superhuman attention to detail. But this would be to miss the point. All of these virtues are manifestations of a Virgo's desire for purity and perfection – a world without Virgos would have ruined itself long ago.

A vice is nothing more than a virtue turned inside out, misapplied or used in the wrong context. Virgos' apparent vices come from their inherent virtue. Their analytical powers, which should be used for healing, helping or perfecting a project in the world, sometimes get misapplied and turned against people. Their critical faculties, which should be used constructively to perfect a strategy or proposal, can sometimes be used destructively to harm or wound. Their urge to perfection can turn into worry and lack of confidence; their natural humility can become self-denial and self-abasement. When Virgos turn negative they are apt to turn their devastating criticism on themselves, sowing the seeds of self-destruction.

Finance

Virgos have all the attitudes that create wealth. They are hard-working, industrious, efficient, organized, thrifty, productive and eager to serve. A developed Virgo is every employer's dream. But until Virgos master some of the social graces of Libra they will not even come close to fulfilling their financial potential. Purity and perfectionism, if not handled correctly or gracefully, can be very trying to others. Friction in human relationships can be devastating not only to your pet projects but – indirectly – to your wallet as well.

Virgos are quite interested in their financial security. Being hard-working, they know the true value of money. They do not like to take risks with their money, preferring to save for their retirement or for a rainy day. Virgos usually make prudent, calculated investments that involve a minimum of risk. These investments and savings usually work out well, helping Virgos to achieve the financial security they seek. The rich or even not-so-rich Virgo also likes to help his or her friends in need.

Career and Public Image

Virgos reach their full potential when they can communicate their knowledge in such a way that others can understand it. In order to get their ideas across better, Virgos need to develop greater verbal skills and fewer judgemental ways of expressing themselves. Virgos look up to teachers and communicators; they like their bosses to be good communicators. Virgos will probably not respect a superior who is not their intellectual equal – no matter how much money or power that superior has. Virgos themselves like to be perceived by others as being educated and intellectual.

The natural humility of Virgos often inhibits them from fulfilling their great ambitions, from acquiring name and fame. Virgos should indulge in a little more self-promotion if they are going to reach their career goals. They need to push themselves with the same ardour that they would use to foster others.

At work Virgos like to stay active. They are willing to learn any type of job as long as it serves their ultimate goal of financial security. Virgos may change occupations several times during their professional lives, until they find the one they really enjoy. Virgos work well with other people, are not afraid to work hard and always fulfil their responsibilities.

Love and Relationships

If you are an analyst or a critic you must, out of necessity, narrow your scope. You have to focus on a part and not the whole; this can create a temporary narrow-mindedness. Virgos do not like this kind of person. They like their partners to be broad-minded, with depth and vision. Virgos seek to get this broad-minded quality from their partners, since they sometimes lack it themselves.

Virgos are perfectionists in love just as they are in other areas of life. They need partners who are tolerant, open-minded and easy-going. If you are in love with a Virgo do not waste time on impractical romantic gestures. Do practical and useful things for him or her – this is what will be appreciated and what will be done for you.

Virgos express their love through pragmatic and useful gestures, so do not be put off because your Virgo partner does not say 'I love you' day-in and day-out. Virgos are not that type. If they love you, they will demonstrate it in practical ways. They will always be there for you; they will show an interest in your health and finances; they will fix your sink or repair your video recorder. Virgos deem these actions to be superior to sending flowers, chocolates or Valentine cards.

In love affairs Virgos are not particularly passionate or spontaneous. If you are in love with a Virgo, do not take this personally. It does not mean that you are not alluring enough or that your Virgo partner does not love or like you. It is just the way Virgos are. What they lack in passion they make up for in dedication and loyalty.

Home and Domestic Life

It goes without saying that the home of a Virgo will be spotless, sanitized and orderly. Everything will be in its proper place – and don't you dare move anything about! For Virgos to find domestic bliss they need to ease up a bit in the home, to allow their partner and children more freedom and to be more generous and open-minded. Family members are not to be analysed under a microscope, they are individuals with their own virtues to express.

With these small difficulties resolved, Virgos like to stay in and entertain at home. They make good hosts and they like to keep their friends and families happy and entertained at family and social gatherings. Virgos love children, but they are strict with them – at times – since they want to make sure their children are brought up with the correct sense of family and values.

Horoscope for 2013

Major Trends

As with Gemini, the past ten years have been all about deal-ing with change – sudden, dramatic, personal earthquake kind of change – and learning to deal with the fear and in-security that this brings. When something happens a couple of times we can chalk it up to coincidence. But when some-thing keeps happening over and over, there is something behind it. You were like the major league ball player who had trouble hitting the curve ball. So, naturally, when the opposing team saw that, all the player ever got was curve balls. He had no option but to learn to hit the curve ball. Once he mastered the art, he didn't see too many more of them. Your curve ball was change and insecurity. Change kept coming and coming, until it ceased to ruffle you, until you actually became comfortable with it. Now that you are comfortable with it, the activity abates. You won't have to deal with this kind of phenomenon for another 20 years or so.

Things began to stabilize for you in 2011 as Uranus left its stressful aspect to you; 2011 was easier than 2010, and 2012 was easier than 2011. This year is slightly challenging, but a piece of cake compared to 2008–2010. Everything is relative.

In June 2012 Jupiter crossed your Mid-heaven and entered your 10th house of career. This initiated a period of great career success and achievement. The career horizons broadened and expanded and very happy opportunities came to you. And this trend continues for the first half of 2013. There's more on this later.

Uranus spent a lot of time – over seven years – in your 7th house of love. Thus the love life has been highly unsta-ble. Many a divorce or break up took place from 2003 to 2010. Things are much calmer now and relationships have a much better chance of enduring now and in the coming years. In March 2011 Neptune made a major move into your

7th house and the whole love life is becoming more refined, elevated and spiritualized. More on this later.

The year begins with two long-term planets in stressful aspect to you: Jupiter and Neptune. On June 27 Jupiter will move away from his stressful aspect and start making harmonious aspects to you. So your health will be better after June 27. Details later.

Now that Saturn has moved out of your money house (in October 2012) you should feel an immediate increase in earning power. Finances are lot easier this year than last. Again, there's more on this later.

Your areas of greatest interest this year are communication and intellectual interests; children, creativity and leisure activities; love and romance; sex, occult interests, personal reinvention and transformation, past lives and reincarnation; career (until June 27); friends, groups and group activities (from June 27 onwards).

Your paths of greatest fulfilment in the year ahead are communication and intellectual interests; career (until June 27); friends, groups and group activities (from June 27).

Health

(Please note that this is an astrological perspective on health and not a medical one. In days of yore there was no difference, these perspectives were identical. But now there could be quite a difference. For a medical perspective, please consult your doctor or health practitioner.)

Health is always important to a Virgo, but with your 6th health house empty, this year less so than usual. Basically health looks good. As we mentioned, there are two long-term planets stressing you out – Jupiter and Neptune – but these planets are not malefic, and by themselves they are not enough to cause major problems. And as you will end the year with only one long-term planet stressing you, health and energy will steadily improve.

Good though your health is, you can make it even better. Give more attention to the vulnerable areas in the year

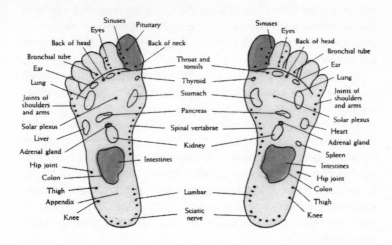

Reflexology

Try to massage the whole foot on a regular basis, but pay extra attention to the points highlighted on the chart. When you massage, be aware of 'sore spots', as these need special attention. It's also a good idea to massage the ankles and top side of the feet.

ahead, where problems are most likely to begin. These are the small intestine (diet is important in your life, meals should eaten more slowly and calmly to aid the digestion); the heart (until June 27; avoid worry and anxiety as much as possible, which are the root causes of heart problems); the ankles and calves (massages these regularly and give the ankles more support when exercising); the head, face and scalp (scalp and face massages are powerful therapies this year, and as the head and face contain reflexes to the entire body you are energizing the whole body when you do this); and the adrenals (avoid anger and fear, which that tend to stress out the adrenals).

Your health planet, Uranus, is in the 8th house of transformation all year. Thus you benefit greatly from detox regimes. Good health is not so much about adding new things to the body, but getting rid of things that don't belong there. Often with this aspect people tend towards surgery – perhaps they are a bit too quick to jump into this. Always get second opinions.

The health planet in the 8th house shows that good health for you also means a healthy sex life. Sexual activity should be kept in balance – neither too much nor too little. But if you listen to your body, you will know when enough is enough.

With your health planet in the sign of Aries, the musculature is very important. A weakness in a muscle is will create a weakness in an organ as the kinesiologists have shown. Vigorous physical exercise is important these days. A day at the gym, will, in many cases, do you as much good as visiting the doctor's.

Home and Family

Though your 4th house of home and family is not a house of power this year, the ruler of the 4th house, Jupiter, is very prominently positioned in this year's Horoscope. He is right near the Mid-heaven in the 10th house. So you're paying attention here, at least for the first half of the year.

In many cases, this indicates that the home and family is becoming the career, the most important thing in your life. Sometimes it shows that you are working from home: the career is pursued in the home. Many of you already have home offices but these could be expanded in the year ahead.

The home is being made more prestigious this year. You want your home to reflect your status – your actual status in many cases, but sometimes just what you aspire to. This can get quite expensive and many go overboard in this direction. Happily this trend won't last too long. By the end of June the home will be more like a home, a place of comfort and nourishment, and not so much a showplace to impress others. However, moves don't seem likely.

The distinctions between the home and office lose meaning this year, as one merges into the other. The home is made like an office and the office like a home. Moves don't seem likely, but the upgrading of the home is more likely.

A parent or parent figure seems personally very involved in your career. This parent or parent figure is also having a banner social year and seems very popular. If the parents are still married the marriage should be more harmonious. There is great devotion by one of the parent figures that make things work. A parent or parent figure prospers greatly in the year ahead; however, they should drive more defensively during the latter part of the year.

Siblings or sibling figures in your life – those who play that role in your life – are having a difficult year. They are asked to carry extra burdens that they can't escape. They seem a bit cold, stand offish and distant. If you understand the astrology behind this you can be more tolerant of it. You can encourage them to make an effort to be more warm and loving with others. Moves don't seem likely. This is a good year for them to get their body and image in shape and to lose weight if necessary.

Children or children figures are moving (and they probably moved last year as well). They have multiple moves in coming years and seem restless and nomadic. Meditation will help them control volatile emotions and mood changes.

A Lunar Eclipse on May 25 will test the present home situation. If there are hidden flaws in need of repair, you will learn about it then. These changes seem short term. If you're redecorating or beautifying the home, or buying objects of beauty for the home, January 1 to 9, October 7 to November 5 and November 22 to December 21 are good times for this.

Finance and Career

As we mentioned, you had Saturn in your money house for the past two years – a difficult transit for finance. You felt tight, squeezed and probably had extra financial burdens placed on you. It was a period of financial consolidation. You needed to get leaner and cut out waste. Assets needed to be managed better. When you made the adjustments, the resources that were needed were there.

Much of the effect of this transit depended on you. If you have been responsible in your financial affairs, the transit, though not comfortable, made you richer. You learned new principles of financial management and you became the 'master of money' (as was always intended) instead of being enslaved by it. However, for those who have been irresponsible in financial matters, well, the last two years were quite traumatic. The lucky breaks were not there. Debts came due. Financial sins ripened into unpleasant events. Often people go bankrupt under such a transit. But this too was leading to eventual long-term financial health. It was educational. And once the karma is paid off and the errors corrected, you are in a position to build a healthier, more stable, financial life.

Most of us are a mix of financial responsibility and irresponsibility. Most of us have areas that could be corrected, and this is what was happening over the past two years. Happily this period is over with and you should see an improvement in the financial life now. I wouldn't call the period 'bullish', but it will be much less stressful than it has been.

As we mentioned, in June of last year Jupiter crossed your Mid-heaven and moved into your 10th house of career. The career, your status, your position in your company or industry was elevated. Often this translates into more money but not always. Sometimes people get honours or recognition with no tangible bottom-line benefit. This could have happened last year and is likely this year as well. (However, it does look good on the resume!)

There are still very nice career opportunities happening this year. You have good family support for your career; there is no conflict between family obligations and your career. Career opportunities are coming from family or family connections. Many of you will get involved in the family business this year.

Job seekers have good fortune in the first half of the year. The latter half seems more challenging, though. Jobs will come but more effort is involved.

Venus, a very fast-moving planet, is your financial planet. And, as our regular readers know, she will move through the entire Horoscope in any given year. Thus there are many short-term trends in finances depending on where she is and the aspects she receives. This is best dealt with in the monthly reports.

Love and Social Life

Your 7th house of love and marriage (and social activities) has been strong for many years. But this year things are less complicated, less stressful and much more stable. For many years love was there but there was always much insecurity involved. Love came like a lightning flash and often disappeared just as quickly. And this kept happening again and again. Happily, this is now stabilizing. It seems to me that you've had enough excitement in love, and a little security – perhaps even some boredom – would be welcome these days. It might be boring, but it's nice to know that your beloved will be there for you when you get home; that when you make long-term plans, the beloved will be there.

Neptune is your love planet, and last year he made a major move into his own sign (Pisces) and his own house (your 7th). You have always been idealistic about love and always had very high standards, but now even more so. Your love planet is now in his own sign and house and thus is much more powerful on your behalf. This is good news on the love front.

You are in a period now – for the next 13 or so years – where 'ideal' love is likely to happen. And this will be very educational. Most people think that the purpose of life is the happiness of the physical body, the carnal self. Thus when they meet a 'twin flame' they expect happiness ever after. But since life has much deeper purposes than carnal well being, the meeting with the ideal love – the twin flame – can bring many psychological shocks. The twin flame will uncover areas of unconsciousness, areas of darkness, in the soul that were holding it back. It can be a very stormy kind of experience, as Judith Hall points out in *The Soul Mate Myth*. To have the ideal love, you have to be your ideal self, and the cosmos is working towards that end.

Spiritual compatibility in love has always been important, but now even more so. If the relationship is just carnal with no spiritual dimension to it, you are not likely to be interested.

In general spiritual-type friends are coming into the picture now. You are attracted to psychics, ministers, spiritual channels, ministers, gurus and yogis. You also like the poet, the mystic, the creative artist and the inspired musician.

Singles find love in spiritual settings now; don't even waste a second on the bars and clubs. Love is at the meditation seminar, the spiritual lecture or workshop, the prayer meeting or at the charity event. Get more involved in altruistic causes that you believe in and love will find you.

On June 27 Jupiter will enter your 11th house of friends. Thus new and significant friends are coming into the picture this year (and next year). The social life will be much more active. After June 27, Jupiter will be making beautiful aspects with your love planet for some months, and this is when romance – serious romance – is likely to happen. This will have marriage potential.

Self-improvement

Neptune in your 7th house of love has a few downsides which need to be kept in mind. Neptune is often associated with 'deception' and scandal. Now the truth is that Neptune never sets out to deceive anyone. Neptune is being who he is. He projects a very high and refined kind of energy which the human mind cannot understand. It is far above the human mind. So, the human mind is often deceived by the energy, much in the way that it will misinterpret a dream or prophecy. So the people in your love and social life might not be who they appear to be and you have to do more homework, get more facts about them. Don't take things at face value.

Neptune is the planet of revelation. He reveals the hidden, secret things. Thus, he is often associated with scandal. So the year ahead will likely bring some unpleasant kinds of revelations about friends or lovers. However, the good things will also be revealed. These revelations are likely to test love and commitment and this is good. If you still love the person in spite of these things, love is likely to be real. Business-type partnerships also need more scrutiny this year and in coming years. Don't take things at face value.

Those of you who are on a spiritual path will most likely attract spiritual-type people into the life, but if not, there is a tendency now to attract alcohol or drug abusers.

It is good that you are having ideal love this year. Ideal human love is wonderful and it teaches many things, but you will also see the limitations of it. Real ideal love is a spiritual condition. It is the love that we experience when in contact with the Higher Power –unconditional and unconditioned. This power, if relied upon, will fulfil all your love needs perfectly, often through people, but not always. This is the love that Neptune is teaching about for the next thirteen or so years.

Saturn is now in your 3rd house of communication and intellectual interests for the next two years. The intellect is getting deepened. The thought process is being re-organized. You are becoming a more disciplined kind of thinker. Perhaps learning will be slower, but you will go deeper into any subject that you study. Students will have to work harder as the educational system doesn't reward depth of thought but the memorization of superficial facts and knowledge. If you are having problems in your studies, slow things down; don't be in a rush. Take it sentence by sentence, paragraph by paragraph and understand it. Try to make learning more fun as well. Work more with audio books and with films or documentaries on the subjects you need to learn. You will learn more from a film about a subject than from a book.

Month-by-month Forecasts

January

   Best Days Overall: 2, 3, 10, 11, 19, 20, 29, 30
   Most Stressful Days Overall: 8, 9, 14, 15, 21, 22, 23
   Best Days for Love: 6, 8, 9, 14, 15, 18, 19, 24, 29, 30
   Best Days for Money: 4, 5, 8, 9, 12, 18, 19, 22, 29, 30, 31
   Best Days for Career: 2, 3, 10, 11, 21, 22, 23, 31

You are in a very powerful career year and much success is happening, but now with most of the planets below the horizon of your chart, it is best to prepare yourself emotionally and mentally for the success that you want. This emotional preparation will ensure that when the outer success comes (and it will) you will be able to handle it. The good news here is that there is no conflict between family life and the career. Family members, and especially a parent or parent figure, actively support your outer ambitions. They could be actually fuelling your ambitions. They seem more ambitious than you.

Most of the planets are in the Western, social sector of your chart as your year begins. Personal independence is not what it should be, so it is more difficult to have things your way. The planetary power is flowing towards others, not to you. So long as it isn't destructive let others have their way for now. The good thing about many planets in the West is that it broadens the horizons and the perspective. Life isn't all about us. The cosmos is concerned with the good of the whole and so we get a more holistic view of life. It's best now to adapt to situations as best you can. If certain conditions are unpleasant, make a note, and when your period of personal independence comes you can easily make any changes necessary. It is good every now and then to take a vacation from ourselves and our personal interests. This is one of those periods.

You begin your year in the midst of a yearly personal pleasure peak. New Year celebrations seem to go on longer than usual. The party doesn't end on New Year's Day; in fact it continues until the 19th.

Finances are basically good this month. There are some bumps on the road, some challenges, but basically they are good. Your financial planet is in Sagittarius until the 10th, which can make you overly speculative, and overly optimistic in financial matters. Speculations are best avoided. Still, you earn more and spend more. Overspending is the main danger until the 10th. After the 10th the Venus moves into Capricorn and your 5th house, and financial judgement becomes more sober. The good news is that you are enjoying your money after the 10th. You are having fun with it. Money is earned in fun kinds of ways. Your personal creativity can be marketable during this period.

Health is good all month. With your 6th house strong after the 19th you are in Virgo heaven, focused on work and health. Virgos will focus on health even if nothing is wrong with them. Health regimes are good for their own sake. You can enhance the health even further by giving more attention to the heart (after the 19th); to the head, face and scalp (all month); and to the lungs, small intestine, arms, shoulders and respiratory system (after the 19th). You are most likely more concerned with the health of a parent or parent figure than with your own health. Moreover, Virgos of childbearing age are more fertile now than usual.

February

Best Days Overall: 7, 8, 15, 16, 17, 25, 26
Most Stressful Days Overall: 2, 3, 9, 10, 23, 24
Best Days for Love: 2, 9, 10, 11, 12, 18, 19, 20
Best Days for Money: 1, 9, 10, 18, 19, 27, 28
Best Days for Career: 1, 11, 12, 18, 19, 21, 22

The planets are now in their most Westerly aspect this month. Cosmic power flows away from you towards others.

Personal power is lessened, perhaps self-esteem and self-confidence as well, but your love and social life is very much strengthened. You get an opportunity now to cultivate your social skills. Review our discussion of this last month.

This month the planets make an important shift. The power moves from the lower to the upper half of your Horoscope. This will happen on the 18th, though you will undoubtedly feel it before this date. Dawn is breaking in your year. It is time to be up and about, to pursue the activities of the day – your outer goals and aspirations. Hopefully over the past six or so months you have found your point of emotional harmony. You have got emotionally prepared for what you want, and now you can start acting in physical and tangible ways to achieve your goals.

On the 18th you enter a yearly social peak. Your 7th house is easily the most powerful in the Horoscope, with at least half and sometime more of the planets either there or moving through there in the month ahead. You are more popular than usual as well. Mercury, the Lord of your Horoscope, will be in the 7th house from the 5th onwards. You are dedicated to others – and especially to the beloved. You put others ahead of yourself (which is what you should be doing) and people respond to this.

Romance for singles is likely all month, but the 6th and 7th, the 19th to the 21st and the 26th to the 28th seem especially good for romance. The problems in love are good problems to have. There is too much opportunity, too many choices, too many functions to attend, and this is often confusing. The relationships that happen now are more likely to endure. The cosmos presents you with a smorgasbord of lovers, all different types and kinds. You seem attracted to all of them. The best are the ones where spiritual compatibility is as strong as the other attractions.

Health becomes more delicate after the 18th, so rest and relax more. Enhance the health in the ways mentioned in the yearly report.

Though career is not highlighted early in the month, it still seems very good. There is success this month. Your work ethic attracts the attention of your superiors and seems to be approved by them. There is luck in the career this year, but your work ethic seems the most important thing this month. Later on in the month, after the 5th, your social connections play an important role. You should attend the right parties and gatherings. It might be advisable to host parties with the right people too.

March

Best Days Overall: 6, 7, 15, 16, 24, 25, 26
Most Stressful Days Overall: 4, 5, 10, 11, 17, 18, 19, 31
Best Days for Love: 1, 2, 3, 10, 11, 20, 21, 22, 29, 31
Best Days for Money: 1, 2, 3, 8, 9, 10, 11, 17, 18, 21, 22, 27, 28, 31
Best Days for Career: 2, 3, 10, 11, 17, 18, 19, 20, 21, 29, 30

Now that most of the planets are in the upper half of the Horoscope, career is becoming important. However, Mercury (both your career and personal planet) went retrograde on February 23 and will be retrograde until the 17th. So until the 17th your main focus should be on attaining mental clarity on career issues and goals. With Mercury retrograde, the career situation might not be as it appears so clarity is very important.

Your career planet spends the month in the 7th house, in the sign of Pisces. Like last month, this shows that you further your career goals by social means, by attending the right parties and perhaps by hosting them as well. The 'likeability' factor is more important careerwise than even your personal skills. With the planets in their maximum Western, social position for most of the month, 'likeability' is important in general, but especially in career matters. However, don't be deceived. Having friends in high places (which seems the case right now) opens doors, but ultimately it is your performance that counts. The social factor is very important, but it's not everything.

Health still needs watching until the 20th. Try to rest and relax more and maintain high energy levels. Enhance the health in the ways mentioned in the yearly report. Health and energy improve after the 20th.

You are still in the midst of a yearly social peak. Like last month, the problem seems to be one of excess – too many romantic and social opportunities.

The family situation got stressful last month. A parent or parent figure seems very stressed out and passions are running high in the family. You don't seem in synch with them. They don't seem to approve of your friends, a current love or your social focus in general. Perhaps they feel you need to focus on other things. The stress is still there this month, but it gets easier as the month progresses.

Earnings look very good this month. Venus, your financial planet, is strong both celestially and terrestrially. She is in her sign of exaltation and in a powerful house – the 7th – until the 23rd. Your social connections are not only helping the career but your finances as well. You socialize with the people you do business with and vice versa. Your friends tend to be wealthy. Your 8th house of transformation becomes strong after the 20th and your financial planet moves into this house on the 23rd. This shows a need to focus on the prosperity of others, to make other people rich and to put their financial interests ahead of your own. Though this is counter-intuitive, such a practice will bring personal prosperity to you, by the law of karma.

April

Best Days Overall: 2, 3, 11, 12, 21, 22, 29, 30
Most Stressful Days Overall: 1, 6, 7, 8, 14, 15, 27, 28
Best Days for Love: 1, 6, 7, 8, 9, 10, 16, 21, 22, 25, 29, 30
Best Days for Money: 1, 4, 5, 9, 10, 14, 15, 21, 22, 23, 24, 29, 30
Best Days for Career: 7, 8, 14, 15, 19, 27, 28

Your 8th house is strong until the 19th of this month. This house has many levels of meaning and each is valid. On the purely mundane level it shows a greater interest in sex. Libido is more aroused than usual (no matter what your age or stage in life), and this active sex life shows that there is much happening on the social front. Sex and love are two different things, but your needs are being met. Often power in the 8th house brings encounters with death – not necessarily personal death but more involvement with these matters. There is a tendency to attend more funerals or memorial services. Perhaps there are near-death kinds of experiences, or perhaps a death that you read about in the papers affects you particularly deeply. There is a need to come to a better understanding of it and the cosmos has many ways to arrange this.

The 8th house also deals with personal transformation. We all have an ideal self that we would like to manifest. In order to do this the old self has to be detoxed, and eventually has to die. For the pauper to become a prince, the pauper self needs to die (on a psychological level) so that the prince can be born. Some refer to this process as resurrection, some as metamorphosis, some as transformation. Whatever label is used, the meaning is essentially the same. The old self doesn't die easily; it puts up a terrific fight. Thus when the 8th house is strong, life tends to be more stormy. Detoxing is seldom pleasant. The effete material that surfaces is shocking and ugly. Yet, the end result of the process is wonderful – a clean body, a clean mind, a new self. The stresses and strains that you feel this month are the birth pangs of a new self.

Many areas of life are getting detoxed this month: the body (from the 14th onwards); the financial life (until the 15th, but the process has been going on since March 22); the career and career path; and the spiritual life. Those of you on the spiritual path will find that a good mental, emotional and physical detox will change the whole quality of your spiritual practice. Meditation will go much better.

Detox regimes have been important healthwise since 2011, but this month even more so. Detox regimes done this month will be more powerful than at other times, and the results will be better and deeper. This is a great month to lose weight if you need to. Health is good all month, but especially after the 19th.

The financial trends are pretty much the same as last month, until the 15th. After that, Venus moves into Taurus, your 9th house. Since Venus will be in adverse aspect with Saturn, speculations should be avoided. You could have some delays in finances, in getting paid, or in getting customers, but be patient – all will work out. The stresses are temporary and not trends for the year or even the month. Your spouse, partner or current love is in a yearly financial peak. Prosperity is happening now. His or her financial ups and downs will be extreme this year, but now they are on the upswing.

May

    Best Days Overall: 8, 9, 10, 18, 19, 27, 28
    Most Stressful Days Overall: 4, 5, 11, 12, 25, 26, 31
    Best Days for Love: 4, 5, 10, 11, 13, 21, 22, 23, 29, 30, 31
    Best Days for Money: 2, 3, 10, 11, 12, 21, 22, 29, 30
    Best Days for Career: 8, 9, 10, 11, 12, 21, 22, 29, 30

There is an exciting, eventful and turbulent month ahead. Keep the seatbelts buckled! We have two eclipses this month, a guarantee that major change is happening both personally and for the world at large. (And these are coming on the heels of a previous Lunar Eclipse on April 25). Also, the planetary power makes a major shift from the West, where it has been all year, to the East. Thus there are psychological changes in you. You are entering a period of personal independence. The planetary power starts to flow in your direction. Self-confidence and self-esteem will improve. The problems in love this month will serve a good purpose. They will actually make you aware of your personal power and independence. And as if all this wasn't enough, on the 20th you enter a yearly career peak.

The Solar Eclipse of the 10th occurs in your 9th house. Foreign travel is best avoided during this period. Students make dramatic changes in their educational plans; sometimes it brings upheavals in the school hierarchy, changes in the curriculum or important administrative changes. Your personal philosophy of life, your core beliefs, will get a good testing now. Some will need to go into the dustbin, others will need some modification. This is when you find out what is what. The Sun is your spiritual planet, thus there are important spiritual changes going on (and this is behind the revamping of your core beliefs). Often there is a change of teachers and teachings, and changes in the spiritual practice, attitudes and ideals. There are dramas in the lives of the guru figures in your life and upheavals in a spiritual or charitable organization that you are involved with. Mars is affected by this eclipse, so avoid risky kinds of activities or elective surgery.

Love is getting tested from the 20th onwards. The transiting planets are causing this, but the Lunar Eclipse of the 25th doesn't help. Good relationships survive these sort of things – in fact they emerge stronger and better. But the fundamentally flawed ones tend to dissolve. Even in a good relationship there is more tension. The beloved is more temperamental. Dirty laundry tends to surface during the eclipse period which needs to be dealt with. In this sense there is change in the relationship, but in a positive way. It is not just love that is getting tested, but friendships as well.

This Lunar Eclipse affects you more strongly than the previous Solar Eclipse, so reduce your schedule during this period, especially as your health is more delicate after the 20th too.

You are very successful this month. You seem above everyone in your world. Thus you are a natural target for the critics and stone throwers. Valuable lessons are being learned through these experiences.

June

Best Days Overall: 5, 6, 15, 16, 23, 24
Most Stressful Days Overall: 1, 7, 8, 21, 22, 27, 28
Best Days for Love: 1, 10, 19, 20, 27, 28
Best Days for Money: 8, 9, 10, 17, 18, 19, 20, 26, 27, 28
Best Days for Career: 1, 7, 8, 10, 11, 19, 20, 27, 28

You are still in the midst of a yearly (and perhaps life time) career peak, until the 21st. There is much success happening, with elevation, honour and recognition for your achievements. You are elevated in your company and perhaps in your industry. Mars in your 10th career house shows that you are working very hard on the career, fending off competitors, personal and corporate. Being successful can be stressful. There is always something to deal with, always some crisis. But in the process, detox happens. Impurities surface and get removed.

By the 27th your career goals (at least for now) have been achieved. Jupiter moves out of your career house and into your 11th house of friends. You are now reaping the rewards of career success. You are making new and important friends. The social life becomes more active. You start to manifest your fondest hopes and wishes. Often the career is the means to an end. We have certain hopes and wishes and we feel that only through the career can these be made manifest. The career was never the main objective – it was these hopes and wishes. And these will start to be realized this month and in the year ahead.

Health and vitality will start to improve after the 21st as well. You will really feel the difference. If there have been health problems in the past month, now you hear good news about them.

A parent or parent figure needs to take it easy these days. Perhaps there has been surgery or near-death kind of experience. He or she seems energetic, but is perhaps more impatient and irritable. This can lead to accidents on the physical plane.

The love life starts to improve dramatically after the 21st, and especially after the 27th. If the eclipse of last month broke up a relationship, someone new (and better) is coming into the picture. If your relationship survived, there is more love and romance within it now. Virgos of child-bearing age become much more fertile after the 27th.

There is no need now to rush love. Your love planet goes retrograde on 7th and will be retrograde until November 15. This is not going to stop all the wonderful love experiences that are happening, but only slow things down a bit (which is probably a good thing). Your spouse, partner or current love seems to lack direction, seems undecided, so allow love to develop as it will. Enjoy the now without projecting too far into the future.

July

Best Days Overall: 2, 3, 12, 13, 21, 22, 29, 30
Most Stressful Days Overall: 4, 5, 6, 19, 20, 25, 26
Best Days for Love: 1, 7, 10, 11, 16, 17, 19, 20, 25, 26, 29, 30
Best Days for Money: 1, 7, 8, 10, 11, 14, 15, 16, 17, 19, 20, 25, 29, 30
Best Days for Career: 4, 5, 6, 7, 8, 17, 25, 26

Your 11th house continues to be powerful this month and you are in a very social period, both romantically and with friends, groups and organizations. Power in the 11th house shows an interest in science and technology. Your knowledge will increase in both these areas. New computers, gadgets and software will come to you and you seem more active online than usual. A parent or parent figure is in a yearly financial peak (since June 21). There is prosperity for the rest of the year too, but this month it is especially strong. He or she needs to be more careful on the physical plane until the 18th. Review the comments from last month.

Virgos are rational, logical people. However, the Water element is strong in the Horoscope this month, with up to 70 per cent of the planets either in water signs or moving through them. People are 'feeling' based these days: logic and rationality count for nothing. It is the mood of the moment, the sentiment, that carries the day. This is what matters. If I feel that the earth is flat, then that's how it is for me! This is a little hard to deal with. Yet at times like this, the world needs more Virgo rationality. You are very important these days. On the other hand, this is a good period to get more in touch with your feelings. Virgos, more than most, can live in the mind and thus miss out on an important dimension of themselves. This is a very good period for making psychological progress.

Love is very happy this month. Singles seem to have a choice between committed, serious relationships or mere love affairs. Both offer themselves to you. Fertility is still very strong now (for those of you of child-bearing age). Romantic opportunities happen in the online world, through social networking sites, online dating services, and through friends who play matchmaker. Romantic opportunities also happen as you get involved in groups, group activities and professional or social organizations.

Finances are good this month and there is prosperity. Until the 23rd, your financial planet is in your spiritual 12th house. Thus the spiritual dimensions of wealth are important. Intuition – inner guidance – is important. On the 23rd, Venus moves into your own sign. This brings financial windfalls and opportunity. Financial opportunities will seek you out. With most of the planets now in the independent Eastern sector and your financial planet in your own sign, prosperity is up to you – it is in your hands. You know best what needs to be done. Shape the financial life (and the other circumstances of your life) according to your specifications. With Venus in your own sign, you tend to spend on yourself, on your body and image. This is a good time for this, as the aesthetic sense is good.

If you need to borrow or negotiate a mortgage, between the 19th and the 24th is a good time.

August

Best Days Overall: 8, 9, 17, 18, 25, 26, 27
Most Stressful Days Overall: 1, 2, 15, 16, 21, 22, 28, 29
Best Days for Love: 3, 8, 9, 13, 19, 21, 22, 25, 26
Best Days for Money: 3, 8, 9, 10, 11, 12, 13, 14, 19, 21, 22, 25, 26, 30, 31
Best Days for Career: 1, 2, 3, 4, 15, 16, 24, 25, 28, 29

Mars is square to Uranus on the 1st and 2nd, which is an extremely dynamic aspect. Take it nice and easy. Avoid arguments, dangerous places or dangerous people. This is not a time for taking risks. This period could bring some kind of health drama, but health is basically good this month, so it is probably nothing serious. Watch the temper at work and with co-workers too. If you employ others, there are probably dramas in the lives of employees.

Your 12th house became very powerful on July 22 and is powerful until the 22nd of this month. It is a spiritual month, a time for getting closer to the Higher Power within you, and for achieving spiritual goals. On the mundane level it is good to be more active in charities or altruistic causes now. The cosmos is pushing you to clear the decks of the past year and start your new year (which begins on your birthday) with a clean slate. Any practice that helps you do this is good. Pay attention to the dream life this month, as dreams will tend to be both prophetic and revelatory. All of you, whether on the spiritual path or not, will have supernatural kinds of experiences this period. Those on the path will recognize them for what they are; those not on the path will pass them off as 'coincidence'.

On the 22nd you enter one of your yearly personal pleasure peaks. Virgos are work horses, so periods of personal pleasure – of pampering – are more beneficial for them than most.

Also on the 22nd the planets move into their maximum Eastern position. So you are in a period of maximum personal independence and power now. Use it to your advantage by channelling this extra energy into building the conditions that you want. You can and should have things your way now; personal happiness and fulfilment are up to you. You have plenty of planetary support for this.

Love becomes more delicate after the 22nd. You and the beloved seem distant with each other. This can be physical distance or psychological distance. The effect is more or less the same. You have opposite perspectives and opinions. Neither is right or wrong. Sometimes you will have to go with your partner's wishes, sometimes he or she will have to give in to you. If you can bridge these differences your relationship can become stronger than before. In astrology, it is the opposites that are the natural marriage partners. Real power comes from the union of opposites. The ancients understood that opposites were merely two sides of the same coin. On the surface they seem to conflict, but in reality they complement each other. Part of the problem is that the current love is focused on his or her interest and you are focused on your interest, and these are divergent. Compromise, compromise, compromise.

September

Best Days Overall: 4, 5, 6, 13, 14, 22, 23
Most Stressful Days Overall: 11, 12, 18, 19, 24, 25, 26
Best Days for Love: 1, 8, 9, 17, 18, 19, 27, 28
Best Days for Money: 1, 7, 8, 9, 10, 17, 18, 19, 27, 28
Best Days for Career: 5, 6, 15, 16, 24, 25, 26

The trend in love is as we mentioned last month, so review our previous discussion. Your challenge is to rise above your differences and see the validity of the beloved's point of view. He or she needs to do the same. Love gets easier after the 22nd. Your challenges are not permanent things.

You are still in one of your yearly personal pleasure peaks – a time for enjoying all the sensual delights, and a time for getting the body and image the way you want it to be. The spiritual planet (the Sun) in the 1st house since August 22 gives great beauty and glamour to the image. Many actors, actresses and models have this position by birth. It gives an unearthly, celestial kind of beauty. I have seen this even in old people. The body is aged, but the person is enfolded in a beautiful aura and when you look at the whole effect, the person is beautiful. This position also sensitizes the body. So, although you are enjoying the carnal pleasures, it's best to avoid alcohol or drugs. Your body can overreact to these things now.

On the 22nd you enter a yearly financial peak. Finances have been good last month, but now they get even better. However, there is much work, much challenge involved here. It is a hectic, active kind of month. You are dealing with many competing interests that pull you in different directions. It's like having a gang of unruly teenagers in the house each wanting to do something different. Your job is to make them all cooperate with each other, make them pull in one direction – easier said than done. In spite of this, you should be richer at the month's end than at the beginning. The 27th and 28th seem like nice paydays. There is luck in speculations then too.

Happily health is good, and you have the energy to deal with all these challenges. It won't hurt, though, to enhance the health in the ways mentioned in the yearly report (page 197).

Mercury moves into a dynamic aspect with Uranus and Pluto from the 15th to the 17th. Take it easy that period. Drive more carefully and avoid dangerous situations or people. Watch the temper and avoid conflict as much as possible. This goes for parents or parent figures as well. A child or child figure in your life should be given extra protection from the 7th to the 11th.

October

Best Days Overall: 2, 3, 11, 12, 19, 20, 29, 30
Most Stressful Days Overall: 8, 9, 15, 16, 22, 23
Best Days for Love: 6, 7, 8, 15, 16, 17, 18, 24, 27, 28
Best Days for Money: 4, 5, 6, 7, 8, 15, 16, 17, 18, 24, 25, 27, 28, 31
Best Days for Career: 6, 7, 15, 16, 22, 23, 24, 25

You remain in a yearly financial peak until the 23rd. Your spiritual planet, the Sun, is in your money house until then, so pay attention to your intuition. This is a period for operating the spiritual laws of wealth, for accessing the supernatural sources of supply rather than the natural ones. To the degree that you succeed in this, there will be true financial freedom. If you feel a sense of lack, increase your giving. Give money to charity or some altruistic cause, and watch how financial doors magically open for you. On the spiritual level the doors open instantly, but you might not see it tangibly right away. Have no fear; it will happen.

Be more patient with the beloved after the 15th. Avoid needless conflict. He or she seems more temperamental that period. Perhaps the beloved is disturbed by financial challenges or conflicts with friends. He or she should be more careful driving between the 15th and the 22nd. Also there is a need to avoid dangerous people or dangerous situations.

You and the beloved have harmony between you; the problems stem from other sources.

There is a Lunar Eclipse on the 18th that occurs in your 8th house of transformation, so take it nice and easy that period. This eclipse can bring encounters with death (generally psychological encounters), surgery or near-death kinds of experiences. There's no need to take on extra risks that period. If an activity is stressful or dangerous, re-schedule it for another time. As with every Lunar Eclipse, friendships get tested. It is not always the relationship that is the problem, but often it's dramas that happen in the lives of friends. Friends should avoid dangerous activities now. Computers, software and hi-tech equipment get tested. These things are more temperamental this period and in many cases they need to be replaced. Since this eclipse impacts on Jupiter, there are family dramas happening as well. Be more patient with family members this period.

Your 3rd house of communication becomes powerful after the 23rd. You will feel this even sooner as Mercury is there all month. This is a month for pursuing your intellectual interests, for taking courses in subjects that interest you, and for gaining or disseminating knowledge. Good communication is not only fun and good in its own right, it seems important financially – especially until the 7th. After that the family and family connections are important financially. You spend more on the home and family, but you earn from here as well. Professional investors might want to look at real estate, restaurants, the food business and hotels for profit opportunities.

November

Best Days Overall: 7, 8, 16, 17, 25, 26, 27
Most Stressful Days Overall: 5, 6, 11, 12, 18, 19
Best Days for Love: 3, 7, 11, 12, 16, 17, 20, 26, 27, 30
Best Days for Money: 1, 3, 4, 7, 11, 12, 16, 17, 21, 22, 26, 27, 28, 29, 30
Best Days for Career: 3, 4, 11, 12, 18, 19, 20, 21, 22, 30

Mars entered your sign on the 15th of last month and will be there all of the month ahead. This has some good points and some less good points. On the positive side, it is great for losing weight (if you need it) and for detox regimes. Mars is the ruler of your 8th house of transformation. He gives energy and courage, the fighting spirit. You are ready to overcome all challenges. You get things done quickly. You are more magnetic and charismatic and the sex appeal is much stronger than usual (which the opposite sex picks up on and sometimes this can be a problem). You excel in athletics and exercise regimes. Whatever your skill level, it is improved these days.

On the downside, courage and the fighting spirit can make for belligerence – and, if you look for a fight you will certainly find one. It can increase the tendency to anger, rush and impatience and this can lead to injuries on the physical plane. When Mars is near the Ascendant we can sound gruff, angry and belligerent even if we don't mean to be. So it will take conscious work to soften your approach to others. You are going to be more active physically, but be more mindful in your actions. Avoid violent people and situations.

There is a Solar Eclipse on the 3rd which occurs in your 3rd house of communication. This eclipse is mild on you as eclipses go, but like every Solar Eclipse it brings spiritual changes – changes in practice, teachers and teachings. Generally this happens as a result of some new insight into things. Sometimes there are scandals and shake-ups in a spiritual organization or charity you're involved with.

Sometimes a drama in the life of your teacher or guru causes the change.

Communication equipment will get tested by this eclipse and might need replacement or upgrading. There are dramas in the lives of siblings or sibling figures, and perhaps shake-ups in your neighbourhood. Students (below college level) change schools or their educational plans. There are prob-ably dramas, shocking events at school. This eclipse impacts on Saturn, your planet of children. Children or children figures should take things easier during this period. Do your best to keep them out of harm's way and out of dangerous situations. They don't need to be taking undue risks now.

Your 3rd house of communication and intellectual inter-ests is still powerful until the 22nd, so review our discussion of this last month.

Career seems in abeyance this month. Mercury, your career planet, is retrograde until the 10th. Most of the plan-ets are still in the lower half of the chart. Your 4th house of home and family was powerful last month and gets even more powerful on the 22nd, so a pause in the career is in the stars. This is a pause that refreshes. The focus should be on the home, the family and the emotional wellbeing. When this is good, the outer career will naturally become good in due course.

Health is delicate after the 22nd. Be sure to rest and relax more and be mindful to maintain high energy levels. Enhance the health in the ways mentioned in the yearly report.

December

Best Days Overall: 4, 5, 13, 14, 23, 24
Most Stressful Days Overall: 2, 3, 8, 9, 15, 16, 17, 30, 31
Best Days for Love: 1, 4, 5, 8, 9, 13, 14, 18, 23, 24, 28
Best Days for Money: 1, 4, 5, 8, 9, 13, 14, 18, 19, 23, 24, 25, 26, 28, 29
Best Days for Career: 1, 10, 11, 15, 16, 17, 21, 22

Last month on the 22nd, the planetary power began to shift from the Eastern sector to the social West. This month, as Mercury moves into Sagittarius, the power in the West is increased. Your period of personal independence is over with (for now). Hopefully, you have used the past six months to create desirable conditions for yourself. Now it is time to live in them. It is more difficult now (though not impossible) to make changes, so it's best to adapt to things as best you can. Make a note of what irks you and when your next period of personal independence comes, you will be able to make changes and adjustments. The planetary power is now flowing away from you and towards others. It is a time to develop and hone your social skills. Personal ability, personal merit, is not that important right now. It is your ability to get on with others, to attain their cooperation and support that matters.

Your 4th house is still powerful until the 24th. The focus is thus on the home and family. Your emotional wellbeing and domestic stability is important. These need to be in some semblance of order if you are to attain your career goals later on.

This is a time for psychological-type breakthroughs. Those of you undergoing therapy should be successful now. With your spiritual planet in your 4th house, mere secular-oriented psychology will not be enough. The spiritual dimension has to be applied here. Past-life regression might be in order. Many family conundrums have their origins in past lives. Generally we have a long karmic history with our families and have incarnated with them in order to adjust things. Seeing this perspective will be a big help. The Horoscope is also saying that your spiritual understanding will help with family issues right now.

Although this is a party time of year, you enter your party period a bit later – on the 21st. Work can take a back seat then. Re-create yourself through leisure and creativity. Virgos of child-bearing age enter another period of enhanced fertility this month.

Love is much improved over previous months. Your love planet is now moving forward again and receiving benevolent aspects. There is more clarity in love as well. A current relationship is much happier. Singles are dating more and attracting happy romantic experiences. There is some temporary stress with the beloved from the 5th to the 8th, but it is soon over with.

Your financial planet is well placed in the sign of Capricorn, so financial judgement is sound. You get value for your money and you manage your money well. It's best to do all your holiday shopping early in the season before the 21st, as your financial planet goes retrograde on that date.

Be careful driving from the 29th to the 31st and avoid dangerous people and situations. In fact, more quiet time at home would be best. Mercury, your ruling planet, makes dynamic aspects to Uranus and Pluto this period.

Libra

☖

Personality Profile

LIBRA AT A GLANCE

Element – Air

Ruling Planet – Venus
  Career Planet – Moon
  Love Planet – Mars
  Money Planet – Pluto
  Planet of Communications – Jupiter
  Planet of Health and Work – Neptune
  Planet of Home and Family Life – Saturn
  Planet of Spirituality and Good Fortune –
    Mercury

Colours – blue, jade green

*Colours that promote love, romance and social
  harmony* – carmine, red, scarlet

Colours that promote earning power –
  burgundy, red–violet, violet

Gems – carnelian, chrysolite, coral, emerald, jade, opal, quartz, white marble

Metal – copper

Scents – almond, rose, vanilla, violet

Quality – cardinal (= activity)

Qualities most needed for balance – a sense of self, self-reliance, independence

Strongest virtues – social grace, charm, tact, diplomacy

Deepest needs – love, romance, social harmony

Characteristic to avoid – violating what is right in order to be socially accepted

Signs of greatest overall compatibility – Gemini, Aquarius

Signs of greatest overall incompatibility – Aries, Cancer, Capricorn

Sign most helpful to career – Cancer

Sign most helpful for emotional support – Capricorn

Sign most helpful financially – Scorpio

Sign best for marriage and/or partnerships – Aries

Sign most helpful for creative projects – Aquarius

Best Sign to have fun with – Aquarius

Signs most helpful in spiritual matters – Gemini, Virgo

Best day of the week – Friday

Understanding a Libra

In the sign of Libra the universal mind – the soul – expresses its genius for relationships, that is, its power to harmonize diverse elements in a unified, organic way. Libra is the soul's power to express beauty in all of its forms. And where is beauty if not within relationships? Beauty does not exist in isolation. Beauty arises out of comparison – out of the just relationship between different parts. Without a fair and harmonious relationship there is no beauty, whether it is in art, manners, ideas or the social or political forum.

There are two faculties humans have that exalt them above the animal kingdom: their rational faculty (expressed in the signs of Gemini and Aquarius) and their aesthetic faculty, exemplified by Libra. Without an aesthetic sense we would be little more than intelligent barbarians. Libra is the civilizing instinct or urge of the soul.

Beauty is the essence of what Librans are all about. They are here to beautify the world. One could discuss Librans' social grace, their sense of balance and fair play, their ability to see and love another person's point of view – but this would be to miss their central asset: their desire for beauty.

No one – no matter how alone he or she seems to be – exists in isolation. The universe is one vast collaboration of beings. Librans, more than most, understand this and understand the spiritual laws that make relationships bearable and enjoyable.

A Libra is always the unconscious (and in some cases conscious) civilizer, harmonizer and artist. This is a Libra's deepest urge and greatest genius. Librans love instinctively to bring people together, and they are uniquely qualified to do so. They have a knack for seeing what unites people – the things that attract and bind rather than separate individuals.

Finance

In financial matters Librans can seem frivolous and illogical to others. This is because Librans appear to be more concerned with earning money for others than for themselves. But there is a logic to this financial attitude. Librans know that everything and everyone is connected and that it is impossible to help another to prosper without also prospering yourself. Since enhancing their partner's income and position tends to strengthen their relationship, Librans choose to do so. What could be more fun than building a relationship? You will rarely find a Libra enriching him- or herself at someone else's expense.

Scorpio is the ruler of Libra's solar 2nd house of money, giving Libra unusual insight into financial matters – and the power to focus on these matters in a way that disguises a seeming indifference. In fact, many other signs come to Librans for financial advice and guidance.

Given their social grace, Librans often spend great sums of money on entertaining and organizing social events. They also like to help others when they are in need. Librans would go out of their way to help a friend in dire straits, even if they have to borrow from others to do so. However, Librans are also very careful to pay back any debts they owe, and like to make sure they never have to be reminded to do so.

Career and Public Image

Publicly, Librans like to appear as nurturers. Their friends and acquaintances are their family and they wield political power in parental ways. They also like bosses who are paternal or maternal.

The sign of Cancer is on Libra's 10th house (of career) cusp; the Moon is Libra's career planet. The Moon is by far the speediest, most changeable planet in the horoscope. It alone among all the planets travels through the entire zodiac – all 12 signs and houses – every month. This is an important key to the way in which Librans approach their careers, and also to what they need to do to maximize their career potential. The Moon is the planet of moods and feelings – Librans need a career in which their emotions can have free expression. This is why so many Librans are involved in the creative arts. Libra's ambitions wax and wane with the Moon. They tend to wield power according to their mood.

The Moon 'rules' the masses – and that is why Libra's highest goal is to achieve a mass kind of acclaim and popularity. Librans who achieve fame cultivate the public as other people cultivate a lover or friend. Librans can be very flexible – and often fickle – in their career and ambitions. On the other hand, they can achieve their ends in a great variety of ways. They are not stuck in one attitude or with one way of doing things.

Love and Relationships

Librans express their true genius in love. In love you could not find a partner more romantic, more seductive or more fair. If there is one thing that is sure to destroy a relationship – sure to block your love from flowing – it is injustice or imbalance between lover and beloved. If one party is giving too much or taking too much, resentment is sure to surface at some time or other. Librans are careful about this. If anything, Librans might err on the side of giving more, but never giving less.

If you are in love with a Libra, make sure you keep the aura of romance alive. Do all the little things – candle-lit dinners, travel to exotic locales, flowers and small gifts. Give things that are beautiful, not necessarily expensive. Send cards. Ring regularly even if you have nothing in particular to say. The niceties are very important to a Libra. Your relationship is a work of art: make it beautiful and your Libran lover will appreciate it. If you are creative about it, he or she will appreciate it even more; for this is how your Libra will behave towards you.

Librans like their partners to be aggressive and even a bit self-willed. They know that these are qualities they sometimes lack and so they like their partners to have them. In relationships, however, Librans can be very aggressive – but always in a subtle and charming way! Librans are determined in their efforts to charm the object of their desire – and this determination can be very pleasant if you are on the receiving end.

Home and Domestic Life

Since Librans are such social creatures, they do not particularly like mundane domestic duties. They like a well-organized home – clean and neat with everything needful present – but housework is a chore and a burden, one of the unpleasant tasks in life that must be done, the quicker the better. If a Libra has enough money – and sometimes even if not – he or she will prefer to pay someone else to take care of the daily household chores. However, Librans like gardening; they love to have flowers and plants in the home.

A Libra's home is modern, and furnished in excellent taste. You will find many paintings and sculptures there. Since Librans like to be with friends and family, they enjoy entertaining at home and they make great hosts.

Capricorn is on the cusp of Libra's 4th solar house of home and family. Saturn, the planet of law, order, limits and discipline, rules Libra's domestic affairs. If Librans want their home life to be supportive and happy they need to develop some of the virtues of Saturn – order, organization and discipline. Librans, being so creative and so intensely in need of harmony, can tend to be too lax in the home and too permissive with their children. Too much of this is not always good; children need freedom but they also need limits.

Horoscope for 2013

Major Trends

The raw ore probably doesn't enjoy the smelting process too much. The heat is beyond all endurance. Yet, the final product is a pure metal. Everyone with high aspirations goes through crucible-type years, and the higher the aspiration, the more intense the crucible will be. The past two years were like that. Perhaps you thought that you were being pushed over the limit, but this was not the case. The Higher Power and his agents, the planetary forces, are intelligent. Every ordeal is carefully measured. Just enough heat is applied to do the job and not an iota more. These ordeals were not punishments as you may have thought, nor bad luck. These were actually the answers to prayer. You wanted certain high things and in order to have them in a proper way these testings were necessary. Certain psychological impurities had to be melted away. Only the crucible experience can bring this about. You see this now, but at the time it wasn't that apparent.

Happily you got through the worst of it. 2011 was the most difficult part; 2012 less so. There are still challenges in 2013, but nothing like you've already been through.

In March 2011 Uranus entered your 7th house of love. Existing relationships were severely tested and many did not make it. Uranus will be here in 2013 and for another five years or so. Love is highly unstable. The whole social sphere is being dramatically changed. More details later.

Neptune, the most spiritual of all the planets, entered your 6th house of health in 2012. This is a positive development. You need to be focused more on health these days. But also it shows that you are exploring the abundant spiritual resources of health and energy. You are being shown how to tap into them and solve many problems. There's more on this later.

You begin your year with Jupiter in your 9th house, which indicates much foreign travel. This is also a nice transit for college or postgraduate students: it shows success. Later on in the year in June, Jupiter will cross your Mid-heaven and enter your 10th house of career. So the career is going to blossom this year, each according to their stage in life. Details to follow.

Your most important areas of interest this year are finance; home and family; health and work; love and romance; religion, metaphysics, higher learning and foreign travel (until June 27); career (from June 27 onwards).

Your paths of greatest fulfilment in the year ahead are finance; religion, metaphysics, higher learning and foreign travel (until June 27); career (from June 27 onwards).

Health

(Please note that this is an astrological perspective on health and not a medical one. In days of yore there was no difference, these perspectives were identical. But now there could be quite a difference. For a medical perspective, please consult your doctor or health practitioner.)

Health is much improved over the past two years, but still needs watching. You begin the year with two powerful long-term planets in stressful alignment. On June 27, Jupiter will move into stressful alignment with you as well. So health is still delicate. Happily, your 6th house of health will be strong – Neptune, as we mentioned, is there all year. So you are watchful, alert and on the case. You are paying attention, which is exactly what needs to be done now.

Stressful health aspects don't necessarily mean sickness. It only means that more focus and attention needs to be given. You can't just take health for granted these days. If you pay attention and watch your energy levels, you will get through with little bother.

There is much you can do to enhance the health and prevent problems from developing. Give more attention to the vulnerable areas in the year ahead. These are the heart (avoid worry or anxiety and enjoy your life); the feet (foot reflexology and foot massage are always powerful therapies

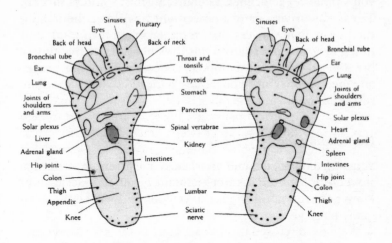

Reflexology

Try to massage the whole foot on a regular basis, but pay extra attention to the points highlighted on the chart. When you massage, be aware of 'sore spots', as these need special attention. It's also a good idea to massage the ankles and top side of the feet.

for you, and be sure to keep the feet warm in the winter; regular visits to a podiatrist might also be good); and the kidneys and hips (these areas are always important for you as well, and the hips should be regularly massaged).

As important as these organs are, the most important thing is to maintain high energy levels. Avoid burning the candle at both ends. Learn to pace yourself better and rest when tired. Work in a rhythm and alternate activities. Different activities use different faculties and different muscles and when you alternate, you give some of the faculties a rest. Delegate tasks as much as possible and plan your day so that more gets done with less effort.

As we mentioned, the most important health development is Neptune's move into your 6th house. This shows the spiritual dimensions of healing. This is a huge subject and you should read as much as you can on it. Spiritual healing is really about accessing a power which is above the mind – the power that 'powers' the mind, enabling it to think and function. There are rules to this. It is not just positive thinking and positive affirmation. It is accessed through prayer and meditation. Once you get the hang of it, your life will be revolutionized.

Home and Family

Your 4th house of home and family has been powerful for some years now and is not something you can just ignore. Pluto has been in this house since 2008 and will be there for many more years.

We have discussed this in past years but it is worth repeating, as this is a long-term trend. The whole family situation is going through a cosmic detox. This is happening on the deepest levels. Old patterns are being eliminated. Unhealthy kinds of relationships, co-dependency, bondages within the family are going. These things are seldom pleasant while they're happening. Ask anyone who has had a colonic or colonoscopy what it feels like when the colon is being discharged. What comes out is often very shocking. Was all that 'gook' in me! I can't believe it! Yes, there is a lot of repressed material in the family situation, and in order for healing to happen, for a positive family pattern to manifest, these things have to go.

Because of the human condition – the state of fallen humanity – family dysfunction seems more or less the norm. It is rare to have a truly functional family – those who have it should thank their lucky stars. Yet, everyone deserves this. And so, the cosmos, at certain times, comes into play and starts to clean up the situation.

There are many scenarios as to how this detox happens; the specifics can vary from person to person. Sometimes there is an actual death in the family and this changes the whole pattern. Sometimes the family unit breaks up and then regroups again on a better level. Sometimes family members have near-death kinds of experiences, and these change patterns. The chances are that over the course of the Pluto transit (which lasts about 15 years) all of these things will happen.

A person doesn't know that he needs healing until confronted with the illness. In the same way, Pluto first brings up the toxic pattern, makes it conscious, and then eliminates it. The family situation will be resurrected, but death comes before resurrection.

What we say about the family situation also applies to the personal emotional life. Major detoxing is going on. It's best to cooperate with the process rather than resist it – it will go much easier. By bringing up repressed emotional material, Pluto will show you why you are in the condition you are in. People often wonder why something is happening, but when the repressed material is seen, the answer is obvious. Subconsciously we have been creating the pain and negative experience. It is wonderful (though not always pleasant) that these hidden causes, these emotional creations, get flushed to the surface and cleared out.

On the mundane level, you are spending more on the home this year, investing in it and probably renovating, but you can also earn money from the home.

Finance and Career

This will be an important area of life for the next two years. Saturn moved into your money house in October 2012. This indicates a period of financial consolidation – not a time for expanding earnings as for managing the earnings that you do have. Right management will do more for your bottom line than just expansion. Experienced business people know that unbridled expansion is not a healthy thing. It sounds nice, but in actual practice it leads to all kinds of abuses and impurities. As with all the areas of life, a healthy financial life is a living, breathing thing. There are times when we are in the 'in breath', expanding earnings and markets, and there are times when we are in the 'out breath', consolidating, re-organizing and shifting things around in a healthier way. The consolidation periods are just as important as the expansion periods, and if done properly, the next expansion (and it will come) will be much healthier and larger than the previous one.

This is a time for gaining control and mastery over the financial life. You were meant to be the master of money, not its slave. Yet, few people are. Saturn, will help you here.

Finances probably feel tight right now. There are probably extra financial burdens and responsibilities on you now, and assets you own might be going down in value. However, if you re-organize, eliminate wasteful expenditure, and shift things around a little here or there, you will find that you have all the resources that you need.

Saturn is putting cosmic order in your financial life. A right order. His intent is to educate, not punish. But sometimes people don't learn except through drama – and if this is the case, dramas will be provided. His intention is to bestow long-term, enduring wealth upon you. So he will teach you important financial principles now – how to attain wealth over the long haul, systematically and methodically, step by step. Though you are lucky in speculations the first half of the year, this is not an aspect for winning lotteries. These kinds of winnings are short-term things. Saturn is interested in the long term.

This is a period for starting systematic, orderly and regular savings and investment plans. A certain percentage of income should go to saving or investment. If there are redundancies in your financial life – multiple bank accounts, etc. – now is the time to get rid of the excess. Slim down and consolidate. Perhaps you have separate cable, mobile and land line bills. There are plans that consolidate all these into one, and for less. Learn to create a good budget – something that allows for both needful things and fun things. Budgeting gives you some control over spending.

If you cooperate with Saturn there will be prosperity this year. Family and family connections seem important financially. The family – and especially a parent figure – seems supportive. You are spending more on the family, but you can also earn from the home and family too. There is good fortune in buying or selling a home. Real estate, food, hotels and industries that cater to the home all seem like good investments this year.

Uranus will be in pretty exact square aspect with your financial planet Pluto for a few months this year, so there are major, dramatic financial changes happening. In the end they will be good.

Career is slow during the first half of the year – you are getting prepared. On June 27, Jupiter crosses your Mid-heaven and enters your 10th house of career – a classic signal of career success. Generally this indicates promotion and pay rises. Often it indicates honours and recognition. Always it brings happy and lucrative career opportunities. However, this may not translate to the bottom line right away; it looks like it will take time. You will have the honour and prestige, but the money will come later on down the road.

Love and Social Life

As we mentioned, ever since Uranus moved into your 7th house in 2011, the love and social life has been unstable. Existing relationships were and are being severely tested. Many have not made it. Singles most likely found love in 2011 as Jupiter moved through this house, but it doesn't seem stable or lasting. In fact, the whole social circle is undergoing radical, revolutionary change this year, and for the next few years – a long-term trend.

Good relationships – relationships where love is true and which are fundamentally sound – will probably survive all this; they always do. Even so, it won't be easy and you and your partner will be stretched to the limit.

For singles the love life has been very exciting. With Uranus, the unexpected is the norm. Love can happen anywhere, at any time, with no advance warning. You can be innocently taking out the rubbish and there on the way is

Mr or Miss Right. (Best to maintain a good appearance at all times – you never know when love will arrive.)

Though you will date and have fun, marriage is not advisable these days. You have the aspects for serial love affairs, not for long-term committed relationships. If you see Uranus in the 7th house in a birth chart, the tendency is to multiple marriages or to no marriages – and the reasons for both are the same. The person needs change, variety. The person needs to experiment in love. One partner is often not enough for this. So they either have serial love affairs or serial marriages.

If you talk to a Libra (or someone very strong in the 7th House) they will say: 'Relationships are the most important thing in life. You can only learn about yourself in relationships. It is the road to self knowledge.' There is some truth to this – we do learn about ourselves in relationships – but it is not the only road to self knowledge. Talk to a Pisces or a Scorpio and you'll get a different perspective on things. This experimentation in love is really a journey into self-knowledge these days. You are throwing out all the rule books about love and learning what works for you personally. Much new knowledge will be gained this way, but you can also expect a few explosions.

Your tastes in love are unconventional these days. Older people might gravitate to the very young and vice versa. You want something 'different'. Often with this aspect people have romances with people of different religions, nationalities or races. You gravitate to unconventional people as well – genius types: the inventor, the mathematician, the media person, the computer whiz, the astronomer or astrologer – people outside the norm.

If you want to win the heart of Libra these days, do the unconventional.

Self-improvement

Jupiter in your 9th house until June 27 is, as we mentioned, a wonderful aspect for students. There is success and good fortune in their studies. Those applying to colleges or universities have good fortune. It is also good for anyone who wants to further their education. This transit shows an enlargement of knowledge and of the mental horizons. Happy educational opportunities will come and they should be taken.

When Jupiter enters your 10th house on June 27, the career will expand almost on its own. Of course you do the normal things – slacking is not an option – but assuming you are doing your job, success will just happen. Your abilities will be recognized by those in authority.

It is in the financial realm where real effort and struggle is happening. You're going to have to work harder and go the extra mile to achieve your financial goals. Mere physical work by itself will not do the trick; you need to do mental and spiritual work here.

This is a good year to make a master financial plan. Set it down on paper. List your financial goals. How much do you want to earn over the next few years? Regardless of your age, with Saturn in the money house it is good to think financially about your later years – how much do you want or need? How do you plan on getting there? How much needs to be saved or invested per month to get you to your goals? Then set about doing it on the physical level. If doing anything seems impossible, look at your list and imagine that you have already attained it. This is a form of meditation. The visualizing sets the spiritual law into motion. As you practice the visualization for a while (and never deny what you are visualizing) the ways and means will manifest themselves. Ideas will come to you. Though it is difficult to predict exact timings, it will happen in due course. Patience, persistence and discipline are needed.

If debts plague you, visualize them as paid. Don't try to evade them, especially if they are legitimate and especially with Saturn in your money house – just see them in your mind's eye as paid. Eventually they will be, often in miraculous kinds of ways.

Month-by-month Forecasts

January

Best Days Overall: 4, 5, 12, 13, 21, 22, 23, 31
Most Stressful Days Overall: 10, 11, 17, 18, 24, 25
Best Days for Love: 4, 5, 8, 9, 12, 13, 17, 18, 19, 22, 23, 29, 30, 31
Best Days for Money: 2, 3, 4, 6, 7, 10, 11, 12, 19, 20, 22, 29, 30, 31
Best Days for Career: 2, 3, 10, 11, 21, 24, 25, 31

You begin the year with between 70 and 80 per cent of the planets below the horizon. Your 4th house of home and family is jam packed with planets, while your 10th house of career is empty (only the Moon moves through here on the 24th and 25th). This is a very clear message. Career matters can be let go of. Keep the focus on the home, family and emotional life. This is a time to set up the interior infrastructure for future success. Career is going to be very powerful in six months' time, but now is the time to get emotionally ready for this success. If you are not ready emotionally, the success will be fleeting.

With the 4th house strong you have more 'psychic' energy available to you. Physically, this is not your best period, and you need to rest and relax more until the 19th. But psychically, emotionally, you are very strong now. Your moods are more intense than usual, and it's very important to keep them positive and constructive. You can use this enhanced psychic energy to your advantage this month. In a quiet mood, picture yourself at your highest point of success. Get into the feeling of this (and it will be easier to do this period). Live in this feeling as long as possible. This will actually create future tangible success later on. You might not see it immediately on the physical level, but you will see it eventually, if you persist.

You are in a personal waxing solar cycle this month. Also on a universal level, since December 21, the Sun is in its waxing yearly phase. Thus you are in an excellent period for starting new projects or launching new products into the world. The planetary momentum is very much forward as well, further increasing the favourability. The 11th to the 27th (as the Moon is also waxing) is the best time for starting things this month.

Last month, on the 21st, the planets shifted from the Eastern to the Western sector of your chart. This is actually your best sector. It is the sector of other people, of relationships – and Libra more than any other sign understands the importance of the 'likeability' factor in life. You get the opportunity to exercise your social genius even more and to develop it further.

This is not your best financial year. As we mentioned, there is a lot of re-organization happening. But this month you are in one of your best financial periods. Your financial planet gets much positive stimulation. Earnings should increase. There is support from the family and family connections. There are opportunities to earn money from home, and there is a nice payday from the 15th to the 18th.

Libras of child-bearing age are more fertile this month and next month. Enhance the health in the ways described in the yearly report.

February

Best Days Overall: 1, 9, 10, 18, 19, 27, 28
Most Stressful Days Overall: 7, 8, 13, 14, 20, 21, 22
Best Days for Love: 1, 9, 10, 11, 12, 13, 14, 18, 19, 20, 21, 22
Best Days for Money: 2, 3, 7, 8, 9, 15, 16, 18, 25, 26, 27
Best Days for Career: 1, 9, 10, 20, 21, 22

The aspects for starting new projects or ventures or for launching new products are even better this month than last month. The solar cycles, both personal and universal, are waxing. The planetary momentum is even more forward than last month – ALL the planets are moving forward. Thus, if you are planning these things, this is the time. The 10th to the 18th is the best period in the coming month.

Last month on the 19th, your 5th house of fun, creativity and children became powerful. This is a time to explore the rapture side of life; a time to create and build up your forces for later on. Personal fertility is at the maximum for the year right now.

This is not a year for speculations. Some years are like that. But this month, until the 18th, is one of the best periods in the year for this. You seem luckier. You are also more involved with children this period, either your own or others'. You get on with them better. They gravitate to you more. Those of you in the creative arts (and many Librans are) have enhanced creativity now. The creative juices are stronger than usual.

Love wasn't serious last month, nor does it seem serious this month. However, you don't seem to mind and you seem active in that department. On the 2nd your love planet, Mars, enters your 6th house. This indicates opportunities for the office romance. There are also romantic opportunities with health professionals in general, or with those who are involved with your health. The 3rd to the 5th seems especially strong for this. Singles are likely to meet someone they consider their 'ideal' during this period. But of course one must look deeper: he or she could also be your biggest illusion. Love is spiritual this month – idealistic and very tender. There is a great desire to serve the beloved. He or she will certainly appreciate this. Spiritual milieus are also scenes for romance or romantic meetings.

On the 18th, your 6th house of health becomes powerful, and so you are more focused here. This is a wonderful thing. Health is much better than in 2011 or 2012, but still pays watching. Spiritual healing has become very important ever since Neptune moved into your 6th house last year, but this month it is even more important. Mercury, your spiritual planet, also moves into this house on the 5th and stays there for the rest of the month. Apply the spiritual techniques you have learned now and you will get good results.

Finances will be better, easier, after the 18th. There are wonderful job opportunities out there for job seekers this period. Those who employ others seem to attract good quality employees as well.

March

Best Days Overall: 1, 8, 9, 17, 18, 19, 27, 28
Most Stressful Days Overall: 6, 7, 12, 13, 14, 20, 21
Best Days for Love: 2, 3, 10, 11, 12, 13, 14, 21, 22, 31
Best Days for Money: 1, 2, 3, 6, 7, 8, 9, 15, 16, 17, 18, 24, 25, 27, 28, 29, 30
Best Days for Career: 2, 3, 10, 11, 20, 21, 22, 31

Saturn, your family planet, went retrograde on the 18th of last month and will be retrograde for many more months. Now is the time to review your home and family situation with a view to making improvements. Important decisions in these matters should be delayed now. Wait for mental clarity to happen first. Things are not the way they seem. Take your time here.

In a way it is good that your family planet is retrograde now, for on the 20th the planets will begin to shift from the lower half to the upper half of the Horoscope. The shift will be more complete next month, but you are feeling it now. It's time to let go of family issues and focus on the career and the outer goals. Dawn is breaking in your year. It's time to be up and about; time to make those dreams manifest through personal effort.

You still have excellent aspects for starting new projects. After this month, the aspects become less favourable, so, if you haven't yet started your new project, now is the time. The period from the 11th to the 27th is best.

On the 20th you enter a yearly love and social peak. You are in the Elysian Fields for a Libran – the place of ultimate joy. It is a very active social month. There is someone you seem to be pursuing. Perhaps you haven't caught him or her yet, but it seems that you will. The only problem is the continued instability in the love life. Even when you make the catch, how long will it last? It doesn't seem to matter much to you at the moment. It's the adrenalin rush of the conquest that is enjoyable.

Libras of child-bearing age enter another period of fertility after the 20th. This will be the maximum for the year ahead.

Health needs more watching after the 20th, when 50 and sometimes 60 per cent of the planets are in stressful alignment. Be sure to rest and relax more and maintain high energy levels. Spend more time in a health spa and get massages and the other treatments they offer. And, of course, enhance your health in the ways mentioned in the yearly report. Especially try to relax more on the 20th and 21st.

Finances become more stressful after the 20th. You just have to work harder to attain your financial goals. Meditation on the affluence of God will be powerful and will alleviate much of the stress.

Mars is conjunct to Uranus from the 18th to the 21st. You and your spouse, partner or current love need to avoid risky kinds of activity. Avoid losing your temper, avoid confrontations and drive more carefully.

April

Best Days Overall: 4, 5, 14, 15, 23, 24
Most Stressful Days Overall: 2, 3, 9, 10, 16, 17, 29, 30
Best Days for Love: 1, 9, 10, 21, 22, 29, 30
Best Days for Money: 2, 3, 4, 5, 11, 12, 14, 15, 21, 22, 23, 24, 25, 26, 29, 30
Best Days for Career: 1, 9, 10, 16, 17, 21, 29, 30

Finances are still stressful, but who cares? As long as love is going well, Libra is happy. This is what life is all about. As long as Libra is in the 'feeling' of love, everything else will work out. You are still in a yearly love and social peak until the 19th. Romance is happening for singles – the 14th to the 20th seems especially good. Even children of an appropriate age seem romantically involved now. Love has been exciting for some years now, but this month even more so. Romance can happen anywhere at any time, in the most unexpected places or situations. The only problem in love is the stability of these things. Lightning flashes light up a dark sky, but they fade out very quickly. You have many lightning flashes these days, and seem content to wait for the next one when one dies out. Librans are much more popular than usual this period. You are really going out of your way for others (and especially the beloved) and this is appreciated – if not outwardly, it is inwardly.

Finances will improve after the 19th. In fact, this period – from the 19th onwards – is one of your most prosperous periods this year. (Your yearly financial peak will happen in October–November, but now is almost as good.) You are making very dramatic financial changes these days and this brings feelings of insecurity. A Lunar Eclipse on the 25th in your money house reinforces what we are saying here. Yes, there are financial bumps, but the end result is prosperity. The Lunar Eclipse also shows career changes happening.

Health needs more watching until the 19th. Like last month, many short-term planets are in stressful alignment with you. Your overall energy is not up to its usual standards and thus there is greater vulnerability to problems. Review our discussion of last month. Health and vitality will improve dramatically after the 19th, and if you've been having health problems you should hear good news after this date. Librans of the appropriate age are still fertile until the 19th.

Your family planet Saturn is still retrograde and most of the planets are still above the horizon. So continue to focus on your career and outer objectives. The New Moon of the 10th brings career opportunities though friends or the current love. It's good to further your career goals by social means that day. A conflict with a family member from the 20th to the 23rd is short lived – don't make long-term judgements based on this.

Your 8th house of transformation becomes powerful after the 19th, initiating a sexually active period, regardless of your age and stage in life. The beloved enters a yearly financial peak and will be more generous with you. It is easier to borrow if you need to.

May

Best Days Overall: 2, 3, 11, 12, 21, 22, 29, 30
Most Stressful Days Overall: 6, 7, 13, 14, 15, 27, 28
Best Days for Love: 6, 7, 8, 9, 10, 11, 18, 19, 21, 22, 27, 28, 29, 30
Best Days for Money: 2, 3, 8, 9, 11, 12, 18, 19, 21, 22, 23, 24, 27, 28, 29, 30
Best Days for Career: 8, 9, 10, 13, 14, 15, 19, 20, 29

Two eclipses this month are going to shatter many obstacles and obstructions on your career path. While they happen the events are not usually pleasant, but the end result will be good. Some obstructions need dramatic medicine and these are supplied by the eclipses. The stage is being set this month for career success – the next act of the play will begin next month.

The Solar Eclipse of May 10 occurs in your 8th house, so do reduce your schedule and avoid unnecessary risk-taking or stress. This kind of eclipse brings encounters (generally psychological) with death. Sometimes it brings near-death kinds of experiences or surgery. There is a need to understand death and to overcome one's fear of it. When this happens, we will live better and more fully. This eclipse brings dramatic events to the lives of friends. They too can have some encounters with death, and they too should take life a bit easier. Children or children figures in the life, of appropriate age, have their relationships or marriages tested. Computers and electronic equipment are more temperamental now. Sometimes they need replacement. It would be good to invest in better anti-virus or anti-hacking software.

The Lunar Eclipse of the 25th is basically benign to you, but it won't hurt to take an easier kind of schedule. This eclipse impacts strongly on Neptune, your planet of health and work. Thus there are job changes, career changes, shake-ups in your company or industry, and dramas in the lives of bosses, parents or parent figures. Stay calm through all this – your career is going to be great. This is just stage setting. This eclipse occurs in your 3rd house of communication, so drive more carefully this period. Cars and communication equipment will get tested. If there are flaws, now is the time that you find out about them so that you can make corrections. Important changes are happening in the health regime and diet as well.

Finances are still good (in relative terms) this period. There are still many changes, many challenges and much reorganization going on. The feeling of insecurity is still there. From the metaphysical perspective, this is your main challenge – to develop more faith, to cultivate the feeling of security. Meditation will be a big help here.

Health is reasonable this month. But keep in mind that two powerful long-term planets are still in stressful alignment. Happily the short-term planets are leaving you alone early on in the month and making good aspects after the 20th.

Venus travels with Saturn from the 27th to the 29th – a very happy aspect for you. You could be getting a new car or communication equipment. There is travel this period, either foreign or domestic, and this also seems happy. It also brings a nice payday and luck in speculations.

June

Best Days Overall: 7, 8, 17, 18, 25, 26
Most Stressful Days Overall: 2, 3, 10, 11, 23, 24, 30
Best Days for Love: 2, 3, 7, 8, 10, 17, 18, 19, 20, 25, 26, 27, 28, 30
Best Days for Money: 5, 6, 8, 9, 15, 16, 17, 18, 19, 20, 23, 24, 26, 27
Best Days for Career: 7, 8, 10, 11, 17, 18, 27

Your 9th house became powerful on May 20 and is still powerful until June 21. The 9th House is considered the most fortunate of all the houses by the Hindu astrologers. Here in the west we consider it fortunate, but not necessarily the most fortunate. Power in the 9th house brings travel and travel opportunities, and also happy opportunities for higher education. It's a very nice aspect for students at the college level, or who are applying for college. There is good news on that front. It is also fortunate for legal matters. When this house is powerful our 'Higher' mind is activated. We are more in touch with it consciously or subconsciously. Thus it is time for religious and philosophical breakthroughs – many 'aha' moments will happen this month. The mental horizons expand, and when this happens, the whole life expands.

When the 9th house is powerful we want more meaning in life. People become more interested in a good juicy theological discussion than a night out on the town. The advent of a visiting guru or minister is often more exciting than that of a rock star. We discover the great pleasures in the mind under a powerful 9th house transit. In fact, you have been experiencing these things all year, but this month (and last month) more so than ever.

On the 21st many important things happen. First, you enter a yearly career peak. The planets are at the 'highest', most elevated position in your Horoscope. There is much career progress happening and many happy opportunities. New jobs or job offers are coming. On the 27th Jupiter crosses the Mid-heaven and enters your 10th house of career. This adds to the success. It brings rises, promotions, honours and recognition and initiates a year-long cycle of career success and elevation. So focus on the career now.

In the short term, all this success doesn't seem to help the finances – perhaps it even puts more stress on them. Sometimes career elevation requires outlays of money, for clothing, for new equipment, for memberships in the appropriate organizations. The home might need upgrading too. Make all the investments necessary though it might be stressful. If you shift things around, you will find that you have the resources you need. A move could be happening now, or in the coming months.

Health needs more watching after the 21st. Do your best to maintain high energy levels and enhance the health in the ways mentioned in the yearly report.

July

Best Days Overall: 4, 5, 6, 14, 15, 23, 24
Most Stressful Days Overall: 1, 7, 8, 21, 22, 27, 28
Best Days for Love: 1, 5, 6, 10, 11, 16, 17, 19, 20, 25, 26, 27, 28, 29, 30
Best Days for Money: 2, 3, 7, 8, 12, 13, 16, 17, 21, 22, 25, 29, 30
Best Days for Career: 7, 8, 17, 18, 27

Like last month, career is the major headline. Your 10th house is easily the strongest in the Horoscope all month. Push forward boldly to your goals. Shoot for the moon. Lady Luck is with you and you are catching the breaks. Students are also doing well this month, attaining their goals.

Last month on the 21st the Water element became very strong. You experienced this in February and March as well. While this will produce a comfortable 'era of good feeling' –

we have a Grand Trine in the water signs – it also makes everyone more sensitive and easily hurt, so be mindful about this. Another issue (and this is a bit more difficult to handle) is that rationality and logic are out. Only the feeling of the moment matters. Everyone goes with their feelings. This isn't so easy for an Air sign such as yourself to handle. But don't get too swept up in all this; now is the time when rationality is most needed.

A parent or parent figure is prospering these days. He or she lacked direction for quite a few months, but that is changing now as your family planet starts to move forward on the 8th. He or she is having spiritual kinds of breakthroughs now and this is helping. You seem in conflict with this parent figure but it is short term and passes after the 23rd.

Your spouse, partner or current love also seems successful this period, especially after the 18th. Last month you were calling the shots in love, but now it seems to be the beloved's turn. Love is more delicate this month. There is more instability than usual after the 18th. The good news is that you are making love a great priority – almost like your career – and this can help keep things together. Your spouse, partner or current love seems active in your own career, helping and supporting you.

Singles find love opportunities in religious or educational settings until the 18th, and perhaps in foreign countries or with foreigners. After the 18th singles find romance as they pursue their normal career goals and with people who are involved in their career. There are romantic opportunities with bosses and superiors. In general there is much socializing with high and important people. The career seems the centre of your social life, and you are working to integrate your social life with your career.

Your love planet travels with Jupiter from the 18th onwards, and the conjunction is especially exact from the 19th to the 24th. This is an especially happy romantic period. Singles will meet a special someone. Those in a relationship will have more romance within it, and the spouse, partner or current love prospers that period.

Moves or renovations of the home could still happen this month. It might be necessary because of your new career position.

Like last month, health is delicate until the 22nd. The problem is that you're so busy you find it difficult to slow down, even though you need it. However, you'll discover that if you push yourself when you are tired, you don't really accomplish more – you just tend to make mistakes. Rest when tired and then go back to your work.

August

Best Days Overall: 1, 2, 10, 11, 12, 19, 20, 28, 29
Most Stressful Days Overall: 3, 4, 17, 18, 23, 24, 30, 31
Best Days for Love: 3, 4, 8, 9, 13, 14, 19, 22, 23, 24, 25, 26
Best Days for Money: 3, 8, 13, 14, 17, 21, 22, 25, 26, 30, 31
Best Days for Career: 3, 4, 6, 7, 15, 16, 25, 30, 31

Like the last two months, the element of Water is still strong. Good feeling is wonderful, but there is still a need for rationality. You and the other Air signs are the ones to supply it these days.

In spite of your success, finances still seem stressed. However, they will get easier from the 22nd onwards. I won't say they'll be great, but they will improve. It is still good to focus on the career and boost your professional status. The financial increase from this will happen down the road, not right away. Your financial planet has been retrograde since April and will be retrograde for the rest of the month. In finance, the most important thing is mental clarity. This is what you need to work for. Do your homework and get the facts. Clarity will come eventually and then it will be safer to make important moves. In the meantime it is good to manage what you have in a better way.

On June 21 the planetary power made an important shift from the Western, social sector, to the Eastern sector of the self. You are basically comfortable when the planets are in the West – gaining the good graces of others is your strong point. You handle this better than most. But now you have a more difficult lesson. The planetary power is flowing towards you. Your happiness, your success is up to you now. Your personal merit, your personal abilities, rather than who you know, are what are important now. It's time to develop some independence and act from what you think is right, to create conditions according to your personal specifications.

You have been in a spiritual period ever since July 23 when Venus entered your 12th house. This month the spirituality gets even stronger as the Sun and Mercury enter this house too. This is a time to achieve spiritual-type goals, to focus more on your spiritual practice, to get more involved in charity and altruistic causes, and to clear the inner blockages to the flow of the Higher Power. Librans are basically party people, but now you feel a need for more solitude. There's nothing wrong with you – it's just natural when the 12th house of spirituality is strong. Spiritual activities are always solitary experiences. You can be in a group or attending a prayer service or meditation seminar, but the inner experience will always be something personal to you. The growth that happens now will be interior, but still very powerful.

You have been very much in the world for the past few months, very focused on your outer life, and this was good. But now it's time to collect yourself, to feel your own aura, and receive guidance and inspiration from above.

Health is much improved this month, but still needs watching. Review our discussion of last month and enhance the health in the ways mentioned in the yearly report.

September

Best Days Overall: 7, 8, 15, 16, 24, 25, 26
Most Stressful Days Overall: 1, 13, 14, 20, 21, 27, 28
Best Days for Love: 2, 3, 8, 11, 12, 17, 18, 20, 21, 27, 28, 29, 30
Best Days for Money: 1, 4, 5, 9, 10, 13, 14, 18, 19, 22, 23, 27, 28
Best Days for Career: 1, 4, 5, 13, 14, 24, 27, 28

Last month on the 16th when Venus entered your sign, a Grand Square formed in the heavens – a rare aspect. This Grand Square becomes even stronger this month as more short-term planets enter the picture, indicating a hectic, hyperactive month ahead. Things are complicated. Many competing interests have to be balanced. The least little disturbance can crash the edifice that you're trying to build. You are involved in some big, big project. Happily, health is much better now than it has been in the past few months so you have the energy to handle all this activity. However, don't fall for the illusion that if you push yourself when you're tired you'll get more done. The reverse is more likely. When tired, rest. Take a break. When you feel rested, go back to what you were doing.

The planets are now in their maximum Eastern position this month. This means that personal independence is at its maximum for the year. So make use of this. If there are conditions that you don't like, that are uncomfortable, take the bull by the horns and make the changes.

On the 22nd, as the Sun crosses the Ascendant, you enter a yearly personal pleasure peak. So pamper yourself a little. Librans don't need lectures from me about pampering; they know very well how to do this. This is a time to get the body and image the way you want it to be, to buy the clothing and accessories you need, to get those massages and manicures, and to look the success that you are.

Love seems complicated this month. You and the beloved are on different pages after the 11th and not in agreement.

But Libra knows how to bridge these conflicts – there is no one out there who can do this better than you. Love opportunities happen through friends, groups and group activities. The online world, social networking sites and dating sites also seem good for love. Even if you are in a relationship, much of it is happening online.

Finances are still stressful, but you seem more focused on them after the 11th and this is a help. You are giving this area the attention and focus that is needed and this tends to success.

On the 22nd, the planetary power shifts from the upper half to the lower half of the Horoscope. By now you have achieved your important career goals. Sure, there is always more to achieve, but now it is good to focus on your home, family and emotional wellbeing. Now it is time to create the psychological infrastructure for future career success. Career is still excellent this month. There are job opportunities too. But now you can be more choosy. You need a career that allows for emotional harmony and which doesn't overly stress the family.

Venus makes fabulous aspects to Jupiter on the 27th and 28th. This brings a nice payday and luck in speculations.

October

  Best Days Overall: 4, 5, 13, 14, 22, 23, 31
  Most Stressful Days Overall: 11, 12, 17, 18, 24, 25
  Best Days for Love: 1, 7, 8, 9, 17, 18, 19, 27, 28, 30
  Best Days for Money: 2, 3, 6, 7, 11, 12, 15, 16, 19, 20, 24, 25, 29, 30
  Best Days for Career: 4, 5, 13, 14, 23, 24, 25

Uranus has been square to Pluto, your financial planet, all year, but now the aspect is very exact. Major financial changes are going on. Happily Pluto is now moving forward (this began on September 20). Thus, there is more financial clarity and the changes should be good. In the short term it's probably not pleasant – you seem to be forced into the changes by circumstances – but in the long term they will be good. It's not advisable to be speculating now or next month. Expenses related to children (or children figures) seem to be causing the stress and the change.

A Lunar Eclipse on the 18th affects you strongly, so take it nice and easy during that period. Avoid risky activities. Like every Lunar Eclipse this brings career changes and dramas, and shake-ups in your company or industry. Parents or parent figures are also affected and they should also take a nice, easy, relaxed schedule. This eclipse impacts on Jupiter, the ruler of your 3rd house of communication, so there could be communication breakdowns and glitches this period. Cars and communication equipment will get tested. There are dramas in your neighbourhood, with neighbours and siblings. With Jupiter still powering your career, this eclipse will probably boost the career later on down the road. Since this eclipse occurs in your 7th house of love, your current relationship gets tested. Be more patient with the beloved this period as he or she is more temperamental. Business partnership or joint ventures also get tested.

Since June 27 job seekers have had magnificent aspects. Jobs don't seem a problem. However, if you are still looking, do more homework before accepting any position. With your work planet retrograde for the past few months, things are not what they seem or the way they are being presented. This applies to those who employ others as well. Do more than the usual checks before hiring anyone.

Love is a bit of a roller-coaster this month. For a start, you are in a period of personal independence and want things your way, and this tends to stress relationships. Until the 7th there is conflict in love. From the 7th to the 15th it quiets down a bit, but the conflict resumes from the 15th onwards. The eclipse is also complicating things. Your social genius will handle these things, but it will take more work.

You are still in a personal pleasure peak until the 23rd. After that you enter a yearly financial peak. The financial changes are happening, as we mentioned, but you are more focused on finance, and you have the help of friends and family, so earnings will be greater than usual.

Children or children figures (of the appropriate age) need more patience in their relationships from the 2nd to the 4th. Love is very stormy for them during that period.

November

Best Days Overall: 1, 9, 10, 18, 19, 28, 29
Most Stressful Days Overall: 7, 8, 13, 14, 20, 21, 22
Best Days for Love: 7, 8, 13, 14, 16, 17, 26, 27
Best Days for Money: 3, 4, 7, 8, 11, 12, 16, 17, 21, 22, 25, 26, 30
Best Days for Career: 3, 4, 11, 12, 20, 21, 22, 23

With all the financial changes going on and with your great focus on finance, valuable financial lessons are being learned. Uranus is exploding many false assumptions and expectations. He is also showing you a lot of hidden financial stratagems – all legal of course – that you can resort to. It is the pressure, the difficulty, that is forcing you to a new and higher financial level. Later on you will be very thankful for these challenges. With the money house so powerful I feel you will prevail in spite of all the challenges.

A Solar Eclipse on the 3rd occurs in your money house, reinforcing what we mentioned above. The financial changes are truly dramatic. You still have the help of family and friends and the law also seems on your side. As with every Solar Eclipse, friendships get tested and bad or flawed ones fall by the wayside. There are dramas in the lives of friends. Computers and hi-tech gadgets get tested. Often under these aspects they start to behave erratically. Sometimes you get a new upgrade that is not really an upgrade but actually sets you back. Be patient with these things and do your best.

This eclipse impacts on Saturn, your family planet, so there are dramas with family members or with a parent figure. If there are hidden flaws in your home, you find out about it now. This eclipse is basically benign to you as far as eclipses go. It seems stronger on friends and family than on you.

The planetary power is still mostly below the horizon, so continue to focus more on the home, family and your emotional wellbeing. Without emotional stability, career success will be fleeting indeed.

The love life starts to improve after the 5th. You and the beloved have achieved some kind of balance. Your love planet entered your 12th house on October 15 and will be there for the rest of this month. Thus love is very idealistic these days. The standards and expectations seem very high, and not too many people can live up to them. Be careful of criticism and perfectionism. Love opportunities are in spiritual milieus for singles – at prayer meetings, meditation seminars, yoga retreats, charity events and things of this nature.

Health is good. The pace of life seems a bit slower than last month. Most of the planets are kind to you. Continue to enhance the health in the ways mentioned in the yearly report.

Finances are challenging as we've said, but you have a nice payday from the 14th to the 16th. The money people in your life seem kind to you. Avoid speculations this month. Friends are supportive all month but especially from the 12th to the 14th. They have a nice payday then too.

December

Best Days Overall: 6, 7, 15, 16, 17, 25, 26
Most Stressful Days Overall: 4, 5, 10, 11, 12, 18, 19
Best Days for Love: 4, 5, 10, 11, 12, 13, 14, 15, 16, 23, 24, 25, 26
Best Days for Money: 1, 4, 5, 8, 9, 13, 14, 18, 19, 23, 24, 28, 29
Best Days for Career: 2, 3, 11, 12, 18, 19, 22, 23

Another hectic, hyperactive month. On the 8th, as Mars enters your sign, the Grand Square pattern in the heavens reforms. Again there is a need to manifest something big in the world, a big complicated kind of project. Many competing and conflicting interests have to be reconciled. One false move and the whole edifice can collapse. The physical activity is one thing, but the mental stress seems more of a problem. Health needs more attention now, and especially after the 21st. It's OK to be busy, but try to schedule frequent breaks. Enhance the health in the ways mentioned in the yearly report.

Mars's move into your sign is wonderful for the love life. Your spouse, partner or current love is bending over backwards to please you, and seems very devoted to you. But you don't seem pleased. You seem in conflict or disagreement with the beloved in spite of his or her best efforts and you seem a bit uncomfortable with it. Singles find that love pursues them, but again, you don't seem pleased or thrilled. There is nothing much you need to do in the love department – love will find you. But the challenge will be to smooth out the differences with the beloved and to enjoy the love that comes. Love seems especially stormy towards the end of the month, from the 23rd to the 31st. Be more patient. Try not to make things worse than they need to be.

This month on the 21st the planetary power shifts from the independent East to the social Western sector. This is your favourite sector. Personal independence is not a big issue for Libra, though you need to develop this more.

Librans prefer getting their way through consensus and the cooperation of others.

Finances improve this month, especially after the 21st. But you're not out of the woods just yet. Your lesson is to develop financial faith and confidence. There is much insecurity these days.

Venus makes one of her rare retrogrades on the 21st. This is a time to review your personal goals and desires. Some goals should be scrapped; some should be modified; some should be upgraded and improved. Avoid making major personal decisions until mental clarity comes to you. And especially avoid important love decisions.

Your 4th house of home and family is easily the most powerful in the Horoscope this month. So the focus is on the family and emotional wellbeing. The career, which is still going great guns, can take a back seat for now.

The beloved and your friends should drive more carefully from the 23rd to the 31st. They should avoid risky kinds of activities as well. This is not a time for daredevil stunts or for testing the limits of the body.

Scorpio

♏

THE SCORPION

Birthdays from
23rd October to
22nd November

Personality Profile

SCORPIO AT A GLANCE

Element – Water

Ruling Planet – Pluto
  Co-ruling Planet – Mars
  Career Planet – Sun
  Love Planet – Venus
  Money Planet – Jupiter
  Planet of Health and Work – Mars
  Planet of Home and Family Life – Uranus

Colour – red–violet

Colour that promotes love, romance and social
  harmony – green

Colour that promotes earning power – blue

Gems – bloodstone, malachite, topaz

Metals – iron, radium, steel

Scents – cherry blossom, coconut, sandalwood, watermelon

Quality – fixed (= stability)

Quality most needed for balance – a wider view of things

Strongest virtues – loyalty, concentration, determination, courage, depth

Deepest needs – to penetrate and transform

Characteristics to avoid – jealousy, vindictiveness, fanaticism

Signs of greatest overall compatibility – Cancer, Pisces

Signs of greatest overall incompatibility – Taurus, Leo, Aquarius

Sign most helpful to career – Leo

Sign most helpful for emotional support – Aquarius

Sign most helpful financially – Sagittarius

Sign best for marriage and/or partnerships – Taurus

Sign most helpful for creative projects – Pisces

Best Sign to have fun with – Pisces

Signs most helpful in spiritual matters – Cancer, Libra

Best day of the week – Tuesday

Understanding a Scorpio

One symbol of the sign of Scorpio is the phoenix. If you meditate upon the legend of the phoenix you will begin to understand the Scorpio character – his or her powers and abilities, interests and deepest urges.

The phoenix of mythology was a bird that could recreate and reproduce itself. It did so in a most intriguing way: it would seek a fire – usually in a religious temple – fly into it, consume itself in the flames and then emerge a new bird. If this is not the ultimate, most profound transformation, then what is?

Transformation is what Scorpios are all about – in their minds, bodies, affairs and relationships (Scorpios are also society's transformers). To change something in a natural, not an artificial way, involves a transformation from within. This type of change is a radical change as opposed to a mere cosmetic make-over. Some people think that change means altering just their appearance, but this is not the kind of thing that interests a Scorpio. Scorpios seek deep, fundamental change. Since real change always proceeds from within, a Scorpio is very interested in – and usually accustomed to – the inner, intimate and philosophical side of life.

Scorpios are people of depth and intellect. If you want to interest them you must present them with more than just a superficial image. You and your interests, projects or business deals must have real substance to them in order to stimulate a Scorpio. If they haven't, he or she will find you out – and that will be the end of the story.

If we observe life – the processes of growth and decay – we see the transformational powers of Scorpio at work all the time. The caterpillar changes itself into a butterfly; the infant grows into a child and then an adult. To Scorpios this definite and perpetual transformation is not something to be feared. They see it as a normal part of life. This acceptance of transformation gives Scorpios the key to understanding the true meaning of life.

Scorpios' understanding of life (including life's weaknesses) makes them powerful warriors – in all senses of the word. Add to this their depth, patience and endurance and you have a powerful personality. Scorpios have good, long memories and can at times be quite vindictive – they can wait years to get their revenge. As a friend, though, there is no one more loyal and true than a Scorpio. Few are willing to make the sacrifices that a Scorpio will make for a true friend.

The results of a transformation are quite obvious, although the process of transformation is invisible and secret. This is why Scorpios are considered secretive in nature. A seed will not grow properly if you keep digging it up and exposing it to the light of day. It must stay buried – invisible – until it starts to grow. In the same manner, Scorpios fear revealing too much about themselves or their hopes to other people. However, they will be more than happy to let you see the finished product – but only when it is completely unwrapped. On the other hand, Scorpios like knowing everyone else's secrets as much as they dislike anyone knowing theirs.

Finance

Love, birth, life as well as death are Nature's most potent transformations; Scorpios are interested in all of these. In our society, money is a transforming power, too, and a Scorpio is interested in money for that reason. To a Scorpio money is power, money causes change, money controls. It is the power of money that fascinates them. But Scorpios can be too materialistic if they are not careful. They can be overly awed by the power of money, to a point where they think that money rules the world.

Even the term 'plutocrat' comes from Pluto, the ruler of the sign of Scorpio. Scorpios will – in one way or another – achieve the financial status they strive for. When they do so they are careful in the way they handle their wealth. Part of this financial carefulness is really a kind of honesty, for

Scorpios are usually involved with other people's money – as accountants, lawyers, stockbrokers or corporate managers – and when you handle other people's money you have to be more cautious than when you handle your own.

In order to fulfil their financial goals, Scorpios have important lessons to learn. They need to develop qualities that do not come naturally to them, such as breadth of vision, optimism, faith, trust and, above all, generosity. They need to see the wealth in Nature and in life, as well as in its more obvious forms of money and power. When they develop generosity their financial potential reaches great heights, for Jupiter, the Lord of Opulence and Good Fortune, is Scorpio's money planet.

Career and Public Image

Scorpio's greatest aspiration in life is to be considered by society as a source of light and life. They want to be leaders, to be stars. But they follow a very different road than do Leos, the other stars of the zodiac. A Scorpio arrives at the goal secretly, without ostentation; a Leo pursues it openly. Scorpios seek the glamour and fun of the rich and famous in a restrained, discreet way.

Scorpios are by nature introverted and tend to avoid the limelight. But if they want to attain their highest career goals they need to open up a bit and to express themselves more. They need to stop hiding their light under a bushel and let it shine. Above all, they need to let go of any vindictiveness and small-mindedness. All their gifts and insights were given to them for one important reason – to serve life and to increase the joy of living for others.

Love and Relationships

Scorpio is another zodiac sign that likes committed clearly defined, structured relationships. They are cautious about marriage, but when they do commit to a relationship they tend to be faithful – and heaven help the mate caught or even suspected of infidelity! The jealousy of the Scorpio is legendary. They can be so intense in their jealousy that even the thought or intention of infidelity will be detected and is likely to cause as much of a storm as if the deed had actually been done.

Scorpios tend to settle down with those who are wealthier than they are. They usually have enough intensity for two, so in their partners they seek someone pleasant, hardworking, amiable, stable and easy-going. They want someone they can lean on, someone loyal behind them as they fight the battles of life. To a Scorpio a partner, be it a lover or a friend, is a real partner – not an adversary. Most of all a Scorpio is looking for an ally, not a competitor.

If you are in love with a Scorpio you will need a lot of patience. It takes a long time to get to know Scorpios, because they do not reveal themselves readily. But if you persist and your motives are honourable, you will gradually be allowed into a Scorpio's inner chambers of the mind and heart.

Home and Domestic Life

Uranus is ruler of Scorpio's 4th solar house of home and family. Uranus is the planet of science, technology, changes and democracy. This tells us a lot about a Scorpio's conduct in the home and what he or she needs in order to have a happy, harmonious home life.

Scorpios can sometimes bring their passion, intensity and wilfulness into the home and family, which is not always the place for these qualities. These traits are good for the warrior and the transformer, but not so good for the nurturer and family member. Because of this (and also because of their need for change and transformation) the Scorpio may be prone to sudden changes of residence. If not carefully constrained, the sometimes inflexible Scorpio can produce turmoil and sudden upheavals within the family.

Scorpios need to develop some of the virtues of Aquarius in order to cope better with domestic matters. There is a need to build a team spirit at home, to treat family activities as truly group activities – family members should all have a say in what does and does not get done. For at times a Scorpio can be most dictatorial. When a Scorpio gets dictatorial it is much worse than if a Leo or Capricorn (the two other power signs in the zodiac) does. For the dictatorship of a Scorpio is applied with more zeal, passion, intensity and concentration than is true of either a Leo or Capricorn. Obviously this can be unbearable to family members – especially if they are sensitive types.

In order for a Scorpio to get the full benefit of the emotional support that a family can give, he or she needs to let go of conservatism and be a bit more experimental, to explore new techniques in child-rearing, be more democratic with family members and to try to manage things by consensus rather than by autocratic edict.

Horoscope for 2013

Major Trends

Last year was a strong love and social year. Many of you married, met a special someone, or got involved in serious romance. Love and social goals have more or less been attained and your focus is elsewhere now.

Ever since Pluto, the Lord of your Horoscope, entered your 3rd house of communication in 2008, communication and intellectual interests have been important. You are into learning and teaching, expanding your knowledge and sharing it with others. Now with the ruler of the 3rd house in your own sign, these interests are even stronger and seem very successful in the year ahead. It's a very nice period for writers, journalists or teachers. Students below college level have good fortune in their studies now. The mind is sharp, learning goes well.

In 2012, Neptune made a major (once in 14 years) move, into your 5th house of children and fun, and will be there for the long term. Personal creativity will be unusually good. You need to be alert for the inspiration that is pouring down upon you continuously. It also makes Scorpios of child-bearing age much more fertile than usual, especially after June 27.

Last year in October Saturn moved into your own sign and will be there for the next two years. This shows that you are taking on more responsibility, more burdens. You have a need to be more serious about life. Health will be good, but more delicate than last year. More on this later.

On June 27 Jupiter will move into your 9th house and into a beautiful aspect with your Sun. This is another wonderful aspect for students, but here it affects those at college or university level. It shows success in their studies and in gaining entrance to the right courses. There will be foreign travel after June 27. The opportunities are coming.

Your major interests this year are the body, image and personal pleasures; communication and intellectual interests; children, creativity and leisure activities; sex, personal transformation and reinvention, occult studies, re-incarnation and life after death (until June 27); religion, metaphysics, higher education and foreign travel (from June 27 onwards); health and work.

Your paths of the greatest fulfilment in the year ahead are the body, image and personal pleasure; sex, personal trans-formation and reinvention, occult studies, reincarnation, life after death (until June 27); religion, metaphysics, higher education and foreign travel (after June 27).

Health

(Please note that this is an astrological perspective on health and not a medical one. In days of yore there was no difference, these perspectives were identical. But now there could be quite a difference. For a medical perspective, please consult your doctor or health practitioner.)

Your 6th house of health has been important since 2011 and this trend continues in the year ahead (and for many

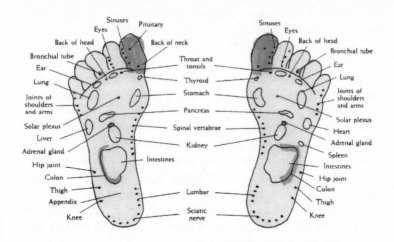

Reflexology

Try to massage the whole foot on a regular basis, but pay extra attention to the points highlighted on the chart. When you massage, be aware of 'sore spots', as these need special attention. It's also a good idea to massage the ankles and top side of the feet.

more years). So there is a good focus on health. Health is basically good these days. But Saturn in your own sign makes it more delicate than last year and so it is good that you are focused here.

On a personal level you are much more conservative than usual. But not when it comes to health matters; here you seem very experimental and perhaps even a bit rebellious with medical orthodoxy. You gravitate to new and experimental therapies and you benefit greatly from them. Generally this shows a preference for alternative therapies and medicine, although sometimes it indicates cutting-edge technologies within orthodox medicine.

Your job these days is to learn how you personally function. We are all wired up differently, uniquely. There are no universal rules that will work for everyone. We learn about ourselves through trial, error and experimentation, and though there are some failures, in the end we wind up with true and valid knowledge.

There is much you can do to enhance your basically good health. Give more attention to the vulnerable organs this year. These are the heart (avoid worry and anxiety and develop more faith and trust); the colon, bladder and sexual organs (safe sex and sexual moderation are always important for you, and colonics on a regular basis are also good); the head, face and scalp (you benefit from regular head and face massage, which strengthens the head and brain and also the whole body, as the head and scalp contain reflexes to the rest of the body); the adrenals (avoid anger and fear, the emotions that stress the adrenals); and the ankles and calves (these should be regularly massaged, and give the ankles more support when exercising).

Uranus, your family planet, moved into your house of health in 2011. His involvement in health shows a need for family and domestic harmony. If health problems arise (God forbid) this area will need to be restored to harmony as quickly as possible. It also shows a need for 'emotional harmony'. Moods need to be constructive and peaceful. Avoid depression like the plague.

There are many short-term trends in health depending on where Mars, your health planet, is and the aspects he receives. These are best covered in the monthly reports.

Saturn in your own sign, though challenging, does have a few good points. It is great for disciplined health regimes, for losing weight if you need to, and for getting the body and image in shape.

Uranus will be squaring the Lord of your Horoscope for a few months in the year ahead. Actually it is square all year, but the square will become very exact in October and November. This is a highly dynamic aspect. Avoid daredevil-type stunts and risky activities. Drive carefully. If you must experiment with your body, do it in a safe, controlled and mindful manner.

Home and Family

Your 4th house of home and family, though powerful for many years, is no longer a house of power. Your intense focus here has probably produced the desired results (more or less) and you have no need to make dramatic changes here. It tends to the status quo for this year.

Personal relations with family members, especially a parent or parent figure, seem very strained in the year ahead, in particular in October and November. This could produce a family rift. Even if the relationship survives it will take much hard work to keep it going. This seems like a clash of egos. Someone will have to swallow their pride to keep the harmony here.

Uranus, your family planet, is in your 6th house of health and work for years to come. This shows a focus on making the home a healthier place. Are there dangerous substances in the paint or building materials? Harmful mites or other pests in the beds or linen? Now is the time to deal with these things. You also seem to be installing all kinds of health gadgets in the home. The home is becoming as much a health spa as a home. You have a fancy for these things now.

A parent or parent figure could have moved or renovated the home last year. This year moves are not advisable. Children or children figures in your life seem to be moving however, and the moves seem happy. They would benefit from a spiritual path these days. Otherwise, they could be prone to drug or alcohol abuse – for many this is a substitute for true spirituality. They are under very intense spiritual energies right now and for years to come. They seem 'dreamy' and 'other worldly'. There's nothing wrong with this per se, but when dealing with the mundane world they need to force themselves to be mindful in the here and now.

Siblings or sibling figures in your life are moving and renovating the home, perhaps multiple times. They are nomadic now. They might be living in various places for long periods of time and it will be 'as if' they have moved multiple times. There is romance in the year ahead for them, and possibly marriage if they are single. You and your siblings are getting along very well; there is great mutual devotion and mutual support.

Grandchildren (if you have them) are having a very good year. They seem prosperous. Those of child-bearing age are very fertile now.

If you are planning serious repairs or construction in the home, January 1 to February 1 is a good time. If you are beautifying the home, repainting, redecorating or buying objects of beauty for the home, January 19 to February 28 is a good time.

Finance and Career

The money house is not strong this year Scorpio. Sometimes this is a good thing. It shows that you are more or less satisfied with the status quo and have no need to make special efforts here. But sometimes this is a weakness – you might not be giving this area the attention it deserves and thus earnings can suffer. Most likely both these scenarios are true for you, at different times.

There is a Lunar Eclipse on May 25 in your money house and this will produce long needed changes; it will force you to give more focus here. It will present you with situations that you can't ignore.

Jupiter, your financial planet, spends the first half of the year in your 8th house of transformation – your favourite house. I consider this positive for earnings. It shows that though you might not be too focused on finance, your spouse or partner is – and he or she is prospering and likely to be generous with you.

The financial planet in the 8th house doesn't favour personal earning power that much. He is in 'exile', furthest away from his true home. However this aspect does favour earning from insurance claims, royalties, inheritances, spousal support or through borrowing. It shows good access to outside money. Whatever the credit situation is in your given economy, you seem unaffected. You have access to credit. This also favours attracting outside investors to your projects.

Jupiter in the 8th house is all about making money for others, with other people's money. It's all about making other people rich, helping them to attain their financial goals and putting the financial interest of others ahead of your own. This might seem 'sacrificial' and counter-intuitive, but as you succeed at this your own prosperity manifests naturally and easily by the karmic law. This is the position of the high corporate executive, the investment banker, financial planner or hedge-fund manager. They use other people's assets for the enrichment of others. To the degree that they succeed, they prosper.

Jupiter will move into your 9th house on June 27. Basically this is a good financial transit. The 9th house is considered very fortunate – lucky. However, Jupiter will receive stressful aspects and this complicates things. Yes, earnings should increase, but there is more work and more challenge involved. From July onwards you seem to be making very dramatic and sudden financial changes. Earnings will be more erratic – sometimes sky high, sometimes very low. Perhaps a parent figure or family developments cause these changes. You are not much in agreement with this parent figure, neither personally nor in regard to finance.

You seem very lucky in speculations that period (from June 27 onwards) and it might be advisable to invest harmless, affordable sums on the lottery or sweepstakes. There will be happy financial opportunities with foreign companies, foreign investments and with foreigners in general. The people at your place of worship seem supportive financially and provide opportunities. And as Jupiter makes beautiful aspects to Neptune after June 27, the financial intuition is very sharp.

This is not an especially strong career year. It is more of a preparation year. Do your homework – career success is coming next year.

Love and Social Life

As we mentioned, last year was a very strong love and social year. Jupiter moved through your 7th house in 2011 and 2012. No one can take this much intensity for too long, so a bit of a cooling off of the social activity is in order. In many cases this cooling off is not what it seems. Many of you got involved in serious romantic relationships, and this tends to narrow the social focus. Many got married under this transit. Whether you are married or single, the year ahead is a sexually active period.

Most of you seem content with things as they are and have no need to make major changes in the love life. Singles will probably remain single. Those who are married will probably remain married – a status quo kind of situation. If you are already in a romantic relationship, the status quo is good news.

Your love planet, Venus, is a fast-moving planet. So there are many short-term trends in the love life which are best dealt with in the monthly reports. Much depends on where Venus is at any given time and the kind of aspects she is receiving.

One of the challenges in love right now is Saturn in your own sign. It tends to make a person 'stand offish'. People get the feeling that you don't want to get too close. Sometimes you come across as cold and distant to others. You are not doing this consciously and you are certainly not this kind of person. However, you could be unconsciously projecting this because of Saturn's influence. You will have to work to project warmth and love to others. This projection of love is something you build up, like a muscle. It gets stronger through practice.

Sometimes Saturn's influence makes a person overly serious, and understandably so. Many of you are thinking of old age or taking on extra burdens and responsibilities. Many of you are carrying on out of a sense of duty and not from the joy of what you are doing. Thus, others can be put off by all this seriousness. When you are with the beloved or at a party, let go of all that and have some fun. Don't carry your burdens into the bedroom or party.

Though love is status quo this year, a Solar Eclipse on May 10 will test the current relationship. This is not enough to cause a break up, but it does show the 'airing of dirty laundry' – a good emotional expelling will happen for both you and the beloved.

Those of you working on the second marriage have beautiful romantic opportunities after June 27. You are meeting people with marriage potential. Those working on the third marriage have a status quo kind of year, and those working on the fourth marriage will probably not marry. Even a current relationship seems stressed out and will get tested.

Parents or parent figures are having a status quo love year. Children (or children figures) of marriageable age likewise. Grandchildren of the appropriate age (if you have them) are having their marriages or romantic relationships tested this year.

Self-improvement

Neptune, the most spiritual of all the planets, moved into your 5th house of children and fun last year and will be there for another 13 or so years. This has a profound effect on the children or children figures in your life. They are now coming under intense spiritual influences. They will be having prophetic kinds of dreams, which can sometimes be disturbing. They need to know how to handle this. They are not crazy – they are seeing into dimensions that other people don't see. Rather than just dismiss these things or berate the child, help him or her cope with it. Be a good listener. Don't judge. If you personally can't help them understand these things take them to a counsellor – preferably a spiritual counsellor – who does. A good spiritually oriented psychic will do more good than a conventional therapist.

Children are apt to be more dreamy and otherworldly these days. It might seem that they live in a dream world, a world of fantasy. Of itself this is OK, but train them that when they are in the world, in everyday life, they are to be mindful and alert. Give them spiritual exercises in mindfulness. They will also be more sensitive than usual. Voice tone and body language will have a greater impact on them than what you actually say. Be more careful about this.

Neptune in the 5th house indicates an inspired kind of creativity. Those of you in the art field will be producing your best work. The only problem here is whether the world can accept it. The creativity is not of this earth. Keep in mind though that 'accepted' people rarely change the world.

Saturn in your own sign indicates a major area for self-improvement for the next two years. The ego is getting a reality check. This is going to be adjusted in the next two years. If the self-esteem has been unrealistically high, it will be reduced; if unrealistically low it will be raised. Saturn is just in all things.

It might be a good idea to take a lower profile these days. Yes, we are to 'let our light shine' as scripture says, but not to make it shine through bombast or arrogant behaviour. The Sun is very brilliant, yet it is silent. Let your light shine by all means, but quietly and unobtrusively.

Month-by-month Forecasts

January

Best Days Overall: 6, 7, 14, 15, 24, 25
Most Stressful Days Overall: 12, 13, 19, 20, 26, 27, 28
Best Days for Love: 8, 9, 18, 19, 20, 29, 30
Best Days for Money: 4, 8, 9, 12, 22, 31
Best Days for Career: 2, 3, 10, 11, 21, 26, 27, 28, 31

The year ahead is very much a communication kind of year – a year for learning, studying and teaching, a year to expand your knowledge base. And this month your 3rd house of communication and intellectual interests is easily the strongest in the Horoscope until the 19th. The mind is sharp and clear. It absorbs and communicates information easily. It's a great month for students. If these aspects happened for a different sign – say Gemini, Libra or Aquarius – your phone and texting bills would be sky high. But Scorpio is not much of a talker by nature so these should be reasonable. However, you are talking much more than usual.

The main health danger this month is a hyperactive mind that refuses to quieten down. It goes on and on and on like a machine, which can drain energy that the body needs for other vital functions. So you need to keep a lid on this. Turn the mind off when not in use. Meditation is a big help for this.

Health is basically good until the 19th, but afterwards you need to rest and relax more. Vitality is not up to its usual standards. Enhance the health in the ways mentioned above and also give more attention to the stomach and breasts (for women). Diet is more of an issue this month and the stomach seems more sensitive than usual. You seem very involved in the health of family members, perhaps more than with your own health. Family harmony is very important as problems in the family can impact on your own health. If this happens (God forbid) restore the harmony as quickly as you can. Alternative, experimental therapies seem powerful for you this month.

You begin your year with most of the planets below the horizon in the lower half of the Horoscope. Career can be downplayed now. Give your attention to the home, family and your emotional wellbeing. Work on your career by interior methods like visualization and feeling having your goals realized. This is daydreaming but controlled, conscious, wilful daydreaming. Your real career right now is your family and emotional life, especially after the 19th. Until the 19th it involved education, writing, sales, marketing and communication. Pursuing outer career goals from home also seems likely this month. Now, with all the modern technology available, one can be just as effective working from home as in the office.

You are in a strong period for launching new projects or products. Both your personal and universal solar cycles are in their waxing phase. The planetary momentum is forward this month and the Moon will wax from the 10th to the 27th. This is the optimum time to launch those new projects.

February

Best Days Overall: 2, 3, 11, 12, 20, 21, 22
Most Stressful Days Overall: 9, 10, 15, 16, 17, 23, 24
Best Days for Love: 9, 10, 15, 16, 17, 18, 19
Best Days for Money: 5, 9, 18, 27
Best Days for Career: 1, 9, 10, 20, 23, 24

On January 19 the planetary power began to shift from the independent Eastern sector to the social West. This month, as Venus moves westward, the shift is even stronger. Now is the time to cultivate your social skills, to gain your ends through cooperation and consensus rather than by independent action. Now you have to live with the conditions you created over the past six months as it is much more difficult to make changes. Best to adapt to situations as best you can.

This is another very good month – perhaps even better than last month – to launch new products or ventures. ALL the planets are moving forward until the 18th. Thus the best time for doing this is from the 10th to the 18th (as the Moon waxes).

Love was bittersweet last month. On the one hand there was happy opportunity from January 15 to 18, but also great instability. There were many mood changes in love. Love becomes more stable this month. You are socializing more from home. A nice quiet dinner at home is more romantic than a night out on the town. Scorpios are very sexual people, but this month you also crave emotional intimacy. Emotional sex – sex on the feeling level – is probably more important than actual physical sex. Often when the love planet is in the 4th house of home and family, people meet up with old flames from the past. Sometimes it is the actual person; sometimes someone who reminds you of the person. The purpose here is to resolve old unfinished business.

Health still needs watching, especially until the 18th. Your health planet Mars moves into Pisces on the 2nd. Thus you can enhance the health through spiritual-type therapies such as meditation, prayer, the laying on of hands, reiki and the manipulation of subtle energies. You get very good results from this all month, but especially from the 3rd to the 5th. Water-based therapies are also very powerful. Health becomes wonderful after the 18th. You have all the energy you need to achieve whatever you put your mind to.

Though you are not in your yearly financial peak, finances have been good and earnings have increased since January 19. This prosperity continues until February 18. After the 18th finances become more challenging. Your goals will be attained but through overcoming obstacles. The financial trends are pretty much as we have described in the yearly report.

Home and family is still the major focus until the 18th. Scorpios of the appropriate age entered a cycle of fertility on the 19th of last month, which will continue for another few months yet.

March

Best Days Overall: 2, 3, 10, 11, 20, 21, 29, 30
Most Stressful Days Overall: 8, 9, 15, 16, 22, 23
Best Days for Love: 2, 3, 10, 11, 15, 16, 21, 22, 31
Best Days for Money: 1, 4, 5, 8, 9, 17, 18, 27, 28, 31
Best Days for Career: 2, 3, 10, 11, 22, 23, 31

On February 18 you entered one of your yearly personal pleasure peaks, a time for enjoying life on all levels, a time for leisure and recreation. This lasts until the 20th. By then you will be 'partied out' and ready to get down to work.

When the 5th house is strong, people become more speculative. They are drawn to casinos, gaming rooms and lotteries. But this time speculations are not advisable, although they will become more favourable after the 20th.

If you have new products or ventures and still haven't launched them, the 11th to the 27th is an excellent time for this. There will be a lot of cosmic power behind your efforts.

Love is happy and romantic until the 22nd. Your love planet is celestially powerful so you and the beloved are capable of experiencing nuances in love that few mortals ever experience. If you are in a relationship you are having more fun with the beloved, enjoying the relationship and doing fun kinds of things. If you are unattached, love opportunities happen in the usual places – resorts, parties, clubs and places of entertainment. Singles most likely are attracting non-serious kinds of people and seem OK with this.

You still need to work hard to achieve your financial goals until the 20th. Perhaps you are overspending on leisure activities. Children or children figures can be more expensive than usual. But things get much easier after the 20th. Job seekers had good aspects at the beginning of last month, and the aspects once again become good after the 20th. The job is perhaps not as enjoyable as you would like – perhaps you feel it is beneath you – but you are doing it and seem successful. Self-esteem and self-confidence could be better, but in a way it is good that the ego is weaker. Most of the planets are in the social West, and your way is probably not the best way these days. Adapt to others so long as it isn't destructive.

Mars and Uranus travel together from the 18th to the 21st. Do your best to make the home safer. Keep dangerous objects away from children. Make sure your smoke detectors are functioning properly. Family members (especially a parent or parent figure) need to avoid temper, confrontations and risky kinds of activities.

Venus travels with Uranus from the 26th to the 29th. This will test a current relationship. If it is just a casual kind of relationship, it is in danger. Serious relationships will survive, although the beloved will be more temperamental. Singles will have unexpected love meetings.

Career changes or shake-ups are happening from the 27th to the 30th.

April

Best Days Overall: 6, 7, 8, 16, 17, 25, 26
Most Stressful Days Overall: 4, 5, 11, 12, 19, 20
Best Days for Love: 1, 9, 10, 11, 12, 21, 22, 29, 30
Best Days for Money: 1, 4, 5, 14, 15, 23, 24, 27, 28
Best Days for Career: 1, 9, 10, 19, 20, 21, 29, 30

A Lunar Eclipse on the 25th occurs in your own sign, so reduce your schedule during this period as you will feel the eclipse strongly. Do your best to keep children and children figures out of harm's way. Over the next six months you will be redefining your image and personality – your whole look and outer demeanour. This needs to be done periodically, but often it takes an eclipse or some other kind of shock to force us into it.

Self-esteem and self-confidence are much weaker this period – even more so than last month. The Lord of your Horoscope, Pluto, goes retrograde on the 12th, and Saturn is in your own sign. Most of the planets are in the West and entering their maximum Western position, so a low profile is in order. Too much self-assertion is not advisable, nor is it easy for you. The planetary power flows away from you and towards others. So, let others have their way now.

It is good every now and then to take a vacation from the ego and its desires. This is the kind of month where your perspective gets widened. You are part of a larger whole and it is the cosmic concern with the wellbeing of the whole that temporarily downplays your personal importance. Adapt to situations as best you can. If they are unpleasant, make a note of what needs to be changed and when your period of personal independence comes (as it will) you will more easily make the changes.

On the 19th you enter a yearly love and social peak. Love seems very happy whether you are married or single. Singles are dating more and meeting romantic partners. Marriage itself is not likely this month, but you will meet people you would consider marrying. Those who are married – and many of you married in the past year or two – are having more harmony and romance within the marriage. Venus makes a very beautiful aspect to Pluto from the 23rd to the 26th. This would show an important romantic meeting or romantic experience. But it seems a bit complicated: Saturn is in the picture. There is uncertainty about this relationship. You might be feeling blocked from showing your true warmth and love. You (or your partner) seem more inhibited. It's very important to make conscious efforts to show love and warmth to others this period. It will not happen naturally.

The social life seems varied and interesting. You are mingling with people of status and power, people who might be celebrities in your world. These connections will help the career. There are athletic types and the 'beautiful' people, also doctors and health professionals. All these types attract you and there are romantic and social opportunities with all of them.

Finances are OK this month. They are better before the 19th than after, but they are still OK – no disasters happening.

Health is more delicate after the 19th. Happily your 6th house of health is strong all month and so you are pretty focused here. The most important thing, as always, is to maintain high energy levels. Enhance the health in the ways mentioned in the yearly report (page 270). Until the 15th give more attention to the kidneys and hips. From the 15th onwards give more attention to the lungs, small intestine, arms and shoulders. The neck and throat are important all month.

May

Best Days Overall: 4, 5, 13, 14, 15, 23, 24, 31
Most Stressful Days Overall: 2, 3, 8, 9, 10, 16, 17, 29, 30
Best Days for Love: 8, 9, 10, 11, 21, 22, 29, 30
Best Days for Money: 2, 3, 11, 12, 21, 22, 25, 26, 29, 30
Best Days for Career: 8, 9, 10, 16, 17, 19, 20, 29

Health is still delicate this month and it is probably good to take a more reduced kind of schedule. Two eclipses this month reinforce this need. Enhance the health in the ways mentioned in the yearly report. This month give more attention to the neck, throat and cervical vertebrae. Craniosacral therapy would be a good idea, as would neck massage. Problems in love can be impacting on the health as well. If problems arise, restore harmony in love as quickly as possible. Health will improve after the 20th, but until then take it nice and easy.

The Solar Eclipse of the 10th affects you strongly, so avoid risky kinds of activities. Do what needs to be done, but re-schedule what you can. This eclipse occurs in your 7th house of love and marriage. Thus a current relationship will get tested. Be more patient with the beloved this period and try not to make matters worse. As we mentioned, it's very important to keep the harmony in love. Sometimes there is nothing wrong with the relationship per se, but problems in the personal life of the partner create stress. Business partnerships get tested as well.

There are career changes happening too – shake-ups in your company or industry. Sometimes there is a near-death kind of career experience – something that seems like a disaster but, if handled properly, actually enhances the résumé. Parents and parent figures need to reduce their workload too. There can be dramatic events in their lives these days. Mars, your work planet, is impacted by this eclipse, so there are job changes, changes in the conditions of work, and perhaps lay offs of fellow workers. Sometimes these aspects produce a health scare. The health regime will undergo dramatic change over the next six or so months.

The Lunar Eclipse of the 25th is more benign to you. It too impacts on the career, reinforcing the career changes we saw earlier. This eclipse occurs in your money house, so there are important financial changes happening. Some shake-up, some surprise occurs that forces you to change your strategy and thinking. These changes have long needed to be made, but now you are forced into it. Students make important changes in their educational plans.

Since the Moon rules your 9th house of religion, philosophy and metaphysics, important changes are going on here too. Your philosophy of life and your beliefs get tested – there is a 'crisis of faith'. Beliefs get discarded or modified in light of new knowledge. Children and children figures are affected by this eclipse. They should be kept out of harm's way this period. Let them spend more quiet time at home or close to home. They are apt to be more temperamental, so be patient with them.

June

Best Days Overall: 1, 10, 11, 19, 20, 27, 28
Most Stressful Days Overall: 5, 6, 12, 13, 25, 26
Best Days for Love: 5, 6, 10, 19, 20, 27, 28
Best Days for Money: 8, 9, 17, 18, 21, 22, 26, 27
Best Days for Career: 7, 8, 12, 13, 17, 18, 27

Your 8th house of transformation became very powerful last month on the 20th and is powerful until the 21st. Scorpios are natural '8th house personalities' so this is comfortable for you. Death is something you always want to know more about. You have encountered death many times in your life. Though you might never admit this in polite society, you kind of enjoy dealing with this subject. The power in the 8th house also shows a more sexually active kind of period, although it's not necessarily romantic. The lusts are intensified these days.

This month is good for all Scorpio activities – detoxing the mind and body, working on personal transformation and reinvention. Those of you on the spiritual path will get deep insights into the nature of 'resurrection' – and no doubt many of you will be resurrecting various aspects of your life.

The spouse, partner or current love has been having a banner financial year, and right now (since May 20) is in a yearly financial peak. He or she seems more generous with you. Finances in general are very good. While you are not yet in the yearly financial peak (this will happen in November and December) this is one of your best financial periods. There is a very nice payday from the 19th to the 22nd. Perhaps a pay rise or promotion is happening. The career is involved here. This period brings career success and opportunity as well.

On the 27th your financial planet moves into the sign of Cancer, your 9th house. The 9th house is considered very fortunate, so there is financial increase and good luck for the rest of the year. Perhaps you are not enjoying the prosperity as much as you would like. Perhaps you are not enjoying the way that it is happening, but still it is happening. (The act of money-making seems to distract you from your studies or from the pursuit of your intellectual interests; you will have to balance these things in the coming year and give each their due.)

On May 20 the planets began to shift from the lower half to the upper half of your Horoscope. This shift is even stronger this month. You can safely downplay home and family issues now and focus on your career.

Health is good all month, but especially after the 21st. You can enhance it even further by giving more attention to the lungs, small intestine, arms and shoulders; arm and shoulder massage will be especially powerful now. Detoxing is always good, but especially this month.

July

Best Days Overall: 7, 8, 17, 25, 26
Most Stressful Days Overall: 2, 3, 9, 10, 11, 23, 24, 29, 30
Best Days for Love: 1, 2, 3, 10, 11, 19, 20, 29, 30
Best Days for Money: 7, 8, 16, 17, 19, 20, 25
Best Days for Career: 7, 8, 9, 10, 11, 17, 18, 27

On June 27 Jupiter moved into a very beautiful aspect with both Neptune and Saturn. These aspects are in effect all month (and pretty much for the rest of the year). The aspect with Neptune shows luck in speculations. It might be advisable this month to invest harmless sums of money on these things. Children and children figures in your life are prospering. Your personal creativity becomes very marketable these days. If you are a writer or teacher you earn more than usual from these things. A new car and new communication equipment is coming to you. Siblings and sibling figures have nice paydays this month and will enjoy financial increase for the rest of the year. Job seekers have beautiful opportunities from the 19th to the 24th. Finances are happy, but there are a few challenges. Family responsibilities dent the bottom line. Perhaps there are some financial disagreements with family members.

The family situation does seem stressed. Perhaps the parents or parent figures are not getting along. But this is temporary. By the 22nd it passes.

On the 22nd the Sun crosses your Mid-heaven and enters your 10th house of career, initiating a yearly career peak. It's a time for great progress and success. Next year your success will be even greater, but it is good now too. Let go of the family for a while; do what needs to be done but give your main focus to your career.

Your love planet Venus spends most of the month in the 10th house too, and this gives us many messages. Career is important, but so is your marriage or current relationship. This transit spells success in love – it is high on your priorities – and indicates a need to integrate the career and the social life. One merges into the other. You socialize more with people in your company or industry. You progress in your career by your merits but also by your social connections. You are attracted to people of power and prestige. Often this aspect shows romantic opportunities with bosses or superiors or with people who are involved in your career. Mainly it shows that as you follow your career path, love will await you. It shows that your spouse, partner or current love is also very ambitious these days and seems very successful. He or she is supportive of your career goals.

Health is good until the 22nd but after that becomes more delicate. So, as usual, rest and relax more, pace yourself, and do your best to maintain high energy levels. Don't allow ambition to push you beyond your physical limits. Until the 18th enhance the health in the ways mentioned last month. After the 18th give more attention to the stomach. Women should give more attention to the breasts too. Diet is more of an issue these days. Most importantly, there is a need for emotional equilibrium – peace and harmony in the feeling body.

August

Best Days Overall: 3, 4, 13, 14, 21, 22, 30, 31
Most Stressful Days Overall: 6, 7, 19, 20, 25, 26, 27
Best Days for Love: 8, 9, 19, 25, 26, 27
Best Days for Money: 3, 13, 14, 15, 16, 21, 22, 30, 31
Best Days for Career: 6, 7, 15, 16, 25

On July 22 the planetary power began shifting from the West to the East. This month the shift gets stronger as Mars and Mercury also cross from the West to the East. You are entering a period of personal independence that will get stronger in the coming months. Now it will be much easier to shape conditions and circumstances to suit yourself. With Pluto still retrograde the challenge is not about power but about mental clarity, being clear as to what you want to create for yourself. Light always precedes creation. Get light.

Get clarity. Then proceed with your creation from that space.

You are still in the midst of your yearly career peak. Success, advancement and opportunity are happening. Mars crosses the Mid-heaven on the 28th and this shows that you are earning your success through hard work. Your work ethic attracts the notice of your superiors. Mercury crosses the Mid-heaven on the 8th and this shows that friends are succeeding and supporting the career goals. Your hi-tech expertise is very important.

Finances are still great. Your financial planet is part of a rare Grand Trine in the Water signs. There is luck in speculations. Children are prospering. Sales people make important sales these days. You are on a roll. Like last month, though, there is still a need for financial compromises with family members.

Health still needs attention until the 22nd. Enhance the health by giving more attention to the stomach, which seems more sensitive these days. Women should also give more attention to the breasts. There are pressure points on the feet that energize the breasts and body massage will also strengthen them. Pay more attention to the diet as well. Like last month emotional tranquillity is important. A short-term disturbance will probably not matter too much, but if it is prolonged, good health can be impacted. Do your best to keep your moods positive and constructive.

Love seems happy until the 16th. There is harmony with the beloved and happy social meetings. The only problem now (and you need to pay special attention to this) is being too perfectionist, too critical, too analytical. This attitude tends to kill any feelings of romance. Until the 15th love opportunities come through friends, groups and group activities. Some friends want to be more than that. Some friends are playing cupid. Online social networking and dating sites also seem a likely venue for romance. On the 16th Venus moves into Libra, which is a much better position for love than Venus in Virgo but she moves into an adverse aspect with Pluto, your ruling planet. So there is conflict and disagreement with the beloved. While you might find it easier to express feelings of love under this aspect, the disagreements cloud the picture. It will take more work, more effort (on both sides) to transcend the differences. It can be done however.

September

Best Days Overall: 1, 9, 10, 18, 19, 27, 28
Most Stressful Days Overall: 2, 3, 15, 16, 22, 23, 29, 30
Best Days for Love: 8, 17, 18, 22, 23, 27, 28
Best Days for Money: 1, 9, 10, 11, 12, 18, 19, 27, 28
Best Days for Career: 2, 3, 4, 5, 13, 14, 24, 29, 30

The Grand Square that began forming last month becomes stronger this month, leading to an active and complicated month. There will be great achievement but also many challenges. Everything has to be handled just right; the least mistake can crash the magnificent edifice that you are working to build. Balance, balance, balance. Many areas of your life are pulling you in different directions. Each must be given their due but you can't go too far in any one direction.

Your life is basically good these days. But events in the world are highly turbulent this month and you could be affected indirectly.

You have been in a period of personal independence since July 21. But the retrograde of Pluto has hampered things. It is one thing to have the power to create, but there is need to be clear on WHAT to create. Gaining this clarity has been your main job since then. By now, as Pluto starts to move forward on the 12th, this clarity is there. You can proceed with confidence to create the conditions that you desire for yourself. You have much cosmic power behind you. You can have things your way these days. Self-esteem and self-confidence are much improved towards the end of the month. You know who you are and what you should have, and you act on it.

Finances are basically good this month, but become more complicated and challenging from the 22nd onwards. There have been financial disagreements with family members since July. This month there could be disputes with bosses, authority figures and friends. But these are all short term and will pass by next month.

Mars will spend the month in your 10th house of career. This shows that you are working hard, fending off competitors in your industry and perhaps personal competitors as well. You are earning success the hard way. You simply outwork and out-produce the competition.

Mars will square Saturn from the 7th to the 11th, so drive more carefully then. Try to avoid arguments. If you disagree with someone, take a few deep breaths and express your opinion in a calm, rational way.

Love is stressful until the 11th, but then changes dramatically. Venus enters your sign and starts to make beautiful aspects with Jupiter and Neptune. Love is in the air and you can't escape it. It will find you. Someone is pursuing you avidly. Between the 27th and 28th Venus trines Jupiter. Singles meet a special someone. Those who are married have more romance in the relationship. There are opportunities for business partnerships or joint ventures. There's a nice payday then, both personal and for the current love.

October

Best Days Overall: 6, 7, 15, 16, 24, 25
Most Stressful Days Overall: 1, 13, 14, 19, 20, 27, 28
Best Days for Love: 7, 8, 17, 18, 19, 20, 27, 28
Best Days for Money: 6, 7, 8, 9, 15, 16, 24, 25
Best Days for Career: 1, 4, 5, 13, 14, 23, 24, 27, 28

Last month the planetary power started to shift from the upper to the lower half of your Horoscope. The shift technically began on September 29 and will become stronger on the 23rd of this month as the Sun crosses from the upper to the lower half. It is sunset in your year. The day is over with and it is time to prepare for the activities of the evening – time to shift attention from the career to the home, family and the emotional wellbeing. By the 15th the hectic activity in the career is finished: Mars leaves the career house and moves into the 11th house of friends. The career house will be mostly empty after that date (only the Moon will move through there on the 27th and 28th), and so it seems safe to downplay this now.

By the 23rd the planets will be in their maximum Eastern position for the year. Personal independence and power is at its maximum. Your mission now is to create conditions that are comfortable and pleasing to you. The cosmos desires your happiness. Take the initiative and create your personal Nirvana now. You have much support for this.

There is a Lunar Eclipse on the 18th that occurs in your 6th house of health and work. This shows job changes, changes in the workplace and in conditions of work. If you employ others there can be employee turnover now. This eclipse also announces major changes in your health regime and diet over the next six months. Since the Moon is ruler of your 9th house, every Lunar Eclipse affects students. There are important changes in their educational plans. There are shake-ups in your place of worship and in the lives of the people there. Avoid foreign travel during this period.

The family situation has been tense all year and this eclipse will most likely exacerbate things. Do your best not to make things worse than they need to be. Jupiter, your financial planet, is affected by this eclipse. Thus there are important financial changes happening. These will work out well in the long run, but in the short term they can be uncomfortable. Finances are challenging anyway until the 23rd, the eclipse only brings things to a head. Finances will improve dramatically after the 23rd.

Regardless of the short-term financial stresses, you are in a year of great prosperity. These are just bumps on the road. If you use them correctly, you will actually increase your prosperity.

Health is good this month. But you can enhance the health further by giving more attention to the heart until the 15th and to the small intestine after that.

November

Best Days Overall: 3, 4, 11, 12, 20, 21, 22, 30
Most Stressful Days Overall: 9, 10, 16, 17, 23, 24
Best Days for Love: 7, 16, 17, 26, 27
Best Days for Money: 3, 4, 5, 6, 11, 12, 21, 22, 30
Best Days for Career: 3, 4, 11, 12, 23, 24

The main headline this month is the Solar Eclipse of the 3rd that occurs in your own sign. All of you will feel this, but those of you born between the 1st and the 5th will feel it strongest. A nice, easy, relaxed schedule is called for. Do whatever needs to be done, but re-schedule anything you can and spend more quiet time at home. This eclipse shows that you are redefining your personality and image. You are going to change how you think about yourself (your self-concept) and how you want others to think about you. You will be presenting a 'new you' in coming months. Generally this involves important wardrobe changes, changes of hair-style, etc. If you haven't been careful in dietary matters this eclipse can produce a detox of the body.

As at every Solar Eclipse there are career changes happening. Sometimes the career itself is changed and you enter a new path. Sometimes there are shake-ups in the hierarchy of your company or industry and so the rules of the game change and you have to revise your tactics and strategy. Parents and parent figures need to reduce their schedule during this period and avoid risky types of activities.

Last month on the 23rd you entered one of your yearly personal pleasure peaks. This continues until the 22nd of this month. This is a period for enjoying all the carnal delights, and for getting the body and image in shape the way you want it. It is still a very good time for creating the conditions that you want in life. You have maximum personal power.

The Sun moving through your sign shows that career opportunities are seeking you out. But now you can be choosier about these things. Career paths or opportunities that violate your emotional peace and harmony should be avoided or amended in the right way.

Finances are super all month. Until the 22nd, Jupiter is receiving fabulous aspects from the Sun, Mercury, Saturn and Neptune. You have a lot of financial firepower these days. This indicates pay rises, the financial favour of bosses, elders and superiors – even the government. If you have issues with the authorities, try to schedule meetings before the 22nd. There is good fortune then and you are more likely to get a 'best case scenario'. On the 22nd, as the Sun enters your money house, you begin a yearly financial peak – a prosperous period in a prosperous year.

There is only one real financial complication. Jupiter starts to go retrograde on the 7th. This is not going to stop the prosperity but it will slow things down a bit and introduce some complications. Avoid financial short cuts. Handle all the details perfectly. It is important now to attain mental clarity on your finances. The economic situation is probably not as you imagine it to be. New facts will give you new opinions.

Health is good all month, though the eclipse period could make you feel under the weather. You can enhance the health by giving more attention to the small intestine. There are reflex points that can help this (see page 269).

December

Best Days Overall: 1, 8, 9, 18, 19, 28, 29
Most Stressful Days Overall: 6, 7, 13, 14, 20, 21, 22
Best Days for Love: 4, 5, 13, 14, 23, 24
Best Days for Money: 1, 2, 3, 8, 9, 18, 19, 28, 29, 30, 31
Best Days for Career: 2, 3, 11, 12, 20, 21, 22, 23

Another hectic, active, frenetic kind of month. There is turbulence in the world at large, especially after the 8th. Your life is basically good, but you can be affected indirectly by these things.

Health is good, but we see more dramatic changes to the health regime happening this month. The Lunar Eclipse of October 18 indicated this, as does your health planet in opposition to Uranus and square to Pluto. Job changes could be happening too, either actual job changes or changes in the workplace or conditions of work. It seems very volatile and insecure right now. Those who employ others are also experiencing instability with their workers.

The financial trends are pretty much as we described last month. You are still very much in a prosperity cycle. Jupiter, your financial planet, is still retrograde. So refer to our discussion of this last month. Finances become more challenging after the 21st. But these challenges and complications seem to be coming from prosperity rather than lack. Prosperity can be as stressful as lack, but of the two problems, the former is the better one. Finance is the major focus until the 21st. The New Moon of the 3rd occurs in your money house and this should clarify the financial situation. Clarity is what you most need right now, although real clarity won't happen until Jupiter starts moving forward again in a few months. Your finances are under review. This is the time to see where improvements can be made. When Jupiter starts moving forward you will be in a good position to implement your plans.

On the 21st, as the Sun enters your 3rd house, your focus shifts to communication and intellectual interests. These have been important all year, but now even more so. For students (especially below college level) this indicates success in their studies. Grades should be better than usual. The mind is sharper and clearer and retains information better. It's a good period for writers, journalists, teachers and sales people too. Their skills are enhanced.

Love has been good the past few months. In September and October love was pursuing you. Last month, from the 5th onwards, love was found (for singles) in the pursuit of financial goals. Material wealth was a turn on in love. This month it is mental compatibility that attracts. Love is about good communication, the sharing of thoughts and ideas. You need to love the mind and thought process as much as the body. Love is found close to home this month – there's no need to travel far for it. Venus in Capricorn shows more caution in love. No need to rush into things too quickly. Venus's rare retrograde on the 21st reinforces this need for caution. Date, enjoy, but avoid making major commitments.

Sagittarius

♐

THE ARCHER
*Birthdays from
23rd November to
20th December*

Personality Profile

SAGITTARIUS AT A GLANCE

Element – Fire

Ruling Planet – Jupiter
　Career Planet – Mercury
　Love Planet – Mercury
　Money Planet – Saturn
　Planet of Health and Work – Venus
　Planet of Home and Family Life – Neptune
　Planet of Spirituality – Pluto

Colours – blue, dark blue

*Colours that promote love, romance and social
　harmony* – yellow, yellow–orange

Colours that promote earning power – black,
　indigo

Gems – carbuncle, turquoise

Metal – tin

Scents – carnation, jasmine, myrrh

Quality – mutable (= flexibility)

Qualities most needed for balance – attention to detail, administrative and organizational skills

Strongest virtues – generosity, honesty, broad-mindedness, tremendous vision

Deepest need – to expand mentally

Characteristics to avoid – over-optimism, exaggeration, being too generous with other people's money

Signs of greatest overall compatibility – Aries, Leo

Signs of greatest overall incompatibility – Gemini, Virgo, Pisces

Sign most helpful to career – Virgo

Sign most helpful for emotional support – Pisces

Sign most helpful financially – Capricorn

Sign best for marriage and/or partnerships – Gemini

Sign most helpful for creative projects – Aries

Best Sign to have fun with – Aries

Signs most helpful in spiritual matters – Leo, Scorpio

Best day of the week – Thursday

Understanding a Sagittarius

If you look at the symbol of the archer you will gain a good, intuitive understanding of a person born under this astrological Sign. The development of archery was humanity's first refinement of the power to hunt and wage war. The ability to shoot an arrow far beyond the ordinary range of a spear extended humanity's horizons, wealth, personal will and power.

Today, instead of using bows and arrows we project our power with fuels and mighty engines, but the essential reason for using these new powers remains the same. These powers represent our ability to extend our personal sphere of influence – and this is what Sagittarius is all about. Sagittarians are always seeking to expand their horizons, to cover more territory and increase their range and scope. This applies to all aspects of their lives: economic, social and intellectual.

Sagittarians are noted for the development of the mind – the higher intellect – which understands philosophical and spiritual concepts. This mind represents the higher part of the psychic nature and is motivated not by self-centred considerations but by the light and grace of a Higher Power. Thus, Sagittarians love higher education of all kinds. They might be bored with formal schooling but they love to study on their own and in their own way. A love of foreign travel and interest in places far away from home are also noteworthy characteristics of the Sagittarian type.

If you give some thought to all these Sagittarian attributes you will see that they spring from the inner Sagittarian desire to develop. To travel more is to know more, to know more is to be more, to cultivate the higher mind is to grow and to reach more. All these traits tend to broaden the intellectual – and indirectly, the economic and material – horizons of the Sagittarian.

The generosity of the Sagittarian is legendary. There are many reasons for this. One is that Sagittarians seem to have an inborn consciousness of wealth. They feel that they are rich, that they are lucky, that they can attain any financial goal – and so they feel that they can afford to be generous. Sagittarians do not carry the burdens of want and limitation which stop most other people from giving generously. Another reason for their generosity is their religious and philosophical idealism, derived from the higher mind. This higher mind is by nature generous because it is unaffected by material circumstances. Still another reason is that the act of giving tends to enhance their emotional nature. Every act of giving seems to be enriching, and this is reward enough for the Sagittarian.

Finance

Sagittarians generally entice wealth. They either attract it or create it. They have the ideas, energy and talent to make their vision of paradise on Earth a reality. However, mere wealth is not enough. Sagittarians want luxury – earning a comfortable living seems small and insignificant to them.

In order for Sagittarians to attain their true earning potential they must develop better managerial and organizational skills. They must learn to set limits, to arrive at their goals through a series of attainable sub-goals or objectives. It is very rare that a person goes from rags to riches overnight. But a long, drawn-out process is difficult for Sagittarians. Like Leos, they want to achieve wealth and success quickly and impressively. They must be aware, however, that this over-optimism can lead to unrealistic financial ventures and disappointing losses. Of course, no zodiac sign can bounce back as quickly as Sagittarius, but only needless heartache will be caused by this attitude. Sagittarians need to maintain their vision – never letting it go – but they must also work towards it in practical and efficient ways.

Career and Public Image

Sagittarians are big thinkers. They want it all: money, fame, glamour, prestige, public acclaim and a place in history. They often go after all these goals. Some attain them, some do not – much depends on each individual's personal horoscope. But if Sagittarians want to attain public and professional status they must understand that these things are not conferred to enhance one's ego but as rewards for the amount of service that one does for the whole of humanity. If and when they figure out ways to serve more, Sagittarians can rise to the top.

The ego of the Sagittarian is gigantic – and perhaps rightly so. They have much to be proud of. If they want public acclaim, however, they will have to learn to tone down the ego a bit, to become more humble and self-effacing, without falling into the trap of self-denial and self-abasement. They must also learn to master the details of life, which can sometimes elude them.

At their jobs Sagittarians are hard workers who like to please their bosses and co-workers. They are dependable, trustworthy and enjoy a challenge. Sagittarians are friendly to work with and helpful to their colleagues. They usually contribute intelligent ideas or new methods that improve the work environment for everyone. Sagittarians always look for challenging positions and careers that develop their intellect, even if they have to work very hard in order to succeed. They also work well under the supervision of others, although by nature they would rather be the supervisors and increase their sphere of influence. Sagittarians excel at professions that allow them to be in contact with many different people and to travel to new and exciting locations.

Love and Relationships

Sagittarians love freedom for themselves and will readily grant it to their partners. They like their relationships to be fluid and ever-changing. Sagittarians tend to be fickle in love and to change their minds about their partners quite frequently.

Sagittarians feel threatened by a clearly defined, well-structured relationship, as they feel this limits their freedom. The Sagittarian tends to marry more than once in life. Sagittarians in love are passionate, generous, open, benevolent and very active. They demonstrate their affections very openly. However, just like an Aries they tend to be egocentric in the way they relate to their partners. Sagittarians should develop the ability to see others' points of view, not just their own. They need to develop some objectivity and cool intellectual clarity in their relationships so that they can develop better two-way communication with their partners. Sagittarians tend to be overly idealistic about their partners and about love in general. A cool and rational attitude will help them to perceive reality more clearly and enable them to avoid disappointment.

Home and Domestic Life

Sagittarians tend to grant a lot of freedom to their family. They like big homes and many children and are one of the most fertile signs of the zodiac. However, when it comes to their children Sagittarians generally err on the side of allowing them too much freedom. Sometimes their children get the idea that there are no limits. However, allowing freedom in the home is basically a positive thing – so long as some measure of balance is maintained – for it enables all family members to develop as they should.

Horoscope for 2013

Major Trends

After eight or so years of intense stress, of challenge, disruptions, psychological earthquakes and insecurity, 2011 and 2012 were like a picnic in the park. It's as if you had paid your dues to life and now you are an accepted member. No need anymore to deal with the previous challenges. Many of the other signs – Cancer, Libra, Capricorn – had the opposite phenomenon. They are facing what you have already faced. Previously they were coasting and you were struggling. Now it's the other way round. Because you have gone through many, many tests, you are now in a position to help others go through them.

The cosmos was not punishing you. It was actually making you ready for real love (which happens this year) and for the role you are to play in life. The Olympic athlete probably doesn't enjoy the gruelling – and often painful – training schedule. It is only when it is time to compete that he or she recognizes the value of it. Many of you were pushed to the edge, but happily you were not pushed over it.

Love is the main headline this year. This has been the case ever since Jupiter, your ruling planet, moved into your 7th house of love in June 2012. This not only brings romance, and possibly marriage, but an expansion of the whole social life, the whole social sphere. There's more on this later.

Health is much, much improved since 2011. You have your normal vim, vigour and vitality. With more energy at your disposal, more possibilities open to you. Hitherto impossible things are now eminently doable. This spells success in the year ahead.

Pluto – the cosmic detoxer – has been in your money house for some years now and will be there in the year ahead. So there is a need to purify the financial life, eliminate waste and inefficiencies and, most importantly, negative financial attitudes. More details later.

You have many areas of interest this year – Sagittarius heaven. On the one hand, this is good as you get bored very easily. You need to have many projects in progress, so when you get bored with one you can go to another. However, the danger (as always) is dispersing your energy in too many directions. Success requires focus.

Your main areas of interest this year are finance; home and family; children, creativity and leisure activities; love and romance (until June 27); sex, personal transformation and reinvention, occult interests, death and rebirth, life after death (from June 27 onwards); spirituality.

Your paths of greatest fulfilment this year are love and romance (until June 27); sex, personal transformation and reinvention, occult interests, death and rebirth, life after death (after June 27); and spirituality.

Health

(Please note that this is an astrological perspective on health and not a medical one. In days of yore there was no difference, these perspectives were identical. But now there could be quite a difference. For a medical perspective, please consult your doctor or health practitioner.)

Health, as we said, is much improved over the past few years. The year begins with two long-term planets in stressful alignment with you. But these planets – Neptune and Jupiter – are lightweights compared to the ones that hit you in previous years – Saturn, Pluto and Uranus. So there is a great improvement. Also, on June 27 Jupiter will move away from his stressful aspect, so health should improve even further as the year progresses. The fact that your 6th house of health is empty is also a positive. There's no need to pay too much attention here. Health is basically good.

Good though your health is, you can make it even better. Give more attention to the vulnerable areas this year. These are the heart (avoid worry and anxiety like the plague, as they drain energy and are the spiritual root causes of heart problems); the liver and thighs (these are always important

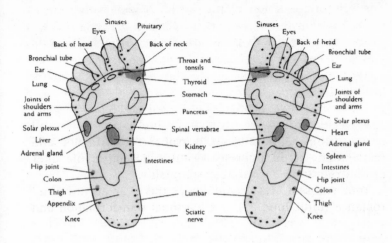

Reflexology

Try to massage the whole foot on a regular basis, but pay extra attention to the points highlighted on the chart. When you massage, be aware of 'sore spots', as these need special attention. It's also a good idea to massage the ankles and top side of the feet.

for you and the thighs should be regularly massaged); and the neck, throat, kidneys and hips (the neck and hips should be regularly massaged, craniaosacral therapy and chiropractic are excellent therapies this year).

Venus is your health planet. Generically she rules love and social activities. Thus problems in love – discord in the marriage or with friends – can actually cause health problems. Thus, if problems arise, restore the harmony here as quickly as you can.

Venus does double duty in your solar Horoscope. She is your health planet and also ruler of the 9th house. This indicates a strong connection between health and religion, philosophy and metaphysics. The most obvious interpretation is that you, more than most, benefit from metaphysical-type therapies – prayers, affirmations and the like. The deeper interpretation of this health-religion connection is that false ideologies – errors in religious beliefs – can be a root cause for health problems. These can not only cause havoc in our outer lives, but if held long enough can actually manifest as physical illness. So, if problems arise (God forbid) this area will need to be explored and set right.

Venus, as our regular readers know, is a fast-moving planet. She will move through all the signs and houses of your Horoscope in any given year. Thus there are many short-term trends in health that are best dealt with in the monthly reports.

Home and Family

For many years, from 2002 to 2010, Uranus was moving through your 4th house, signifying a turbulent time at home and with the family. There have been many moves, many changes of residence, many family upheavals, shake-ups and break-ups. There were many dramatic, life-changing events in the lives of parents, parent figures and family members. In March 2011 Uranus moved out of your 4th House, and in 2012, Neptune moved in. Things are much quieter, more serene. You are still very much focused here, but there is much less drama; it is an easier time.

Neptune is the most spiritual of all the planets. He refines and idealizes any area he touches. He brings the spiritual perspective into it. Thus (and this is a long-term trend) there is a spiritual revolution going on in the family and with parents or parent figures. They are subject to very intense spiritual energies these days.

Neptune's effect is interior in nature. Great inner change is happening with family members. You might not see it overtly yet, but it is happening on the internal level. In due course, when the time is right, you will see it. They should become kinder, more compassionate, more idealistic about life.

The home is becoming as much a spiritual centre as a home. These are the aspects for someone who holds meditation seminars, spiritual-type lectures, yoga classes or prayer meetings at home. You entertain spiritual figures – yogis, gurus, ministers or priests – at home. Perhaps they come to stay for a while. Many of you are setting up home altars or special rooms for meditation, prayer and spiritual activities.

On June 27, Jupiter will move into the sign of Cancer and into beautiful aspect with Neptune. This aspect will be in effect for the rest of the year, but will be strongest in July. This shows many things. A move or opportunity to move will happen. As regular readers know, it doesn't always show a literal move. Sometimes it indicates the purchase of an additional home or a home renovation. This all seems happy. There is great harmony between you and the family. If there have been break-ups (and this seems almost certain), there will be reconciliation, or at least a softening of the antagonisms.

Sagittarians of child-bearing age are much more fertile during this period. Pregnancy would not be a surprise. Other family members of child-bearing age also seem more fertile. The family circle expands, either through birth, marriage or through meeting people who are 'like' family to you.

With Neptune in your 4th house there are many things going on behind the scenes in the lives of family members. Don't take things at face value. Before making important decisions, do your homework thoroughly. This applies to buying a home or buying expensive items for the home as well.

If you are planning major repairs or renovations, February 1 to March 12 is a good time, and also the month of July. If you are redecorating or buying art objects for the home, February 28 to March 22 and June 3 to June 28 are good times.

Finance and Career

Ever since Pluto moved into your money house in 2008 money has been a great focus. For the past two years, your financial planet, Saturn, has been on the receiving end of some very stressful aspects. Sure, you earned, and most likely prospered, but it was a difficult road, with many challenges and dramatic changes. This is difficult for a Sagittarius to handle. They like everything quick. Happily finances are much improved this year. Saturn moved into Scorpio in October 2012, your 12th house of spirituality. This year he is receiving mostly harmonious aspects, so prosperity will be greater than in past years, and will also come much easier. Many of the impediments you faced are no longer there.

On June 27, Jupiter will move into Cancer and into harmonious alignment with Saturn. This will be a very prosperous period. The first half of the year is OK, but the latter half is much, much better. You will end the year richer and in better financial circumstances than when you began.

The most interesting thing this year (and for the next two years) is the spiritual connection to earnings. Pluto is your spiritual planet and he has been in your money house since 2008. Saturn, your financial planet, is now in your spiritual 12th house: the two planets are in 'mutual reception' with each the guest in the house and sign of the other. There is great mutual cooperation between these two planets. Each is showing 'hospitality' to the other. Thus you are in a period for going deeper into the spiritual dimensions of wealth and you should read as much as you can on this subject. (There is much literature on it, but it might be good to start with the works of Emmet Fox and Ernest Holmes. Napoleon Hill also has some interesting books on this.)

Your challenge these days is to access the supernatural sources of supply, not so much the natural. This is a period for 'miracle' money. Natural money, earned by hard work, is a wonderful thing and we should be grateful for it. But miracle money is so much more joyful and interesting. The year ahead is about trusting the Divine Providence – the Divine

Supply – which, if invoked, will never fail a person. The financial intuition was shaky the past few years. But now it becomes much better, much sharper and much more trustworthy. Intuition will do in an instant what years of hard work cannot do.

On a more mundane level, you have an affinity for commercial real estate, bonds and the bond market, and large traditional companies (especially the bonds of these companies). You have the aspects for inheritance over the next few years. Hopefully no one has to actually die, but you could be named in someone's will, or receive a trust fund, large insurance payment, or be named the executor of a will. There are many scenarios as to how this can happen. You also have an affinity for troubled properties or troubled companies. You see value where others see only death and decay and can profit from the turnaround.

If you have good ideas, this is a great year (especially after June 27) to attract outside investors or outside funding for your projects.

The Pluto-Scorpio connection with wealth shows a need to cut out waste. You prosper by cutting back on the wasteful and the unneeded. (Don't cut back on essentials.) It's good to get rid of old possessions that you no longer need. They're just clogging up the works. Make room for the new wealth that wants to come in.

Love and Social Life

We mentioned earlier that you have been in a very powerful love and social period since June of last year. For singles this is a signal for romance – serious romance. This is not about fun, games and entertainment (though you are certainly enjoying things) but something with real marriage potential. However, Jupiter in the 7th house doesn't always mean literal marriage. Often it shows relationships that are like marriage, or meeting people who are 'marriage material'.

Since last June you are the proactive one in love. You are doing the courting. You are creating your ideal social life through personal effort. You're not sitting around waiting for the phone to ring or for the next text message. You go after what you want and tend to get it.

In general you are more popular this year. You are 'other oriented'. You put the interests of others ahead of your own. You are there for the beloved and for your friends. People respond to this. The only problem here is that you feel in 'exile' from yourself. Many of you are saying, 'What about me? What about my needs?' But you need not concern yourself too much about this. Your needs will be met by the karmic law.

It is good every now and then to take a vacation from the self and its personal desires and interests. Many of the problems in life come precisely from too much self focus, too much 'me'. Letting go of 'me' for a while is a liberating kind of experience.

On June 27, Jupiter will leave the house of love and marriage and move into the 8th house of transformation. For most of you this means that the love goals are achieved and you are on to the next thing. The latter half of the year is a more sexually active kind of period. Whatever your age or stage in life, libido will be stronger than usual.

With Mercury as your love planet there are many short-term trends in love. Mercury will move through your entire Horoscope in the course of a year. These trends are best dealt with in the monthly reports.

Mercury goes retrograde three times a year and this tends to complicate love matters. It's unwise to make important love decisions then. These are times to review the current relationship or the love life in general and to see where improvements can be made. It is good to understand this, as it explains the sometimes bizarre behaviour of a loved one or the glitches in social matters. This year, these periods are February 23 to March 16, June 26 to July 19, and October 21 to November 9.

Self-improvement

Earlier we discussed the spiritualization of the family, which is a long-term trend. But there is more to it than just that. We all have two families. We have our biological family and our spiritual family. Generally these are two separate things. The biological family tends to be karmic in nature. We are brought together with the people of our family in order to adjust and balance past karmas, past negative momentums. As this is going on, it can be quite painful. Buddhists say that bitter enemies from past embodiments are brought together in the same family – the quickest way to balance old karma. And who hasn't felt this way at times with various family members. This is the reason why the vast majority of families are considered dysfunctional!

Painful though family life is sometimes, we can take solace in the fact that we have a spiritual family. This is a perfect family. These people love and support you unconditionally. They behave as a perfect family would behave. These people are generally not related to you by blood. Sometimes they are incarnate, sometimes not. But they are there with you all the time, loving, supporting and nurturing you. With Neptune now in your 4th house of home and family for the long term, you are going to start meeting up with these people. In most cases it will be a physical kind of meeting. You meet someone who feels and behaves as a perfect father, mother or sibling would feel and behave. Sometimes it is not an actual physical meeting but a dawning awareness that you have a spiritual family on the inner levels and that they are with you. Often there will be telepathic contact in meditation and prayer.

Sometimes people find their spiritual families at ashrams, convents, monasteries or in spiritual groups. Many of them are set up to run like a family. And many of you will be comfortable in those settings. You are looking for the 'ideal' family these days. Most likely, over the next 12 or so years, you will find it.

Month-by-month Forecasts

January

  Best Days Overall: 8, 9, 17, 18, 26, 27, 28
  Most Stressful Days Overall: 2, 3, 14, 15, 21, 22, 23, 29,
    30
  Best Days for Love: 2, 3, 8, 9, 10, 11, 18, 19, 21, 22, 23,
    29, 30, 31
  Best Days for Money: 4, 6, 7, 10, 11, 12, 14, 15, 22, 24,
    25, 31
  Best Days for Career: 2, 3, 10, 11, 21, 29, 30, 31

You begin your year with most of the planets in the Eastern
sector of your chart, the sector of self and personal independence. The planetary power is flowing towards you and thus
there is more personal power available to you. This will
change in a month or two, so if there are conditions in your
life that displease you, make any changes necessary. Have
your way. We are always respectful to others, but there's no
need right now to sacrifice your personal interests on behalf
of others. No question you are doing this – this has been the
case for the past six months – but this month start thinking
more of number one. The only problem is that Jupiter, the
Lord of your Horoscope, is still retrograde until the 30th.
What good is creative power if we are not sure what to
create? So the need now is for mental clarity. By the time
Jupiter moves forward on the 30th you will have it.

    Last month the planetary power shifted from the upper to
the lower half of your Horoscope. You are in the evening of
your year. The day is over. Outer goals have been achieved
up to a point and now the activities of night begin. It's time
to let go of the outer world for a while and focus on the
home, family and your emotional wellbeing; time to focus
on the inner conditions that make outer success possible.

    Your personal solar cycle began its waxing phase on your
birthday. The universal solar cycle began its waxing phase

last month on the 21st. Both these important cycles are waxing at the same time, thus this is a great period to launch those new products or ventures you have in mind into the world. As 90 per cent of the planets are moving forward this month, this adds to the favourability. And when the Moon waxes from the 11th to the 27th the favourability increases even further. New projects are always complicated and need much energy; why not swim with the cosmic tide instead of against it?

Your year begins as you are in the midst of a yearly financial peak; up to half of the planets are either in or moving through your money house. Prosperity is happening now. You have the financial favour of your spouse, partner or current love, of bosses, parents or parent figures, and the religious and spiritual people in your life. Prosperity will be greater later in the year, after June 27, but this is one of your high points now. Finances become more complicated and challenging after the 19th, but this only means that you need to work harder to achieve your financial goals.

The love life has been excellent for the past six months and it is good this month too. The period after the 19th seems best. Love and social goals are attained easily, smoothly, with little fuss. Marriage could happen this month or next month. Romance is there. For those who are married, this indicates harmony in the marriage and more romance with the partner. Until the 19th singles find love opportunities as they pursue their normal financial goals and with people involved in their finances. Wealth and material gifts are romantic turn-ons. After the 19th, as the love planet moves into the 3rd house of communication, love is found close to home, in the neighbourhood. Wealth ceases to be the major attraction. Mental ability, good communication, is more alluring. You need to fall in love with the mind, with the thought process as much as with the body.

Health is good all month.

February

Best Days Overall: 5, 13, 14, 23, 24
Most Stressful Days Overall: 11, 12, 18, 19, 25, 26
Best Days for Love: 1, 9, 10, 11, 12, 18, 19, 21, 22
Best Days for Money: 2, 3, 7, 8, 9, 11, 12, 18, 20, 21, 27
Best Days for Career: 1, 11, 12, 21, 22, 25, 26

You are still in a period of personal independence until the 18th. Jupiter is now moving forward. Make those changes that you want to make before the 18th as after that the planets shift to the Western, social sector and it will be more difficult. Once again you become more at the mercy of others, their decisions and actions. You have been cultivating your social skills for many months now, and after the 18th it is time to go even deeper here. There is something to be said for not being in control. For many this produces stress and anxiety but it need not. Allow a higher power to be in control and trust its workings. Being in control these days can actually be detrimental for you in the long run.

Finances are still challenging until the 18th, but this is temporary. By the 18th, prosperity resumes with a vengeance. Earnings and opportunities could actually be better now than in your last financial peak. Mars makes beautiful aspects to your financial planet from the 15th to the 17th. This brings luck in speculations. Some of you might want to invest harmless sums of money on a lottery or some other kind of speculation. (Please don't play with rent or grocery money.) This aspect shows earning money in happy ways, as you are enjoying yourself. If you have creative skills, whether music, writing, painting, sculpture, etc, they seem more marketable now. Children are supportive of financial goals. The Sun trines your financial planet on the 28th, bringing more of the same.

The planets are at the lowest point of the chart this month from the 18th onwards. You are in the magical midnight hour of your year. This is when you recharge your inner batteries and get emotionally prepared for future success.

Interior activities go better than exterior activities, thus if you have career or financial goals, build the inner conditions for them now. Visualize, speak the word, fantasize – get into the feeling of what you want. It seems like mere daydreaming, but since it is conscious and directed by the will, it is much more than that – it is magic.

Your career planet will be in your 4th house of home and family from the 5th onwards, which reinforces what we're saying here. Your real career, spiritually speaking, is your family and emotional life now. On the more mundane level, this indicates working more from home, pursuing the career from home. Family is your career, but they are also helping the career in subtle ways. Perhaps you don't see it just yet, but it is happening.

Health needs more watching from the 18th onwards, and you could feel lowered energy levels even before that. Until the 2nd enhance the health by giving more attention to the spine, knees, teeth, skin and bones. Back massage will be powerful. From the 2nd to the 26th massage the ankles and calves regularly. From the 26th onwards pay attention to the feet. Foot reflexology will be especially powerful.

March

Best Days Overall: 4, 5, 12, 13, 14, 22, 23, 31
Most Stressful Days Overall: 10, 11, 17, 18, 19, 24, 25, 26
Best Days for Love: 2, 3, 10, 11, 17, 18, 19, 20, 21, 22, 29, 30, 31
Best Days for Money: 1, 2, 3, 6, 7, 8, 9, 10, 11, 17, 18, 20, 21, 27, 28, 29, 30
Best Days for Career: 2, 3, 10, 11, 20, 21, 24, 25, 26, 29, 30

Your 4th house of home and family is still powerful until the 20th, so review our discussion of this last month.

Last month, on the 18th, the element of Water became very strong. And this is still the case for most of the month ahead, until the 20th. Being a Fire sign you are not especially comfortable with all this Water energy – emotionalism, nostalgia, the exaltation of every little nuance of feeling. But if you are aware of it, you will handle it better. You tend to be open and honest. You speak the truth regardless of consequences. But now, this attitude can have explosive consequences that you don't need. Speak the truth by all means, but temper it with sensitivity. People are hypersensitive this period. Often they will read things into simple statements that were never said or intended.

You are still in a very powerful time for launching new products and ventures. Most of the planets are moving forward (between 80 and 90 per cent), and both your personal and universal solar cycles are in their waxing phases. In addition, the Sun will be moving into Aries, the best starting energy of the zodiac. If you can launch these things from the 18th to the 27th – as the Moon waxes – you have even stronger auspices.

Finances are still excellent this month. They are better before the 20th but after the 20th they are still very reasonable.

Neptune has been in good aspect with your financial planet all year. This shows good family support. It shows the prosperity of the family as a whole and of a parent or parent figure in your life. Residential real estate, restaurants, hotels and the food business are all interesting investments for those who invest professionally. On February 18 your financial planet went retrograde and will be retrograde for some months. So your finances are under review now. Prosperity is still happening. Earnings are coming, but there are more glitches and complications. For the next few months your job is to attain mental clarity on these things. Your financial picture – and economic conditions in general – are not what they seem. Major financial decisions, large purchases or major investments, need more study and research. Best to delay them until your mind is clear about things. This clarity will come if you are patient.

Health needs more watching until the 20th. Like last month, foot massage is powerful until the 22nd. After the

22nd, vigorous physical exercise and scalp and facial massages are good.

April

Best Days Overall: 1, 9, 10, 19, 20, 27, 28
Most Stressful Days Overall: 6, 7, 8, 14, 15, 21, 22
Best Days for Love: 1, 7, 8, 9, 10, 14, 15, 19, 21, 22, 27, 28, 29, 30
Best Days for Money: 2, 3, 4, 5, 6, 7, 14, 15, 16, 17, 23, 24, 25, 26, 29, 30
Best Days for Career: 7, 8, 19, 21, 22, 27, 28

The planetary power is still mostly in the Western, social sector of the chart. The Lord of your Horoscope, Jupiter, is in your 7th house of love since the beginning of the year. You are in a very strong love and social period these days. It is important to you; you focus on it, you are active here and thus success is likely. In the past two months the love life was complicated by emotional and psychological issues – perhaps family problems interfered as well. You and the beloved were not in synch. It was harder than usual to express feelings of love. Your love planet was also retrograde from February 23 to March 17 and this complicated matters even more.

On April 14 Mercury moves away from its stressful aspect with Jupiter and is also now moving forward again, so the love life is moving forward too, and is much happier. Mercury will be in your 5th house from the 14th onwards. Thus you are enjoying your social life, and you are scheduling fun kinds of activities with the beloved and with friends. Those who are married might want to go on a second honeymoon now. Romance in general is honeymoonish. Singles find love opportunities in the usual places after the 14th – at parties, resorts, clubs and places of entertainment. The gym or the athletic event is also a valid venue for romance. Sagittarians of appropriate age have been more fertile (more than usual) since February 5 and this is still the case this month.

On March 20 you entered a yearly personal pleasure peak. This is a fun time of year which continues until the 19th. This is a time to explore your personal creativity, to get more involved with your children or the children figures in your life and to explore the joy of life. Follow the joy and you will attract everything needful into your life. Even career opportunity will come as you are having fun. Those of you already involved in a career seem to be having fun in the career – perhaps you are entertaining clients, or superiors. Those looking for their career path should follow their joy – an unerring guide this period. Job seekers also have good aspects from the 19th onwards.

Health is much improved this month. Vitality is strong and you have all the energy you need to achieve any goal you set for yourself. You can enhance the health further by giving more attention to the head and face (until the 15th) and the neck and throat afterwards. Head, face, neck and throat massages are especially powerful this month.

Finances are more delicate after the 19th. Avoid speculations then. Saturn, your financial planet, is still retrograde, so keep in mind our previous discussion. The temporary stress doesn't necessitate drastic moves just yet. Take things day by day and try not to project too far into the future. As we mentioned, the financial life is not as it appears to be. Drastic moves now, made out of desperation and with your financial planet retrograde, will most likely make matters worse.

A Lunar Eclipse on the 25th occurs in your 12th house of spirituality, so important spiritual changes are happening now. Avoid risk-taking activities for a few days before and after the eclipse.

May

Best Days Overall: 6, 7, 16, 17, 25, 26
Most Stressful Days Overall: 4, 5, 11, 12, 18, 19, 31
Best Days for Love: 8, 9, 10, 11, 12, 21, 22, 29, 30
Best Days for Money: 2, 3, 4, 11, 12, 13, 14, 21, 22, 23, 27, 28, 29, 30, 31
Best Days for Career: 8, 9, 10, 18, 19, 21, 22, 29, 30

There are lessons we learn from self-reliance and personal independence, and there are lessons we learn from self-sacrifice and putting others first. In many philosophies and religious teachings, either one or the other is exalted as the ideal. Not so in the Horoscope. Both positions are equally valid; only at certain times we are developing one or the other side. Right now you are learning the lessons of self-sacrifice. Logically one would think that such an attitude would deprive you of your personal comfort or personal aspirations. Not so, as you are learning now. Your good will comes to you by the karmic law. The planetary power is now in its maximum Western position (this will be the case next month as well). At times like this you discover that you don't even need to think about yourself. You don't need to concern yourself with personal interests. These have all been worked out. Your job is other people.

Love is one of the main headlines of the month. On the 20th you enter a yearly love and social peak. Marriages or engagements are likely this month or next. Singles will meet special someones now. All the planets are aligned for love.

The other headlines are the two eclipses this month. The Solar Eclipse of the 10th is relatively benign to you as far as eclipses go. You have gone through many stronger ones in recent years. It occurs in your 6th house, which indicates job changes, changes in the workplace and instability in the workplace. In many cases it indicates a new job; in other cases it shows losing a job and getting another one. The status of the job situation is changed, and often by dramatic means. This aspect also generally produces important changes in the health regime or health scares. These changes will occur over the next six months. The Sun rules your 9th house of religion, philosophy and metaphysics. Students (at the college level or beyond) are most affected here. There are dramatic changes in educational plans or shake-ups in the schools they attend. Belief systems – personal philosophies – get tested now. Many beliefs will go by the wayside, and many will be amended or deepened.

The Lunar Eclipse of the 25th affects you more strongly, so reduce your schedule over that period, from the 20th onwards. This eclipse occurs in your own sign, bringing a redefinition of your body and image, of your personality and self-concept. In coming months, you will present a new look and new image to the world. The Moon rules your 8th house of transformation, thus there can be encounters with death (generally on the psychological level). As this will happen anyway, there is no need to tempt fate by indulging in risky kinds of activity. The family, and especially a parent or parent figure, gets shaken up by this eclipse – there are life-changing events happening there. Family members are likely to be more temperamental this period, so be more patient.

June

Best Days Overall: 2, 3, 12, 13, 21, 22, 30
Most Stressful Days Overall: 1, 7, 8, 15, 16, 27, 28
Best Days for Love: 1, 7, 8, 10, 11, 19, 20, 27, 28
Best Days for Money: 1, 8, 9, 10, 17, 18, 19, 23, 24, 26, 27
Best Days for Career: 1, 10, 11, 15, 16, 19, 20, 27, 28

Health became more stressful on May 20 and remains so until June 21. As always, do your best to maintain high energy levels. Delegate tasks wherever possible. Rest when tired. Don't think that by pushing yourself you will get more done. Most likely you will only increase your work load because of mistakes. Enhance the health by giving more attention to the lungs and respiratory system until the 3rd and to the stomach afterwards. Women should give more attention to the breasts after the 3rd. Diet and emotional tranquillity become important after the 3rd. Health improves after the 21st though.

Love is still the main headline until the 21st. Many a marriage or engagement is happening these days. This is serious, committed love. Those already married or in a relationship are having more romance within that relationship and attending more parties and gatherings. The social scene cools down a bit after the 21st – probably your love and social goals have been attained. The Sun leaves your 7th house on the 21st and Jupiter, the Lord of your Horoscope, leaves that house on the 27th, having spent a year there. This is a major move, a major shift.

Pluto, the planet of personal transformation, was in your sign for many years until 2008. So you have been involved in personal transformation, personal reinvention for many years. You had a brief hiatus for the past four years but now you are again involved in this. You are giving birth to a new you – an ideal you. This can be hard work at times. One must be willing to 'die' to the old ways and old thought and emotional patterns. Often the process brings crises but you are enjoying all of this; though painful, the birth of a child is considered a happy event. So it is with you.

Finances are OK until the 21st. There are no disasters, but nothing special either. But after that date, earnings soar. Keep in mind though that your financial planet is still retrograde. There can be delays and misunderstandings, but this won't stop the prosperity. You still need to work on your mental clarity here. Financial opportunities (and there will be many) need a lot more homework. Your spouse, partner or current love enters a yearly financial peak on the 21st. In fact, the whole year ahead is a prosperity period. He or she will be more generous with you. You are in a good period for paying down debt. If you need to borrow, get a mortgage or other kind of business loan, it is very good for that too. An inheritance is likely for many of you – if not this month, then in the coming year.

Moves could also happen now. The family circle expands either through birth, marriage or through meeting people who are like family to you. Sagittarians of appropriate age are unusually fertile after the 21st.

July

Best Days Overall: 1, 9, 10, 11, 19, 20, 27, 28
Most Stressful Days Overall: 4, 5, 6, 12, 13, 25, 26
Best Days for Love: 1, 4, 5, 6, 7, 8, 10, 11, 17, 19, 20, 25, 26, 29, 30
Best Days for Money: 7, 8, 16, 17, 21, 22, 25
Best Days for Career: 7, 8, 12, 13, 17, 25, 26

On May 20 the planetary power began to make a major shift from the lower to the upper half of the Horoscope, the sector of outer activities. Home and family are still important, but you can start shifting your attention to the career and the outer goals. It is daytime in your year, and time to be about the affairs of the day.

Basically this is a happy and successful month. Finances continue to soar, personally and for the beloved. Saturn, your financial planet, which has been retrograde for many months, starts moving forward on the 8th. Thus there is clarity in financial matters and major moves, purchases or investments will go better. The family as a whole (and especially a parent or parent figure) is also prospering now. You are catching the lucky breaks in financial matters. Things that you already own increase in value. Something that you thought was worthless turns out to be valuable. Speculations are favourable, after the 8th; the 19th to the 24th seems especially favourable.

Health is also much better now, and after the 22nd it gets even better. If there have been health problems you hear good news after the 22nd. You can enhance your health further by giving attention to the heart until the 23rd. Avoid worry and anxiety. Take positive steps to improve your situation and reduce stress. After the 23rd give more attention to the small intestine. Right diet will be a help.

Love is not that important this month, though it is a sexually active kind of month, so you are not idle in that department. Social goals seem to have been attained, so there is no need for dramatic actions or changes. Your love planet is retrograde until the 20th, so the beloved seems to lack a sense of direction these days. Mercury also makes a square to Uranus from the 17th to the 26th which will test your present love. Your spouse, partner or current love will be more temperamental, so exercise more patience – no need to make matters worse than they need to be. He or she needs to be more careful driving, and to avoid risky situations. Foreign travel is not advisable that period. This transit also seems to bring career changes and shake-ups. Ultimately these will prove beneficial for you.

Venus crosses your Mid-heaven on the 23rd – basically a happy aspect. It brings career opportunity to you. Friends are succeeding personally and are helpful in your career. Your good work ethic is noted by superiors.

On June 21 the Water element once again became unusually strong. You experienced this in February and March as well. People are hypersensitive these days. Bluntness and honesty is likely to be seen as 'insensitive' – so watch what you say.

August

Best Days Overall: 6, 7, 15, 16, 23, 24
Most Stressful Days Overall: 1, 2, 8, 9, 21, 22, 28, 29
Best Days for Love: 1, 2, 3, 4, 8, 9, 15, 16, 19, 24, 25, 26, 28, 29
Best Days for Money: 3, 13, 14, 17, 18, 21, 22, 30, 31
Best Days for Career: 3, 4, 8, 9, 15, 16, 24, 25

Your 9th house became powerful on the 22nd of last month and is still powerful until the 22nd of this. This is Sagittarius heaven. No doubt you will be travelling this period. The doors are wide open. Sagittarians have a natural interest in theology, religion and metaphysics. In many cases it is not that developed, but the innate interest is there. So this is a month to go deeper into metaphysics and philosophy. There are philosophical breakthroughs for those who seek them. Happy opportunities for higher education will also come and you should take them. If you are involved in legal issues, this is a good month to deal with them. Students (at college level or beyond) are successful in school. Those seeking admittance to college should hear good news too.

On the 22nd, as the Sun crosses your Mid-heaven and enters your 10th career house, you enter a yearly career peak. Mercury, your career planet (as well as love planet) moves into the 10th house on the 24th. Venus has been there since July 23 and remains until the 16th. So your house of career is packed with benefic planets. You have much help in the career and in the attainment of career goals. You have the support of friends, the current love, and the ministers and religious people in your life. This is a successful month in the outer world.

Until the 22nd prepare yourself. Take courses in subjects that will enhance your career, attend seminars and work-shops. Be willing to mentor those beneath you and to be a disciple of those above you. The authority figures in your life will make note of this. The love planet on the Mid-heaven shows many things. First, that love is high on your priorities.

Your marriage and relationship ranks right up there with your career goals. This is good for the love life. Your focus tends to spell success. This also indicates that you further your career by social means, by attending or hosting parties, and by making friends with the people who can help you. Your ability to get on with others and gain their cooperation (and you've had a lot of practice with this in the past year) is a major factor in your success. Your personal abilities matter of course, but not as much as your social skills. They play a decisive role these days.

Health is more delicate after the 22nd, so be sure to rest and relax more. Yes, you are very busy these days, but try to schedule breaks and rest periods. Don't burn the candle at both ends or push the body beyond its natural limits.

Avoid speculations on the 1st and 2nd, and drive more carefully then (this especially applies to children of appropriate age). Also drive more carefully from the 18th to the 25th. Avoid risky, daredevil-type activities then too.

September

Best Days Overall: 2, 3, 11, 12, 20, 21, 29, 30
Most Stressful Days Overall: 4, 5, 6, 18, 19, 24, 25, 26
Best Days for Love: 5, 6, 8, 15, 16, 17, 18, 24, 25, 26, 27, 28
Best Days for Money: 1, 9, 10, 13, 14, 18, 19, 27, 28
Best Days for Career: 4, 5, 6, 15, 16, 25, 26

The month ahead is a fast-paced, hectic kind of month – just the way you like. Action and change make life interesting. However, be careful not to overdo all this activity, especially until the 22nd. Health is still delicate. The danger now is that you will push the body beyond its natural limits. The kidneys and hips are always important for you healthwise, but especially until the 11th. After then, pay more attention to the colon, bladder and sexual organs. You will also get powerful results from spiritual healing – prayer, meditation, the laying on hands, reiki and the manipulation of subtle energies. Health will improve very naturally after the 22nd. Make sure to get more rest though.

Last month on the 22nd the planetary power shifted from the West to the East. You entered a period of personal independence which is getting stronger day by day and month by month. With Jupiter still very much in the Western sector (and this has been the case since 2010), you are still very much putting others first. But now you can shift some attention to your own interests and desires. This is not selfishness, but more an attitude of self-reliance. The cosmos is expecting you to develop more of this quality now. If you want to help others, you yourself must become more effective, more balanced, and more personally happy. The more effective you are as a person, the greater the service you can perform. More independence means more power to create conditions and circumstances as you want them to be. There is less of a need to answer to others. You can do it on your own.

You are still very much in a yearly career peak until the 22nd. Review our discussion of this last month. The New Moon of the 5th occurs in your 10th house and this is an especially powerful career day, bringing success and opportunity. Also this New Moon will clarify career issues as the month progresses. Information will come to you that will help your decision-making.

Finances are still good this month. Though you are generally lucky with money, speculations are not advisable now, and especially avoid them from the 7th to the 11th. Expenses related to children or children figures could create some short-term problems, but this doesn't change the overall prosperity of the year.

Love is delicate until the 29th. Criticism, exactingness and perfectionism need to be avoided and are probably complicating the love life. Keep in mind that perfection is never handed to us on a silver platter; it is a road that we travel and it happens as a gradual process. Mercury makes dynamic aspects with Uranus and Pluto from the 15th to the 17th. This will test a current relationship. Be more patient with the beloved (who is apt to be more temperamental that period) and try not to make matters worse. The beloved and parents or parent figures should avoid risky activities during that period and need to drive carefully.

October

Best Days Overall: 1, 8, 9, 17, 18, 27, 28
Most Stressful Days Overall: 2, 3, 15, 16, 22, 23, 29, 30
Best Days for Love: 6, 7, 8, 15, 16, 17, 18, 22, 23, 24, 25, 27, 28
Best Days for Money: 6, 7, 11, 12, 15, 16, 24, 25
Best Days for Career: 2, 3, 6, 7, 15, 16, 24, 25, 29, 30

The main headline this month is the Lunar Eclipse of the 18th. Its affect is strong on you as it impacts on Jupiter, the Lord of your Horoscope. Take it nice and easy that period. This eclipse occurs in the 5th house and impacts on children or children figures in your life. Do your best to keep them out of harm's way. Let them avoid risk-taking activities and spend more quiet time at home. Speculations are best avoided that period as well. Since Jupiter is affected you are going to once again redefine your personality, image and self-concept. Things that were not attended to after the eclipse of May 25 will get attended to now. Like every Lunar Eclipse, this one brings encounters with death – not necessarily literal death, but psychological encounters. Sometimes this happens through personal near-death kinds of experiences or surgery.

Your 11th house of friends became powerful on September 22 and is powerful until the 23rd. It is a social kind of month. Not necessarily a romantic period – though romance seems much happier than last month – but more about friendship and group activities. The 11th house rules friendships of the mind, while the 7th house rules friendships of the heart. So this is a good month to reconnect with your friends and to get involved in group kinds of activities. New friends are coming into the picture too. Your circle of friends expands these days. (This can be on the physical level or in the online world.) It's a good month to upgrade your technology, your software, computers and gadgetry, and also to take courses or read books on science and technology. Astrology and astronomy become more interesting.

On the 23rd you enter a more spiritual period. Your 12th house of spirituality becomes the strongest in the Horoscope. Spiritual changes have been going on all year, but now they happen even more so. Your spiritual practice, your path, your commitment is being tested. You seem to be facing stiff opposition from the scientific community in your world, and also from siblings and neighbours. They don't seem at all receptive to your ideals and practice. A true path, a true teaching, will easily withstand these challenges and the very attacks will actually strengthen the practice. But a teaching or path that is less true (or partially true) will have to be modified.

After the 23rd you enter into greater prosperity. Finances are super. The financial intuition is super. There are nice paydays happening.

Love is also much happier this month. Mercury will camp out in beautiful aspect to Jupiter from the 17th to the 26th. Singles will meet significant romantic partners. Those already in a relationship will have more harmony and more romance within the relationship. Mercury, your love planet, starts to retrograde on the 21st, so avoid making important love decisions after that date. There's no need to rush love (or career matters); let things develop as they will. Your work should be to attain to clarity.

November

Best Days Overall: 5, 6, 13, 14, 23, 24
Most Stressful Days Overall: 11, 12, 18, 19, 25, 26, 27
Best Days for Love: 7, 16, 17, 18, 19, 26, 27
Best Days for Money: 3, 4, 7, 8, 11, 12, 20, 21, 22, 30
Best Days for Career: 3, 4, 11, 12, 20, 21, 22, 25, 26, 27, 30

A Solar Eclipse on the 3rd occurs in your spiritual 12th house. Uranus (both this month and last) is EXACTLY square to your spiritual planet, Pluto. So the eclipse is reinforcing the changes that have been going on in your spiritual life all year, and especially in the past month. The gurus, ministers, or priests in your life – your spiritual mentors – are experiencing dramatic, life-changing events, probably on a personal level. But there are also upheavals and shake-ups in a spiritual or charitable organization that you are involved with. Personal finances also seem affected here. There are important financial changes. Probably you have been too pessimistic about finances or the economy. Your actual situation is much better than it seems. Most likely you have to revise your strategy and planning. Students make important educational changes now (and over the next six months). There are dramatic events in the lives of the people at your place of worship. Legal issues will take a dramatic turn now and reach a climax.

Your house of spirituality was strong last month and is strong this month too, until the 22nd. This is a good period to achieve your spiritual and idealistic goals and for making spiritual progress. You are much closer to the spiritual, invisible world these days. You more easily access this world. Generally when the 12th house is strong, the dream life is more active and revelatory. This is so now, but around the eclipse period your dreams shouldn't be trusted – the dream world (the astral plane) is upset by the energies of the eclipse.

A happy travel or educational opportunity occurs between the 12th and 14th, but give it more thought. If you do
travel, allow more time for getting to and from your destination. Spiritual healing is very powerful during that particular
period, but the job situation seems unstable then. Be more
patient with co-workers or employees.

Your love planet goes forward on the 10th so the love
situation becomes clearer. It still looks very happy. Mercury
is trine to Jupiter on the 27th to the 29th, which brings
happy love meetings for singles and happy career opportunities.

From the 25th to the 27th, Mercury travels with Saturn.
This has some good points and some difficult points. You
need to work harder to show love and warmth to others.
Your normal sunny disposition might not be coming across
as it should. However, it is a nice financial period and there
are opportunities for partnerships or joint ventures. The
current love seems financially supportive. Bosses, parents
and authority figures are also supportive of your financial
goals.

December

Best Days Overall: 2, 3, 10, 11, 12, 20, 21, 22, 30, 31
Most Stressful Days Overall: 8, 9, 15, 16, 17, 23, 24
Best Days for Love: 1, 4, 5, 10, 11, 13, 14, 15, 16, 17, 21,
    22, 23, 24
Best Days for Money: 1, 4, 5, 8, 9, 18, 19, 28, 29
Best Days for Career: 1, 10, 11, 21, 22, 23, 24

Last month on the 22nd, as the Sun crossed your Ascendant
and entered your 1st house, you began a yearly personal
pleasure peak. This is a time for pampering, for taking care
of number one, for getting the body and the image the way
you want it to be. You are also in your period of greatest
personal independence now for this year. (In future years
you will have stronger periods of independence.) So now is
the time to have things your way and to create conditions

the way you want them to be. Though it might not seem like it, you really have no one to answer to but yourself. You've been adapting to the world all year – let the world adapt to you for a change.

Another important shift began last month, with the planetary power moving from the upper to the lower half of the Horoscope. It is evening in your year. The day is over, the activities of the day have more or less been completed and now you are ready for the interior, unseen activities of the night. It's time to start focusing on your emotional wellbeing and to get the home in order, to build the interior conditions for future career success, and to find your personal point of emotional harmony.

Mars spent the month of November in your 10th house of career. He is still there until the 8th. This shows hard work careerwise, but also fun. Children and children figures advance in their careers as well.

Health is better than last month. You can enhance it by giving attention to the spine, knees, teeth, bones, skin and overall skeletal alignment. Regular back and knee massages will be powerful. Don't allow financial worries or cares to affect your health. The fact is you are still in a very prosperous period (both you and family members). On the 21st you enter a yearly financial peak which will continue into next month. The money is rolling in. The financial judgement is sound. Remember, spiritually speaking, there is no limit to wealth. The Divine supply is unlimited. The only limitation lies with us, with our personal capacity to receive. If you can open up to receive more, you will have more.

Love is happy from the 5th to the 24th. The beloved is going out of his or her way to please you. You are having love on your terms. There's nothing much you need to do to attract love – just go about your normal routine. After the 24th, Mercury moves into your money house, and the beloved seems very generous and supportive.

Capricorn

♑

THE GOAT
*Birthdays from
21st December to
19th January*

Personality Profile

CAPRICORN AT A GLANCE

Element – Earth

Ruling Planet – Saturn
   Career Planet – Venus
   Love Planet – Moon
   Money Planet – Uranus
   Planet of Communications – Neptune
   Planet of Health and Work – Mercury
   Planet of Home and Family Life – Mars
   Planet of Spirituality – Jupiter

Colours – black, indigo

*Colours that promote love, romance and social
   harmony* – puce, silver

Colour that promotes earning power –
   ultramarine blue

Gem – black onyx

Metal – lead

Scents – magnolia, pine, sweet pea, wintergreen

Quality – cardinal (= activity)

Qualities most needed for balance – warmth, spontaneity, a sense of fun

Strongest virtues – sense of duty, organization, perseverance, patience, ability to take the long-term view

Deepest needs – to manage, take charge and administrate

Characteristics to avoid – pessimism, depression, undue materialism and undue conservatism

Signs of greatest overall compatibility – Taurus, Virgo

Signs of greatest overall incompatibility – Aries, Cancer, Libra

Sign most helpful to career – Libra

Sign most helpful for emotional support – Aries

Sign most helpful financially – Aquarius

Sign best for marriage and/or partnerships – Cancer

Sign most helpful for creative projects – Taurus

Best Sign to have fun with – Taurus

Signs most helpful in spiritual matters – Virgo, Sagittarius

Best day of the week – Saturday

Understanding a Capricorn

The virtues of Capricorns are such that there will always be people for and against them. Many admire them, many dislike them. Why? It seems to be because of Capricorn's power urges. A well-developed Capricorn has his or her eyes set on the heights of power, prestige and authority. In the sign of Capricorn, ambition is not a fatal flaw, but rather the highest virtue.

Capricorns are not frightened by the resentment their authority may sometimes breed. In Capricorn's cool, calculated, organized mind all the dangers are already factored into the equation – the unpopularity, the animosity, the misunderstandings, even the outright slander – and a plan is always in place for dealing with these things in the most efficient way. To the Capricorn, situations that would terrify an ordinary mind are merely problems to be managed, bumps on the road to ever-growing power, effectiveness and prestige.

Some people attribute pessimism to the Capricorn sign, but this is a bit deceptive. It is true that Capricorns like to take into account the negative side of things. It is also true that they love to imagine the worst possible scenario in every undertaking. Other people might find such analyses depressing, but Capricorns only do these things so that they can formulate a way out – an escape route.

Capricorns will argue with success. They will show you that you are not doing as well as you think you are. Capricorns do this to themselves as well as to others. They do not mean to discourage you but rather to root out any impediments to your greater success. A Capricorn boss or supervisor feels that no matter how good the performance there is always room for improvement. This explains why Capricorn supervisors are difficult to handle and even infuriating at times. Their actions are, however, quite often effective – they can get their subordinates to improve and become better at their jobs.

Capricorn is a born manager and administrator. Leo is better at being king or queen, but Capricorn is better at being prime minister – the person actually wielding power.

Capricorn is interested in the virtues that last, in the things that will stand the test of time and trials of circumstance. Temporary fads and fashions mean little to a Capricorn – except as things to be used for profit or power. Capricorns apply this attitude to business, love, to their thinking and even to their philosophy and religion.

Finance

Capricorns generally attain wealth and they usually earn it. They are willing to work long and hard for what they want. They are quite amenable to foregoing a short-term gain in favour of long-term benefits. Financially, they come into their own later in life.

However, if Capricorns are to attain their financial goals they must shed some of their strong conservatism. Perhaps this is the least desirable trait of the Capricorn. They can resist anything new merely because it is new and untried. They are afraid of experimentation. Capricorns need to be willing to take a few risks. They should be more eager to market new products or explore different managerial techniques. Otherwise, progress will leave them behind. If necessary, Capricorns must be ready to change with the times, to discard old methods that no longer work.

Very often this experimentation will mean that Capricorns have to break with existing authority. They might even consider changing their present position or starting their own ventures. If so, they should be willing to accept all the risks and just get on with it. Only then will a Capricorn be on the road to highest financial gains.

Career and Public Image

A Capricorn's ambition and quest for power are evident. It is perhaps the most ambitious sign of the zodiac – and usually the most successful in a worldly sense. However, there are lessons Capricorns need to learn in order to fulfil their highest aspirations.

Intelligence, hard work, cool efficiency and organization will take them a certain distance, but will not carry them to the very top. Capricorns need to cultivate their social graces, to develop a social style, along with charm and an ability to get along with people. They need to bring beauty into their lives and to cultivate the right social contacts. They must learn to wield power gracefully, so that people love them for it – a very delicate art. They also need to learn how to bring people together in order to fulfil certain objectives. In short, Capricorns require some of the gifts – the social graces – of Libra to get to the top.

Once they have learned this, Capricorns will be successful in their careers. They are ambitious hard workers who are not afraid of putting in the required time and effort. Capricorns take their time in getting the job done – in order to do it well – and they like moving up the corporate ladder slowly but surely. Being so driven by success, Capricorns are generally liked by their bosses, who respect and trust them.

Love and Relationships

Like Scorpio and Pisces, Capricorn is a difficult sign to get to know. They are deep, introverted and like to keep their own counsel. Capricorns do not like to reveal their innermost thoughts. If you are in love with a Capricorn, be patient and take your time. Little by little you will get to understand him or her.

Capricorns have a deep romantic nature, but they do not show it straightaway. They are cool, matter of fact and not especially emotional. They will often show their love in practical ways.

It takes time for a Capricorn – male or female – to fall in love. They are not the love-at-first-sight kind. If a Capricorn is involved with a Leo or Aries, these Fire types will be totally mystified – to them the Capricorn will seem cold, unfeeling, unaffectionate and not very spontaneous. Of course none of this is true; it is just that Capricorn likes to take things slowly. They like to be sure of their ground before making any demonstrations of love or commitment.

Even in love affairs Capricorns are deliberate. They need more time to make decisions than is true of the other signs of the zodiac, but given this time they become just as passionate. Capricorns like a relationship to be structured, committed, well regulated, well defined, predictable and even routine. They prefer partners who are nurturers, and they in turn like to nurture their partners. This is their basic psychology. Whether such a relationship is good for them is another issue altogether. Capricorns have enough routine in their lives as it is. They might be better off in relationships that are a bit more stimulating, changeable and fluctuating.

Home and Domestic Life

The home of a Capricorn – as with a Virgo – is going to be tidy and well organized. Capricorns tend to manage their families in the same way they manage their businesses. Capricorns are often so career-driven that they find little time for the home and family. They should try to get more actively involved in their family and domestic life. Capricorns do, however, take their children very seriously and are very proud parents – particularly should their children grow up to become respected members of society.

Horoscope for 2013

Major Trends

You have just come through a very rough two years. Three powerful long-term planets were arrayed against you and there were times when 60 per cent (and sometimes 70 per cent) of the planets were in stressful alignment. Your mettle was tested. You were pushed to the limit. Not everyone came through this, but if you're reading this you did. Give yourself a pat on the back. This was an achievement.

Much of the stress came from instability within the family. There were many dramatic events in the lives of family members. The family unit could have broken up, or come near breaking up; even now it is held together with 'string and chewing gum' – very tenuous and delicate bonds. More details on this later.

Much stress came, curiously, from your success. In many cases, Capricorn, you were at the pinnacle of achievement, so you stood out like a target. The person on top is always the natural target. You had to deal with a lot of flak from underlings and competitors. Being on top is not all that it's made out to be. Not being on top has its challenges, but being on top has perhaps greater challenges. Every decision was scrutinized and criticized. In many cases, you were on top, but you aspired to be and this created tensions. You had to be reminded, sometimes dramatically, of your true status.

Health could have suffered these past two years. Happily, this area is much improved. If you have had health problems you should be hearing good news about it. There's more on this later.

Pluto has been in your own sign since 2008. And so you are in process of reinventing yourself, giving birth to the 'you' that you really want to be. This trend is continuing this year and for many more years.

Your most important interests in the year ahead are the body, the image and personal pleasure; communication and intellectual interests; home and family; health and work (until June 27); love and romance (from June 27 onwards); friends, groups, group activities and organizations.

Your paths of greatest fulfilment this year are health and work (until June 27); love and romance (after June 27); and friends, groups, group activities and organizations.

Health

(Please note that this is an astrological perspective on health and not a medical one. In days of yore there was no difference, these perspectives were identical. But now there could be quite a difference. For a medical perspective, please consult your doctor or health practitioner.)

Health as we mentioned is much improved these days. In 2011 and 2012 you were subjected to unusual and rare health stresses. This year health is still delicate, but nothing compared to the past two years. Happily, this year your 6th house of health is strong, especially until June 27, so you are paying attention and this is exactly what is needed. When the health aspects are stressful, we need to make health a priority. If we just ignore things problems are likely to arise.

You begin the year with two long-term planets in stressful alignment. On June 27, Jupiter will move into stressful alignment as well. Jupiter's opposition to your Sun is not as serious as what was happening over the past two years, but it still needs to be taken into account.

There is much that can be done to improve and enhance the health and stamina. The first and most important thing is to be more mindful of your energy. Don't waste it frivolously. Invest it in things that are important to you and let lesser things go. Rest and relax more. If you're tired take a nap, and delegate tasks wherever possible. Plan your day so that more gets done with less effort. Mental and emotional activity takes energy. It requires energy to think, feel and talk. Keep these things in check. The powerful people are silent and placid. They don't fritter their power

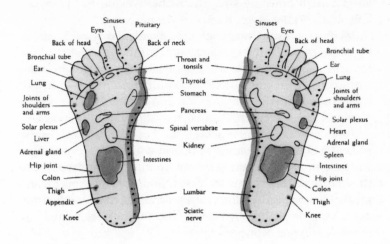

Sinuses · Pituitary · Eyes · Back of head · Back of neck · Bronchial tube · Throat and tonsils · Ear · Thyroid · Lung · Stomach · Joints of shoulders and arms · Pancreas · Solar plexus · Spinal vertebrae · Liver · Heart · Kidney · Adrenal gland · Hip joint · Spleen · Colon · Intestines · Thigh · Lumbar · Appendix · Sciatic nerve · Knee

Reflexology

Try to massage the whole foot on a regular basis, but pay extra attention to the points highlighted on the chart. When you massage, be aware of 'sore spots', as these need special attention. It's also a good idea to massage the ankles and top side of the feet.

away in useless speech or emotion, which is why they are powerful.

Give more attention to the following organs: the heart (avoid worry and anxiety, the two emotions that are the root causes of heart problems); the spine, knees, teeth, bones, skin and overall skeletal alignment (regular back and knee massage will be powerful on the energetic level, and therapies such as yoga, Pilates, Alexander Technique or Feldenkrais are good – as are regular visits to a chiropractor or osteopath; give the knees more support, and when out in the sun use a good sun screen); the lungs, small intestine, arms, shoulders and respiratory system (arms and shoulders should be regularly massaged, air purity is important for you and breathing exercises are good); the liver and thighs (these are important until June 27. Regular thigh massage is good. It will not only strengthen the liver on the energetic level but also the lower back.)

Mercury is your health planet. As regular readers know, he is a very fast-moving planet and in the course of the year he will move through all the signs and houses of your Horoscope. Thus there are many short-term trends in health that depend on where Mercury is and the kinds of aspects he receives. These are best dealt with in the monthly reports.

Jupiter, your spiritual planet, has been in your 6th house of health since June of last year, and will be there until June 27. So you are in a period where you are going deeper into the spiritual dimensions of health and healing. You benefit greatly from spiritual kinds of therapies such as meditation, the laying on of hands, prayer, visualization, reiki and the manipulation of subtle energies.

Home and Family

This will be a turbulent and important area of life this year, and for years to come. Family unity – the family situation – is highly unstable, as we mentioned. There is much unrest and rebellion going on and in coming years the whole family situation will be dramatically changed.

Uranus, the planet of sudden and revolutionary change, has been in this house since March 2011. So there is a liberation process happening here. Family is very important, a survival mechanism that we can't do without. However, it is a two-edged sword and at certain times it can be a form of bondage. A seed is very comfortable in the ground. But at a certain point of growth, it must emerge from it or die. As it leaves the ground and flowers, it is still rooted in the ground, but the relationship is different. This is what is happening in the family. In the end you will still have your family relationship, but it will be very different. There will be more freedom and less bondage. Everyone will be able to flower as they should and yet still be connected. Sometimes dramatic events are needed to bring this about and Uranus knows how to supply this.

There is a need now, in general, for more freedom in the family unit. Give each other maximum space, so long as it isn't destructive.

Many of you are working to create a team spirit in the family and this is good. For Capricorn this is a bit of challenge (you tend to be more authoritarian) but it is a good challenge. Family members need to understand the rules, and the reasons for the rules. Take the time to explain these things. If they understand the logic behind them they are more likely to comply. If you take the authoritarian route, you are likely to have rebellion on your hands.

Uranus is the planet of experimentation and innovation. So you are experimental with the family and with the domestic life in general. The standard rule books don't apply any more; you are learning what works here through trial and error.

This aspect also shows that you are modernizing the home, networking, broadbanding and installing all kinds of hi-tech gadgetry. Even your taste in furniture is modern. Uranus is your financial planet. This indicates that you are investing in the home and family, but that you can also earn from it as well. A home-based business seems likely. And even if you are in a 'bricks and mortar' kind of business, you will be earning more from home. Many of you are setting up home offices.

Uranus in the 4th house shows many moves. Moves probably already happened in the past two years, but more are likely. It shows a constant upgrading of the home, a never-ending process of perfection. Every time you think you have things 'perfect' a new idea comes along. Either you move or renovate.

Finance and Career

Finance and career are always important to Capricorn, but this year less so. Neither the 10th house of career nor the 2nd house of money is a house of power.

I read this as a good thing. You are leaving a multi-year focus on these things. Most likely you have achieved your major career and financial goals and have no need to make major changes. There's no need to pay too much attention here. Other things are more important.

Uranus, your financial planet, has been in Aries since March 2011 and will be there for many years to come, so this is a long-term trend. Uranus in Aries suggests new ventures, start-up types of ventures. These have probably already happened, but if not they can still happen – the opportunities come. There is a need now for financial inde-pendence, for being in personal control of your financial destiny. You seem to be working towards this end. Generally this is not so good for business partnerships. You prefer to operate solo as you have more control. However, business partnerships are likely in the year ahead so you need to take this into account in your decision-making.

Here's another interesting trend. Capricorns are stable, methodical people. They are cautious and conservative by nature. They like to attain wealth step by step, methodically, over time. To them, in general, wealth is a 'process' not a 'thing' or 'object'. But now with your financial planet in dynamic Aries you seem more in a hurry, more willing to speculate and take risks. And perhaps you need to be this way at this time. Your basic attitudes are good but a little boring and you need to add a little excitement to the finan-cial life. Sometimes in life, bold moves are called for. Often these conservative attitudes are fear based. This is not always so but the line that separates healthy caution from fear is a thin one. This is a period where you will learn about your-self. This is a period for overcoming financial fear, for devel-oping faith and courage, and for taking giant leaps into the unknown.

As we mentioned earlier, your chart favours a home-based kind of business. It also shows 'family' businesses – your own, or another's. Residential real estate, restaurants, the food business, hotels and motels – companies that cater to the home and homeowners – are all favoured these days.

Uranus is also the planet of technology. Thus you are spending more on technology, but you also earn from this.

Gadgets for the home would fit the symbolism of the Horoscope these days. You always need to be up to date with the latest technology. Your technological skills and expertise are always important. This year is no different.

An ongoing conflict with friends seems to stress the bottom line. This has been going on for some time but gets more intense later in the year. If you have invented something make sure you are well covered legally.

Financial intuition is a wonderful thing, but after June 27 it needs more verification. Take time to see that you have grasped the true intent of the guidance.

Love and Social Life

Your 7th house of love and marriage becomes strong in the latter part of the year, after June 27. In the meantime love is more or less status quo. For singles this should be a period for preparation and self-improvement, to become clear in your mind as to what you want in love, the kind of person you want to be with, etc. It's also a good time to make yourself more lovable. All of us can use more work on this, and now is a good time to get into it.

When Jupiter enters your 7th house on June 27 the whole love and social life is going to expand in a very positive way. Often it brings marriage. Sometimes it brings marriage opportunity. Sometimes it brings a relationship that is like a marriage. Sometimes it brings meetings with people that you would consider 'marriage material' or relationships that have marriage potential. Often it brings business partnerships or joint ventures. Always, though, it expands the social life and the social circle. New and significant friends come into the picture now. There is more dating and going out, more parties and social gatherings.

Jupiter is your spiritual planet. Thus his move into the house of love is giving us other messages as well. Your social circle is becoming more refined and spiritualized. You are attracting spiritual kinds of friends – mystics, yogis, psychics, spiritual channels, ministers, gurus. You will also be attracted to poets, musicians and dancers. In other words you are going to attract spiritual kinds of relationships. The spiritual dimension becomes very important in the romantic life as well. Mere physical attraction is not enough for you. You and the beloved have to be on the same spiritual path, and have more or less compatible spiritual values and ideals. If this is the case the relationship has a better chance of enduring.

This year you find love in both the usual and unusual kinds of places. The usual places are parties, social gatherings and through introductions from friends. But love also awaits you in spiritual-type settings – at retreats, prayer meetings, yoga studios, meditation seminars and so forth. It also awaits you in charitable kinds of activities and functions and as you get involved in causes that you believe in.

Love is idealistic these days. There is a need to feel that your relationship is 'sanctioned from on high' and not just a matter of chemistry, and many of you will find 'ideal' love this year or in 2014. However, keep in mind that one must be ready for such love otherwise impurities in the psyche will mar it and cause many complications.

For those already married, the spouse or partner is becoming more spiritual, so the relationship will be spiritualized.

For those of you in or working on the second marriage, the year ahead will be a status quo one. Singles will tend to remain single and those who are married will tend to remain married. However the social life will still be much expanded. For those of you in the third marriage this is a year of testing. For those of you working on the third marriage, you seem proactive about it, but marriage is probably not advisable this year.

There are many short-term trends in love which we will deal with in the monthly reports. Your love planet, the Moon, is a fast-moving planet and moves through all the signs and houses of your Horoscope every month.

Self-improvement

Your spiritual planet Jupiter spends the first half of the year in your 6th house of health. Thus, this is a year for going deeper into spiritual healing. You benefit from spiritual-type therapies as well, as we have mentioned, and it's good to read all you can about this subject. There is much literature on it, but I recommend that beginners should start with the works of Emmet Fox and Ernest Holmes.

Spiritual healing is a bit different from 'Mind-Body' medicine, which is all about positive thinking and holding positive images. Spiritual healing involves something deeper: it is about accessing a healing force that is above the mind, a supernatural force, if you will. We access this awesome and stupendous power through prayer and meditation. Sometimes, if a person can't access it directly, they are led to others – spiritual healers – who can. This too can happen for many of you.

On June 27, as we mentioned, your spiritual planet will enter your 7th house of love. We have discussed the mundane meanings of this earlier. But there are spiritual meanings to this transit. Love is always a doorway to the Divine, but this year even more so. When you are in a state of love, the doors are open. When you are involved in romance you feel close to the Divine. The problem with romantic love, though, is that it tends to be 'conditional', so lovers' spats, irritations and annoyances can close the door if you are not careful. This is a year for practising unconditional love. Intuition – the inner guidance – is very important in health matters this year, and also in love and social matters. The short cut to romance is to follow your intuition.

If love problems get too overwhelming, cast the entire burden of the love life upon the Divine, and do it sincerely. Watch how everything starts to straighten out. The sincerity though is very important. If you only surrender with the mouth but not the heart, nothing much will happen.

Month-by-month Forecasts

January

Best Days Overall: 2, 3, 10, 11, 19, 20, 29, 30
Most Stressful Days Overall: 4, 5, 17, 18, 24, 25, 31
Best Days for Love: 2, 3, 8, 9, 10, 11, 18, 19, 21, 24, 25, 29, 30, 31
Best Days for Money: 4, 8, 12, 13, 17, 22, 26, 27, 31
Best Days for Career: 4, 5, 8, 9, 18, 19, 29, 30, 31

You begin your year with personal independence at its greatest extent for the year. Not only is the Eastern half of the Horoscope strong, but your 1st house is very powerful until the 19th. When the Eastern sector is strong the cosmos urges us to cultivate self-reliance, to shape our destiny to our personal specifications. There will be some mistakes, but no matter. These mistakes will be learning experiences and you will find out about them when the planets move West and you are forced to live with your creation. Then when the planets move East again you will create anew and in a better way. This is the cosmic rhythm of growth and development. You can have things your way now, and you should. You know better than anyone what will make you happy and you should follow your path of bliss (so long as you don't hurt others). You are also in one of your yearly personal pleasure peaks until the 19th. This is the time to enjoy all the sensual delights of the body and to get your body and image in shape.

Last month on the 21st, the planets shifted from the upper half of the Horoscope to the lower half. The sun is setting in your year. The activities of the day are finished and you are getting ready for the activities of the night. It is time to focus on your home base – your family, the domestic situation and your emotional wellbeing. Like a good night's sleep, this temporary withdrawal from the outer world allows you to build up the forces for future career success.

Happy career opportunities are pursuing you this month after the 10th. But now you can be a bit more choosy about them. These opportunities should not violate your emotional harmony or family situation.

Health is excellent this month and you seem focused here. Good health is like a cosmetic – it enhances the personal appearance. Back and knee massage (always good for you) is even more powerful until the 19th, as are detox regimes. After the 19th enhance the health with ankle and calf massages. Give the ankles more support. Don't allow financial ups and downs to affect your health. It might be advisable to invest in health gadgets after the 19th.

Job seekers have beautiful aspects all month, but especially until the 19th. There's nothing much you need to do; job opportunities are seeking you out. On the 19th you enter a yearly financial peak. It's a time to build up the bank balances and the investment accounts, but use your economic power constructively – to bless and heal yourself and others, not to punish, dominate or control.

February

Best Days Overall: 7, 8, 15, 16, 17, 25, 26
Most Stressful Days Overall: 1, 13, 14, 20, 21, 22, 27, 28
Best Days for Love: 1, 9, 10, 18, 19, 20, 21, 22
Best Days for Money: 4, 5, 9, 10, 13, 18, 23, 27
Best Days for Career: 1, 9, 10, 18, 19, 27, 28

Since the 19th of last month all of you have been in a personal waxing solar cycle. The universal solar cycle is in its waxing phase now too (until June 21). So, you are in a great period for starting new projects, businesses or other kinds of ventures. Most of the planets are moving forward now and this adds to the favourability. If you're thinking of starting something new, between the 10th and 18th is best. On the 18th Saturn, your ruling planet, starts to retrograde and more caution is needed.

You are still in the midst of a yearly financial peak and prosperity is strong – a good period to pay down debt. But if you need to borrow, the aspects are good for that as well. There is luck in speculations too. You have the financial favour of bosses, elders, parents or parent figures – even the government. The New Moon of the 10th will bring all kinds of financial information and clarification, allowing you to make astute financial moves.

The love situation is more or less status quo. Last month was better for love. Venus spent from January 10 onwards in your own sign, which is always good for love. On the 2nd Venus moves into Aquarius and out of your sign. In general, you are socially more magnetic from the 10th to the 25th as the Moon is waxing. You are more in the mood for love that period. You are in a preparation period these days. Serious love for singles will start happening at the end of June. In the meantime, enjoy whatever is happening.

Health is good this month. Energy is not as high as last month, but still adequate. You can enhance the health by giving more attention to the ankles and calves until the 5th and to the feet from the 5th onwards. Your health planet goes retrograde on the 23rd so avoid making drastic changes to the diet or health regime after then. Things need more study. Claims being made are not what they seem. Job offers or opportunities also need more scrutiny after the 23rd. Resolve all doubts before accepting a position.

The family situation has been unstable for a few years now. There is spiritual guidance on these matters from the 3rd to the 5th. Perhaps a dream explains the true inner situation to you. You have good opportunities to create family harmony from the 15th to the 17th.

There is luck in speculations from the 6th to the 7th. Money is earned in happy ways. A nice career opportunity happens then too. Parents, children, parent figures or children figures have a nice payday.

March

Best Days Overall: 6, 7, 15, 16, 24, 25, 26
Most Stressful Days Overall: 1, 12, 13, 14, 20, 21, 27, 28
Best Days for Love: 2, 3, 10, 11, 20, 21, 22, 31
Best Days for Money: 1, 4, 8, 9, 12, 13, 17, 18, 22, 27, 28, 31
Best Days for Career: 1, 2, 3, 10, 11, 21, 22, 27, 28, 31

Though Saturn, the Lord of your Horoscope, is still retrograde you are still in an excellent period for starting new projects or ventures. Sure, more homework has to be done with these things, but if you've done it, you can let them loose now. The 17th to the 27th would be the best time. The Moon is waxing and Mercury is moving forward. The momentum of the planets is forward and you should make faster progress towards your goals.

On February 18 the Water element became very strong, which continues until March 20. People tend to be hypersensitive under this aspect. Little, inconsequential things can set them off. You need to be aware of this and tread very carefully with people's feelings. A little forethought can prevent many needless explosions later on. Logic, rationality, even practical issues mean little these days – it is the mood of the moment that people respond to, even if it is costly.

Your 3rd house of communication and intellectual interests became powerful on the 18th of last month and is powerful until the 20th. This is a good period for students. They do better in their studies. The mind is sharper and clearer. It is also very good for writers, journalists, sales people and teachers. The communication faculties are much stronger. It's a good period to catch up on those letters, emails and texts that you owe, and for taking courses in subjects that interest you. This month you discover the joy of learning, the joy of mental satisfaction.

Health is good until the 20th but afterwards becomes more delicate. Relax, keep your focus on the important things and drop the trivia. If you do this, you will discover that you have all the energy you need to achieve what is important in your life. Until the 22nd enhance the health in the ways mentioned in the yearly report (page 340), but also give more attention to the feet. Regular foot massage is very powerful then. Also you respond well to spiritual therapies – prayer, meditation, the laying on of hands, invocation, reiki and the manipulation of subtle energies. After the 22nd you prefer more 'hands on' kinds of therapies and you respond better to them. Physical exercise is good. The muscles need to be toned. Head and face massage is also very good.

Finances are OK until the 20th – nothing special, but no disasters either. Finances improve but are more volatile after the 20th as your financial planet gets much stimulation. Mars will conjunct Uranus from the 18th to the 21st. Avoid risk-taking or impulse buying or spending. There can be unexpected expenses at home or with the family. Make sure the home is safer that period. Smoke detectors should be in good order and keep dangerous objects away from children. Speculations improve from the 26th to the 29th. You also have the financial favour of those in authority that period. If you need to borrow or pay down debt, the 1st and 2nd and the 27th to the 30th are good.

Love is pretty much status quo this month, though your social magnetism will be much stronger from the 11th to the 27th.

April

Best Days Overall: 2, 3, 11, 12, 21, 22, 29, 30
Most Stressful Days Overall: 9, 10, 16, 17, 23, 24
Best Days for Love: 1, 9, 10, 16, 17, 21, 22, 29, 30
Best Days for Money: 1, 4, 5, 9, 10, 14, 15, 19, 20, 23, 24, 27, 28
Best Days for Career: 1, 9, 10, 21, 22, 23, 24, 29, 30

Your 4th house of home and family became very strong last month and is still strong until the 19th. Your 10th house of career, by contrast, is basically empty – only the Moon will pass through on the 23rd and 24th – and at least 80 per cent of the planets are in the lower half of your chart. This is a very clear message. Let go of career for a while and focus on the home and family. You are in the midnight hour of your year. The body (which is the instrument for outer activities) is still, but interior activities are very strong. The subconscious mind is working overtime now. It is setting the stage for future career success. Your emotional wellbeing and your stable home base take priority now.

This is a month where people make major psychological breakthroughs. The memory body is very active now and people become more nostalgic. There is a reason for this. As the past gets reviewed old issues get resolved. We look at the past from our present perspective and thus can revise and amend many of our old opinions. That event you categorized as a failure (and which perhaps caused you much pain), when seen in hindsight was really a great blessing and a stepping stone to success. It is great to review the past and resolve old issues. However, it is not so great to be 'living in the past': this is the danger of a powerful 4th house. Always keep in mind that you are in the 'now' reviewing your past, much like you would watch a movie.

Finances are still good this month, but erratic. They can go sky high or ultra low. The moves in your financial life are extreme.

There are dramas in the lives of your friends and life-changing kinds of experiences. This is testing friendships in spite of the fact that you seem very devoted to them. Financial disagreements seem a problem here, but family problems are also a factor. These dramas are going on all year, but now they seem extreme. A Lunar Eclipse on the 25th reinforces what we say. This eclipse will also test love and marriage.

Uranus square to Pluto shows that your computers, software and hi-tech gadgetry are being tested. They seem erratic and some of it will need replacement. It's good to invest in good anti-virus, anti-spyware and anti-identity theft software nowadays.

Health has been more delicate since March 20. Rest and relax more. Keep in mind last month's discussion. Health can be enhanced in the ways mentioned in the yearly report. In addition, until the 15th give more attention to the head and face, like last month. After the 15th give more attention to the neck and throat. Regular neck massage will be powerful. Health and vitality improve after the 20th.

Last month on the 20th, the planetary power began to shift from the independent East to the social Western sector. Until then you were developing self-reliance; now the cosmos urges you to develop the social skills. Both are equally important.

May

Best Days Overall: 8, 9, 10, 18, 19, 27, 28
Most Stressful Days Overall: 6, 7, 13, 14, 15, 21, 22
Best Days for Love: 8, 9, 10, 11, 13, 14, 15, 19, 20, 21, 22, 29, 30
Best Days for Money: 2, 3, 6, 7, 11, 12, 16, 17, 21, 22, 25, 26, 29, 30
Best Days for Career: 10, 11, 21, 22, 29, 30

Last month on the 19th you entered another one of your yearly personal pleasure peaks and this continues until May 20 – a happy time. Capricorns can be workaholics so a period of leisure is very important. It recharges the batteries. This is a period for doing the things that you love to do. Capricorns of the appropriate age are more fertile this period than usual.

Health is good this month. You can enhance it further by giving more attention to the neck and throat (neck massage and craniosacral therapy is powerful) until the 15th and to the lungs, respiratory system, arms and shoulders afterwards. On the 5th and 6th pay attention to the spine and knees.

We have two eclipses this month. This will be a turbulent time for the world at large, but for you these seem basically benign. (Your personal Horoscope, cast for your actual time of birth, could modify what we say here.) Eclipses tend to roil up the psychic energies on the planet and thus it is always good to avoid risk-taking kinds of activities. People are not up to par these periods and though you might be OK, others are not. The Solar Eclipse of the 10th occurs in your 5th house of children, so there will be dramas in the lives of your children or children figures in your life. Do your best to keep them out of harm's way this period. A parent or parent figure makes important financial changes, perhaps due to some upheaval or surprise. Your spouse, partner or current love is also making dramatic financial changes. Since the Sun is ruler of your 8th house of transformation, Solar Eclipses often bring encounters with death or near-death kinds of experiences. Sometimes surgery is recommended, or they happen. The angel of death pays a visit. Most likely he is not after you, but he lets you know that he is around.

The Lunar Eclipse of the 25th occurs in your 12th house of spirituality and it will bring dramatic spiritual changes – changes in your practice or changes of teachings or teachers. There are dramas with the guru or minister figures in your life and shake-ups in spiritual or charitable organizations that you belong to. Like every Lunar Eclipse, love is tested, business partnerships as well. These testings can happen in various ways. Sometimes old resentments surface so they can be corrected. Sometimes the relationship gets tested because of dramas that occur in the life of the beloved or partners. Be more patient with these people this period. They are more temperamental. This Lunar Eclipse impacts on Neptune, which again indicates spiritual changes are happening. But it also tests cars and communication equipment. Drive more carefully this period.

June

   Best Days Overall: 5, 6, 15, 16, 23, 24
   Most Stressful Days Overall: 2, 3, 10, 11, 17, 18, 30
   Best Days for Love: 7, 8, 10, 11, 17, 18, 19, 20, 27, 28
   Best Days for Money: 2, 3, 8, 9, 12, 13, 17, 18, 21, 22, 25, 26, 27, 30
   Best Days for Career: 10, 17, 18, 19, 20, 27, 28

Last month your 6th house of health and work became powerful. It is still powerful until the 21st of this month, indicating an excellent period for job seekers (job seekers have had good aspects all year) and for those who employ others. Workers are more productive this period and are easily found. You are more into personal health now – right eating and health regimes. Children or children figures are prospering this period.

Testings in love, which happened at the end of last month, are rarely pleasant. But sometimes these are necessary so that the right relationship can come to you. Too much attachment for the wrong reasons blocks the good that would naturally come to you. Many a relationship broke up last month. Good ones survived and got even better. If your relationship broke up, take heart – you are entering one of the best love periods of your life this month. There is a Mr or Ms Right coming into the picture now. Marriage or relationships that are like a marriage could easily happen.

On the 21st you enter a yearly love and social peak. This one will be much stronger than the usual (which you generally experience at this time of year), as Jupiter is moving into the 7th house on the 27th.

Aside from the romance that is happening, there is a general increase in your socializing. You are going out more, attending more parties, weddings and gatherings. New and important friends are coming into the picture as well. The exciting social life could be distracting you from finance, so keep your eye on the ball.

You seem to be getting a new car and new communication equipment. (This could happen next month as well.) Siblings and sibling figures have very nice paydays at the end of the month.

Health needs more watching from the 21st onwards, so be sure to rest and relax more, especially on the 30th. Seventy per cent of the planets are in stressful aspect with you. Enhance the health by giving more attention to the stomach, and women should give more attention to the breasts. The stomach seems more sensitive these days, so right diet is important. The emotions need to be kept in harmony.

The planets are now in their maximum Western position this month. Avoid self-will and self-assertion. Let others have their way so long as it isn't destructive. Take a vacation from yourself and your personal interests and focus on others.

July

Best Days Overall: 2, 3, 12, 13, 21, 22, 29, 30
Most Stressful Days Overall: 1, 7, 8, 14, 15, 27, 28
Best Days for Love: 1, 7, 8, 10, 11, 17, 18, 19, 20, 27, 29, 30
Best Days for Money: 1, 7, 8, 12, 13, 16, 17, 21, 22, 23, 24, 25, 27, 28
Best Days for Career: 1, 10, 11, 14, 15, 19, 20, 29, 30

Many of the trends we wrote of last month are still in effect now. You are still in the midst of a powerful love and social peak until the 22nd. Love will be good afterwards too, but is most active until then. Love and social goals are being attained now.

Health still needs watching, especially until the 22nd. Keep in mind our discussion of this last month. Your health planet went retrograde on June 26 and is retrograde until the 21st. If you are making dramatic changes to the diet, research it more carefully. The same goes for any major change in the health regime. Changes might be necessary but get more information.

Jupiter, your spiritual planet, is making beautiful aspects to Saturn this month. So this is a spiritual period for you. You are meeting spiritual kinds of friends and perhaps they are the instrument the cosmos is using. You seem very receptive to spiritual influences this month and this tends to produce new understandings. Singles have many choices in love, but the spiritual dimension – the spiritual compatibility – is most important. Many problems can be assuaged if there is spiritual compatibility.

Last month on the 21st the Water element became strong again, and this is the situation until the 22nd of this month. You went through a similar period in February and March. The emotional energy is very powerful now. When emotions are positive things are happy. But if they turn negative, and this can happen very easily, it can be very painful. Be more aware of people's sensitivities now: they are hypersensitive.

Logic and practicality – your strong points – can be seen as cruel or unfeeling these days. So take this into account when dealing with people; state your case, but with more sensitivity. It is at times like this that your sound judgement is most needed, but will others listen?

Finances are still stressful until the 22nd. You have to work harder to achieve your financial goals. On the 17th your financial planet Uranus goes retrograde as well, meaning the financial life is under review for most of the year ahead, until December 17. This will not stop earnings, but it does slow things down a bit. The financial judgement is not at its optimum. Handle your normal financial responsibilities but avoid making major purchases or investments. Your job is to attain mental clarity on your finances and this will take time. The financial picture is not as you believe it to be and many assumptions are not correct – as you will find out in the coming months.

On the 22nd your spouse, partner or current love enters a yearly financial peak. He or she will most likely make up any short fall. A parent or parent figure has a nice payday on the 19th–20th and seems generous with you too. You have the financial favour of bosses, elders and authority figures that period.

August

Best Days Overall: 8, 9, 17, 18, 25, 26, 27
Most Stressful Days Overall: 3, 4, 10, 11, 12, 23, 24, 30, 31
Best Days for Love: 3, 4, 6, 7, 8, 9, 15, 16, 19, 25, 26, 30, 31
Best Days for Money: 3, 6, 7, 13, 14, 15, 16, 19, 20, 21, 22, 23, 24, 30, 31
Best Days for Career: 8, 9, 10, 11, 12, 19, 25, 26

Finances are improving but they are still not what they should be or will be. There are still many challenges to deal with. A sudden expense in the home or with a family member at the beginning of the month is difficult to deal with. This is not a good period for speculation or risk-taking, though you seem more inclined to this these days. There is financial disagreement with a parent figure then. Jupiter will square the financial planet from the 18th to the 25th. Overspending is the main danger here. Financial deals need more scrutiny for the rest of the year, but especially during that period. The beloved is still in the midst of a yearly financial peak and is likely to be generous with you. Continue to work for financial clarity – this is the most important thing. Once this happens, decision-making will be easy.

The home needs to be made more safe on the 1st and 2nd. Keep sharp or dangerous objects out of the reach of children. Make sure safety devices in the home are working properly. Parents or parent figures (and other family members) need to drive more carefully and avoid taking risks. Temper needs to be watched too. People are likely to overreact during this period.

On June 21 the planetary power shifted from the lower to the upper half of the Horoscope, so you are in a more ambitious, outer-oriented period now. Home and family are still important but you can safely shift attention to the career. You seem ready to get involved in some major project – something big or something delicate.

Love is still happy but not as active as in previous months. Singles find love opportunities in spiritual settings such as meditation seminars, prayer meetings and charity events. Your social magnetism will be strongest from the 6th to the 21st as the Moon is waxing. You are more in the mood for love that period.

The element of Water is still very strong this month, so keep in mind our previous discussion of this. What is perceived as insensitivity can cause all kinds of delays and needless complications. Watch your voice tone and body language.

Health needs attention from the 16th onwards. Enhance the health in the ways mentioned in the yearly report. In addition, until the 8th give more attention to the stomach, breasts and diet. After the 8th pay attention to the heart and after the 24th give more attention to the small intestine. Detox regimes are powerful from the 8th to the 24th.

You are still in a very spiritual period. Take a note of your dreams and pay attention to your hunches. You are being guided step by step.

September

Best Days Overall: 4, 5, 6, 13, 14, 22, 23
Most Stressful Days Overall: 1, 7, 8, 20, 21, 27, 28
Best Days for Love: 1, 4, 5, 8, 13, 14, 17, 18, 24, 27, 28
Best Days for Money: 1, 2, 3, 9, 10, 11, 12, 15, 16, 18, 19, 20, 21, 27, 28, 29, 30
Best Days for Career: 7, 8, 17, 18, 27, 28

Health needs even more watching than last month, especially after the 22nd. The problem seems to be overwork, hyperactivity. You flit from one activity to the next with nary a break. Everything is go-go-go. A lot of this has to do with the career. On the 22nd you enter a yearly career peak and so you are very busy and taking on more responsibilities. Many busy people think that if they push themselves they will achieve more. But this is not usually the case. When work is done from a tired state it generally has to be redone. More mental mistakes happen. So the advice is simple: rest when tired.

Enhance the health by giving more attention to the small intestine until the 9th and to the kidneys and hips from the 9th to the 29th. Hip massage will be powerful then. Be especially careful from the 15th to the 17th. Take it nice and easy then; spend more time at the health spa, get massages. Watch the driving. Foreign travel is not so advisable; reschedule it for a better time if you can.

There is good career success happening all month. A meeting or discussion with a boss or superior goes well between the 12th to the 14th – there is good communication between you. The superior seems open to your ideas. He or she could have some good ideas for you as well. Venus travels with Saturn from the 17th to the 20th, which shows career success and elevation. You are in favour with your superiors. Happy career opportunities pursue you. Venus's trine with Jupiter on the 27th and 28th also brings success and opportunity.

The family situation has been unstable all year. Emotions run high in the family, especially between the 7th and 11th. Be more patient with family members.

Finances are still stressful. You will get through the month but reaching your financial targets requires more work and effort. Right now, career – your status and professional life – is more important to you than money. Perhaps you are not giving finance the attention it deserves. Overspending still seems a problem. Continue to work for mental clarity.

You remain in a very spiritual period. You easily access the invisible world. There are all kinds of spiritual help and support available to you and this will help you get through the month.

October

Best Days Overall: 2, 3, 11, 12, 19, 20, 29, 30
Most Stressful Days Overall: 4, 5, 17, 18, 24, 25, 31
Best Days for Love: 4, 5, 7, 8, 13, 14, 17, 18, 23, 24, 25, 27, 28
Best Days for Money: 1, 6, 7, 8, 9, 13, 14, 15, 16, 17, 18, 24, 25, 27, 28
Best Days for Career: 4, 5, 7, 8, 17, 18, 27, 28, 31

You are still in a yearly career peak, still involved in delicate, complicated projects, and still in a hectic period. Health still needs watching, especially until the 23rd. Your career is furthered through involvement with groups and organizations. Online activities and networking also boost the career until the 9th. Friendships are still being tested and there are many life-changing dramas in the lives of friends, but they seem helpful in career matters. After the 9th, as the career planet moves into your 12th house, it is good to be more involved in charities and non-profit kinds of causes. This boosts your image and connects you to important people. (For those on the spiritual path, the spiritual practice is the real career this period.)

With you, career peaks tend to also bring crises. The crisis now is not what you think it is. Right behind it is some fabulous success, some breakthrough. The crisis is the message that progress is happening. No major success ever happens without going through a few 'nightmare' scenarios. These are the fears and worries that hold us back. Rejoice when they are surfacing.

Health is delicate until the 23rd. Enhance it by giving more attention to the colon, bladder and sexual organs. Safe sex and sexual moderation is important this period, and detoxing will be useful.

The family situation has been unstable all year. Now a Lunar Eclipse on the 18th adds fuel to the flames as it occurs in the 4th house of home and family. So be very patient with family members and especially with a parent or parent figure. Passions have been running high all year, but now even more so, so try hard not to make matters worse than they need to be. Do your best to make the home more safe. Smoke detectors and alarm systems should be checked, and if there are dangerous objects lying around get rid of them. Often hidden flaws in the home are revealed under an eclipse and repairs or corrections need to be made. This eclipse affects you strongly, so make sure you have a nice easy schedule that period – family members too. This eclipse also impacts on Jupiter, your spiritual planet, so there are spiritual changes happening too, in teachings or practice, and shake-ups in a spiritual or charitable organization you belong to.

Finances are still stressed, but will improve after the 23rd. Your finances are still under review, so keep working to attain mental clarity on the matter.

November

Best Days Overall: 7, 8, 16, 17, 25, 26, 27
Most Stressful Days Overall: 1, 13, 14, 20, 21, 22, 28,
    29
Best Days for Love: 3, 4, 7, 11, 12, 16, 17, 20, 21, 22, 23,
    26, 27
Best Days for Money: 3, 4, 5, 6, 9, 10, 11, 12, 13, 14, 21,
    22, 23, 24, 30
Best Days for Career: 1, 7, 16, 17, 26, 27, 28, 29

As with family, the situation with friends has also been unstable all year. A Solar Eclipse on the 3rd adds more fuel to the fire. It occurs in your 11th house of friends, further testing friendships and bringing more dramatic, life-changing events into their lives. An eclipse in the 11th house tends to make your computers and gadgets more temperamental. They start behaving strangely for no apparent reason. (I have found that these sensitive kinds of devices are highly susceptible to the cosmic energy and when the cosmic energy is roiled up they don't work as they should.) Make sure your anti-virus, anti-hacking software is up to date.

As with every Solar eclipse, the angel of death pays a visit. He lets you know that he is around. He reminds you that life here on earth is short and fragile. Time to get down to the really serious matters of life. Your spouse, partner or current love has some financial crisis and is forced to make important changes.

Health is much improved this month, but still needs watching. Enhance the health in the ways mentioned last month: give more attention to the colon, bladder and sexual organs. Detoxes have been good all year, but especially from the 4th to the 7th this month. Be more careful driving that period as well. Avoid dangerous or risky kinds of activities. Weight loss programmes go better during this time, and it's a good time to start one if you need to. There are sexual encounters this period as well. Your health planet is still retrograde until the 10th so avoid making major changes to the diet or health regime, or major medical decisions, until after that date. This is a time to gain clarity in health matters, to get second and third opinions and to read up more on these things. Many new fads or supplements are not as they are being presented.

On September 22 the planetary power began to shift from the West to the East, and the shift is even more pronounced now. You are in a period of personal independence. By now you have built up your social muscles and it is time to develop more self-reliance and personal initiative. With more personal independence comes great self-confidence and self-esteem. You are being 'boosted' by the planetary power. You have more personal power these days and can change conditions more easily to the way that you like them.

Love seems good this month. Venus moves into your sign on the 5th. Thus the personal appearance, the manner, the outer demeanour is more glamorous, beautiful and graceful. (Whatever your age or stage in life, there is more beauty and grace in the image now than usual.) The opposite sex takes notice. The social magnetism will be strongest from the 3rd to the 17th, as the Moon waxes.

December

Best Days Overall: 4, 5, 13, 14, 23, 24
Most Stressful Days Overall: 10, 11, 12, 18, 19, 25, 26
Best Days for Love: 2, 3, 4, 5, 11, 12, 13, 14, 18, 19, 22, 23, 24
Best Days for Money: 1, 2, 3, 6, 7, 8, 9, 10, 11, 18, 19, 20, 21, 28, 29, 30, 31
Best Days for Career: 4, 5, 13, 14, 23, 24, 25, 26

The planetary power approaches the maximum Eastern position for the year, so keep in mind our discussion last month. Now you don't need to give in to others all the time. You can and should have your own way, so long as it isn't destructive. Now is the time to assert yourself in a positive way, to create the conditions of life as you would like them to be. Personal initiative matters now.

Ever since Jupiter moved into Cancer at the end of June you have been in a very spiritual kind of period. On November 22 your 12th house of spirituality also became powerful and it is powerful until the 21st of the month ahead. For a down-to-earth Capricorn this is unusual. You are experiencing all kinds of synchronistic events, spiritual phenomena, and supernatural phenomena. The dream life becomes more active and prophetic, and you can't just dismiss it. Your dreams are vivid and real on their level. Sometimes the 'impractical' – the unworldly – is the most practical path. You are seeing how the world and the universe really work. Many spiritual breakthroughs are happening. The vast invisible world is letting you know that it is around and in charge. You are especially seeing this in health matters and healing and respond very well to spiritual therapies. But it seems to me you are seeing the power of this for other people as well.

Your personal health is relatively good this month, and it gets even better after the 21st as the Sun moves into your own sign. You look good. There is more sex appeal and glamour to your image and the opposite sex takes notice. Love should be good. You still have strong marriage aspects this year – and well into next year.

Your Financial Planet starts to move forward on the 17th after many months of retrograde motion. This is good news. Mental clarity should start to happen. The financial judgement becomes trustworthy again. Still, finances seem stressful this month. You are dealing with many, many challenges. Friends and family don't seem supportive of your financial goals and family expenses are higher than usual. You just need to work harder and exert more effort to attain your goals. Your spiritual understanding will be a big help in dealing with this.

On the 8th, Mars, the family planet, crosses the Midheaven and enters your 10th house. This shows that family is now becoming the number one priority. The family seems to support your career, but not your finances. This focus on the family is good. On the 21st the planetary power starts to shift to the lower half of the Horoscope, also signalling a need to focus on home, family and emotional wellbeing.

There are some dynamic aspects at the end of the month from the 23rd to 31st. These affect friends and family very much. They should stay out of harm's way as much as possible. Drive more carefully and avoid risk-taking activities.

Aquarius

≋

THE WATER-BEARER

Birthdays from
20th January to
18th February

Personality Profile

AQUARIUS AT A GLANCE

Element – Air

Ruling Planet – Uranus
  Career Planet – Pluto
  Love Planet – Venus
  Money Planet – Neptune
  Planet of Health and Work – Moon
  Planet of Home and Family Life – Venus
  Planet of Spirituality – Saturn

Colours – electric blue, grey, ultramarine blue

*Colours that promote love, romance and social
  harmony* – gold, orange

Colour that promotes earning power – aqua

Gems – black pearl, obsidian, opal, sapphire

Metal – lead

Scents – azalea, gardenia

Quality – fixed (= stability)

Qualities most needed for balance – warmth, feeling and emotion

Strongest virtues – great intellectual power, the ability to communicate and to form and understand abstract concepts, love for the new and avant-garde

Deepest needs – to know and to bring in the new

Characteristics to avoid – coldness, rebelliousness for its own sake, fixed ideas

Signs of greatest overall compatibility – Gemini, Libra

Signs of greatest overall incompatibility – Taurus, Leo, Scorpio

Sign most helpful to career – Scorpio

Sign most helpful for emotional support – Taurus

Sign most helpful financially – Pisces

Sign best for marriage and/or partnerships – Leo

Sign most helpful for creative projects – Gemini

Best Sign to have fun with – Gemini

Signs most helpful in spiritual matters – Libra, Capricorn

Best day of the week – Saturday

Understanding an Aquarius

In the Aquarius-born, intellectual faculties are perhaps the most highly developed of any sign in the zodiac. Aquarians are clear, scientific thinkers. They have the ability to think abstractly and to formulate laws, theories and clear concepts from masses of observed facts. Geminis might be very good at gathering information, but Aquarians take this a step further, excelling at interpreting the information gathered.

Practical people – men and women of the world – mistakenly consider abstract thinking as impractical. It is true that the realm of abstract thought takes us out of the physical world, but the discoveries made in this realm generally end up having tremendous practical consequences. All real scientific inventions and breakthroughs come from this abstract realm.

Aquarians, more so than most, are ideally suited to explore these abstract dimensions. Those who have explored these regions know that there is little feeling or emotion there. In fact, emotions are a hindrance to functioning in these dimensions; thus Aquarians seem – at times – cold and emotionless to others. It is not that Aquarians haven't got feelings and deep emotions, it is just that too much feeling clouds their ability to think and invent. The concept of 'too much feeling' cannot be tolerated or even understood by some of the other signs. Nevertheless, this Aquarian objectivity is ideal for science, communication and friendship.

Aquarians are very friendly people, but they do not make a big show about it. They do the right thing by their friends, even if sometimes they do it without passion or excitement.

Aquarians have a deep passion for clear thinking. Second in importance, but related, is their passion for breaking with the establishment and traditional authority. Aquarians delight in this, because for them rebellion is like a great game or challenge. Very often they will rebel strictly for the fun of rebelling, regardless of whether the authority they defy is right or wrong. Right or wrong has little to do with the rebellious actions of an Aquarian, because to a true Aquarian authority and power must be challenged as a matter of principle.

Where Capricorn or Taurus will err on the side of tradition and the status quo, an Aquarian will err on the side of the new. Without this virtue it is doubtful whether any progress would be made in the world. The conservative-minded would obstruct progress. Originality and invention imply an ability to break barriers; every new discovery represents the toppling of an impediment to thought. Aquarians are very interested in breaking barriers and making walls tumble – scientifically, socially and politically. Other zodiac signs, such as Capricorn, also have scientific talents. But Aquarians are particularly excellent in the social sciences and humanities.

Finance

In financial matters Aquarians tend to be idealistic and humanitarian – to the point of self-sacrifice. They are usually generous contributors to social and political causes. When they contribute it differs from when a Capricorn or Taurus contributes. A Capricorn or Taurus may expect some favour or return for a gift; an Aquarian contributes selflessly.

Aquarians tend to be as cool and rational about money as they are about most things in life. Money is something they need and they set about acquiring it scientifically. No need for fuss; they get on with it in the most rational and scientific ways available.

Money to the Aquarian is especially nice for what it can do, not for the status it may bring (as is the case for other signs). Aquarians are neither big spenders nor penny-pinchers and use their finances in practical ways, for example to facilitate progress for themselves, their families, or even for strangers.

However, if Aquarians want to reach their fullest financial potential they will have to explore their intuitive nature. If they follow only their financial theories – or what they believe to be theoretically correct – they may suffer some losses and disappointments. Instead, Aquarians should call on their intuition, which knows without thinking. For Aquarians, intuition is the short-cut to financial success.

Career and Public Image

Aquarians like to be perceived not only as the breakers of barriers but also as the transformers of society and the world. They long to be seen in this light and to play this role. They also look up to and respect other people in this position and even expect their superiors to act this way.

Aquarians prefer jobs that have a bit of idealism attached to them – careers with a philosophical basis. Aquarians need to be creative at work, to have access to new techniques and methods. They like to keep busy and enjoy getting down to business straightaway, without wasting any time. They are often the quickest workers and usually have suggestions for improvements that will benefit their employers. Aquarians are also very helpful with their co-workers and welcome responsibility, preferring this to having to take orders from others.

If Aquarians want to reach their highest career goals they have to develop more emotional sensitivity, depth of feeling and passion. They need to learn to narrow their focus on the essentials and concentrate more on the job in hand. Aquarians need 'a fire in the belly' – a consuming passion and desire – in order to rise to the very top. Once this passion exists they will succeed easily in whatever they attempt.

Love and Relationships

Aquarians are good at friendships, but a bit weak when it comes to love. Of course they fall in love, but their lovers always get the impression that they are more best friends than paramours.

Like Capricorns, they are cool customers. They are not prone to displays of passion or to outward demonstrations of their affections. In fact, they feel uncomfortable when their other half hugs and touches them too much. This does not mean that they do not love their partners. They do, only they show it in other ways. Curiously enough, in relationships they tend to attract the very things that they feel uncomfortable with. They seem to attract hot, passionate, romantic, demonstrative people. Perhaps they know instinctively that these people have qualities they lack and so seek them out. In any event, these relationships do seem to work, Aquarian coolness calming the more passionate partner while the fires of passion warm the cold-blooded Aquarius.

The qualities Aquarians need to develop in their love life are warmth, generosity, passion and fun. Aquarians love relationships of the mind. Here they excel. If the intellectual factor is missing in a relationship an Aquarian will soon become bored or feel unfulfilled.

Home and Domestic Life

In family and domestic matters Aquarians can have a tendency to be too non-conformist, changeable and unstable. They are as willing to break the barriers of family constraints as they are those of other areas of life.

Even so, Aquarians are very sociable people. They like to have a nice home where they can entertain family and friends. Their house is usually decorated in a modern style and full of state-of-the-art appliances and gadgets – an environment Aquarians find absolutely necessary.

If their home life is to be healthy and fulfilling Aquarians need to inject it with a quality of stability – yes, even some conservatism. They need at least one area of life to be enduring and steady; this area is usually their home and family life.

Venus, the planet of love, rules the Aquarian's 4th solar house of home and family as well, which means that when it comes to the family and child-rearing, theories, cool thinking and intellect are not always enough. Aquarians need to bring love into the equation in order to have a great domestic life.

Horoscope for 2013

Major Trends

Last year was basically a good year – not perfect by any means, but more easy than difficult. The long-term planets were mostly leaving you alone or were in harmonious aspect to you. Health and energy were basically good and this should have translated to the achievement of your goals. Late in 2012 Saturn made a major move into Scorpio and into a stressful alignment to you. While this by itself is not enough to cause sickness, it does show a need to watch the energy more. Saturn might slow you down, but he won't stop you. There's more on this later on.

Pluto has been in your spiritual 12th house since 2008. We have discussed this in previous years but the trends continue in the year ahead. A cosmic detox is taking place in your spiritual life, in your attitudes and practice. A lot of 'effete material' is being removed from the spiritual life so that spiritual power can flow freely.

In 2012 Neptune, your financial planet, made a major move into your money house. This basically accentuated a trend that has been happening for many years: you are going deeper into the spiritual dimensions of wealth, tapping into the supernatural sources of supply and learning how spirit works to produce material wealth. This trend continues this year and for many more years. More details later.

In 2011, Uranus, your ruling planet, made a major move out of Pisces and into Aries, your 3rd house of communication. Always a great communicator and networker, now these skills are even further enhanced. You tend to be experimental in most things but these days it is happening in communication. Your originality here, in your writing, speech and online activities, is very much enhanced these days.

Jupiter has been in your 5th house of fun, children and creativity since June of last year and he will be there until June 27 of this year. So you are in a party kind of year. You are exploring the 'joy of life' and getting involved in fun kinds of activities. Aquarians of child-bearing age are unusually fertile these days.

Jupiter will move into your 6th house of work in June. This is a wonderful aspect for job seekers or those who employ others. Dream job opportunities are coming. And for those who employ others there is an abundance of good help available.

Saturn moved into your 10th house of career late last year. Career is challenging now. Success comes through sheer merit and for no other reason. Also, two eclipses in this house indicate career changes in the year ahead. There's more on this later.

Your most important areas of interest this year will be finance; communication and intellectual interests; fun, children and personal creativity (until June 27); health and work (from June 27 onwards); career; spirituality.

Your paths of greatest fulfilment this year will be career; fun, children and creativity (until June 27); and health and work (from June 27).

Health

(Please note that this is an astrological perspective on health and not a medical one. In days of yore there was no difference, these perspectives were identical. But now there could be quite a difference. For a medical perspective, please consult your doctor or health practitioner.)

Health, as we mentioned, should be good this year. There is only one major long-term planet (Saturn) in stressful alignment with you. Still, energy is not as high as it was last year and this relative difference could be a concern. Saturn

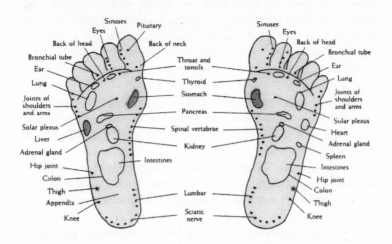

Reflexology

Try to massage the whole foot on a regular basis, but pay extra attention to the points highlighted on the chart. When you massage, be aware of 'sore spots', as these need special attention. It's also a good idea to massage the ankles and top side of the feet.

by himself is not enough to cause sickness or disease, but when the short-term planets join him in stressful aspect this could make you more vulnerable. Make especially sure to rest and relax more from April 20 to May 20, July 22 to August 22 and October 23 to November 21. These are your most vulnerable periods in the year ahead.

You don't seem too focused on health issues the first half of the year. But when Jupiter moves into your 6th house on June 27, you start to pay more attention. This is basically good.

There is much that can be done to improve the health and prevent problems from developing. Give more attention to the following: the stomach and breasts (these are always important to you as the Moon is the Health Planet). Diet is always an issue for you as the stomach tends to be sensitive, and HOW you eat is perhaps just as important as what you eat; As we have mentioned in previous years, WHAT you eat is important, but meals should be taken calmly in a state of peace, and try to if possible have beautiful, harmonious music playing as you eat. Give praise and gratitude for the food in your own words, bless the food and elevate the act of eating from a mere animal appetite into something higher – an act of worship. This will ensure that you get only the highest energy vibrations of the food and the digestion should be better.

For ankles and calves regular massage would be wonderful, and give the ankles more support when exercising; and for the heart, avoid worry and anxiety as much as possible. Whatever positive actions that can be taken about a situation should be taken, but after that drop the worry. After June 27; thighs should be regularly massaged, and a liver detox in the year ahead might be a good idea.

Jupiter in your health house shows that you benefit greatly from metaphysical kinds of therapies – prayer, speaking of the word and positive affirmations. It shows a need for philosophical purity. Errors in the upper mental body will not only cause havoc in worldly affairs, but if held long enough will actually manifest as illness. The Horoscope is showing us the root cause of problems as well as the problem itself. The best cure for philosophical or religious error is LIGHT. Invoke the light often. Think of light. See it coming into the mind and body.

Home and Family

Your 4th house of home and family is not a house of power this year, in contrast to 2011 and 2012. Many of you moved, renovated the home or bought additional homes. By now everything is in order and there is no need to make any dramatic kinds of changes.

There is a Solar Eclipse in your 4th house on May 10 and this will shake things up a bit, but it doesn't seem to bring major change. This eclipse will test the present home and domestic situation. If there are hidden flaws there (such as rodents, toxic substances, bad wiring or plumbing) this is when you find out about it so that you can make repairs. The eclipse will tend to bring dramatic events into the lives of family members. But once the dust settles from the eclipse the status quo prevails once again.

A parent or parent figure seems gloomy and pessimistic this year. He or she seems cold and unfeeling. He or she is taking on extra responsibilities and perhaps experiencing life-changing kinds of event. Be more patient with this person.

You seem very close to a sibling or sibling figure this year – very devoted, very involved with this person, much more so than usual. This sibling or sibling figure will likely move in the coming year and it seems happy.

Neither of the parent figures seems to be moving this year. Children (or children figures in your life) are likewise having a status quo kind of year. They are prospering and successful and travelling, but moves are not likely.

If you are planning major repairs, April 20 to May 31 is a good time. If you are planning cosmetic kinds of changes – a new paint job, new furniture and things of this nature – April 15 to May 9 is a good time. This latter period is also good for buying art or beautiful objects for the home.

Since fast-moving Venus is your family planet, there are many short-term family trends that are best covered in the monthly reports.

Finance and Career

As we mentioned earlier, Neptune, now in your money house for the long term, is extending and reinforcing your interest in the spiritual sources of supply. This interest has been going on for many years now, and is merely getting deeper. Neptune rules intuition – inner guidance – and thus this is ultra-important in finance right now. Regular readers know that one millisecond of real intuition is worth many years of hard labour. Indeed it is the short cut to wealth. With Neptune now in his own sign and house (a position that makes him stronger) your financial intuition is super. You are being guided moment to moment to your financial goals. Intuition can be trusted now. (However, Neptune will go retrograde for a few months in the year ahead, and those are times when the intuition will need more verification.)

With your financial planet now strong both celestially and terrestrially, earning power is stronger than usual – a good prosperity signal. On June 27 Jupiter will start to make fabulous aspects to Neptune, which is another prosperity signal. You will be catching the lucky financial breaks when this happens. July seems especially fortunate and some of you might want to invest harmless amounts of money in the lottery or some other speculation. (Please just use spare money that you can afford to lose. The cosmos might want to prosper you in another way.)

Just making a lot of money is not enough for you these days; you have to earn it in ways that are beneficial to all. This is your challenge now. I see the same trend in your career as well. It's not enough just to be successful in the worldly way, it has to be in ways that are idealistic and beneficial to all.

Jupiter in your 5th House shows luck in speculations and it might be advisable to invest harmless sums of money on this – especially when the intuition comes to you.

You have the aspects of someone who follows a spiritual kind of career these days. Ministry, charity, full-time work for an altruistic cause or non-profit organization is very appealing now. This is all over the Horoscope. Neptune, the planet of spirituality, rules the finances. Your spiritual planet, Saturn, is right on the Mid-heaven of the career. Your career planet, Pluto, is in your spiritual 12th house. So most likely you will follow a spiritual, altruistic kind of career path now. But even if you are in a conventional kind of career, being involved in charities and good causes will be helpful in the worldly way too. First, you will get satisfaction from doing good, from helping others and the world;

secondly, you will meet people and make connections that will help the worldly career, enhance it and elevate it.

Career is challenging this year – much more challenging than finance. Saturn in the career house indicates a demanding boss, someone who is stern and who pushes you to the limit. This is a year where you earn career success the hard way, through sheer merit.

Uranus is making a square to Pluto, your career planet, all year. This aspect will be most exact in October and November. Thus there are sudden and dramatic career changes happening. Aside from this there are two eclipses in the 10th house of career: a Lunar Eclipse on April 25 and a Solar Eclipse on November 3. This also indicates career changes. While this is going on there are probably many insecurities, but the end result will be just fine. As we mentioned, Jupiter in your 6th house of health and work from June 27 onwards shows very happy job opportunities.

One of the parents or parent figures in your life is prospering this year – it's a banner financial year. Children or children figures are prospering and otherwise enjoying the high life. Siblings are having a status quo financial year.

Love and Social Life

As in 2012, the 7th house of love and marriage is not a house of power. Marriage and committed relationships are not such a big issue this year. This tends to be the status quo. Those who are married tend to stay married; singles tend to stay single. The empty 7th house could be read as a positive thing. You are basically content with the love life as it is and you have no need to make major changes or give it undue attention.

Though marriage is not in the stars this year, love affairs are. But these are not serious things, just another form of entertainment. There will be many opportunities for love affairs this year. Singles probably prefer this anyway.

The Sun is your love planet. He is a fast-moving planet and during the course of the year ahead he will move through all the signs and houses of your Horoscope. Thus love and social opportunities can happen in many ways and with a variety of people. Your needs in love tend to change month by month, so the many short-term trends in love are best dealt with in the monthly reports.

The Sun will get eclipsed twice this year, once on May 10 and again on November 3. These eclipses will test the current relationship. Good relationships tend to survive, although the dirty laundry comes up for cleansing. The spouse, partner or current love will tend to be more temperamental during those periods. Hopefully you'll be ready to handle this when it comes.

A parent or parent figure is having their marriage or current relationship severely tested. Love is very challenging this year. Siblings (or sibling figures in your life) seem very freedom oriented. This tendency could test a current relationship. Their spouse, partner or current love needs to give this sibling much space, much elbow room. Children (or children figures) of marriageable age are likely to marry or get involved in a serious romance this year. (It could have happened last year as well.) This seems a very happy relationship. There's nothing special that the child needs to do to attract love, it will find him or her. He or she probably can't even escape it. Even if the child is too young for marriage there is love this year. The social life seems happy. Grandchildren of appropriate age (if you have them) are not likely to marry this year, nor does it seem advisable. They have aspects for serial love affairs not marriage. If they are already married, the marriage is being severely tested. Financial issues seem a root cause, but not the only one.

Self-improvement

The career seems the most challenging area of life this year. Yet, at the same time it is the most fulfilling. How can this be? There is a tremendous joy and satisfaction that comes when we succeed at something difficult; when we exerted ourselves to the full and finally prevailed. Few people know this kind of joy, as for the most part it is known by people who take on difficult challenges. The adrenalin rush that comes at the moment of success makes all the previous effort, struggle and pain worthwhile, and they are forgotten in the moment of victory. This is the kind of joy that awaits you in your career – if you stay the course and keep your discipline.

Bosses will be demanding. The work will be hard. You will have to deal with a lot of behind-the-scenes activity and there will be a lot of outright deception too. There will be changes of rules, changes of policy and most likely changes in your corporate hierarchy and industry. Yet, if you stay the course, you will prevail. Saturn demands that you succeed in spite of all the obstacles. Saturn demands that your success comes from sheer merit and no other reason. If you have the merit, if you are the best at what you do, you have little to fear from all the behind-the-scenes shenanigans. Saturn will ensure that you are in your rightful place in your industry and profession, whether it is with the present company or another one. So, the object this year is to cultivate merit – excellence – in your profession.

No great achievement ever happened over night. With Saturn on your Mid-heaven, forget about this in the year ahead. Take a step by step, methodical approach to success.

Many of you are already on a spiritual path. This is a year for making your personal spiritual practice your number one priority. In truth, it is your mission this year and for many years to come. Spiritual practice is never really personal, though it seems that way. The work is on oneself, but the effect goes into your neighbourhood, your community and eventually the whole world. The lone meditator who makes a spiritual breathrough – perhaps in a shabby unfashionable home, perhaps in a cave in the Himalayas – does more to change the world than presidents or kings. The meditator is cause; the president or king will only ratify the change that has already occurred. Generally the effect doesn't happen right away and there are few who can see the connection. But eventually it happens. Many of the trends that seem mainstream today were once unthinkable; they became mainstream because a few hardy souls made the spiritual breakthrough. So don't discount your spiritual work.

Those of you not on a spiritual path should make the effort to find one. Let this effort be your priority.

Month-by-month Forecasts

January

Best Days Overall: 4, 5, 12, 13, 21, 22, 31
Most Stressful Days Overall: 6, 7, 19, 20, 26, 27, 28
Best Days for Love: 2, 3, 8, 9, 10, 11, 18, 19, 21, 26, 27, 28, 29, 30, 31
Best Days for Money: 4, 6, 12, 14, 15, 22, 24, 31
Best Days for Career: 2, 3, 6, 7, 10, 11, 19, 20, 29, 30

You begin your year with the planets in their maximum Eastern position. This will be the case next month as well. You are in a period of maximum personal independence and creative power. You can and should have things your own way, so long as it isn't destructive. Your personal initiative and self-reliance is being developed this period. You know who you are, you know what you believe and what is right for you and you follow that path, regardless of whether it is popular or not. Now is the time to create the conditions of your life according to your personal taste. You are in a period for 'making karma'. Later – in a few months – you will have to live with your creation, so build wisely.

Many of you have birthdays this month. If so, you are in an excellent period for starting new projects and ventures. The universal solar cycle is waxing (since December 21) and on your birthday, your personal solar cycle will also be waxing. The planetary momentum is also forward which helps matters. If you can schedule these new start-ups from your birthday until the 27th (as the Moon waxes) you'll have the most favourable period of the month. Those who have birthdays after the 27th or next month, have an equally favourable period in February.

Health is good this month. It gets even better after the 19th as your own sign gets powerful. You can enhance the health further in the ways mentioned in the yearly report.

You are in a very spiritual period until the 19th. It's a good period to achieve your spiritual and altruistic goals, and for spiritual pilgrimages, visits to holy places and retreats in exotic kinds of places. These opportunities open up to you after the 10th. Your career needs a spiritual-type breakthrough and this kind of thing is available now. This is a time to get more connected to the higher power within and to allow it to operate freely in your mind, body and affairs. This will start to bring all the affairs of life into harmony. Even love (for singles) awaits you in spiritual settings, especially until the 19th. Love is at the yoga studio, the prayer meeting, the meditation seminar, the charity event this period.

On the 19th, the love planet Venus enters your own sign. Thus love is pursuing you and will find you. Just go about your everyday life.

February

   Best Days Overall: 1, 9, 10, 18, 19, 27, 28
   Most Stressful Days Overall: 2, 3, 15, 16, 17, 23, 24
   Best Days for Love: 1, 9, 10, 18, 19, 20, 23, 24
   Best Days for Money: 2, 9, 11, 12, 18, 20, 27
   Best Days for Career: 2, 3, 7, 8, 15, 16, 25, 26

Last month on the 19th you entered one of your yearly personal pleasure peaks. The pleasures of the senses pursue you and you can indulge. It is also a good time for getting the body and image in shape, the way you would like them to be. You have more personal control over the body this period and this helps. Personal pleasure is strong until February 18. You look good, you dress well and have more personal charisma – that invisible something that is the essence behind all beauty.

As we mentioned, you are still in a powerful period for launching new projects or ventures. ALL the planets are moving forward until the 18th (highly unusually). So you have a rare window to launch that new venture. The 10th to the 18th is best for this, but the 18th to the 25th is a good second choice.

Last month also on the 19th, the planetary power began to shift from the upper half to the lower half of your Horoscope. This shift gets even stronger after the 2nd as Venus moves below the horizon of your chart. It is time to de-emphasize the career and focus on the home, family and emotional wellbeing; time to build up the forces for your next career surge, which will happen in six months or so. These pauses are very healthy. It is like a good night's sleep. The body is still. Outer world objectives are left behind. The forces are built up to handle the next day. The person who deprives him or herself of sleep will not function well the next day. Of course, you still handle the basic needs of the career – you don't completely abandon it – but you shift attention to the home and the emotional life.

On the 18th you enter one of your yearly financial peaks. Your prosperity will be even greater in July (and after) but this month is excellent too. Your money house is easily the most powerful in the Horoscope this month, with 50 and sometimes 60 per cent of the planets either there or moving through there. The financial intuition is super. Your gut instincts are good. You have a lot of help, a lot of financial favour, from friends, from the current love, neighbours, foreigners and foreign companies. The money is rolling in. The gates of heaven have opened and there is a down pour-ing of wealth. It comes in many ways and through many people. Enjoy! With these kinds of aspects wild and wonder-ful things start to happen. You might invoice someone for an amount and they send you twice that and tell you to keep the change. You might ask the beloved for something and he or she gives you double what you asked for.

Aquarians are rational, logical people, but after the 18th this strength that you have doesn't seem to matter. The Water element gets very powerful. People are feeling oriented and they go with the mood of the moment. Logic doesn't sway them, but if you can appeal to their feelings – to their imagination – you will connect. Keep in mind that people are hypersensitive this month. Watch your words, your body language and facial expressions. People overreact to these things now.

March

Best Days Overall: 1, 8, 9, 17, 18, 19, 27, 28
Most Stressful Days Overall: 2, 3, 15, 16, 22, 23, 29, 30
Best Days for Love: 2, 3, 10, 11, 21, 22, 23, 31
Best Days for Money: 1, 2, 8, 9, 10, 11, 17, 18, 20, 27, 28, 29
Best Days for Career: 2, 3, 6, 7, 15, 16, 24, 25, 29, 30

You are still in an excellent period for launching new projects, products or ventures into the world. All of you are now in a personal waxing solar cycle (it began on your birthday). The Moon will wax from the 11th to the 27th, adding to the favourability. Until the 17th, 80 per cent of the planets are moving forward, which rises to 90 per cent after the 17th. The planetary momentum is overwhelmingly forward, which is another good omen for new projects. The 17th to the 27th would be the best time to start things in the coming month.

The Water element is still very strong until the 20th, so keep in mind our discussion of this last month. Tread very carefully around people's feelings. When hypersensitivity is this strong, even good natured humour is not always appreciated.

Finance is still the major headline until the 20th. It is time to build up the bank balances, the investment and savings accounts and to do your financial planning. Keep in mind our discussion of this last month.

Love is still happy. Since February 18 singles have found love as they pursue their normal financial goals and with people involved in their finances. Wealth – material gifts and support – seems the primary turn on in love this period. This is how you feel loved. This is how you express love. The good provider, the generous person, the big spender is the most alluring. However it would be a mistake to ignore spiritual compatibility this period. This is equally important. If you could find a person who was both wealthy and spiritual, who was a business person but also a bit of a poet, you would have the ideal.

On the 20th your love planet moves into your 3rd house and this signals a shift in the love attitudes. Money is not that important now. You want someone you can communicate with, someone to share your thoughts with. Mental intimacy is important. You need to fall in love with the beloved's mind as much as with the body. The person with a wealth of knowledge and communication skills allures you. And it seems you are finding such a person.

The 27th to the 30th brings an important romantic meeting. Though your love and social peak will happen later in the year, in July and August, this period could be called a mini-love and social peak. The social life is highly active. Singles are dating more. There are more parties and gatherings. There is a 'mood for love' now, and love is in the neighbourhood, close to home. There's no need to travel far and wide in search of it. Love happens in educational-type settings as well, in school, at the library, at the lecture or seminar.

After the 20th you are in another good period for getting the body and image in shape – a mini personal pleasure peak. Health looks good. Your personal appearance shines. The only health danger is too much of a good thing. You might be pushing the body beyond its limits. Burn out is the main health danger after the 20th.

April

Best Days Overall: 4, 5, 14, 15, 23, 24
Most Stressful Days Overall: 11, 12, 19, 20, 25, 26
Best Days for Love: 1, 9, 10, 19, 20, 21, 22, 29, 30
Best Days for Money: 4, 5, 6, 7, 8, 14, 15, 16, 23, 24, 25
Best Days for Career: 2, 3, 11, 12, 21, 22, 25, 26, 29, 30

There are a lot of career changes going on of late. This has been the case since the beginning of the year and the change intensifies this month. There is more ahead too. There is not much that can be done right now. Your career planet goes retrograde on the 12th and most of the planets are still below the horizon of the chart and entering their maximum lowest position. Keep the focus on the home, family and the emotional life. Get the home base in order. If career issues displease you, make the corrections inwardly, in your thoughts and feelings, rather than by overt actions. The important thing now is to attain more mental clarity about your career situation, about the situation in your company or industry. Things are not as you imagine them to be. Get more facts.

A Lunar Eclipse on the 25th reinforces what we say above. There is much career change going on, possibly even job changes.

You also seem in conflict with a parent or parent figure these days. It could signal a break with this person. However, with more work and effort (a lot more work) this can be harmonized. But without effort, nothing much will happen. You, parents and parent figures need to drive more carefully this month and avoid confrontations or dangerous situations.

Love is tempestuous on the 1st and 2nd, so be more patient with the beloved. The beloved needs to avoid risky activities that period.

Your 3rd house of communication and intellectual interests became powerful last month and is still powerful until the 19th. Your normally sharp mental faculties are even sharper these days. Information and learning are easily assimilated – a good period for students, for taking courses in subjects that interest you and for teaching others too. The only danger now is mental overload – the mind is so power- ful that it easily gets over-stimulated and you can't turn it off. This often causes insomnia or other nervous kinds of problems. Use the mind, but turn it off when not in use. Meditation is a big help for this.

Health needs more watching from the 19th onwards. This is not a long-term problem. It's just not one of your better health periods this year. So rest and relax more. Pace your- self. Spend more time at the health spa and get more massages. Enhance the health in the ways mentioned in the yearly report.

The love trends are the way we discussed last month until the 19th. After then, emotional intimacy becomes more important. The need is to share real feelings, not just intel- lectual concepts: the person with whom you are emotional comfortable with is the most alluring. You need to feel safe expressing your true feelings to the beloved, no matter how crazy they seem. Love is still close to home. Family members enjoy playing cupid and there is more entertaining from home.

May

    Best Days Overall: 2, 3, 11, 12, 21, 22, 29, 30
    Most Stressful Days Overall: 8, 9, 10, 16, 17, 23, 24
    Best Days for Love: 8, 9, 10, 11, 16, 17, 19, 20, 21, 22, 29, 30
    Best Days for Money: 2, 3, 4, 5, 11, 12, 13, 21, 22, 23, 29, 30, 31
    Best Days for Career: 8, 9, 18, 19, 23, 24, 27, 28

Your 4th house, which became strong on April 19, is still strong until May 20. So the focus is on the home and family. A Solar Eclipse on the 10th also occurs in the 4th house reinforcing what we say here.

When the 4th house is strong we make progress by going backwards. We change the future by coming to terms with the past. Many problems in life have their origin in old memories. Though we have long forgotten them consciously, they are operating there on subconscious levels, impeding progress. Often these old memories affect the health as well, so it is good to explore these things and clear them. When this happens, the future is changed. This is a month for these kinds of activities. The past is easily accessed. Those of you who are undergoing therapy will make progress this month. And even if you are not officially in therapy, the cosmic therapist is hard at work this month. Old memories will come up spontaneously for cleansing. Often we meet old flames from the past and get a chance to resolve old issues. Sometimes you don't meet the exact person, but someone who is like that person. The effect is the same. You get to look at an old and perhaps painful situation from your present state of knowledge and understanding, and thus you bring a whole new perspective on it. This is healing.

The Solar Eclipse of the 10th affects you strongly, so reduce your schedule that period. Actually you need to do this until the 20th but especially round the eclipse period. This eclipse will test love, your current relationship. Be more patient with the beloved that period as he or she is likely to be more temperamental. Family members are more temperamental as well. If there are flaws in the home, now is the time you find out about them and can remedy them.

The Lunar Eclipse of the 25th is more benign to you, but it won't hurt to spend more quiet time at home during that period. This eclipse shows job changes, changes in the conditions of work or the workplace. If you employ others, there are dramas with employees. Neptune, your financial planet, is affected strongly by this eclipse, so you are making some dramatic financial changes, usually because of some upheaval or some unexpected kind of event. Your financial planning and strategy needs revision. There will be long-term changes in your health regime and diet too.

Friendships get tested. Often there are dramatic, life-changing events in the lives of friends.

Health still needs watching until the 20th. After that you will see great improvement.

June

Best Days Overall: 7, 8, 17, 18, 25, 26
Most Stressful Days Overall: 5, 6, 12, 13, 19, 20
Best Days for Love: 7, 8, 10, 12, 13, 17, 18, 19, 20, 27, 28
Best Days for Money: 1, 8, 9, 10, 17, 18, 19, 26, 27, 28
Best Days for Career: 5, 6, 15, 16, 19, 20, 23, 24

Health is much improved this month. There is a great focus here and this helps. You are more into healthy living, healthy lifestyles and health regimes in general.

The financial changes you made last month (and perhaps are still making) are working out very well. The financial crisis or disturbance turns out to be a blessing in disguise, a gift from the most high. You will feel the prosperity early in the month, but the major things happen later – after the 27th. Jupiter starts to make beautiful aspects to your financial planet then, and it will be a very prosperous period. You have the financial favour of your spouse, partner or current love and of friends and family. The financial intuition is excellent too, but needs more verification than usual.

The only complication now is the retrograde of Neptune beginning on the 7th. This could create some delays and glitches in earnings, but it won't stop the prosperity. You need to strive to handle financial issues perfectly, and to make sure all the details are correct. Keep copies of all receipts and records of transactions. It might be a good idea to keep a log or diary of your conversations with people involved in your finances. Major changes need more study and homework. The important thing now is to attain mental clarity about your finances. Things are not as they seem.

Until the 21st, you are in a yearly personal pleasure peak – a fun period. Aquarians of the appropriate age are much more fertile than usual (and this has been the case since the beginning of the year). Love also seems happy this period, playful and non-serious. You are enjoying your friends and the beloved more, scheduling more fun kinds of activities with them. For singles it indicates attraction to those who can show them a good time. Material wealth, mental or emotional compatibility are not as important as they were in past months. You gravitate to the 'fun' person. Singles find love in the usual places this period, at the clubs, the resorts and night spots. Children or children figures in your life play cupid during this period. Your love planet travels with Jupiter from the 19th to the 22nd and this brings important opportunities for love.

After the 21st, love is more serious, more touchy-feely and emotional. You and the current love are more 'moody' in love. When the moods are good, love is wonderful. When the mood is bad, love seems nightmarish. The problem is not with your relationship, but with your moods. Work to keep them positive.

Though your spiritual 12th house is not strong this month, this is still a very spiritual kind of period. Your spiritual planet Saturn receives much positive stimulation. So there are spiritual breakthroughs happening especially later in the month. There are many supernatural kinds of experiences as well.

July

> Best Days Overall: 4, 5, 6, 14, 15, 23, 24
> Most Stressful Days Overall: 2, 3, 9, 10, 11, 17, 29, 30
> Best Days for Love: 1, 7, 8, 9, 10, 11, 17, 18, 19, 20, 27,
>   29, 30
> Best Days for Money: 7, 8, 16, 17, 25, 26
> Best Days for Career: 2, 3, 12, 13, 17, 21, 22, 29, 30

Last month on the 21st, the element of Water became unusually prominent, with between 60 and 70 per cent of the planets either in or moving through the Water signs. This situation lasts until July 22. You experienced this kind of energy in February and March. People are feeling-oriented now and if you want to connect you have to engage them at that level. Reason, logic and practical issues mean little now. It is the mood, the feeling of the moment that matters. The world sorely needs some rational people now. Keep in mind our discussion of this in February and March. Be more sensitive to other people's feelings and watch your voice tone, body language and facial expression. People will tend to overreact to these things. Your logic is needed now, but present it in a sensitive way.

Your 6th house of health and work became powerful on the 21st of last month and will be powerful for the rest of the year, but especially until the 22nd. This is a very good period for job seekers. Dream job opportunities are happening these days. You are in the mood for work, you want to be productive and thus there is success at the job. New technology is coming to you that enables you to be more productive at work. This is a good month for those who employ others. The workforce is expanding and the quality of the workers is good. This is another indicator of financial success. Failing companies are usually not hiring new workers.

Finances are still excellent; review our discussion of this last month. There might be delays but financial goals are being achieved now. The question is where do you go from here? What is life like in a 'post-wealth' condition? It's good to start pondering these things after the 17th as Uranus starts to retrograde. Personal goals need more clarification.

The planetary power has been in the Western, social sector since April 19 and this month the planets reach their maximum Western position. Your 7th house of love becomes very strong after the 22nd and you enter a yearly love and social peak. This is a time to put others first; to take a vacation from your self and your personal desires and to allow good to happen rather than trying to coerce it by personal effort. As you do this, you will find that your personal interests are taken care of very nicely and naturally.

Love is happy after the 22nd. You and the beloved are in harmony. Singles will meet new romantic interests. Marriage is more likely next year than now, but you are meeting 'marriage material' – people you would consider marrying. Before the 22nd, love seems stressful. You and the current love are not in synch. You've experienced these situations many times and it is not a long-term problem. Compromise now and let the beloved have his or her way. No need to make things worse than they need to be.

August

Best Days Overall: 1, 2, 10, 11, 12, 19, 20, 28, 29
Most Stressful Days Overall: 6, 7, 13, 14, 25, 26, 27
Best Days for Love: 6, 7, 8, 9, 15, 16, 19, 25, 26
Best Days for Money: 3, 13, 14, 21, 22, 30, 31
Best Days for Career: 8, 13, 14, 17, 25, 26

Take it nice and easy on the 1st and 2nd. Mars is square to Uranus. Drive more carefully and avoid confrontations and risky situations. Watch the temper. People (and you) are more likely to overreact to things. Communications are more difficult then, be patient.

You are still in the midst of a yearly love and social peak until the 22nd – a good period to achieve your social goals. Happy social opportunities come. Singles are dating more.

Whether you are single or in a relationship there are more parties and social functions happening now. Marriage is more likely for singles next year, but you are getting prepared for it.

Health became more delicate on the 22nd of last month and is still delicate until the 22nd of this. Rest and relax more. Spend more time at the health spa. Get more massages. Enhance the health in the ways mentioned in the yearly report. Happily, you are paying more attention to health these days, which is a positive health signal. Energy and vitality return to normal levels after the 22nd.

Friendships get tested from the 4th to the 13th and from the 18th to the 25th. Be more patient with friends. They seem more temperamental. Problems in the relationship could be coming from events happening in their lives and not necessarily be because of you. Hi-tech gadgetry also gets tested. Make sure your anti-hacker, anti-virus software is up to date. Sometimes actual flaws are discovered in your gadgets and they need to be replaced. Sometimes the equipment is just more temperamental than usual.

You are still in a very prosperous financial cycle. Sometime too many opportunities – too much money – is stressful. It can be confusing. This seems to be your problem these days. Continue to work to attain mental clarity on your finances. Things are better than they seem to you.

On the 22nd your spouse, partner or current love enters a yearly financial peak and is likely to be more generous with you. You already have the financial favour of friends. There is some financial disagreement with the beloved from the 22nd to the 27th, but it is short lived. In the end he or she is more generous.

Job seekers still have excellent aspects.

September

Best Days Overall: 7, 8, 15, 16, 24, 25, 26
Most Stressful Days Overall: 2, 3, 9, 10, 22, 23, 29, 30
Best Days for Love: 2, 3, 4, 5, 8, 13, 14, 17, 18, 24, 27, 28, 29, 30
Best Days for Money: 1, 9, 10, 17, 18, 19, 27, 28
Best Days for Career: 4, 5, 9, 10, 13, 14, 22, 23

On July 22 the planetary power began to shift from the lower half to the upper half of your Horoscope. The trend became even stronger on August 28 as Mars crossed from the lower to the upper half. Hopefully in the past few months you've got your home base in some kind of order and you are in your point of emotional harmony. Now you can shift your energy to your outer, career goals.

Career changes have been brewing all year and are very likely to happen in the coming months. The family seems more supportive of your career goals after the 11th. The status of the family as a whole seems elevated after the 11th as well. Family is still ultra-important these days, but you can best serve them by succeeding in the outer world.

The Western social sector of the chart is still stronger than the Eastern sector, so continue to cultivate your social skills and avoid undue self-assertion and self-will. You still need the cooperation of others to attain your goals.

Your 8th house of transformation became powerful on the 22nd of last month and will remain strong until October 22. This heralds a sexually active kind of period. The spouse, partner or current love is prospering and this is a good period to pay down debt or to borrow if you need to. It's also a good month for detox regimes on all levels, physical, emotional and mental.

Death is not an appetizing subject. We tend to avoid thinking about it. But when the 8th house is strong it is unavoidable – the angel of death comes calling. Usually he is not there to take you away, only to remind you that he is around. Sometimes there is a death in the family of business associates or friends. Sometimes there are near-death kinds of experiences. Sometimes people dream of dead relatives or loved ones. Sometimes they seek out mediums to communicate with dead relatives. There is an educational process about death happening, and this is ultimately good.

Love is more challenging this period. You and the beloved are on opposite sides of the universe – you seem more distant. This is especially so after the 22nd. Distance doesn't necessarily mean a break up or separation, but if it is allowed to continue it can lead to this. Your challenge is to bridge your differences, to see the opposite perspective as valid (and even complementary to your position). If you can do this, your relationship will be better than before. In astrology, it is the opposite that is the natural love partner. On the spiritual level we are in love with our opposite. There is a recognition of the essential unity of the opposites on the higher levels.

Children or children figures in your life should be kept out of harm's way from the 15th to the 17th. They should drive more carefully and avoid dangerous situations. Foreign travel is not advisable during this period.

October

Best Days Overall: 4, 5, 13, 14, 22, 23, 31
Most Stressful Days Overall: 1, 6, 7, 19, 20, 27, 28
Best Days for Love: 1, 4, 5, 7, 8, 13, 14, 17, 18, 23, 24, 27, 28
Best Days for Money: 6, 7, 15, 16, 24, 25
Best Days for Career: 2, 3, 6, 7, 11, 12, 19, 20, 29, 30

There are many changes happening this month – a hectic, hyperactive period.

There is a Lunar Eclipse on the 18th that occurs in your 3rd house of communication. Cars and communication equipment will get tested. Drive more carefully that period. Be more patient with siblings or sibling figures: they are apt to be more temperamental. Life-changing events are happening for them. Every Lunar Eclipse tends to bring job changes and changes in the health regime and this one is no different. Those who employ others can have employee turnover at this time. Sometimes it is not literal turnover, but dramatic events in the lives of employees. Be more patient with them now. Long-buried resentments are likely to surface for correction.

This eclipse affects Jupiter, your planet of friends, so friendships are getting tested. Friends are more temperamental and can exhibit strange behaviour. Have patience. Your hi-tech gadgetry gets tested too and is apt to behave in temperamental kinds of ways. The dynamic energies generated by an eclipse often affect physical things. Sometimes the problems are just temporary, but sometimes equipment needs replacement.

The other headline this month is the career. This is hyperactive and very volatile. The hierarchy of your company and industry seems unstable and the rules of the game can change dramatically. The good news is that you are very focused on the career this month, especially after the 23rd. You enter a yearly career peak then. You are focused here and this focus tends to success. You are willing to deal with all the various challenges that arise. Relations with a boss could be a lot better, and the same is true with a parent or parent figure in your life. Relations with government are also not so great. If you have issues here, try to re-schedule meetings for a better time; postpone them for as long as possible.

The love situation is pretty much as we described last month. There is still much distance between you and the beloved. He or she seems to be in charge and calling the shots, and sometimes this is difficult to handle. On the other hand, he or she is supportive of your career goals. The tension in love is reduced after the 22nd, but you are still very distant with the beloved. It's as if you live two separate lives.

In spite of all the challenges, you are prospering. Finances are good all month, but especially after the 22nd. The beloved seems very supportive financially, friends too. The money is coming in, but you still need to work on your mental clarity. Your financial planet is still retrograde.

November

Best Days Overall: 1, 9, 10, 18, 19, 28, 29
Most Stressful Days Overall: 3, 4, 16, 17, 23, 24, 30
Best Days for Love: 3, 4, 7, 11, 12, 16, 17, 23, 24, 26, 27
Best Days for Money: 3, 4, 11, 12, 20, 21, 22, 30
Best Days for Career: 3, 4, 7, 8, 16, 17, 25, 26, 30

Career is still the main headline this month. The instability and volatility are coming to a head now. A Solar Eclipse on the 3rd occurs in your career house. Something is about to blow – the rumblings of the past year now reach a climax. It is not just your personal career that is changing, but the company and industry as well. Try not to make matters worse. Whatever happens, you still have excellent job prospects this month and for the rest of the year ahead. Be more patient with bosses, parents and parent figures; dramas are happening in their lives. These people need to avoid risky kinds of activities this period.

Love, too, is being tested by this eclipse. This doesn't necessarily mean a divorce or break up, and good relationships survive these things. However, flawed ones tend to dissolve (explode is more like it). The cosmos desires the best for you (and for the current love), so anything less than perfect tends to get exploded by the eclipse. This eclipse also impacts on Saturn, your spiritual planet. Thus there are changes in your spiritual attitudes and practice. The guru-mentor figures in your life have dramatic experiences and there are upheavals in a charity or spiritual organization you are involved with. Saturn gives us our sense of security and stability, thus during this period you feel less secure – your routine of life is disrupted. This will pass and you will form a better routine, but in the meantime it is uncomfortable.

You are still in a yearly career peak. Thus you are very focused here. In spite of all the challenges and crises, you are basically succeeding – but earning everything by the 'sweat of the brow'.

Health became more delicate last month, and is still delicate until the 22nd. A reduced schedule is called for, especially during the eclipse period. Enhance the health in the ways mentioned in the yearly report. You are going to be very busy, but schedule in rest periods where ever possible.

In spite of all the challenges, your finances are still excellent. Prosperity is untouched by all the turmoil. Your financial planet will start moving forward on the 18th, which is another good sign. Mental clarity is happening. After the 18th it will be safer to set new financial plans into motion. There is some financial disagreement with the beloved from the 22nd to the 26th, but it passes quickly.

Love will improve after the 22nd. There is harmony with the beloved. Those not in a relationship will meet romantic partners – the 30th looks especially good for that. Make an effort to project more love and warmth to others from the 4th to the 7th. You could be appearing 'cold' without realizing it. On the 22nd your love planet moves into the 11th house of friends, indicating love opportunities online through social networking sites or dating services. It also shows romantic opportunities that happen as you get involved with groups and organizations. Since October 23 you have been attracted by 'power people' – power was the great aphrodisiac for you. But from the 22nd onwards, you want friendship with the beloved – a friend not a boss.

December

Best Days Overall: 6, 7, 15, 16, 17, 25, 26
Most Stressful Days Overall: 1, 13, 14, 20, 21, 22, 28, 29
Best Days for Love: 2, 3, 4, 5, 11, 12, 13, 14, 20, 21, 22, 23, 24
Best Days for Money: 1, 8, 9, 18, 19, 28, 29
Best Days for Career: 1, 4, 5, 13, 14, 23, 24, 28, 29

On October 23 the planetary power began to move to the East. Now the shift is growing stronger. You are in a period of personal independence and this will become even stronger in the coming months. The cosmos aims for a balanced development. Sometimes self-reliance and personal initiative is important. Sometimes we need to put the interests of others ahead of our own. Neither position is absolutely correct all the time. We cannot act on behalf of others unless we are strong and self-reliant. This is a time to exercise your personal power and create the life that you want to live. It seems selfish – you mind your own business and take care of number one. But when number one is satisfied, you will be more effective for others. It is a matter of emphasis.

Last month on the 22nd, your 11th house became powerful, and it is still powerful until the 21st. This is Aquarian heaven. You get to do all the things you most love to do and that you are good at doing. This spells a successful month.

The 11th house is about friendship, groups and group activities. It is a social kind of month, but not the social that we associate with the 7th house of love. This house is about friendships of the mind; the 7th house is about friendships of the heart. The 11th house is about uncommitted kinds of relationships. Everyone is free. No one is beholden to anyone. You get together with people of similar interests and mind sets, you enjoy each other's company, network, and go home to your normal activities. The connections are mental, not emotional.

With your love planet Venus in the 11th house until the 21st, these friendships of the mind have the potential to go further. Perhaps a relationship starts that way but ends up being much more. Groups and group activities are the venue for romance until the 21st. Review our discussion of this last month.

The 11th house is associated with technology, another Aquarian strength. This is a good month to expand your knowledge in this area. The speed of change is breathtaking these days and there's always more to learn.

This has been a year of spiritual progress for you, and after the 21st there is more in store. This is a spiritual period, and spiritual-type activities – meditation, prayer, charity work – all prosper this period. Even love comes to you as you pursue your spiritual path, in spiritual venues and with spiritual people. However, love is a bit tense this period. Be more patient with the current love.

Pisces

)(

Personality Profile

PISCES AT A GLANCE

Element – Water

Ruling Planet – Neptune
   Career Planet – Jupiter
   Love Planet – Mercury
   Money Planet – Mars
   Planet of Health and Work – Sun
   Planet of Home and Family Life – Mercury
   Planet of Love Affairs, Creativity and Children
     – Moon

Colours – aqua, blue–green

*Colours that promote love, romance and social
   harmony* – earth tones, yellow,
   yellow–orange

Colours that promote earning power – red,
   scarlet

Gem – white diamond

Metal – tin

Scent – lotus

Quality – mutable (= flexibility)

Qualities most needed for balance – structure
and the ability to handle form

Strongest virtues – psychic power, sensitivity,
self-sacrifice, altruism

Deepest needs – spiritual illumination,
liberation

Characteristics to avoid – escapism, keeping
bad company, negative moods

Signs of greatest overall compatibility – Cancer,
Scorpio

Signs of greatest overall incompatibility –
Gemini, Virgo, Sagittarius

Sign most helpful to career – Sagittarius

Sign most helpful for emotional support –
Gemini

Sign most helpful financially – Aries

Sign best for marriage and/or partnerships –
Virgo

Sign most helpful for creative projects – Cancer

Best Sign to have fun with – Cancer

Signs most helpful in spiritual matters – Scorpio,
Aquarius

Best day of the week – Thursday

Understanding a Pisces

If Pisces have one outstanding quality it is their belief in the invisible, spiritual and psychic side of things. This side of things is as real to them as the hard earth beneath their feet – so real, in fact, that they will often ignore the visible, tangible aspects of reality in order to focus on the invisible and so-called intangible ones.

Of all the signs of the zodiac, the intuitive and emotional faculties of the Pisces are the most highly developed. They are committed to living by their intuition and this can at times be infuriating to other people – especially those who are materially, scientifically or technically orientated. If you think that money or status or worldly success are the only goals in life, then you will never understand a Pisces.

Pisces have intellect, but to them intellect is only a means by which they can rationalize what they know intuitively. To an Aquarius or a Gemini the intellect is a tool with which to gain knowledge. To a well-developed Pisces it is a tool by which to express knowledge.

Pisces feel like fish in an infinite ocean of thought and feeling. This ocean has many depths, currents and undercurrents. They long for purer waters where the denizens are good, true and beautiful, but they are sometimes pulled to the lower, murkier depths. Pisces know that they do not generate thoughts but only tune in to thoughts that already exist; this is why they seek the purer waters. This ability to tune in to higher thoughts inspires them artistically and musically.

Since Pisces is so spiritually orientated – though many Pisces in the corporate world may hide this fact – we will deal with this aspect in greater detail, for otherwise it is difficult to understand the true Pisces personality.

There are four basic attitudes of the spirit. One is outright scepticism – the attitude of secular humanists. The second is an intellectual or emotional belief, where one worships a far-distant God-figure – the attitude of most modern church-going people. The third is not only belief but direct personal spiritual experience – this is the attitude of some 'born-again' religious people. The fourth is actual unity with the divinity, an intermingling with the spiritual world – this is the attitude of yoga. This fourth attitude is the deepest urge of a Pisces, and a Pisces is uniquely qualified to pursue and perform this work.

Consciously or unconsciously, Pisces seek this union with the spiritual world. The belief in a greater reality makes Pisces very tolerant and understanding of others – perhaps even too tolerant. There are instances in their lives when they should say 'enough is enough' and be ready to defend their position and put up a fight. However, because of their qualities it takes a good deal to get them into that frame of mind.

Pisces basically want and aspire to be 'saints'. They do so in their own way and according to their own rules. Others should not try to impose their concept of saintliness on a Pisces, because he or she always tries to find it for him- or herself.

Finance

Money is generally not that important to Pisces. Of course they need it as much as anyone else, and many of them attain great wealth. But money is not generally a primary objective. Doing good, feeling good about oneself, peace of mind, the relief of pain and suffering – these are the things that matter most to a Pisces.

Pisces earn money intuitively and instinctively. They follow their hunches rather than their logic. They tend to be generous and perhaps overly charitable. Almost any kind of misfortune is enough to move a Pisces to give. Although this is one of their greatest virtues, Pisces should be more careful with their finances. They should try to be more choosy about the people to whom they lend money, so that they are not being taken advantage of. If they give money to charities they should follow it up to see that their contributions are put to good use. Even when Pisces are not rich, they still like to spend money on helping others. In this case they should really be careful, however: they must learn to say no sometimes and help themselves first.

Perhaps the biggest financial stumbling block for the Pisces is general passivity – a *laissez faire* attitude. In general Pisces like to go with the flow of events. When it comes to financial matters, especially, they need to be more aggressive. They need to make things happen, to create their own wealth. A passive attitude will only cause loss and missed opportunity. Worrying about financial security will not provide that security. Pisces need to go after what they want tenaciously.

Career and Public Image

Pisces like to be perceived by the public as people of spiritual or material wealth, of generosity and philanthropy. They look up to big-hearted, philanthropic types. They admire people engaged in large-scale undertakings and eventually would like to head up these big enterprises themselves. In short, they like to be connected with big organizations that are doing things in a big way.

If Pisces are to realize their full career and professional potential they need to travel more, educate themselves more and learn more about the actual world. In other words, they need some of the unflagging optimism of the Sagittarius in order to reach the top.

Because of all their caring and generous characteristics, Pisces often choose professions through which they can help and touch the lives of other people. That is why many Pisces become doctors, nurses, social workers or teachers. Sometimes it takes a while before Pisces realize what they really want to do in their professional lives, but once they find a career that lets them manifest their interests and virtues they will excel at it.

Love and Relationships

It is not surprising that someone as 'otherworldly' as the Pisces would like a partner who is practical and down to earth. Pisces prefer a partner who is on top of all the details of life, because they dislike details. Pisces seek this quality in both their romantic and professional partners. More than anything else this gives Pisces a feeling of being grounded, of being in touch with reality.

As expected, these kinds of relationships – though necessary – are sure to have many ups and downs. Misunderstandings will take place because the two attitudes are poles apart. If you are in love with a Pisces you will experience these fluctuations and will need a lot of patience to see things stabilize. Pisces are moody, intuitive, affectionate and difficult to get to know. Only time and the right attitude will yield Pisces' deepest secrets. However, when in love with a Pisces you will find that riding the waves is worth it because they are good, sensitive people who need and like to give love and affection.

When in love, Pisces like to fantasize. For them fantasy is 90 per cent of the fun of a relationship. They tend to idealize their partner, which can be good and bad at the same time. It is bad in that it is difficult for anyone to live up to the high ideals their Pisces lover sets.

Home and Domestic Life

In their family and domestic life Pisces have to resist the tendency to relate only by feelings and moods. It is unrealistic to expect that your partner and other family members will be as intuitive as you are. There is a need for more verbal communication between a Pisces and his or her family. A cool, unemotional exchange of ideas and opinions will benefit everyone.

Some Pisces tend to like mobility and moving around. For them too much stability feels like a restriction on their freedom. They hate to be locked in one location for ever.

The sign of Gemini sits on Pisces' 4th solar house (of home and family) cusp. This shows that the Pisces likes and needs a home environment that promotes intellectual and mental interests. They tend to treat their neighbours as family – or extended family. Some Pisces can have a dual attitude towards the home and family – on the one hand they like the emotional support of the family, but on the other they dislike the obligations, restrictions and duties involved with it. For Pisces, finding a balance is the key to a happy family life.

Horoscope for 2013

Major Trends

There are many important and positive changes that have been happening the past few years. Neptune, your ruling planet, has moved into your sign. This adds much glamour to the image – an unearthly kind of beauty. It gives more confidence and self-esteem as well. Your whole body is being elevated in energy vibration – more on this later.

In 2011 Uranus moved into your money house, bringing great change to the whole financial life – to your investments, the way you earn and your attitudes towards money. Again, there are more details on this later.

Jupiter has been in your 4th house of home and family since June 2012, and will remain there until June 27 of this year. Thus there are moves, renovations and an enlargement of the family circle going on, which all seem very happy. Jupiter moves into your 5th house of children on June 27. This shows a happy, fun kind of period – a cosmic vacation. You start to experience the joy of life. This brings luck in speculations too. Pisces of child-bearing age are more fertile than usual during that period.

Saturn moved into your 9th house late last year and will be there for another two years. For students, especially at college or postgraduates, this is a difficult period. They need to work much harder on their studies than usual. They are not catching any 'lucky breaks' and only sheer merit will get them through. For non-students it shows a testing of the belief systems, a re-organization of the higher mind. Generally this brings 'crises of faith'.

Your areas of greatest interest this year are the body and image; finance; home and family (until June 27); children, fun, creativity (from June 27 onwards); religion, philosophy, metaphysics, foreign travel; friends, groups and group activities.

Your paths of greatest fulfilment this year are home and family (until June 27); fun, children and creativity (after June 27); and religion, philosophy, metaphysics and foreign travel.

Health

(Please note that this is an astrological perspective on health and not a medical one. In days of yore there was no difference, these perspectives were identical. But now there could be quite a difference. For a medical perspective, please consult your doctor or health practitioner.)

Now that Saturn, Uranus and Pluto have moved away from their stressful aspects, health is much improved over the past few years. In the year ahead, only one long-term planet – Jupiter – is in stressful aspect with you, and that only until June 27. After that date all the long-term planets will either be in harmonious aspect or leaving you alone. Health is good this year and will get even better after June. The empty 6th house of health confirms this good health – there's no need to pay too much attention here as nothing is really wrong. Sure, there will be times during the year when health is less easy than usual. These are caused by temporary planetary transits and are not trends for the year. When the difficult transits pass, the normal good health resumes.

Good though your health is, you can make it even better. Give more attention to the heart and the feet. These two

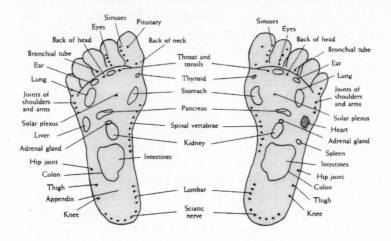

Reflexology

Try to massage the whole foot on a regular basis, but pay extra attention to the points highlighted on the chart. When you massage, be aware of 'sore spots', as these need special attention. It's also a good idea to massage the ankles and top side of the feet.

areas are always important to you. Regular foot massage is excellent therapy and is especially powerful for you. You respond to this better than most. Foot baths – hydro massage – is also very powerful for you. There are many such gadgets out on the market and it might be advisable to invest in one. Avoid worry and anxiety, the two emotions that are the spiritual root causes of heart problems.

Since these are the most vulnerable areas this year, problems (if they happened) would most likely begin there. So keeping them healthy and fit is sound preventive medicine.

The other important health trend is Neptune's move into your own sign last year. This shows a refinement of the physical body. It is, as we mentioned, being elevated in energy vibration. It is becoming more sensitized. Thus dietary habits which never bothered you in the past could bother you now. A more refined diet is in order. It is never advisable to abuse alcohol or drugs and this is especially true for Pisces people. But now, with Neptune in your sign, it is even less advisable. The new sensitivities could easily make you overreact to these things.

Pisces is the most psychic of all the signs (though Scorpio will give you a run for your money). With Pisces even a bad thought is picked up and responded to. And this sensitivity is greatly increased at this time. It will now become 'physical' and tangible. Subtle vibrations will be felt right in the body. If you are experiencing aches and pains, or weird sensations in the body, the chances are these are not coming from you. You are picking things up from the environment, from people you are around, or people you are connected to spiritually. You need to be most careful not to 'identify' with these sensations. If you do you will have all kinds of needless medical adventures. See your body as a gauge that registers certain sensations, but is not itself the sensation. Separate yourself from these sensations. Yes, you feel them, but they are not you.

The Sun is your health planet. As our regular readers undoubtedly know, he is a fast-moving planet and during the course of the year he will move through all the signs and houses of your Horoscope. So there are many short-term trends in health depending on where the Sun is and the aspects he receives, and these are best dealt with in the monthly reports.

Home and Family

This is a very important area of life this year and a major focus in the year ahead. It's not just that Jupiter occupies this house until June 27. It's also the fact that it is the career planet that is in that house – Jupiter being your career planet. We could say that it is your spiritual mission to get the home, domestic and family life in right order this year. Until June 27 this is your highest priority. However, there's no question that you will succeed here. Jupiter is a benevolent planet and he is helping you.

As we mentioned previously, moves could have happened last year and, if not, they are likely in the year ahead. Often people don't literally move but they buy additional homes or renovate or expand the present home. The net effect is the same; it is 'as if' they have moved.

Jupiter in the 4th house shows an expansion of the family circle. Generally this happens through births, marriages or by meeting people who are 'like family' to you. Pisceans of appropriate age are more fertile than usual.

There is good family support in the year ahead, emotionally, financially and in other ways. Family life is basically happy. This transit of Jupiter shows the prosperity and success of the family as a whole. The family is elevated in status. It especially shows the prosperity and generosity of a parent figure.

The career planet in the 4th house has mundane interpretations aside from what we mentioned. It shows following your career from the home – often it shows a home-based kind of business. Even if you work in an outside office, you will be doing more work from the home. The home is becoming as much a place of business as a home.

If the parents or parent figures are married, the relationship seems much happier in the year ahead. One of the parents is making supreme efforts to be devoted to the other. If the parents or parent figures are single, there is serious romance in the year ahead. Parents or parent figures are not likely to move in the year ahead. Siblings and sibling figures likewise.

Children or children figures in your life are having a spiritual kind of year. There is a lot of interior growth and development happening. The inner growth will become evident after June 27 when they start to prosper and catch all kinds of lucky breaks. They enter a two-year cycle of prosperity after June 27.

Finance and Career

Many of the trends that we have written about over the past two years are still in effect for the year ahead. Uranus is in your money house for another five years or so. This shows much financial experimentation as you try out different financial strategies and learn what works for you by trial and error. This makes the financial life very exciting – there's never a dull moment – but it can test your faith. You seem in uncharted territory these days.

In the past two years you have been making dramatic changes in your investments, in the way you handle money, the way you spend and in the way that you earn. These kinds of changes are likely to continue in the year ahead.

Uranus rules the hi-tech industry. Thus these areas are very attractive to you now and you have a good feeling for them. This also shows how important it is for you to stay up to date with latest in technology. Yes, it is expensive, but it is ultra-important in earnings. Uranus also rules the online world – web sites, online businesses – and the electronic media – radio, TV and the internet. So these areas seem important in finance now.

You are in a period in your life where 'same old, same old' just doesn't cut it. You need to make changes, to do things differently. There is a saying, 'If you keep doing what you have always been doing how can you expect a different result?' If you want different results you have to change what you're doing.

Uranus also happens to be your spiritual planet. Thus his move into your money house shows that you are going deeper into the spiritual nature of wealth and supply. You Pisceans already understand these things very well, but now you are going deeper into it. Your challenge these days is to access the supernatural, rather than the natural sources of supply.

Your intuition always tends to be good. You are perhaps the most intuitive of all the signs. But now with Neptune in your own sign and the spiritual planet in the money house, the intuition is even sharper. Follow it to prosperity. It is basically trustworthy (although there are times when it needs more verification, such as when Neptune or Uranus is retrograde or receiving stressful aspects).

Uranus will be square to Pluto for most of the year. The aspect will be most exact, and therefore most powerful, in October and November of this year. This indicates a need to watch all the legalities of what you do in finance. Have important moves checked by an accountant or solicitor. Learn more about the legal ramifications of what you do. A little forethought will save many headaches later on down the road.

Career is so-so early in the year. As we mentioned, it is really about getting the home and family in order. A home-based business is very likely. If you work in an outside office you will probably be doing more work at home. On June 27 Jupiter will move into Cancer and start to make fabulous aspects to Neptune, your personal planet. This shows much career success in the latter part of the year. But first the home life and the emotional life need to be in order. What I like about this transit is that the career seems like fun. You are enjoying the career path. The career could involve entertainment, sports or leisure kinds of activities.

Love and Social Life

Your 7th house of love and marriage is not a house of power this year. As regular readers know, this tends to the status quo. There is a basic contentment in things as they are and there is no special compulsion to make dramatic change. (However if you want to, if you feel strongly motivated, you have more freedom in this area.)

Love and social matters are simply not that important to you this year. Some years are like that. You need to focus on yourself, your finances and family situation. Singles are in a preparation stage for love this year. Timing is very important in love matters. You and your future soul mate could be passing each other on the street every other day and you would not recognize each other – until the right time came.

Marriage or committed relationships are not indicated here this year. Singles will tend to stay single, and those who are married will tend to stay married. However, singles will certainly date more and have love affairs. This is especially so after June 27 when Jupiter enters the 5th house. But these are not serious kinds of relationships; you are just amusing yourself.

For the unattached there are love affair opportunities in the usual places – at parties, resorts, clubs and places of entertainment. You have the aspects for the office romance this year, but with superiors.

Mercury, your love planet, is a very fast-moving planet. During the course of the year he will move through all the signs and houses of your Horoscope. Thus there are many short-term trends in love that are best dealt with in the monthly reports. Mercury goes retrograde three times a year. These are times to go slow in love, to review your love and social life and to see where improvements can be made. They are not times for making important love decisions one way or another. This year the Mercury retrograde periods are from February 23 to March 16, June 26 to July 19 and October 21 to November 9. Love tends to be more complicated during these periods as well, so try to be more patient.

Self-improvement

Saturn moved into your 9th house of religion and metaphysics last October and will be there for the next two years. Not only that, but there are two eclipses in your 9th house this year: a Lunar Eclipse on April 25 and a Solar Eclipse on November 3. This is an area of life that is undergoing great change and ferment.

There is much written about the importance of psychology – mood and feeling – as an influence in life. But you don't read much about the importance of the personal religion, the personal philosophy of life, or the personal metaphysics. This is strange, for in truth the affairs of 9th house are much more powerful than the affairs of the 4th. Your personal religion will shape and mould your psychology. Changes here will change every area of life. You will interpret the meaning of events differently and thus have different psychological reactions to them. The affairs of the 9th house control the affairs of all the other houses.

With stern, reality-loving Saturn moving through this house, your beliefs are getting tested. This is a good thing. They are getting 'reality therapy'. Events will happen in your life that will contradict many things that you believe. This will lead to a review and re-organization of your beliefs. Some will go by the wayside and be discarded; some will get revised; some – the true ones – will be left as they are. In the end you will have a personal philosophy that is solid and can stand the test of time.

We mentioned earlier that you are going deeper into the spiritual dimensions of wealth. Perhaps the most important lesson is to discern between the visible, tangible aspects of wealth – the money, the cars, homes etc. – and the power that produces these things. Unfortunately most of us are worshiping the side effects instead of the source: the power that creates the wealth.

Month-by-month Forecasts

January

Best Days Overall: 6, 7, 14, 15, 24, 25
Most Stressful Days Overall: 2, 3, 8, 9, 21, 22, 23, 29, 30
Best Days for Love: 2, 3, 8, 9, 10, 11, 18, 19, 21, 29, 30, 31
Best Days for Money: 4, 5, 12, 13, 17, 18, 22, 23, 31
Best Days for Career: 4, 8, 9, 12, 22, 31

You begin your year with most of the planets in the upper half of the Horoscope. Though you have passed your yearly career peak (this happened last month) you will have a mini peak after the 19th. Home and family is still very important, but you can shift more attention and energy to the career. The best way to serve your family now is to be successful in the outer world. There is success happening after the 19th. Job seekers have fabulous opportunities. You have the financial favour of bosses, elders, parents and parent figures all month, but especially from the 3rd to the 5th. Speculations are favourable that period as well. A nice payday happening.

Most of the planets are now in the Eastern sector of the self and self-interest. Thus you are now in a period of personal independence. You have more personal power. Other people are always important, but they can't interfere too much with what you want to do or create. You can have your way these days and your way seems the best way. So, if conditions are not satisfying, change them – create what does satisfy you. Your personal independence is getting stronger over the next few months; the world is ready to adapt to you.

Almost all of the planets are moving forward. Things happen quickly. There is much forward progress towards your goals and in the world at large. Normally this would be a great time for starting new projects, but it's best to wait until your birthday. Your personal solar cycle is still in its waning phase right now. On your birthday your solar cycle will start to wax.

The career aspects are very good after the 19th, although they are reasonably even before that date. However, your career planet is still retrograde until the 30th. You still need to do more homework on career matters, especially on new offers or opportunities. Jupiter is also square to Neptune towards the end of the month and this shows much behind-the-scenes activity. Things are not as they seem and you need to do more research and get more facts.

Love is basically happy this month. Singles are not likely to marry, but there are romantic opportunities. The social life seems harmonious. Until the 19th romantic opportunities happen as you get involved with groups, group activities and friends. The online world also brings romantic opportunity. After the 19th, love becomes more spiritual, more idealistic. Romantic opportunities happen in spiritual settings, at the yoga class or spiritual retreat, the meditation seminar, the prayer meeting, the spiritual lecture or charity event. Many love developments are happening behind the scenes. You might not see them outwardly just yet, but progress is happening.

Health is good.

February

Best Days Overall: 2, 3, 11, 12, 20, 21, 22
Most Stressful Days Overall: 5, 18, 19, 25, 26
Best Days for Love: 1, 9, 10, 11, 12, 18, 19, 20, 21, 25, 26
Best Days for Money: 1, 9, 11, 12, 13, 14, 18, 20, 21, 22, 27
Best Days for Career: 1, 11, 12, 18, 19, 21, 22

The spiritual life, the inner life, is the main headline this month. Your 12th house of spirituality is chock full of planets, denoting a strong interest and focus. After the 18th, your own sign Pisces becomes very powerful, and this too enhances the spiritual life. Your challenge will be to keep both feet on the ground and to handle the mundane details of life. You seem more in the spiritual world than here on earth. Those on the spiritual path will have important break-throughs this month. Those not on the path will have many supernatural kinds of experiences too, but generally they'll put it down to 'coincidence'. Those not on the spiritual path could tend to overindulge in alcohol and drugs these days and this is not advisable. The body is more refined than usual and could overreact to these things. Real spiritual practice will get you higher than any drug and you will always have your faculties.

The planets are now in their maximum Eastern position and will be so next month too. You are in your period of maximum personal power. Have your way by all means. Build the life of your dreams. Create what you want. The cosmos is supporting you. In a few months it will be more difficult to do this, so now is the time.

On the 18th you enter one of your yearly personal plea-sure peaks. On one level you are able to enjoy all the sensual delights – enjoy. On another level, this is a great period to get the body and the image in shape the way you want them to be.

This is a happy month. There is prosperity all month with financial windfalls. Financial opportunities are seeking you out – you don't need to do anything special, they will find you. The 3rd to the 5th brings a nice payday or opportunity. The financial intuition (always good) is very good this period. You just need to trust it.

Job seekers still have fabulous opportunities this month, especially after the 18th. The opportunities will come to you; you don't need to do anything special. The 19th to the 21st seems especially good for job seekers.

If you are having your birthday this month, it is very good to launch new projects, ventures or products from your birthday until the 27th. All the various cosmic and personal cycles are in alignment then. If your birthday happens next month, wait until next month.

Health is super. You have all the energy you need to achieve anything you set your mind to. Love is also happy. As with the other things in life, love seeks you out and will find you.

March

Best Days Overall: 2, 3, 10, 11, 20, 21, 29, 30
Most Stressful Days Overall: 4, 5, 17, 18, 19, 24, 25, 26, 31
Best Days for Love: 2, 3, 10, 11, 20, 21, 22, 24, 25, 26, 29, 30, 31
Best Days for Money: 1, 2, 3, 8, 9, 11, 12, 13, 14, 17, 18, 22, 27, 28, 31
Best Days for Career: 1, 4, 5, 8, 9, 17, 18, 27, 28, 31

The Water element, your native element, got very powerful on February 18, and is powerful until the 20th. Basically this is a comfortable energy for you. The only caveat for you is the need to keep your feelings positive and constructive. The feeling, emotional energy is very powerful. When it is constructive, you will see paradise on earth. Your wishes, your prayers, will be answered very quickly. But if the emotions get negative, great damage and destruction can happen. There is more voltage behind your feelings. You can manifest hell very quickly too. The month ahead can be a dream come true or your worst nightmare. It is up to you.

Health is still excellent. You seem more focused on health until the 20th. Your state of health greatly affects your personal appearance, and probably this is the cause for your interest. You can enhance the health even more by giving more attention to the feet (foot massage) until the 20th and to the head, face and scalp (scalp and facial massage) from the 20th onwards. Physical exercise is also good after the 20th. Spiritual healing is very powerful from the 27th to the 30th.

Many of you have your birthday this month. If you are planning to launch a new product or venture do it from the

20th to the 27th. All the various cosmic cycles are well synchronized for this. There will be much 'oomph' behind your efforts.

Prosperity is strong all month. Until the 12th financial opportunities seek you out. Nothing much you need to do. You spend on yourself. You adopt the image of wealth and you dress more expensively. People see you as wealthy and prosperous. On the 20th you enter a yearly financial peak. The doors of heaven are open and the affluence is flowing in from on high. It seems to you that the wealth comes from 'outside', from this world. But these things are only side effects of the down-pouring of spiritual affluence upon you.

Job changes can happen from the 27th to the 30th and these seem sudden. Important financial changes happen from the 18th to the 21st. This often shows a sudden opportunity or windfall that comes 'from nowhere', from an unexpected place.

Drive more carefully from the 26th to the 29th. Siblings and sibling figures in your life should avoid risky kinds of activities then.

Love is still happy this month. You still have love on your terms and love still pursues you. But your love planet went retrograde on February 23 and is retrograde until the 17th. This often shows a 'lack of direction' in the love life. Relationships seem to go backwards instead of forwards. It's a good time to review the love life and current relationship and see where improvements can be made. Avoid making important love decisions until after the 17th when clarity returns.

April

Best Days Overall: 6, 7, 8, 16, 17, 25, 26
Most Stressful Days Overall: 1, 14, 15, 21, 22, 27, 28
Best Days for Love: 1, 7, 8, 9, 10, 19, 21, 22, 27, 28, 29, 30
Best Days for Money: 1, 4, 5, 9, 10, 14, 15, 21, 23, 24, 29, 30
Best Days for Career: 7, 8, 14, 15, 19, 27, 28

The planetary power is still mostly below the horizon. This shift began on February 18 and is getting stronger day by day. Your focus should be on the home, family and your emotional wellbeing. This is the time to prepare the inner psychological and emotional conditions for future career success. People involved in show business or athletics know that the preparation is just as important, if not more so, than the actual event. Your career, your outer success, is built on inner, unseen activity. You are in the 'behind the scenes' phase of your career these days and it should not be discounted.

Prosperity is still strong. You are still in the midst of a yearly financial peak. There are nice paydays (or happy opportunities) from the 5th to the 9th and from the 14th to the 20th. Sales people make a fortunate sale from the 4th to the 9th. Writers and journalists sell their products then. Perhaps you are buying a new car or new communication equipment. A sibling or sibling figure prospers. Children or children figures prosper from the 14th to the 20th. You are spending more on health that period, but can also earn from that field.

Uranus is making a pretty exact square to Pluto this month – a very dynamic aspect. There is turbulence in the world. For you, foreign travel is best avoided (especially if it is elective) this month. Your religious and philosophical beliefs are being challenged. Often this creates a crisis of faith. Students are making dramatic changes to their educational plans.

Health is still good. You can enhance it further by giving more attention to the head, face and scalp (scalp and face massage is very good) until the 19th and to the neck and throat from the 19th onwards. Neck massage and cranio-sacral therapy will be powerful.

Your 3rd house of communication and intellectual interests becomes powerful on the 19th. There is joy in exercising the mind. Learning is good for its own sake, regardless whether it has any practical value or not. In your case it does have practical value, but this is a side effect. Your communication skills, your knowledge, seem important on the financial level that period. Good use of the media – good advertising and good PR – is also important. People need to know what you have to offer.

Job seekers have beautiful opportunities from the 19th to the 25th.

A Lunar Eclipse on the 25th occurs in your 9th house. It is basically benign to you, but children and children figures should be kept out of harm's way. This eclipse will impact on legal matters – they start to move forward in dramatic ways – and on students. They make changes in their educational plans. Avoid foreign travel or speculations this eclipse period.

May

Best Days Overall: 4, 5, 13, 14, 15, 23, 24, 31
Most Stressful Days Overall: 11, 12, 18, 19, 25, 26
Best Days for Love: 8, 9, 10, 11, 18, 19, 21, 22, 29, 30
Best Days for Money: 2, 3, 6, 7, 8, 9, 10, 11, 12, 18, 19, 21, 22, 27, 28, 29, 30
Best Days for Career: 8, 9, 10, 11, 12, 21, 22, 29, 30

We have two eclipses this month. This ensures that the month ahead will be tumultuous and full of dramatic change, mostly on the world level. For you, the second eclipse – the Lunar Eclipse of the 25th – is the stronger one, but it won't hurt to take a reduced schedule for the first one anyway.

The Solar Eclipse on the 10th occurs in your 3rd house and impacts on the financial planet Mars. So there are important financial changes happening. Some shock or surprise forces the change. Most likely your thinking or planning was not realistic and the eclipse shows you why. Cars and communication equipment will get tested. Often there is a need to replace equipment, although sometimes the disturbances are just temporary. Drive more carefully this period. If possible avoid long drives. There are dramas and life-changing events in the lives of siblings, sibling figures and neighbours. Job changes could happen too. Often the job change is within the present company. The workplace is in a state of upheaval. Over the next six months there will be dramatic changes in the health regime as well.

Health becomes more delicate after the 20th. There is no long-term problem, but this is one of your vulnerable periods of the year. You should take a more relaxed schedule from the 20th onwards, but especially around the eclipse period of the 25th.

The Lunar Eclipse of the 25th occurs in your 10th house, indicating career changes. These are not just personal changes but seem to affect the hierarchy of your company and industry as well. This eclipse is a direct hit on Neptune, the Lord of your Horoscope and a very important planet in your chart. Thus the eclipse is going to produce events that force you to redefine yourself, your personality and self-concept. If you don't redefine yourself for yourself, others will, and it probably won't be pleasant. As you start to change the way you think of yourself, your outer image – your presentation to the world – will also change. Thus there will be wardrobe changes, changes in hairstyle, etc. If you haven't been careful in dietary matters, the eclipse could bring a detox of the body. In general, it's good to stay out of harm's way this period. Spend more quiet time at home. This is the best way to handle this kind of energy.

Enhance the health by giving more attention to the neck and throat until the 20th. After the 20th give more attention to the respiratory system, lungs, arms and shoulders. Tension tends to collect in the shoulders and needs to be released. Have them massaged regularly. Breathing exercises and plain old fresh air are also good.

June

Best Days Overall: 1, 10, 11, 19, 20, 27, 28
Most Stressful Days Overall: 7, 8, 15, 16, 21, 22
Best Days for Love: 1, 10, 11, 15, 16, 19, 20, 27, 28
Best Days for Money: 2, 3, 7, 8, 9, 17, 18, 25, 26, 27, 30
Best Days for Career: 8, 9, 17, 18, 21, 22, 26, 27

Your 4th house of home and family became strong on the 20th of last month and is strong until the 21st of this. This is the time to get the home and domestic situation in right order. Many important and happy changes are happening in the career, but your focus should still be on the home, family and emotional life. When you are in emotional harmony and coming from this place, the career will naturally blossom. Your spiritual mission is still your family, as it has been all year. After the 27th, as Jupiter moves into Cancer, the family is still important, but there is more focus on the children or children figures in your life. Your mission is to be there for them.

The element of Water becomes unusually strong after the 21st. We have a situation similar to February and March; 60 to 70 per cent of the planets are either in Water signs or moving through them. People are more emotional and feeling-oriented. The emotional energy on the planet is much stronger than usual. (Often there is more rain and sometimes flooding under these aspects.) While you are very comfortable with a lot of water, you must make sure that your feelings are positive and constructive. When they are positive, you will create and experience heaven on earth.

When they turn negative you will understand the seven circles of hell. Be on guard now.

For those of you on the spiritual path there are important metaphysical implications here. A successful prayer or meditation is when you succeed in entering the 'feeling' of what you are praying for. When this happens, the prayer is answered. Now, it is much easier to enter the feeling of what you want, thus you have more power to manifest what is desirable. Spiritual work will go better.

Health improves tremendously after the 21st. You have all the energy you need to achieve whatever you set your mind to. Goals are achieved much easier now and with much less fuss and bother. You enter a yearly personal pleasure peak which will be stronger than your normal personal pleasure peaks. Jupiter also moves into your 5th house – a fun time.

There will be many opportunities for love affairs although these seem non-serious. Those of you involved in relationships will have more fun with the beloved. Love is honeymoonish this period.

When Jupiter enters Cancer on the 27th you enter a cycle of good fortune. There is luck in speculations; there is fertility for those of appropriate age; there is enhanced personal creativity. Fun kinds of travel will happen.

July

Best Days Overall: 7, 8, 17, 25, 26
Most Stressful Days Overall: 4, 5, 6, 12, 13, 19, 20
Best Days for Love: 1, 7, 8, 10, 11, 12, 13, 17, 19, 20, 25, 26, 29, 30
Best Days for Money: 1, 5, 6, 7, 8, 16, 17, 25, 26, 27, 28
Best Days for Career: 7, 8, 16, 17, 19, 20, 25

Many of the trends that we wrote of last month are still very much in effect. The element of Water is still very powerful (especially until the 22nd). You are still in the midst of a yearly (and perhaps life time) personal pleasure peak until the 22nd too. Life is good these days. Are there a few challenges? You bet. But the good things – the harmony – are much stronger. When problems arise you have plenty of help in dealing with them.

Jupiter is making beautiful aspects to Neptune this month. This brings happy career opportunities to you. You have the favour of bosses, elders, parents, parent figures and those who are the authority figures in your life. If you have issues with these people (or the government) now is the time to deal with them. You should get best case scenarios this period.

You are meeting new and powerful friends and they seem helpful in your career. Your management ability, your ability to manage your own affairs and those of others, is much stronger now. You just have an innate knack for it. Career seems enjoyable. You manage to have fun as you pursue your career path. Many of you will find careers that are more fun-filled as well.

Health is excellent all month. The main danger now is overindulgence in the good life. Weight could be a problem. Indulge, but don't overindulge! You can enhance the health by giving more attention to the stomach and the diet until the 22nd. Women should give more attention to the breasts as well. After the 22nd give more attention to the heart.

Finances are good this month. You have the financial favour of a parent or parent figure. You are spending on the home and family and can earn from here as well. Family connections are also important financially. Mars will travel with Jupiter from the 19th to the 24th – a very strong financial period. A nice payday is happening. This could come in the form of a pay rise (bosses are supportive of your financial goals) or though luck in speculations. Personal creativity is more marketable this period. You have the financial favour of friends. Online activities boost the bottom line. It will also be good to get involved with groups and organizations.

Love is happy but seems to lack direction until the 21st. Mercury, your love planet, is retrograde. Be more patient with the beloved from the 17th to the 24th. He or she is apt to be more temperamental. He or she should stay out of harm's way that period too. There are life-changing events happening for the beloved and love will be tested that period.

On May 21 the planetary power began to shift from the East to the social West. Your period of personal independence is over with. Now and for the next few months, you have to live with what you created and adapt as best you can to conditions. Happily you seem comfortable and this adapting doesn't seem a problem. You are in a period where you don't 'make' things happen, but rather you 'allow' them to occur. Your good is already prepared and it is just a matter of getting out of the way and allowing its manifestation. Your social skills are important these days.

August

Best Days Overall: 3, 4, 13, 14, 21, 22, 30, 31
Most Stressful Days Overall: 1, 2, 8, 9, 15, 16, 28, 29
Best Days for Love: 3, 4, 8, 9, 15, 16, 19, 24, 25, 26
Best Days for Money: 3, 4, 13, 14, 21, 22, 23, 24, 30, 31
Best Days for Career: 3, 13, 14, 15, 16, 21, 22, 30, 31

The party period of the past two months is not over yet, it's just in more of a lull. You are still partying and enjoying life, but are taking a 'work break' since July 22. With your 6th house of health and work still powerful until the 22nd, job seekers have excellent aspects. This is a good month to do all those mundane, detail-oriented, 'boring' chores such as getting your filing system in order, making sure you have copies of important documents, doing your bookkeeping, balancing your accounts, etc. You have a greater ability to handle details these days and you should take advantage of it.

The planetary power is now in its maximum Western position this month. This will be the case next month as well. Keep in mind our discussion of this last month. Self-assertion and self-will won't work these days. Allow good to happen, don't try to force things. Cultivate the good graces of others – they are the instruments of your good.

Love is happy this month. The love planet is moving speedily forward and there is great confidence in love now. Social goals are achieved speedily. Not only that, but you enter a yearly social peak on the 22nd. So the social life is much more active than usual. Singles most likely won't marry this period – the aspects for marriage are much better in 2014 and 2015 – but still there is romance and happiness on the love front. Sometimes there is a meeting with the person that you will marry in the future. Sometimes it just indicates meeting people who are 'marriage material'. There are many possible scenarios.

The main challenge in love – and this happens after the 24th – is bridging the differences between you and the beloved. You are meeting people who are exactly your opposite, with opposite perspectives on life and opposite positions on things. Those already in a relationship are also experiencing this within the relationship. Keep in mind that in astrology, the person most opposite to you is the natural marriage partner. On a higher level opposites are seen as complementary – our other half. When opposites unite you have the most powerful of relationships.

Avoid speculations or financial risk-taking on the 1st and 2nd. Important financial changes are happening then. The financial intuition, though good, needs more verification that period. Try to avoid risky situations in general then.

Be more patient with parents, parent figures and bosses from the 4th to the 13th. They are going through personal changes and are apt to be more temperamental. They should avoid risky situations that period as well.

Health is more delicate after the 22nd. Rest and relax more. Keep your mind on the really important things in life and let go of trivia. Enhance the health by giving more attention to the heart until the 22nd and to the small intestine afterwards. Stresses in love after the 22nd affect the health. If this happens, restore harmony as quickly as possible.

September

Best Days Overall: 1, 9, 10, 18, 19, 27, 28
Most Stressful Days Overall: 4, 5, 6, 11, 12, 24, 25, 26
Best Days for Love: 4, 5, 6, 8, 15, 16, 17, 18, 25, 26, 27, 28
Best Days for Money: 1, 2, 3, 9, 10, 11, 12, 18, 19, 20, 21, 27, 28, 29, 30
Best Days for Career: 1, 9, 10, 11, 12, 18, 19, 27, 28

The planets are still in their maximum Western position this month. The planetary power flows away from you rather than towards you. It is a time to focus on others. Some would say this is a time for 'unselfishness'. You have no need to have your way. Go along with others this month. Their way is probably best right now. Cultivate the likeability factor as this is more important than personal abilities or merit for now.

Health still needs watching until the 22nd. The long-term planets are basically kind to you, so there is nothing major happening; it is just one of your more vulnerable periods in the year. Harmony in love and with friends is still very important all month. Discord here could be a root cause for health problems. Enhance the health by giving more attention to the small intestine (and diet) until the 22nd and to the kidneys and hips after the 22nd. Health should improve after the 22nd. This is a hectic, active kind of month and you will have to be very creative to maintain high energy levels until that date. Dropping the non-essentials from the life liberates much energy, but this requires making tough choices and not everyone will be pleased.

You are still in the midst of your yearly social peak. Even when your 7th house of love weakens after the 22nd, the sign of Libra (which rules love and romance) will be powerful. You tend to have a natural attraction to health professionals and office romances, and this tendency is even stronger until the 22nd. Romantic opportunities not only happen in the usual ways – at parties and gatherings – but in the workplace, or as you handle your normal health goals. Until the 9th there is still a need to learn to bridge differences with the beloved. If you can do this, you will have a very powerful relationship.

On the 22nd, as your 8th house of transformation becomes powerful, you enter into a sexually active period. Whatever your age or stage in life, libido will be stronger than usual. This is good for detox regimes on all levels – physical, emotional, mental and financial. The spiritual and physical circuits tend to get clogged and need a periodic cleansing.

Last month the planetary power began to shift from the lower to the upper half of the chart. It's time to start focusing on the career and outer world objectives.

Though you are in a basically fortunate period in your life, money is earned through work this period. This is not the Horoscope of a lottery winner. A financial disagreement with a friend complicates the financial life, but it will pass next month.

October

   Best Days Overall: 6, 7, 15, 16, 24, 25
   Most Stressful Days Overall: 2, 3, 8, 9, 22, 23, 29, 30
   Best Days for Love: 2, 3, 6, 7, 8, 15, 16, 17, 18, 24, 25, 27, 28, 29, 30
   Best Days for Money: 1, 6, 7, 8, 9, 15, 16, 17, 18, 19, 24, 25, 30
   Best Days for Career: 6, 7, 8, 9, 15, 16, 24, 25

The month ahead is still hectic and hyperactive, but health is good and you are able to handle it. You can enhance the health further through detox regimes, which are powerful all month. Until the 23rd continue to give more attention to the kidneys and hips. Hip massage will be powerful. After the 23rd give more attention to the colon, bladder and sexual organs. Many of you have been more sexually active than usual, but after the 23rd more moderation is called for.

If you listen to your body you will know when you've had enough.

The main headline this month is the Lunar Eclipse on the 18th. Basically this eclipse is benign to you (next month's eclipse is much stronger). It occurs in your money house and shows important financial changes happening. Often the thinking and planning is shown to be unrealistic and needs adjustment. Investments that you thought were good are not so good. Sometimes an unexpected expense arises that forces the change. (Mars enters your 7th house on the 15th and this brings opportunities for business partnerships or joint ventures.) Jupiter is impacted by this eclipse. Thus career changes are brewing too. These changes are not just personal for you but could involve your company or industry. Parents or parent figures should stay out of harm's way this period – children as well. There are life-changing kinds of events for these people in your life. Be more patient with them this period as they are more temperamental than usual. If you are in the creative arts (and many Pisceans are) there is a whole new approach to your creativity happening.

Though the eclipse will produce drama and change, this is basically a happy and successful month. The Water element is strong all month, but especially after the 23rd. You are personally comfortable with this, but keep in mind our previous discussions.

Love is happy this month, but lacks direction. There is harmony with the beloved but neither you nor your partner has a clue as to where you are going. Your love planet goes retrograde on the 21st, so it is a time for gaining mental clarity. Mercury makes beautiful aspects with Jupiter from the 17th to the 26th. For singles this shows an important romantic meeting. For those who are married this shows more harmony and romance within the relationship.

Your 9th house becomes powerful on the 23rd. Thus foreign lands call to you. There are happy travel and educational opportunities and religious and philosophical breakthroughs for those who want them. Theological discussions can be more interesting than a night out on the town these days.

November

Best Days Overall: 3, 4, 11, 12, 20, 21, 22, 30
Most Stressful Days Overall: 5, 6, 18, 19, 25, 26, 27
Best Days for Love: 3, 4, 7, 11, 12, 16, 17, 20, 21, 22, 25, 26, 27, 30
Best Days for Money: 3, 4, 7, 8, 11, 12, 13, 14, 16, 17, 21, 22, 26, 27, 30
Best Days for Career: 3, 4, 5, 6, 11, 12, 21, 22, 30

The Solar Eclipse on the 3rd affects you pretty strongly, so do take it easy and do your best to stay out of harm's way. Drive more defensively and avoid unnecessary trips. Avoid risky activities or confrontations. People tend to overreact under these influences. This eclipse can bring health scares. Both your health planet, the Sun and the Lord of your Horoscope, Neptune, are affected here. Since health is basically good – there are no long-term planets stressing you out – these will most likely be nothing more than scares. Get second opinions and don't rush into anything drastic. Often when the Lord of the Horoscope is affected a detox of the body happens. This is not disease, but is often diagnosed that way – the symptoms seem the same.

This eclipse period spend more quiet time at home. Read a good book, watch a good movie, pray and meditate – pursue your spiritual practice. The best way to go through stressful transits is to be in the highest possible energy vibration. Safety is an 'inner condition'. There can be job changes or changes at the workplace. This eclipse occurs in your 9th house. For students this shows major changes in the educational plans. Sometimes there are upheavals and shake-ups in their school. Sometimes there are major policy changes. Your belief systems and personal philosophy of life get 'reality checked'. Some will have to be revised. Some will go by the wayside and be replaced with better. Many of you have been travelling of late. If so, schedule your flights around the eclipse and try not to fly during that period.

On the 22nd as the Sun crosses your Mid-heaven you enter a yearly career peak. Career has been good all month, but gets even better after this date. There is much progress and much success. You earn success the traditional way, through hard work. Your work ethic is a major factor here. You simply outwork, outperform, your competitors.

Health becomes more delicate after the 22nd. Again there is no long-term problem, but you enter one of your more vulnerable periods of the year. Happily you are paying attention – health is high on your priorities – and this is a positive signal. You are not ignoring things. You can enhance the health by giving more attention to the liver and thighs after the 22nd. From the 4th to the 7th a visit to the chiropractor or osteopath seems a good idea. The spine needs to be kept in alignment.

Love is very happy this month. Mercury makes fabulous aspects to Neptune and Jupiter. Singles are meeting romantic partners. There is harmony with the beloved. Romance happens in foreign countries or with foreigners, and in religious or educational settings. The parents or parent figures are also having more harmony in love. If they are married, there is more harmony in the marriage. If they are single, they are meeting romantic partners.

December

Best Days Overall: 1, 8, 9, 18, 19, 28, 29
Most Stressful Days Overall: 2, 3, 15, 16, 17, 23, 24, 30, 31
Best Days for Love: 1, 4, 5, 10, 11, 13, 14, 21, 22, 23, 24
Best Days for Money: 1, 4, 5, 8, 9, 10, 11, 12, 15, 16, 18, 19, 25, 26, 28, 29
Best Days for Career: 1, 2, 3, 8, 9, 18, 19, 28, 29, 30, 31

On the 22nd of last month the planetary power began to move from the West to the East. On the 5th, Mercury crosses from the West to the East making the shift stronger. You are entering a period of personal independence and power. The planetary power is moving towards you rather than away from you. The cycle of 'people pleasing' is more or less over with and it's time to develop your personal initiative and self-reliance, to take personal charge of your destiny and to create what you want in life. Over the past six months you've seen what needed to be changed – now is the time to start making these changes. There are lessons we learn by creating our worlds and there are lessons we learn from being forced to live with our creations. Now is the time to create.

Health still needs watching until the 21st. The most important thing is to maintain high energy levels. But you can enhance your health by giving more attention to the liver and thighs until the 21st and to the spine, knees, teeth, bones, skin and overall skeletal alignment afterwards. Back and knee massage is powerful after the 21st. A visit to the chiropractor or osteopath might also be a good idea if you feel under the weather.

You are still in a yearly career peak until the 21st. So there is much success happening. Like last month you are basically earning your success through hard work. Career opportunities will come this month, but with your career planet retrograde these things need more analysis and study. There's no need to rush into anything. Take your time and get more facts. On the 5th Mercury, the love planet, crosses the Mid-heaven and enters the career house. This shows that social methods enhance the career. It's important now to attend or host the right parties and to interact socially with those who can help you careerwise.

Love is important that period but problematic. You seem out of sorts with the beloved, but this is a short-term problem and will resolve itself after the 24th. Mercury will be in the career house from the 5th to the 24th. Thus there are romantic opportunities with bosses and superiors. In general you are attracted to those with power and will tend to mix with these people as well. Love seems 'practical' this month. It seems a job like any other. The passion of love seems missing. This will be your job. You will have to consciously project more love and warmth to others – and especially to the beloved.

You have been coping with financial change all year. But there are more changes coming from the 23rd to 31st. The financial intuition needs more verification that period. It might not mean what you think.